D1498341

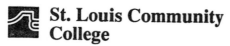

Wives *of the* Leopard

WIVES *of the* LEOPARD

Gender, Politics, and Culture in the Kingdom of Dahomey

Edna G. Bay

University of Virginia Press

Charlottesville & London

First published 1998

∞ The paper used in this publication meets the minimum requirements of the
American National Standard for Information Sciences—Permanence of
Paper for Printed Library Materials, ANSI z39.48-1984.

Library of Congress Cataloging-in-Publication Data

Bay, Edna G.
    Wives of the leopard : gender, politics, and culture in the
Kingdom of Dahomey / Edna G. Bay.
        p.   cm.
    Includes bibliographical references (p.   ) and index.
    ISBN 0-8139-1791-3 (cloth : alk. paper). — ISBN 0-8139-1792-1
(paper : alk. paper)
    1. Political culture—Benin—History.   2. Women in politics—
Benin—History.   3. Benin—Politics and government—To 1960.
I. Title
JQ3376.A91B39   1998
320'.082'096683—dc21   97-45943
                                                               CIP

Frontispiece: The Kpojito Hwanjile in 1972. Author's field photo of the replacement
by positional succession of Dahomey's second Kpojito, Hwanjile, the reign-mate of
King Tegbesu

For Ray

Contents

Illustrations

Preface

This book has been a long time in the making. I first became intrigued with Dahomey more than twenty-five years ago. Looking for a dissertation topic that would allow me to study African women's history, I stumbled upon Dahomey, notorious for its amazons, and quickly discovered that women in Dahomey had been involved in much more than soldiering. Dahomey seemed a place where women prior to the colonial period had enjoyed extraordinary liberties and powers—an ideal subject for a young woman, like so many others at the time, looking for patterns of female autonomy different from the experience of the West. The work that emerged from that initial research was an exploration of women's institutions that I called "The Royal Women of Abomey." Drawing on evidence from the entire history of the kingdom, it reconstructed offices within the palace and elaborated women's importance in kin groups. It spoke in terms of an unchanging ethnographic past, but a past in which it was clear that women had been important, and powerful, in the state.

My findings satisfied my search for women of historical importance, but I was troubled by a nagging sense that not all of my evidence fit. "The Royal Women of Abomey" described women as central to the state, as powerful politically. However, when I had searched the archives and published materials for prominent women in the twentieth century, I had found no one. When I had asked people in the field about women and politics in the colonial period, I had learned nothing. When I attended ceremonies and saw the courts of the men who were claimants to the royal stool, there were few women officials. Most significantly, not one of the three would-be kings of Dahomey in the early 1970s had a kpojito, a female reign-mate and the holder of what I knew had been the most important woman's office. If women had been so important in the kingdom, why had they and their offices disappeared so completely with the imposition of colonial rule? If women had held certain powers, why had they relinquished them so rapidly? Why were the women who were visible in late-twentieth-century Abomey mainly adepts of cults, women who received the spirits of kings and other gods and deified individuals, or priests associated with cults that included the Nesuhwe, which was dedicated to the deified dead of the royal family? Why did twentieth-century women's power seem to be only religious?

Finn Fuglestad turned my thinking in a direction that provided an answer. In an article about the origins of Dahomey, he argued that the Alladahonu, the ruling family, had violated the usual norms followed by newcomers to an area in Africa. By conquering the Abomey plateau and ruling by military might alone, the dynasty had refused to make accommodations with the "owners of the earth," the people established there first who had ritual control over the land. It occurred to me that, to the contrary, the kpojito as a reign-mate to the king might represent just such an accommodation, because the kpojito were women of common birth, and the first one had come from the plateau region. Perhaps she and the king together symbolized the accommodation of the newcomers with the owners of the earth. More broadly, the Fuglestad article prompted me to look at patterns of religion and ritual practice, and I began to realize that changes in the hierarchies of the vodun, or gods, were also comments on change in the world of humanity.

A remark by Joseph Miller at an academic conference provided the other spark that moved me toward the interpretation of Dahomean history presented in this book. I had by that point worked out the lines of my argument, that by reading the changing hierarchy of the vodun and comparing it with historical evidence, one could see that women and men of royal, commoner, and slave background had shared power in the eighteenth century. In the nineteenth, women and men of commoner birth were increasingly excluded from the center, and by the end of the century, men of royal birth were monopolizing power in their own hands. Hence, it was not surprising to find few women in the twentieth century associated with precolonial forms of power. Miller suggested that although all those cultural arguments were fine, there had to be an economic factor that played a significant role in these changes. The transition from the slave trade to the palm-oil trade proved to be that factor.

In fact, it fit the other evidence so nicely that in writing this book I worried at times that I was presenting an argument that was at base one of economic determinism.

Having worked out the argument, I needed time to write. My career track from 1977 to 1995 was an administrative one, with no time for the slow nurturing of ideas and translation to paper (and to electronic impulses) that is essential to book preparation. Emory University and the African Studies Association, my coemployers at the time, provided a sabbatical year in 1993/94. The National Humanities Center in Research Triangle Park, North Carolina, also provided financial support, naming me their Delta Delta Delta fellow for that year. The center proved the perfect place to write and enjoy the intellectual stimulation of a superb body of fellows and staff.

There are many others deserving of recognition and thanks both before and after that key sabbatical year. The Foreign Area Fellowship Program of the Social Science Research Council sponsored my original field research and the National Endowment for the Humanities sent me back to Abomey for a related project in 1984. I made use of subsequent short stays for conferences in Benin sponsored by the University of Benin and by UNESCO to gather additional material. Dozens of generous people have helped me over the years. In Benin, I wish to mention the staff of the National Archives and the Historical Museum of Abomey, including Ernest d'Oliveira, and research colleagues including Amélie Degbelo and Elisée Soumonni. Of so many kind friends in Abomey and Cotonou, I would recognize particularly Angèle and Alexis Feliho, Léonard and Camille Loko and their children, and Grâce d'Almeida and her extended family. Outside of Benin, Robin Law has given me steadfast encouragement and valuable resources over the years. Dr. C. W. Hickcox of Emory University was instrumental in helping me prepare the maps. Finally, I thank Ray Ganga, who is aware of the importance he has played in this project and in my life.⁓

Author's Note

My governing objective in presenting this history of Dahomey has been to balance scholarly accuracy with accessibility, to write a work that can be readily understood by English-speaking persons who are not African studies specialists. Dahomey presents a bewildering number of names, of individuals as well as offices, that threaten readability even for those familiar with African history. There is no firm agreement on the spelling of historical place-names. The name of the kingdom itself, for example, appears in the texts used as sources for this work as Dahomey, Dahomy, Dahomi, Danxome, Danhome, Dan-hô-min, and Danhomé. The spelling of the state and city of Whydah varies perhaps the most among place-names. Whydah, the usual spelling in English, is a corruption of the name of the people, the Hweda. Portuguese sources use Juda and Ajuda, while the French spell the name Ouidah.

Individual names vary, too. The name Glele is sometimes spelled Glélé or Gelele, and Gezo may be Guezo or Ghezo. I have chosen to use the spellings most commonly found in English sources in the expectation that English-speaking readers who want to learn more about the kingdom will find further research less tedious. For less familiar names, I have tended to retain the spelling of the source.

Words and phrases in Fongbe, the language of the area that was Dahomey, have similarly been simplified. There are vowel and consonant sounds in Fongbe that are not used in English. Moreover, Fongbe is a tonal language, with rising, falling, and modulating tones that change the meaning of words. I have not tried to indicate these variations but rather have used spellings with the English alphabet that will convey only an approximate pronounciation. Readers should assume that all vowels and consonants are pronounced, with the letter *i* pronounced *ee, a* as *ah*, and *e* as *ch*.

1
Along the Slave Coast

*The palace of the king was the pivot of political life. In this sense, the
Abomey palace was a microcosm of the kingdom as a whole.*

A. Le Hérissé, *L'Ancien royaume du Dahomey*

Dahomey epitomized everything negative that the Euro-American imagination of the nineteenth and twentieth centuries wanted to believe about Africa. Dahomey was said to be a state grown rich through the slave trade. Over more than 250 years, hundreds of thousands of enslaved Africans were despatched from its beaches across shark-infested waters and into the infamous middle passage. But slavery in the Western Hemisphere was a blessing compared with life in the kingdom, at least as Euro-American observers described it. Slaves were captured by an army of women, amazons who severed their right breasts to be better able to fire arrows at their enemies. Foes not brutally decapitated on the battlefield by machete-wielding amazons, or not sold overseas after capture, were destined to die as sacrifices in horrifying fetish ceremonies. One visitor claimed that the king would sail in a boat on a sea of the blood drained from the severed necks of sacrifice victims. Others told of half-naked men eagerly waiting to eat the flesh of the dead. These rituals were said to have sprung from the evil beliefs that in North America were known as voodoo, and included the worship of snakes and trees. The absolute monarch who presided over this butchery lived in the capital, Abomey, in a palace surrounded by twelve-foot-high mud walls topped with rows of human skulls. He would sit on a throne supported by the heads of princely enemies or recline on a silk-cushioned sofa, where he would be served in oriental opulence by thousands of women. The royal harem in turn was guarded by eunuchs who indulged in intrigues with the wives of the king. As for the remainder of the populace, they were all slaves of the king.

Tales of Dahomey were told by many, and prior to the twentieth century, the storytellers were all outsiders: slave traders, abolitionists, missionaries, diplomats, and officials of European governments. It has of late become fashionable to analyze the texts of such writers and travelers, to explore the ways in which their apparent observations were molded by the cultures of their birth and their life experiences. Like Joseph Conrad's Marlowe, we have relearned in such analyses the truism that the horrors we perceive tend to be the reflections of our own inner darknesses, and that human beings can rarely transcend culture or history. But having said that, we are left with the knotty question of Dahomean realities. What was this place called Dahomey like? Did the dozens of visitors make up these stories? Were their accounts simply creations of the racist imagination of Europe? If not, what did people see when they visited Dahomey? Can Dahomean culture be understood in other ways? And whose words can we trust? Having seen the errors of our predecessors' eyes, how can we be certain of the clarity of our own vision? How can we begin to understand meanings in other cultures, in other times?

Since the turn of the twentieth century, many scholars and writers, both Dahomeans and outsiders, have tried to counteract the negative stereotypes of the kingdom—explaining its customs, praising its governmental organization, admiring its military, describing its religious practices, and lauding its rulers. Yet no one today disputes the essential veracity upon which the stereotypes of savagery were based. Dahomey was a central player in the overseas slave trade from West Africa. In addition to a standing army of men, there were women soldiers in the kingdom's armed forces, at least in the nineteenth century. Despite the perpetuation of a myth of Greek antiquity by many, the women soldiers did not cut off either breast. Some captives of war were sold overseas, others were kept as domestic slaves within the kingdom, and yet others were sacrificed at ceremonies honoring the ancestors of the royal family. However, there were no lakes of blood, and cannibalism was never more than a rumor. Religion in Dahomey was focused on gods who were taken by slaves to the New World; there, the religion was called voodoo, a corruption of *vodun*, the Dahomean word for deity. The palace of the king was surrounded by a massive wall, which at one period in history was decorated with human skulls, as was the throne of one of the kings. And the kings did have many wives who, along with a much smaller number of eunuchs, inhabited a citylike palace. But what visitors saw as intrigue tended to be the actions of women and eunuchs as they performed their roles as officials in the governments of the kings. And the mass of Dahomeans were not slaves but citizens in a hierarchic structure of family and state relations and obligations.

Even when stripped of moralizing and racist condemnations, Dahomey appears to the Western eye exotic at best. Yet exoticism is always in the eyes of the beholder, the outsider whose own culture must appear equally strange to the exotic. Certainly, by the human-rights standards of the late twentieth century, Dahomey is worthy of criticism. On the other hand, compared with the practices of many nations both past and present, Dahomey as a state functioned reasonably well. It guaranteed its citizens basic rights and access to means of livelihood, providing order and protection while demanding specific responsibilities. Dahomeans were able to meet their fundamental material and spiritual needs, producing reasonably abundant surpluses of foodstuffs and crafted goods while having access to imported goods and the stimulation of outside cultural contacts. Though slaves traded into the kingdom and captives of war might be condemned into the overseas trade or executed in the name of the state religion, the kingdom's leadership paradoxically showed great respect in principle for human life, and carefully controlled the taking of life. In short, Dahomey was neither a state that terrorized its citizens, nor a Garden of Eden whose citizens enjoyed an idyllic existence.

This book explores the political culture of Dahomey over nearly two hundred years of the kingdom's autonomous existence, from approximately 1700 to the imposition of French colonial authority in 1894. It traces cultural, economic, and political changes over time and focuses on the changing composition of the coalitions of persons who ruled Dahomey in the name of the kings. It argues that those cultural characteristics that appear to us as oddities—and that were once seen as the bizarre customs of an uncivilized nation—were logical developments of cultural

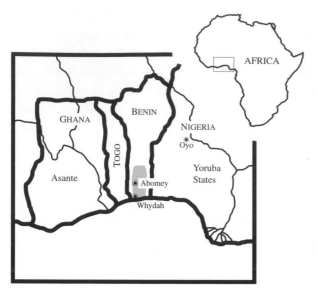

1. Dahomey and the Slave Coast. Contemporary nation-states in all capital letters; precolonial states and cities in upper- and lowercase. Shaded area is estimated greatest extent of Dahomey

traits found elsewhere in West Africa. Dahomey presents a changing picture of how people organize human society, of how a nation comes to be, and of what rulers do to gain and maintain power. In short, what seems to have been unique in Dahomey will often be found to be an intensification of common practices, or subtle alterations in institutions known elsewhere among Dahomey's West African neighbors.

This study of Dahomey differs in many respects from recent studies in African, Dahomean, and women's history. Histories of kingdoms and their rulers were much in vogue in the 1960s, the period when most contemporary African nation-states gained their independence. The early studies that glorified states were gradually replaced by social histories and analyses of class structures, with emphases on peasantries. Women took their place among the oppressed subjects of scholarly scrutiny, and by the mid-1970s attention had turned to the colonial and postcolonial periods. This work returns to a consideration of a precolonial state and the people who controlled it. It is in that sense a history from the point of view of rulers. But it argues that there was a constantly changing set of persons who reached for and gained power in Dahomey, a set of persons that varied by gender, status, ethnic group, and lineage origin. Thus it might be described as a social history of ruling coalitions. Women and men of varying kin origins and social strata interacted at the political center of Dahomey through more than two centuries of history—as the kingdom expanded, as relations of commerce and production changed, as Dahomean society borrowed and adapted social and cultural forms from neighbors, and as the kingdom carried out war, diplomacy, and trade with other nations. This flow of historical events in turn reveals patterns of the intersection of gender, kinship, and class that highlight how power and authority were gained, were exercised, and were lost over the life of the kingdom.

This book highlights women as players in the history of Dahomey's ruling elite, exploring their changing opportunities for autonomous action over the course of two hundred years of Dahomean history. In contrast to what has become a widely accepted vision of precolonial Africa, it does not argue that Dahomean (or African) culture was fundamentally patriarchal and oppressive to women. Rather, it finds women exercising choice, influence, and autonomy, if not in wholly egalitarian relationships with men, in situations where there was clear recognition of their ability and right to do so. It goes beyond previous studies of precolonial African women by tracing the transformation of their powers chronologically and placing women's experience in a broader context that informs and is informed by the history of the kingdom as a whole. It argues that women's status changed over time in precolonial Dahomey, that women experienced a loss of acknowledged authority and power not unlike the losses demonstrated by scholars for African women during the colonial period. In the case of Dahomey, however, changes in women's status were related to cultural and economic factors more complex than simply the imposition of European mores. At the same time, this is much more than a history of women. It goes beyond women's history to explore larger questions of the state, its nature, and how male and female individuals were involved in shaping it.

Finally, this study is unusual in showing changes in the institutions of a precolonial African state. Scholarly analyses of precolonial African state structures have tended to present a static picture, sometimes tracing the origins of institutions but otherwise implying little change over time once an office or function of state had been established. This work focuses on development and change in two overlapping institutions of the Dahomean state, the monarchy and the palace. It uses the practice of religion in part as a lens through which to focus on change. It revisits a number of important issues long debated in Dahomean historiography about the nature of the state: about succession patterns, the organization of offices, militarism, the origins of the ruling lineage, the slave trade, the transition to the trade in palm oil, and the ultimate decline of Dahomey.

The remainer of this chapter includes two parts. The first develops a snapshot of Dahomean political culture as it existed in the late nineteenth century. It focuses on the monarchy and the palace, the instruments through which state power was exercised. In doing so, the snapshot of necessity deals with some of the assumptions and cultural values upon which institutions of state were based. The second part introduces sources for the history of Dahomey, the people whose voices, motives, and misconceptions we will use to create a moving picture of Dahomey over the years.

Power, the Monarchy, and the Palace ∾

Both precolonial observers and twentieth-century scholars have debated the mechanisms of power and control in Dahomey. Apologists for the slave trade, for example, describe the king as an absolutist despot wielding arbitrary power over a hapless population that would have been better off under plantation slavery. Typical was the French observer who comments that "the king of the Dahomeans rules with oriental despotism. His ministers only appear before him covered with dust or mud. They prostrate while receiving his orders. Without trial, without forms of justice, he has the heads of blacks cut off when he is displeased with them." [1] Abolitionists similarly saw a despot, but one made so by the evils of the slave trade. More frequently, travelers and scholars have posited a balance of power, arguing that the king was checked by a class of nobles or powerful priests. Stanley Diamond theorizes a struggle between a civil state and the power of kinship groups. Karl Polanyi sees a two-tier system in which power was exercised over external relations by an authoritarian monarch and "freedom and autonomy" were left to the masses in the countryside.

Maurice Ahanhanzo Glélé, stressing the importance of hierarchical relations, argues that all power was concentrated in the hands of the king and the royal family, so that the history of the kingdom is essentially the story of the royal family. Eighteenth-century Europeans sometimes argue that women played an important role in power relations, whereas twentieth-century writers tend to deny that women exercised any power: "effectively, they [women in the palace] had no active role in the government and no influence whatsoever on the mind of the king."[2] All of these conceptions paint a picture of an individual monarch working alone to establish relations of competition or cooperation with individuals or with groupings of individuals.

I propose a slightly different conception of power in Dahomey. I argue that power in Dahomey was diffuse and multifaceted, and was exercised by coalitions of individuals whose membership changed over time. Those coalitions that succeeded in gaining control of the state will be called here the "monarchy." The monarchy thus is a metaphor for a small and fluid political and economic elite; one of its members was the man who reigned as king and in whose name the country was governed. The monarchy was typically made up of men and women from differing lineages and strata of Dahomean society, all of whom wielded various powers—at times in concert and at times at cross-purposes—and who acted from a variety of motives. All of the individuals who constituted the monarchy were loyal to the person of the king, in the sense that their continued access to power was individually dependent upon him. Yet collectively they could act in face of the king's opposition. The grouping of individuals who constituted the monarchy was constantly reworked in light of changes internal and external to the kingdom.

At the same time, the king himself was neither a prisoner nor a puppet of his monarchy. No one became king of Dahomey through a simple accident of birth. Rather, the king was one of a small group of sons of a king, born after his father had been recognized as heir or enstooled as king. A man of ambition, the prince who became king proved his worth and earned his office through building alliances with siblings, with important common men, and with powerful women within the household of the reigning king.

The women involved in the monarchy were nearly always drawn from the palace, a term used here, as it was in Dahomey, to refer both to royal edifices and to the persons who inhabited them. By the late nineteenth century, the palace as institution included an estimated eight thousand persons who lived in a series of royal residences across the kingdom. The vast majority were women, though there were also some eunuchs. All persons associated with the palace were termed *ahosi* (*aho* = king; *si* = dependent, follower, subordinate), or wives of the king. All were involved in the administration of the kingdom, working for the advancement of the monarchy's interests in a polygynous household that was simultaneously the state's administrative arm. The women of the palace were a cross section of Dahomean society; they included slaves and war captives, freeborn commoners, and women from well-to-do households.

Also resident within the palace, or closely allied to it, were princesses, or *ahovi* (*aho* = king; *vi* = child). Ahovi is a term that refers to all individuals, male or female, whose father was a prince. Birth-rank gave certain female ahovi the authority to exercise power within the royal lineage. For example, ahovi who were eldest daughters or senior sisters of reigning kings at times were centrally involved in the selection of kings and in their installation. Though royal privilege gave ahovi special status in Dahomean society, the distinction between princess and wife, between ahovi and ahosi, sometimes blurred. For example, kings often married princesses of royal lines descended from their predecessors. And in the late nineteenth century, some sisters to the reigning king became prominent members of the palace and hence wives of the king. A few princesses had a significant impact on the history of Dahomey independent of any relationship with the palace. For the most part, though, it was through the palace that women, ahovi or commoner, had the greatest potential for gaining and exercising authority and power.

Certain ahosi exercised extraordinary power as part of the monarchy, and typically they were titled state officers. They and other ambitious wives of the king competed for influence through building power bases within the palace, working to serve the king or to assist princes who were seeking to become king. Their ethnic, class, and kin backgrounds changed over time, and the powers that they effectively wielded changed. They included both ahosi and ahovi, both king's wives and princesses.

The palace, then, was both the king's household, a city of women who carried out the king's orders, and a part of the policy-making apparatus of the state. An ideology of meritocracy promised promotion to all women of ambition and achievement, though they entered the hierarchical ranks of the palace according to their social status of origin. Belief in advancement through merit and the importance of hierarchy were not unique to the palace. Both appear to have run deeply through Dahomean history, and were still visible in the twentieth century.

The Palace as Place

The palace was a spatial entity as well as a political, economic, and social institution. Its center was in the capital city of Abomey and its periphery in royal residences located at strategic points throughout the country. The central palace complex in Abomey was the formal residence of the king, his reign-mate, and their courts; as such, it was also the residence of a large proportion of the ahosi population. In actuality, the central Abomey palace was a series of royal residences, with each new section constructed adjacent to its predecessor by each succeeding king. By the late nineteenth century, it covered nearly one hundred acres of land. It was surrounded by a massive mud wall rising in some places to thirty feet and describing a perimeter of nearly two and a half miles. Inside, tombs of the kings were located in the order of their reigns along a curve running clockwise from northwest to southeast, reflecting the building of each successive palace section.[3] Comparable memorial shrines to the kpojito, the kings' female reign-mates, were ranged from northwest to southwest along the western portion of the enclosure. The reigning king always occupied the latest portion to be built. To his west were the quarters of his kpojito and her entourage. The remainder of the city-sized palace population appears to have lived throughout all areas of the palace complex.

The central Abomey palace was the seat of government in Dahomey and the kingdom's political and religious center. Control over it and its inhabitants was the absolute prerequisite to control over the kingdom. It was in public at the palace that policies were made and sacrifices executed, that wars were planned and rituals performed, and that appoint-

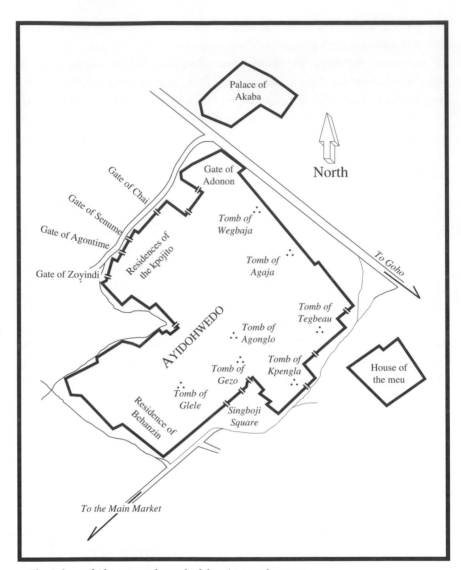

Palace of
Akaba

North

Gate of Chai

Gate of Senume

Gate of Agontime

Gate of Zoyindi

Gate of
Adonon

Residences of
the kpojito

Tomb of
Wegbaja

Tomb of
Agaja

AYIDOHWEDO

Tomb of
Agonglo

Tomb of
Tegbeau

Tomb of
Kpengla

House of
the meu

To Goho

Tomb of
Gezo

Tomb of
Glele

Residence of
Behanzin

Singboji
Square

To the Main Market

2. The Palace of Abomey at the end of the nineteenth century

ments were confirmed and taxes paid. In the privacy of its inner courts, records were kept, treasures were guarded, kings were advised, princes and princesses were conceived, and thousands of tasks in support of the monarchy were performed.

It was mainly in the Abomey palace that the king received his male ministers and governors, along with visiting diplomats and commercial representatives, all of whom otherwise resided outside. As described in the nineteenth century, the large, inner courtyard for audiences with the king was divided in two by a row of midribs of palm branches. The king and his immediate entourage remained on one side, obscured under the low, thatched roof of a long verandah. Outsiders to the palace would wait on the opposite side of the palm-branch boundary, facing the palace-as-organization: a sole man surrounded by thousands of women and a number of eunuchs.

The palm branches described a line that was both sexual and political. It underscored the king's control over his women's sexuality and, because ahosi were drawn from all lineages in the kingdom, it stood by extension for royal control over the entire population. The line also underscored the palace as a separate and secret organization, a virtual city of women experienced in the mechanics of government who, from an outsider's perspective, were capable of blocking or promoting outsiders' interests. Dahomeans summoned to the king's presence moved to the palm-branch line, prostrated there, and spoke to a woman called the *daklo*. She conveyed their words to the king. The spatial arrangement distanced and mystified the person of the king and his entourage—and made literal a truism shared by European visitors, that to gain access to the king, one must work through the women of the palace.

The divided courtyard pointed to another reality of nineteenth-century government in Dahomey. It expressed spatially a fundamental ideological and organizational principle, that any whole is made up of complementary parts: inside/outside, right/left, royal/commoner, male/female. The palace was the center of a universe that was the kingdom of Dahomey, but it was a center that balanced the interests of a periphery, a complementary "outside." Dress reinforced the contrast between outside and inside. Eunuchs appeared in palace audiences in women's dress, signaling their responsibility for activities of the inside. In contrast, women whose function was to oversee the male ministers of state wore *agbada*, men's gowns in Yoruba style, which pointed to their responsibility for functions on the outside. The ideology of complementarity was strikingly visible. However, it was a complementarity of parts of unequal status: inside outranked outside, right took precedence over left, and royal superseded commoner. Gender complementarity was more complex. On the level of popular culture, male was superior to female, though as part of the palace, women took precedence over men.

The palace was also the site of the ritual processes that legitimized the dynasty. The well-being of the kingdom was dependent upon the continued support of the deceased kings and their reign-mates, who needed to be honored at their palace shrines at regular intervals. Ceremonies designed to honor the royal ancestors were noted by visitors to the region of Dahomey from early in the eighteenth century. Called Annual Customs by Europeans, the cycle of ceremonies grew increasingly elaborate over time. Nineteenth-century accounts, when mass public portions of Customs took place at Singboji, a broad triangular plaza fronting the two-story palace entrance, describe human and animal sacrifices, parades of the riches of the king, military demonstrations, political debates, and mutual gift-giving between the king and the population. Early in his reign, a new king was also required to perform particularly elaborate ceremonies in the palace in honor of his predecessor. These Grand Customs constituted the final funeral for the preceding king and the formal installation of his successor. They linked the new king spiritually to the dynasty and ensured the kingdom's continued growth and prosperity. It was only after the completion of Grand Customs that a king was believed to be legitimate in the eyes of his ancestors, because "the king did not owe his title only to his birth: as long as he had not completed the ceremonies in honor of his father, he was not truly linked to the dynasty. An Abomean explained the relationship saying 'it is not enough that a king have a proper relationship with the living, he must also establish a correct relationship with the dead.'" [4]

Annual Customs and Grand Customs were directed to both the living and the dead. They spoke to the royal ancestors, offering them the nourishment of sacrifice and the strength of recognition through prayer. The king's ancestors in turn were expected to respond by assisting their progeny. But Customs spoke equally strongly to Dahomeans who were not of the royal lineage. In their lavishness and their use of human sacrifice, they impressed upon all others the supremacy of the royal line. Moreover, because annual ceremonies for ancestors in other Dahomean lineages could not be performed prior to the king's, they underlined royal control over the kingdom and its population.

The displays of military power and material riches at Customs reminded all that the monarchy and the resources it commanded were paramount in Dahomey. Military power was directly linked to the economic well-being of Dahomey. It allowed the kingdom to expand the territory under its control and to obtain the productive human resources needed to participate in external commerce, most specifically in the slave and palm-oil trades. The debates on political and military decisions reinforced the importance of the palace as a point for policy formation while allowing the tensions of factional viewpoints to be aired and to some extent resolved.

Those who attended Customs—heads of lineages and villages, governors of provinces, merchants, and ministers of state—presented gifts that are called tribute or taxes by writers on Dahomey. The givers in turn received gifts from the king. Gifts or taxes were clearly a major source of revenue for the monarchy, but they were also symbolic recognition of a patron-client relationship between the monarch and his Dahomean subjects. Echoing the relationship of the king to his ancestors, Dahomeans recognized and enriched a powerful patron, the king, who in turn owed them protection and support. Customs thus made visible the three interwoven threads of power that legitimized the rulers of Dahomey: religious/ideological, military, and political/economic.

Of Hierarchy, Merit, and Access to Power

A strong sense of hierarchy meant that individuals within any social structure could always find their rank, which they were then expected to respect. For example, the order of birth established hierarchy among children within families, and the order of arrival in a household fixed hierarchy among wives. No two individuals ever occupied the same rank. Everywhere, the first to arrive, by birth or marriage, outranked all who came later. Not even twins were equal, for the secondborn was considered the elder. Hierarchy promoted a respect for authority that was evident inside and outside the palace; in fact, it was to last beyond the lifetime of the kingdom. The French in the twentieth century found the region of Abomey easy to govern, with a population disinclined to rebel against colonial authority and willing to provide taxes and labor as required. Typical was the missionary resident in Abomey in the early twentieth century who looked around him and saw "everywhere a hierarchic society well ordered and disciplined: masters and servants understand their duties and rights."[5]

Cross-cutting strict hierarchy was a belief that individuals could rise in status through merit. With hard work, skill, and support from spiritual forces, an individual could win wealth and higher status. For some, mercantile success, particularly at the port of Whydah, proved an avenue for advancement. Material success was also linked to service to the monarchy. Both males and females who performed well and loyally in service to the king were rewarded appropriately. The impact of success on hierarchy can best be seen in the structures of kinship.

There were three levels of kin organization. Clans included all persons who traced their ancestry to a mythical being, usually a wild animal, which was the clan *tohwiyo* (*to* = agent; *hwiyo* = worshipped, offered libations). Clans were relatively few in number and had little practical impact on kin relations. Instead, lineages, the subdivisions of clans, were the key kinship organizations. Each lineage traced its ancestry back to a given historical individual. Titular lineage leadership was in the hands of the oldest man and woman, whose responsibilities were both secular and ritual. Major decisions affecting all lineage members—access to land, negotiations of marriage, honoring of ancestors—were taken at the level of the lineage. Households constituted the third level of kinship organization. They were groupings of lineage members and persons attached to the lineage who lived in a single compound; that is, a series of contiguous dwellings on lineage-controlled land. Household heads might be male or female, though men served most often as head. Marriage was strictly patrilocal, and ancestry was traced through patrilineal lines, with one exception. The royal lineage claimed all children born to any of its members, whether female or male.

Hierarchy within a lineage, as noted above, was based on rank. Rank was an ascribed characteristic related to the length of time any person had been a member of a particular lineage. It affected persons born into the group, married into it, or brought into it as slaves or other subordinates. Material success, however, created nodes of wealth and prestige within a given lineage—households where resources were greater, dependents more numerous, and status higher. Though ranked hierarchically by chronological factors, then, people within lineages also were divided by socioeconomic strata. A wealthy individual would show appropriate deference to those of higher rank within the lineage, yet within the kingdom's political system, wealth and a close relationship to the monarchy placed that individual—and members of his or her household—on higher social strata than lineage members who might otherwise outrank them. In short, a class system based on achieved status existed across kinship lines.

The belief that an individual could rise in social status through merit applied to women not only as members of the lineage of their birth but also as wives in their husbands' households. A woman at the time of her marriage moved into the household of her husband. Her deportment there could aid or destroy her own children's chances to win lineage office and, in the case of exemplary behavior, could allow her to rise to the status of honored ancestor in her husband's lineage. Merit as an avenue for women's advancement in the palace was underlined ideologically by stories of the rise of slaves to the position of kpojito, reign-mate to the king and the highest-ranking woman in the kingdom.

Married Dahomean women expected to assist a husband in his endeavors, but also to earn income that was neither controlled by nor inherited by him. Palace women similarly worked at a variety of tasks on behalf of themselves and of the king. They were farmers, food processors, traders, porters, artisans, ritual specialists, and healers. In contrast with other Dahomean women, however, ahosi also worked for the state as guards, soldiers, messengers, spies, prostitutes, performers, political advisors, ministers of state, governmental record keepers, and makers of state policy. They were rewarded by the king for these services with cash, cloth, slaves, land, and control over villages, all of which could contribute to a substantial estate to be left to relatives in the families of their birth. Because distinctions were not made between domestic functions performed in the name of the king as head of household and state functions performed in the name of the king as head of state, many of the activities of members of the palace had implications for national policy and administration. In effect, the palace was at one and the same time a polygynous household and the central administrative institution of the state. And on the highest levels of this institution, women of talent and ambition enjoyed extraordinary opportunities for the acquisition of wealth and the exercise of power.

Of Kinship and Power

The Dahomean monarchy faced constant problems of state integration. Dahomey was an expansionist kingdom bent on conquering and incorporating land and populations in every direction from Abomey. To function, it needed to win and keep the allegiance of people at the center who would cooperate militarily, economically, and politically in the monarchy's goals. With each new conquest, Dahomey had to integrate peoples from outlying areas, allowing the older center to benefit from the spoils of conquest yet incorporating captured land and people into the state and ultimately making them part of the center. The mechanisms of state control directly paralleled principles of social and kin relations. Kinship structures were recognizable in state institutions, and political links between individuals were established through the idiom of kinship. In this sense, the state seemed little more than a lineage writ large, operating under principles widely used and respected in Dahomey and in neighboring areas. But even while invoking principles of kin and commoner society, the monarchy distorted their function and meaning, and thus transformed social and kin relations into devices for the exercise and consolidation of state power.

Kinship met many fundamental human needs at the same time that it made strong economic and emotional claims on its members. In that sense it competed with the state for individuals' allegiance. For example, Dahomeans could look to their patrilineage for basic shelter, protection, and nurturance, along with access to land and training in artisan or other economic skills. The patrilineage identified the ancestral spirit who was responsible for each member's birth and consulted the ancestors as necessary when members were ill or needed to make major decisions. The patrilineage found spouses for its members and helped them rear their children. At death it ushered its members into the world of the spirits and then took responsibility for their eternal well-being by "feeding" them at regular intervals. In return, individuals were expected to accede to the lineage's demands, providing personal services and material support to it and, if necessary, subordinating personal desires and fulfillment to lineage obligations. A woman's obligations in marriage to the lineage of her husband were finite and temporary; it was the patrilineage of her birth that would call on her services in old age, would house her if she chose to return home, and would be responsible for her burial. Individuals, living and dead, had foremost obligations to the patrilineage. They literally received life and livelihood through its good offices; their loyalty of necessity lay with their patrilineage.

The kingdom of Dahomey did not attempt to take over the functions of the patrilineage. Indeed, the state offered Dahomeans complementary forms of sustenance: protection at a national level, security for travel, expanded land area, and opportunities to participate in long-distance commercial relations. Lineage authorities and the kingdom's officials did not necessarily agree, however, on details of how the state could and would work with lineages. And dependents of the king, even if they were among the privileged elite that made up the monarchy, were forced to balance the demands of their participation in the machinery of state with the imperatives of their membership in kin groups. Ahosi who were of slave origin were theoretically without direct family connections. From the perspective of the monarchy, they did not have competing loyalties to families of their birth, and they were thus more to be trusted. Yet because even slave ahosi were guaranteed the product of their industry, slaves could be personally ambitious, driven to found a household or even a new lineage based on the wealth they amassed. Other ahosi came from Dahomean lineages; as such, they remained in reasonably close touch with relatives and might strive to use the palace to enrich their lineage. Many ahosi represented, then, the interests of people other than members of the royal lineage. At times, and in part because of their lack of kinship with royalty, relatively large numbers of them appear to have shared similar perspectives on policy questions. Nevertheless, the women of the king's household did not represent a unified power block.

Though the state did not initially usurp lineage rights and responsibilities, it did adopt the language of kin relations, using it to serve as a series of models and metaphors for institutions of the state and for the obligations of its subjects. To the extent that it was successful, the state reduced the autonomy of Dahomean lineages in favor of greater central control. The palace, for example, echoed the organization of polygynous households common throughout Dahomey. Wives in any household were dependents and subordinates who owed loyalty and service to the lineage of their husband. Wealth was based on control over labor power, and a large polygynous household expressed a fundamental principle of society, that wealth was measured in numbers of dependents. In Dahomey, the king by definition was the wealthiest individual in the kingdom. It was to be expected that he would maintain large numbers of wives. The palace was thus a polygynous household writ large, but it functioned in ways that distorted the meaning of marriage as practiced in Dahomey.

Marriage was normally an alliance between lineages, and the wife who moved into her husband's patrilineal home represented the provisions of the alliance. She established through her behavior the grounds for continued interlineage cooperation. Marriages were arranged by lineage leaders, with at least the tacit approval of the individuals who would become husband and wife. Marriage to the king, on the other hand, was effected in a number of ways, only one of which included the kind of interlineage links that characterized normal Dahomean practices: some women entered the palace as captives of war, others were recruited through levies on Dahomean lineages, and still others were sent there as punishment for misbehavior; but well-to-do lineages sometimes offered daughters to the king, and this provided the closest parallel to the meaning of marriage between nonroyal lineages. Outside the royal line, the gift of a daughter to another lineage was an egalitarian gesture that would normally be reciprocated; a daughter of the recipient lineage would be offered to the giver lineage. At the level of the palace, the offer of a woman to the king confirmed lines of subordination. Such a woman was the gift of a client to a patron, a symbol of the expectation that such a gift would reinforce links of loyalty and obligation.

Once within the palace, ahosi lacked the rights and protections enjoyed by women in normal Dahomean marriage. Their entry into the palace was permanent. Unlike wives in commoner marriages, they could not appeal to their lineages should they be mistreated, nor could they move back to their patrilineal homes to protest poor treatment. Divorce, otherwise a reasonably common option for women, was simply not possible when one's husband was the king. Relatively few ahosi ever became sexual partners of any monarch. Since procreation was the avowed purpose of marriage, and a lack of sexual access to a spouse was grounds for divorce, most palace women were in reality retainers rather than wives of the king.

Wives in polygynous households were ranked according to the date of their arrival in their husband's home. In the palace, women were integrated at levels that reflected the social strata from which they were drawn. Changes in rank would be earned, at least in theory, as women demonstrated their loyalty to the king and worked to further the interests of the monarchy. Royal marriage thus acknowledged and reinforced class relations. Those who had been privileged by origin began their palace lives in privileged positions, with control over resources that gave them greater opportunity to advance themselves and the interests of their own patrilineages. The palace thus distorted the meaning of marriage, and in the place of alliances between lineages conveyed messages of central power and control. Marriage to the king was an idiom that in fact spoke of royal control over all lineages in Dahomey. In this sense, palace women were a metaphor for the position of nonroyal lineages, legally subordinate to the monarchy as wives were legally subordinate to husbands.

Fostering was common in Dahomey, as young people from poorer branches of lineages might be sent to the households of more well-to-do kinspeople to serve and possibly prosper from opportunities in a wealthier household. Thus the homes of people of importance, and the ranks of the palace itself, were augmented by the poor relatives of successful and powerful people in what were effectively client-patron relations among kinspersons. Ambitious youth, too, attached themselves to persons perceived as powerful in client-patron relations that mimicked the mutual obligations of kinship. A French colonial official in Abomey in 1935, for example, observed that Dahomean chiefs had large families and lots of "parasites" working the chiefs' fields [6]

The monarchy also constructed personal political relationships in terms of principles drawn directly from marital, kin, and client ties. As noted above, all women of the palace were technically wives of the king, even though their relationship to the monarch did not fulfill the obligations of marriage as practiced in Dahomey. The kings also "married" men. Prominent artisans and talented leaders from newly conquered areas were integrated into Dahomey through ties based on the idiom of marriage. Along with eunuchs and women of the palace, such men were called ahosi. Male ahosi brought families with them or were granted women and slaves with which to establish a line. However, the lineages that they founded through gifts from their kingly "husband" legally came under the control of the royal line. Lost was the autonomy of independent lineages to move, to contract marriage alliances, or to make fundamental decisions about their future. Metaphors of marriage, then, linked the king to thousands of women and men, but they evoked relationships of subordination without protection that emphasized the loyalty and responsibilities expected of the subordinate party, the ahosi.

Individual Dahomeans could also forge close connections with persons outside their direct kinship connections or even outside their lineages that cross-cut the hierarchy of birth rank and kin position. A form of oath taking created links between persons of different patrilineages that supplanted even the ties between siblings of the same mother. At its simplest level, the oath would allow two friends to pledge lifelong support to each other. The oath created fictive kinship, but with ties that were meant to be stronger than kin. It was guaranteed by the invoking of divine sanction; a friend who betrayed his sibling-by-oath would be killed by a god. At the level of the monarchy, kings and would-be kings distorted the meaning of friendship cemented by oath by using oaths to build political relationships and coalitions. Perhaps the most famous of these political oaths was the one that linked the man who became King Gezo to an Afro-Brazilian slave trader, Francisco Félix de Souza. Gezo was said to have taken the oath with de Souza while the trader was imprisoned in Abomey. After escaping with Gezo's help, de Souza supplied the material goods that enabled the prince to build the coalition that in about 1818 carried out a successful coup to make Gezo king.[7]

At least in the nineteenth century, the kings also used oaths to ensure

the loyalty of low-ranking subordinates. Prior to making war, the Dahomeans would send spies to potential enemy territory; the monarchy
forced each spy to make an oath with the king. As in the case of institutions, the monarchy used the common idiom of personal relationships
to develop associations in the interests of the state. If all went well, those
persons linked to the king received ample material rewards, but at a price.
There was no guarantee that a monarchy strengthened through the relationship would remain faithful to the principles upon which those personal relationships were based. In Dahomey, then, in theory kin links
were paramount, but in fact marriage, client-patron alliances, and oaths
allowed a certain flexibility and fluidity in relationships between people
of differing statuses.

Annual Customs were in their religious essence a ritual performed
each year by every lineage. Gift-giving at Customs—or, in scholarly
terms, the "redistributive" nature of Customs—was not a unique creation of the Dahomean monarchs. Heads of lineages always oversaw the
collection of gifts from family members and the bestowal of largess as
part of annual lineage ceremonies. Like the royal line, nonroyal lineages
used the setting of their annual homage to the ancestors to discuss family
business and to make collective decisions about lineage leadership. At
the level of the monarchy, Annual Customs mimicked but also violated
the meaning of ceremonies in honor of the ancestors. By requiring the
representation of the entire population, and the payment of taxes at that
time, the monarchy used the ceremonial cycle as an integrative device
for the state. The message of Customs was that the well-being of the
royal line and the well-being of the kingdom were synonymous, and
that the entire population had the same obligations to the monarchy that
they had to their own kinspeople. Customs supported the fiction of a
commonality of interests among all Dahomeans, even as it attempted to
undermine the realities of kinship.

Of Religion and Power

From the perspective of the monarchy, the religious life of the kingdom
was paradoxically an opportunity for the state to centralize power and a
threat to central control. Thousands of spiritual beings—vodun—were

recognized in the precolonial period. All vodun can be classified into one of two categories: those that were associated with lineages and those that were not. Religion at the level of the lineage linked kinspeople to their deified ancestors, to the vodun that had founded their clan, and, by the nineteenth century, to powerful and dangerous spirits born into their families in the form of deformed children. But individuals could also participate in extrafamilial congregations associated with the so-called popular vodun, deities often linked to forces of nature. Popular vodun might be worshipped over relatively large areas that crossed political boundaries, and might include followers of different nations and ethnic groups. In Dahomey, many popular vodun were derivative gods imported from Yoruba-speaking country to the east: Gu, the god of iron, Legba, the divine trickster, and Heviosso, the god of thunder, for example.

Religious practice in Dahomey was pragmatic and eclectic. The ultimate test of a vodun, whether ancestral or popular, was its efficacy. If a god delivered—allowed a barren woman to conceive, protected a man on a long and dangerous journey, led a hunter to game, cured a sick child—it deserved prayer and sacrifice. It would be heeded when it demanded that a member of the lineage become its devotee, or *vodunsi* (wife, or follower, of the vodun). Dahomeans were always on the alert for deities of proven capability. A vodun that worked well for another community would be welcomed. Immigrants, including war captives, often carried their vodun with them and installed them in Dahomey. Dahomeans were sometimes sent to neighboring areas to be trained as priests of new gods. Vodun even arrived as spoils of war.

But vodun, whether deified ancestors or independent spirit beings, did not work mechanically to fill all requests of their followers. Vodun were believed to be linked to humanity through complex relationships of mutual interdependence. All vodun inhabited Kutome (literally, the land of the dead), a kingdom of shadows that exactly mirrored the visible world of human beings. The royal dynasty reigned in both worlds, and lineages and their members enjoyed the same relative status and wealth in Kutome as their kinspeople in the visible world. Birth and death were passage points from one world to the other; communications between the two were maintained through prayer and divination. Ancestors in

Kutome were ranked hierarchically according to their date of arrival, just as children in the visible world were ranked according to the date of their birth. Each world could affect the other. If angered or neglected, the ancestors or other vodun could injure or kill humans; alternatively, they could bless people with success in business, a bountiful harvest, or large numbers of healthy children. The living could also modify the well-being of those in Kutome: a woman enriched by the king raised the status of her ancestors; if, as sometimes happened, the king stripped a powerful man of his title, seized his lands, and made his wives and daughters servants in the palace, the ancestors were similarly reduced.[8] Vodun who were not regularly worshipped and nourished gradually weakened; ancestors would cease to exist if a lineage had no more living members to venerate them.

Like other Dahomeans, the kings believed in the efficacy of the gods and recognized the need to harness their power. The monarchy needed spiritual backing to assist in governing, to assure victory in warfare, to punish enemies, to make the earth fertile, and to ensure the king's health. The successes of the monarchy were seen as a sign of divine approval. In effect, spiritual and human powers were mutually reinforcing; earthly success meant that beings in Kutome had helped Dahomey, and the gods and ancestors were treated to sumptuous sacrifices that in turn increased their power and ability to assist the monarchy even more. The blessings of the gods and ancestors were crucial to legitimize a dynasty that had established itself through violence and was expanding through war.

The monarchy approached the vodun in two ways. Some were embraced as allies, pampered and adored, so that their power would develop in support of the kingdom. Ancestors and other deities born to the royal lineage in particular were empowered. Other vodun were ignored or suppressed, in the expectation that their strength would be diminished. Choices of which vodun to revere and which to restrain were made consciously as an attempt to alter power relationships among the gods for the benefit of the monarchy and the state. But Dahomeans believed that the structure of the world of the spirits mirrored the organization of the visible world. Changes induced by the monarchy in the religious hierarchy thus reflected changing conceptions of the nature of power by the kingdom's rulers. In effect, the gods of Dahomey had a history, one that was "written" by the ruling order to parallel its own conceptions of power relations in the visible world. Such a religious history provides insights and confirmations of trends but dimly visible in the history of humanity in the kingdom.

Manipulating vodun in the world of Kutome was one strategy to control and channel spiritual power. The monarchy also recognized that the vodun had an organized presence in the visible world. Each congregation of a vodun was directed by a pair of priests, male and female, both of whom were called *vodunon* (*non* = mother, person responsible for a child or charge). Networks of vodunon and the vodunsi pledged to their god's service were a potential political threat to the monarchy and its concern to consolidate power. For this reason, over time the monarchy attempted to control appointments to priestly office and to prescribe when and if new congregations might be established. The monarchy also appears to have forbidden the establishment of religious traditions whose public manifestation involved masquerades, for masquerade societies in West Africa typically had roles in social control and a degree of political power. The Yoruba societies known as Egungun and Oro, both of which are associated with control over women, are said to have been brought to Dahomey only with the establishment of Yoruba-speaking quarters at Abomey in the nineteenth century. Participation in them remained limited to descendants of Yoruba-speakers into contemporary times.

Of Cultural Contacts and Power

Eclecticism and pragmatism were characteristic of Dahomean approaches to religion. They also characterized Dahomean attitudes to other cultures. Dahomean leaders eagerly looked to friends as well as enemies for innovations that they considered efficacious or simply interesting; not only new gods, but technology, dress, art forms, foods, offices, and titles were tried, adopted, and sometimes discarded. Signs of foreign material culture were frequent. As described over the years, the style of court dress was drawn literally from the four cardinal directions: the Muslim north, the Yoruba-speaking east, the Akan west, and the European-influenced south. An 1849 visitor, for example, noted that in comparison with his courtiers, "the king was plainly dressed, in a loose robe of yellow silk slashed with satin stars and half-moons, Mandingo sandals, and a Spanish hat trimmed with gold lace; the only ornament being a small gold chain of European manufacture."[9] The dress of members of the royal line during ceremonies paralleled dress and its usage among the Akan. The ritual beaded crown of the Yoruba appears to have been considered and rejected, possibly because of its physical inconvenience to its wearer.

Technicians and craftsmen were relocated to Dahomey to practice their skills and teach others. In the late eighteenth century, King Kpengla settled a group of Akan-speaking smiths in a village four miles from Abomey, where they cast brass into tiny, delicately decorative bells. His predecessor, Tegbesu, imported a village that knew pottery making, a women's craft, from Aja country to the west. In the nineteenth century, smiths from Yoruba-speaking areas were set to work in the Yoruba quarter of Abomey to design everything from new weaponry to sacred sculptures.

Firearms were the most visible technological import from Europe, and arguably the one with the most impact on the kingdom's history. But European visitors carried hundreds of other items as gifts to Dahomey. Monopolized by the kings, many were paraded at Customs as part of the display of the king's wealth. Sometimes, the presentation of technologies by Europeans was pointed. A slave trader presented King Tegbesu with a red sedan chair, a gift meant to demonstrate a form of transportation potentially more comfortable than the hammocks that carried European visitors the sixty miles from coast to court. The king was so charmed by the device that he decided to be buried in it, leaving Europeans to swing in their hammocks until well after the French conquest one hundred years later. The Dahomeans' use of European technology was similarly pointed. Toward the end of the nineteenth century, two cuckoo clocks hung on the walls of the *djononho*, the reception room in the outer palace court, where impatient Europeans waited interminably long hours to be summoned into the royal presence.[10]

Dahomey was a tributary of the Yoruba empire of Oyo for seventy years (1748 to c. 1818). During that period, certain court offices derivative of Oyo were reported in Dahomey. The *legede*, for example, were known as half-heads, for the characteristic way that, at any given time, one side of their heads would be shaved; messengers for the kings, their function was modeled on the *ilari* of the court of Oyo.

It is relatively easy to trace elements of material culture, offices of state, and religious institutions brought from abroad. Far more difficult to discern is the process of adoption of foreign ideas and values. What makes one god more attractive than another? What perceived needs are met by a given technology? Are some innovations attractive because they fit into a Dahomean value system? Or is the value system itself changing as a result of foreign influence? Was it in fact a changing value system that led to the changes in the political order that will be the focus of this book?

In the earliest phases of Dahomean history, the monarchy was little more than the royal lineage—a line of strangers to the territory who waged war on village-sized principalities. By the second quarter of the eighteenth century, as the kingdom struggled to establish control over a dramatically expanded territory, women and men of nonroyal lineages became active as part of the monarchy. Women within the palace availed themselves of opportunities to wield great power. As Dahomey expanded, the balancing of lineage and gender interests that characterized the early period gradually changed. The participation of nonroyal men and women in the exercise of power at the level of the state became unattractive to the monarchy and was no longer solicited. Centralization consolidated power in the hands of members of the royal lineage, whose male and female members in turn struggled with each other for access to wealth and power.

How and why did these processes take place? Are we in the presence of a human universal, a process by which societies as they grow larger and more complex inevitably disempower women and certain groups of men? Or are we seeing the effects of particular cultural influences that prompted the changes? Dahomey had constant and profound interactions over two hundred years with two cultural systems—European and Yoruba—both of which are noted for gender and class disparities. Or is this a matter of economics? Cultural changes in Dahomey paralleled a shrinking of resources and consequent wealth. Was the royal lineage simply meeting its own obligations as the total pool of resources contracted? This study cannot fully answer those questions. It will, however, outline the story of the monarchy, a group of persons at or near the centers of power in the kingdom. It will explore the power relationships between and among the members of this elite. Who had power, how did they gain power, how did they lose it? It will construct an image of the offices and institutions that the monarchy built. But even that story, of necessity, is speculative.

Learning about Dahomey ～

The central organs of state power in Dahomey were the monarchy and the palace. The monarchy is a theoretical construction of my own making, a fluid institution made up of those closest to the king whose exercise of power I believe I can demonstrate, though I cannot always name precisely who belonged to it. The palace is in a sense more tangible, as physical entity and as organization, and it is referred to regularly by sources on Dahomey. Nevertheless, it was never described in detail by any traveler. Its operation was part of the deliberately constructed mystery that surrounded the monarchy, and its organization as a political entity lay beyond the conception of most writers about Dahomey. During the lifetime of the kingdom, no one who was a member either of the monarchy or of the palace ever recorded her or his memoirs or was interviewed about power and how it was exercised in Dahomey.

Though twentieth-century writers occasionally mention that a particular woman once lived in the palace of Abomey, only two interviews with former ahosi have ever been published. One had been a soldier and the other was a servant to a high-ranking woman.[11] Until the 1920s, the travelers, missionaries, government officials, and scholars who wrote about Dahomey were without exception non-Dahomean and male. Applying European standards of proper female behavior to what they saw, they tended to notice women in Dahomey only when women's behavior visibly violated European middle-class norms. Women soldiers march in great detail across the pages of their accounts, followed at a distance by women prostitutes, porters, and traders. Though travelers notice female officials at court, particularly by the mid–nineteenth century, they nevertheless tend to see the palace as an enlarged domestic unit rather than a political center. As such, they view women's involvement in politics as a form of meddling. Travelers who have to do business at court frequently complain of the power wielded by palace women, hinting that it is both inappropriate and illegitimate.

How can we understand institutions that were central to the state but that cast only a faint shadow across Dahomean history? Students of sketching are urged to record the shape of an object, not by trying to outline it but by observing and drawing the shape of the space that surrounds it—and Dahomey is richly endowed with evidence about the space that surrounds the monarchy and the palace. Because the palace was in constant interaction with the kingdom as a whole, by looking at the contacts between the more visible outside and the palace inside we can tease form out of the accounts of the many persons who visited, studied, or lived in what was once Dahomey. But the process is not a simple one.

Historians are sensitive to the reality that the building blocks of their trade are both elusive and unreliable. Faulty memory, error-prone eyewitness accounts, rumor, self-aggrandizing autobiography, hearsay, and competing interpretations of events are the stuff from which history is made. The historian in Africa steps even further into a minefield of problems with evidence. Outsiders to Dahomey confront a foreign culture whose signals and symbols are subject to gross misinterpretation by an untutored observer. The information that outsiders learn from Dahomeans is filtered through the eyes of informants who may or may not be knowledgeable about their own culture, and whose interpretations are colored by the nature of their relationship to the outsider in question. All the information gathered is in translated form, from Fongbe to a European tongue, and then it is sometimes translated a second time into another European language before it becomes available for the historian's use. Moreover, outsiders bring with them suppositions about human society and about Africa—assumptions that vary with the culture from which they spring and with particular moments in history and that color their understanding of what they see. But neither are insiders' accounts free of the vicissitudes of time and place. Persons reared in Fon society are also strangers in the past. They also visualize and interpret evidence on the basis of assumptions about the present and the past that need to be examined.

The many voices about Dahomey are in a sense in dialogue with each other. Many writers echo observations of predecessors, giving the unwary reader a false sense of a preponderance of evidence.[12] Some travelers, particularly in the nineteenth century, are well read in the literature about Dahomey and are able to comment on the relative correctness of previous travelers' work. Twentieth-century scholars are similar. But well-read visitors always risk seeing only what their eyes have been prompted to see. Others contradict or, without being aware of it, independently corroborate, repeat, or disagree with predecessors. Our guides to this history will be Dahomeans, travelers, traders, missionaries, officials, and scholars—all of them our models for drawing the space that will reveal an image of the palace of Dahomey, and I therefore here introduce the major players.

Virtually all accounts of Dahomey written up until the end of the eighteenth century were provided by persons associated in some way with the overseas slave trade. Prior to the 1720s, Dahomey was an inland kingdom cut off from direct contact with European slavers. Accounts up to that date provide details of life in neighboring areas, most notably Allada, the kingdom that effectively blocked Dahomey's access to the coast, and Whydah, the major slave-trading kingdom and port that Dahomey would later control. It was only with Dahomey's conquest of Allada in 1724 that Europeans began to come into direct contact with the kingdom. The best known and most useful slave-traders' records published in English are by Bulfinch Lamb, William Snelgrave, Robert Norris, and Archibald Dalzel. All were eyewitnesses to events and observers of the land, people, and politics of Dahomey. All also recorded hearsay evidence, drawing on conversations with persons they met in Dahomey, persons who were sometimes not closely tied to developments at Dahomey's center. And all interpret and judge what they saw and heard, painting a picture of eighteenth-century Dahomey that is best described by the late-twentieth-century idiom *bad press.*

Snelgrave, Norris, and Dalzel take pains to defend the slave trade, arguing that the savagery of Dahomey, ruled by an arbitrary and absolutist monarch who presided over unparalleled human sacrifice, made enslavement and sale in the Western Hemisphere a better alternative for Africans than life in Africa. All assume that Dahomey conquered its way from the Abomey plateau to the port of Whydah in the 1720s in order to be more deeply involved in the slave trade. A lesser-known source from this period, John Atkins, who visited the coast in 1721 as a surgeon on a slaver, views Dahomey with far more sympathy, arguing instead that the kingdom conquered others in order to protect its own people from the slave trade. Atkins in the twentieth century became an instrumental source for the work of a Nigerian historian, I. A. Akinjogbin, who promotes a controversial thesis that argues that Dahomey conquered the coast in order to abolish the slave trade.[13]

The French, along with the English and the Portuguese, maintained a trading establishment, or fort, at Whydah throughout nearly the entire eighteenth century. Two important accounts have come down to us from French personnel. Joseph Pruneau de Pommegorge, a factor at Whydah as early as the 1750s and director of the French fort in the early 1760s, published his *Description de la nigritie* in 1789. A decade after Pommegorge left Whydah, the fort's chaplain and one of its agents wrote their observations in a long document, "Réflexions sur Juda par les Sieurs De Chenevert et abbé Bulet," that found its way into the French archives.[14] A generation later, in 1797, Vicente Ferreira Pires, a Portuguese priest sent to try to convert the king to Roman Catholicism, was in Abomey when the king was assassinated. His record provides invaluable though sometimes ambiguous material on court life just before the turn of the nineteenth century.

European sources are relatively few for the first four decades of the nineteenth century. The relative paucity of travelers' accounts is matched by an absence of information from the oral historical memory of the court. Adandozan, the king whose rise to power was witnessed by Pires in 1797, was removed by a coup d'état in about 1818. His successor, Gezo, eliminated all accounts of Adandozan's reign from the official oral records, leaving a twenty-one year gap in Dahomean oral history. In contrast, the mid–nineteenth century is rich in travelers' accounts. Between 1840 and 1865, well over a dozen envoys of various nationalities visited Abomey to try to negotiate an end to the trade in slaves, to increase other forms of trade, and to gain support for missions and European schools at the coast. The two most important among these visitors who published material in English are Frederick E. Forbes and Richard Burton. Forbes was a naval commander in the British antislavery squadron who welcomed an opportunity to try to negotiate an end to Dahomey's slave exports. Burton was a brilliant but erratic intellectual and explorer who in midcentury was named British consul in the Bight of Benin. Each in his own way contributes to Dahomey's bad press. Now that the slave trade had been outlawed by the British, Dahomey was condemned for continuing it and for continuing its practice of human sacrifice. Burton's account is richest in detail and most erudite. Burton was a keen and experienced observer of foreign cultures, a gifted linguist who quickly learned Fongbe; however, his writings on Dahomey also reflect his arrogance and contempt for West Africans, both of which evidently were apparent when he visited the kingdom. The Dahomeans developed a strong distaste for Burton, ultimately excluding him from ceremonies and refusing to negotiate with him. It is Burton more than any other visitor of the period who pointed the way toward the pseudoscientific racism that characterizes so many accounts of Africa toward the end of the century and beyond.

The depth of the Dahomean dislike for Burton contrasts with the affection Dahomeans expressed for J. A. Skertchly, a British entomologist who arrived in the kingdom to gather specimens but who was effectively detained in Abomey for eight months in 1871. Made a prince by King Glele, Skertchly was entertained and honored at what was probably the happiest period of Glele's reign. Using his time to make observations about human rather than insect society, Skertchly is able to comment on Burton's observations and add new material to the corpus of information about the kingdom. By the late nineteenth century, the French were becoming increasingly active in the area, making continuous representations to Glele to try to assert their claims on the coast. A series of accounts from persons who participated in official missions to the court or who were held hostage by the Dahomeans as negotiations broke down paves the way to numerous descriptions of the war waged by the French against Dahomey in 1892–93, of which the most lucid are those of Alexandre d'Albeca and Edouard Aublet.

With the colonial period comes an important shift in the stance of major contributors to Dahomean historiography. Gone is the bad press of the precolonial period, replaced by accounts that adopt a Dahomean viewpoint or at least show respect for the kingdom: for building and centralizing a state, for administrative efficiency, for military prowess, for artistic creativity. The early colonial period was marked by two major works by French officials, Auguste Le Hérissé and Bernard Maupoil. As representatives of colonial authority who nevertheless displayed great sensitivity toward African culture, the two were participant-observers of Dahomean life long before the term came into vogue as a method for anthropological field research. Le Hérissé served two tours as colonial administrator (*commandant de cercle*) of Abomey in the first decade of the twentieth century. He carefully recorded oral accounts of prominent members of the royal family, drawing most centrally on the knowledge of Agbidinukun, a son of Glele and one of a number of professional court historians responsible for learning and conveying the history of the kingdom. Closely allied to the children of Behanzin through his marriage to a daughter of that king, Le Hérissé helped to shape the twentieth-century history of Dahomey by attempting to integrate an understanding of African culture into administrative and judicial processes. Maupoil, who served in Dahomey from 1934–36, built a monumental study of divination and Dahomean religion around the memoirs of one of Behanzin's chief diviners, Gedegbe. Maupoil writes with uncritical admiration for his subject, even though Gedegbe's memories are as often as not self-serving.

Most prominent among the colonial-era anglophone researchers was the American anthropologist Melville J. Herskovits. Despite remaining only a few months in the field in 1931, Herskovits and his spouse, Frances, contribute valuable anthropological material, though with occasional lapses in understanding that have been noted by subsequent scholars. Herskovits's vision of Dahomey was formed by his major informant, René Aho, a grandson of King Glele who later produced several articles on Fon social structure and who continued to work as guide and informant for scholars and filmmakers until his death in May 1977.[15]

The colonial period also saw the first written contributions from Dahomeans. Two of the earliest authors to deal with the history and culture of the kingdom, Maximilien Quénum and Paul Hazoumé, represented communities that were distant from Dahomey's center. Quénum was born of one of several prominent trading families licensed by the kings of Dahomey who lived and worked in the port of Whydah. His first book, *Au pays des Fons*, a compilation of information about Fon culture, language, and religion, with a brief note on the kingdom's history, appeared in 1936. Quénum's *Les ancêtres de la famille Quénum* (1981) includes an invaluable record of one lineage's changing relations with the kingdom of Dahomey. Paul Hazoumé was born of a father who was a court official in Porto Novo, a rival kingdom to Dahomey. He was a teacher, novelist, journalist, ethnographer, and political activist whose two major works dealing with Dahomean history are the novel *Doguicimi*, first published in 1938, and the ethnographic study of oath taking, *Le pacte de sang au Dahomey*, first published in 1937. Like some of the works of Hazoumé's contemporary négritude writers, *Doguicimi* glories in the virtues of African womanhood. It is a tale of a prince's wife who, in contrast to the king's wives, is absolutely obedient, faithful, and loyal to her husband, even unto death. Rich in ethnographic detail, *Doguicimi* is regularly cited as a historical source, even though some of its assertions are not corroborated by other sources.

French research facilities in West Africa, which after independence in 1960 became African-controlled, were an important support and outlet for research by French and African scholars, particularly after World War II. During its heyday in the 1950s and 1960s, the journal *Études Dahoméennes* and IFAN (the Institut Français—later Fondamental—d'Afrique Noire) published work by Edouard Dunglas, Anatole Coissi, Paul Falcon, Alexandre Adande, Serpos Tidjani, and others. Dahomean history was also published by the professional sociologists and ethnographers associated with the historical museum situated in the remains of the palace of Abomey: Paul Mercier, Jacques Lombard, and Ernest d'Oliveira, among others. Mention needs also to be made of Pierre Verger, a Frenchman beloved by West Africans whose own triangular research career—incorporating Europe, West Africa, and Brazil—allowed him to publish important, cross-cultural field studies of religion and to make major portions of Brazilian archival records accessible to others through translation and publication.

The explosion of interest in African history coupled with the coming of independence in 1960 opened the way for dozens of African and non-African scholars to write about Dahomey in the remainder of the twentieth century. Usually drawing on oral traditions that they collected in their home areas, numerous Africans from the area that had been precolonial Dahomey have written accounts of the kingdom as part of degree programs at the University of Benin and at universities in France. European and American students have drawn more heavily on archival and published sources. Because such a wealth of published information exists on Dahomey, many Americans have used the kingdom as a paradigm for theoretical analyses, usually drawing heavily from the most accessible of the sources in English: Herskovits, Burton, and Forbes.[16] Preeminent among recent scholars has been Robin Law, who in the past two decades has published prolifically on nearly all aspects of Dahomean history and has done valuable historiographical work correlating unpublished correspondence with the evidence provided by published sources.

Though nearly all scholars try to use evidence from both archival/published accounts and from oral narratives collected in the field (by themselves or others), the work of most can be distinguished by a heavy reliance on one or the other major areas of evidence, either oral accounts or archival and travelers' records. What is striking about the work of those who concentrate on the archival record, for example, is the degree to which the concerns of the Europeans who provide their fundamental evidence are reflected in the kinds of questions that the historians ask. Travelers assumed that their central concerns in visiting the kingdom were equally the central concerns of the monarchy. Over the course of the history of Dahomey, those concerns included the regulation of commerce, debates in Europe over the slave trade and its abolition, the need to develop "legitimate" trade, the negotiation of treaties, and the recognition of European territorial claims. The contemporary historians follow their lead. However, were those preoccupations shared by the monarchy of Dahomey?

The oral records suggest something rather different, a kingdom absorbed by concerns for expansion, for consolidation of control over new territory, for celebrating military and cultural prowess, and for maximizing the support of the gods. The twentieth-century collection and integration of oral memory into the Western-style construction of Dahomean history has been a major accomplishment. Principal in importance among those who have collected oral narratives and integrated them with archival documents is Maurice Ahanhanzo Glélé, a direct descendant of Ahanhanzo, the prince chosen as heir by Glele but who died prematurely in the mid-1870s. Glélé unabashedly presents his family's perspective on history, noting correctly the advantages enjoyed by scholars born of the royal family, who can build on cultural and linguistic understandings learned from a very young age to collect oral memoirs.

The oral documentation that Glélé collected is illustrative of the major characteristics of twentieth-century oral history. First, the oral history of Dahomey reflects the perspective of the ruling class, and specifically the ruling dynasty. But the ruling dynasty was itself divided into ten sublineages that included respectively the descendants of the ten kings acknowledged in tradition. Each sublineage preserved its own history, so there are multiple sources; yet all present the dynasty's point of view. Though there are occasional oral records of individuals or villages conquered by Dahomey, those narratives tend to stress positive aspects of their relations with Dahomey; for example, their integration into the kingdom, and the opportunities that conquered peoples were offered to become successful Dahomeans. Rarely do we hear with any clarity the responses of areas and individuals who were victims of Dahomey. Nowhere do we learn details of life in the slave villages that were created in nineteenth-century Dahomey, of the slave revolts mentioned in passing by travelers, or even of the perspectives of Dahomean peasants. In short, Dahomean oral history is essentially the self-serving story of those who held power. Though some of those narratives are based on testimony from villages that were subject to Dahomean exploitation, the historical memory as it is retained is far from critical. Indeed, Dahomean historical memory puts everyone on the "right" side: the narrators of oral history regularly claim that their ancestors were all either directly or by extension a part of the ruling body, all close and favored associates of one king or another.

Secondly, twentieth-century oral narratives describe the kingdom as it existed toward the end of the nineteenth century, essentially during the reign of King Glele. Many characteristics of the kingdom based on the period of Glele are projected backwards over the entire history of the kingdom. The structures of the Dahomean state thus appear to have sprung fully developed from the time of the first king, and to have remained unchanged for more than two hundred years. Even though it is based on the state at the time of Glele, Dahomey's oral history is filtered through the experience of the French conquest and of colonialism. France destroyed Dahomey, incorporated her land into a colony and sent her monarch into exile, making Dahomey both a victim of injustice and a symbol of lost independence, a nation whose glories would be subject to magnification and weaknesses subject to forgetfulness. In 1894, Behanzin, the king who was defeated and deposed by the French, was denounced by the royal family for his disgrace; a century later, he was remembered as a heroic resister of French colonialism. Moreover, by deposing one king and setting up his brother as their puppet, the French precipitated a rift within the ruling family that has yet to be healed. As the twentieth century wore on, the memories of the precolonial era began to be articulated more and more in the idiom of the French administration and the evolving modern institutional state structures. Is the centralization that historians now find to have been characteristic of the Dahomean administration in fact Abomean or Parisian?

As we move farther from the nineteenth century, the accuracy of accounts is increasingly in question. Each generation of scholars collecting traditions has met fewer persons who could personally remember the precolonial era. At the period of my initial field research in 1972–73, for example, more than a dozen sons and daughters of Kings Glele and Behanzin were still living, but they were only a tiny fraction of the persons who had been available to Mercier in the 1950s, to Hazoumé in the 1920s, or to Le Hérissé in the 1900s. None of those still-living princes or princesses had witnessed as adults the last years of the kingdom. By my second research trip in 1984, all of them had gone to Kutome. Heads of lineages and households, the usual repositories of oral history, are increasingly individuals who are Western-educated, including persons who have researched and written Dahomean history. Sophisticated in their understanding of issues of Dahomean history and historic methodology, they can hardly be considered to be repositories of a relatively untouched oral tradition. Yet oral accounts about precolonial Dahomey continue to be collected and are often used uncritically. Recently, researchers have tried to understand how Dahomey was viewed by her neighbors by collecting materials in areas peripheral to the center of the kingdom. Though laudable as an effort, is it reasonable to assume that peasants living in the Weme River valley in the 1980s have retained enough details of eighteenth-century history, for example, to describe accurately the dress of Dahomean women soldiers who purportedly fought against their ancestors some 250 years before? [17]

The widespread and uncritical collection and use of oral narratives is related to another phenomenon of twentieth-century Abomean experience: the commoditization of history. Concerned to minimize the influence of the former kingdom in colonial Dahomean affairs, the French isolated Abomey politically and commercially. The monarchy was abolished in 1900 and the environs of the city were divided into eight cantons to discourage the amassing of political influence by any single chief. The north–south rail line and road were run six miles to the east through Bohicon, a town that also became the site of commercial palm-oil processing. Meanwhile, the French encouraged artisanal activity and the creation of a museum in the remains of the palace and the preservation and promotion of the past became one of the few viable economic activities in the region, apart from farming. Knowledgable Abomeans—guides to the museum, elderly members of the royal family, and others—became middlemen purveying history and culture. How does the commoditization of historical information alter its content and interpretation as it is effectively sold to the succession of scholars, filmmakers, journalists, and tourists who have visited the area throughout the twentieth century?

Finally, too few historians have taken into account the reality that oral history over time works very much like written history. That is, succeeding generations rethink and rework oral history to reflect contemporary concerns, just as literate societies and their historians regularly rewrite the past to fit the present. The history of the kingdom of Dahomey appears always to have been organized and retold through the chronology of the kings and the principal events of their reigns. This seeming precision masks a central concern for legitimacy on the part of the Dahomean monarchy—first, the legitimacy of the dynasty to rule, and then the legitimacy of any individual king to rule vis-à-vis other kingly candidates. With each new king, history of necessity had to be recreated to justify and legitimize the present. Dahomean history claims perhaps the most blatant manipulation of oral memory ever documented—the elimination of the twenty-one-year reign of Adandozan, from 1797 to 1818. But Dahomean oral memory is replete with far more subtle and complex examples of historical manipulation, some of which are corroborated in the written records of the past. The true history of the royal family is said to have been esoteric knowledge, with elements carefully hidden from outsiders to the royal line. The myths of the origin of the royal lineage, for example, were revealed only after the fall of the kingdom and were first published in Le Hérissé's 1911 account. Nevertheless, aspects of the kingdom's known history make clear why suppression of knowledge of the royal lineage's origins would have had instrumental value in precolonial Dahomey. Part of the history of Dahomey thus is the history of the invention of history, and the motives of those who changed it.[18]

Historical evidence for Dahomey includes more than oral narratives about history and written documents by travelers and scholars. Historic realities are embedded in certain social and religious institutions that provide corroboration and clarification of oral narratives and written texts. A practice that anthropologists call positional succession keeps the lines of descent from influential historical figures sharply drawn. Through positional succession, titled and wealthy Dahomeans at their deaths passed their names and estates to direct descendants in their patrilineages. All members of the line then had the same kin relationship to the replacement that they had to the original individual. In effect, the heir *became* his or her predecessor. Positional succession and a related institution, perpetual kinship, insured that major estate holders would survive, literally, into the present, and that branches of the various family lines emanating from Abomey would remain closely linked to their founders. A cult dedicated to the deified dead of the royal family, Nesuhwe, similarly ensures the perpetual remembrance of the prominent children of each king, whose spirits possess trained vodunsi (adepts) during annual rituals. Neither positional succession nor the existence of Nesuhwe ensures that the persons who embody historic figures are deeply knowledgable about their predecessors; it does, however, provide a framework of names and relationships of influential Abomeans during any given king's reign.[19]

Obviously, all historical material, whether written or oral in origin, needs to be treated with skepticism. And all historians similarly must be confronted for their manner and motives in piecing together the past. My particular historical perspective grows out of the selections I have made of written sources, out of my understanding of the accounts of people in Abomey that I as often as not met by chance, out of the vagaries of my memory, and out of a sense of what fits with my own vision of Dahomean culture as I experienced it. My work draws more heavily on published as opposed to archival sources, in large part because the published materials are particularly rich with cultural material. Archival records, in contrast, tend to offer a great deal of detail about commercial and political relations between Europeans and Dahomey. My interpretation of the Dahomean past also relies on oral records collected by me and by others. It particularly privileges points in Dahomean history where outsiders and insiders agree, places where the oral record corroborates or clarifies the written accounts of contemporary outsiders. The history of Dahomey that I write today differs from what I believed about the kingdom twenty years ago, and differs from the way I shall see it two decades hence. Like all history, mine is in a sense fiction, yet it is a fiction informed by records of human experience and perception—fiction that is intended to convey something of what happened and was experienced by people living in a small part of West Africa some time ago.～

2

From Dahomey's Origins to 1740

They generally say that it was Dako who led us to Abomey following a quarrel between him and his brothers at the death of their father. . . . That is not completely true.

Agbidinukun, brother of King Behanzin, as told to Lé Hérissé

The Slave Trade and the Founding of the Kingdom ∽

The period up to the 1720s is the most difficult to construct in the history of Dahomey. It is there that oral narratives and travelers' accounts diverge most widely—that the accounts of insiders differ most from the written observations of contemporary outsiders. Indeed, there is virtually no correspondence between oral traditions and contemporary written records prior to the 1710s, even though oral narratives and some scholars agree that by that period the kingdom may have been in existence for as many as one hundred years.

Part of the reason for the lack of accord between Dahomean oral record and outside observation is the fact that travelers prior to the 1720s had no direct contact with Dahomey as a state. Concentrated near the coast, travelers knew the name Fon or Foin only as one of the several interior nations from which slaves were brought for the Atlantic trade. In the interior, however, that same Fon nation was establishing itself as a political entity named Dahomey and was beginning the expansion that oral memory would recall as a sacred duty, that each king "make Dahomey always larger." [1]

Dahomey arose some sixty miles from the West African coast on a plateau centered in what geographers call the Dahomey gap, a break in the coastal rain forest where savannah climate, mixed with some vestiges of forest, continues down to the sea. The relatively open and well-watered land (more than forty-three inches of rain annually) made viable the cultivation of a wide variety of crops: millet, maize, cassava, beans, cotton, and oil palms, among others. The lack of thick forest also left Dahomey vulnerable to attack, as the Dahomeans discovered when they fell subject to cavalry raids from the Yoruba-speaking kingdom of Oyo, to the east, beginning in the second quarter of the eighteenth century. Nevertheless, Dahomey's plateau heartland was somewhat sheltered by natural barriers, toward which the kingdom expanded. The river Coufo formed a boundary to the west and the Zou to the east and northeast. To the north lay a series of steep hills and to the south was a swamp, the *ko*, which would later become known as Lama, from the Portuguese word for mud. Dahomey over time grew to incorporate territory beyond her natural boundaries, most notably the older kingdoms of Allada and Whydah to the south. But despite the incorporation of those relatively large areas, the capital city of Abomey and the lands that surrounded it remained the core of a kingdom that was effectively centralized only within the roughly one thousand square miles of the Abomey plateau. Other areas, including Allada and Whydah, were in effect tributary states administered by governors appointed in Abomey. As late as the 1870s, a visitor would remark that "the King is but nominal anywhere except in the district immediately surrounding the capital."[2]

No one knows how or why the people of the Abomey plateau came to be called the Fon. The name was recorded in the seventeenth century, though a false etymology dates the term to a much later period, the reign of Tegbesu (1740–74), who is said to have compared the people to the *fontin* tree, before which all the other trees bow down.[3] Linguistically and culturally, the Fon were part of a cluster of peoples speaking dialects of the same language. Different groupings of these peoples are sometimes called the Aja, or Ewe. Recently the term Gbe, drawn from their common word for language, has been utilized to describe the various peoples as a whole. The collective body of the Gbe filled much of the land area of the Dahomey gap between the sea and eighty miles inland. They lived midway between two other major linguistic and culture areas of West Africa,

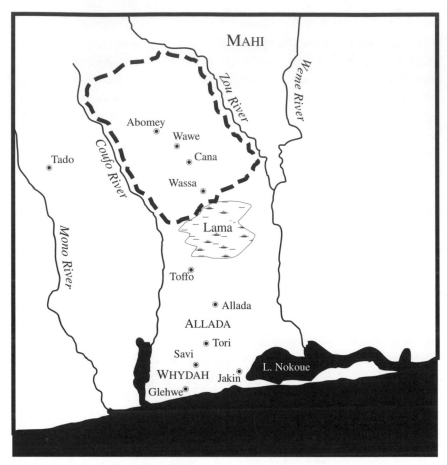

3. Dahomey in the early eighteenth century

the matrilineal Akan to the west and patrilineal Yoruba-speaking peoples to the east, both of whom had major impacts on their culture.

In the period before the 1720s, however, only the odd rumor of the kingdom of the Fon reached European ears, and only as individuals did Dahomeans enter directly into contact with Europeans. Some of those individuals were middlemen traders who accompanied slaves to the coast. A far greater proportion arrived on the coast as commodities destined for the overseas slave trade. Reputed to have been bad slaves—they tended to commit suicide—Dahomeans would have been enslaved as a result of wars, raids into their territory, criminal condemnation, or possibly sale in times of natural crisis. Later in the eighteenth century, Dahomey would become well-known as a slave-trading state, and though scholars disagree about the process by which that occurred, income from the trade was undisputably a central source of state revenue for at least half the life of the kingdom. Given the importance of the export of slaves for Dahomey, it is useful to look for a moment at the experience of the trade of Dahomean individuals. Oral traditions tell us nothing in this area, but the European slave traders, who created virtually all contemporary written records of the time, provide details of what happened to Dahomeans who journeyed to the coast and into the infamous middle passage at the turn of the eighteenth century.

Fon slaves likely traveled to the coast as part of a slave caravan, possibly joining individuals from other areas, a few of whom could have come from as far as a three months' walk inland.[4] They would have walked single file, though travelers in later times would describe wide roads in the area, and they would likely have taken four to five days to reach the coast, as did travelers in later times. If they left Abomey itself, at slightly more than one thousand feet in altitude, and followed one of the two main routes to the south, they would have begun an immediate though imperceptible descent to Cana, passing by intercropped fields and occasional villages of mud houses with thatch roofs. After descending more than eight hundred feet, they would have reached the edges of the Ko swamp, which was roughly six to seven miles wide. The Ko was crossed most easily from December to June; the rains made passage difficult and sometimes impossible in July to November. Once across the Ko, the Fon slaves would have climbed to heights some four hundred feet above sea level, where they entered the partially forested territory controlled by the kingdom of Allada. Slave caravans may have been halted to pay tolls at various towns along the route, and they were most certainly stopped before Allada's capital. Allada was able through much of the seventeenth century to control the roads both north and south, serving as a kind of funnel through which slaves from a relatively wide area of Gbe-, Yoruba-, and Hausa-speaking populations could be channeled to the coast and to any one of a series of coastal settlements from which traders of various European nationalities—French, Dutch, English, and Portuguese—operated trading factories.

At the beginning of the eighteenth century, the coastal area between what is now eastern Ghana and western Nigeria was made up of tiny independent kingdoms, whose heads are descriptively and derisively called *roitelets* (kinglets) in the French sources. These kings rose and fell depending upon their warring skills in face of competing states and upon their ability to maintain comfortable working relationships with European factors, on the one hand, and with more powerful polities in the interior, most often Allada and Oyo, on the other. Their fates were dependent, too, on the demand for slaves, which fluctuated according to economic and political factors in Europe and in the slave-using territories controlled by European states. Even though Whydah was in theory a tributary state, Allada in the late seventeenth century preferred to send slaves southeast to its subordinate states on the coast, initially to Offra and later to Jakin, in the area of contemporary Godomey. Nevertheless, Whydah managed to attract a good portion of the total trade, despite intermittent hostilities with Allada, particularly as the volume of trade dramatically increased near the end of the seventeenth century. Dahomean slaves thus might well have passed from Allada to follow the road that ran slightly to the southwest and through the kingdom of Tori. Along this route they would have passed an occasional European trader traveling up to Allada in a hammock. Hammocks were large; one traveler noted that they were made from cloths nine feet long and seven wide. The hammock was tied to a long, stout pole and balanced on the heads of two male carriers who moved at a near run, switching off from time to time with other pairs of carriers.[5] The traveler was shaded by an awning that projected eighteen inches or so to either side of the pole. Unable to see out and constantly jostled by the rapid motion, travelers grumbled at what must have been one of the least comfortable forms of luxury conveyance ever devised.

A half-mile south of the river that marked the boundary between Tori and Whydah lay Savi, capital of Whydah and a town that might well have impressed Fon slaves at the time. Savi lay seven miles inland from the sea and boasted the trading establishments of the four major European nations. William Smith, who arrived in the town shortly after it had been burned by the Dahomeans in 1727, gleaned this description of its previous prosperity from fellow Europeans:

> All the Factory-houses were built after the European Fashion, being lofty, spacious and very airy; containing many neat commodious Apartments; also to each a fine large open Hall with cool Balconies, etc. all these upon the First Floor. Underneath upon the Ground Floor were their Warehouses. These delightful Dwellings contributed very much, not only to the Comfort and Satisfaction, but also to the Health of the Europeans. The Town was so exceeding populous that it was with Difficulty one pass'd along the Streets, tho' they were very broad. Here were daily Markets wherein many Sorts of European, as well as African Commodities, were exhibited to publick Sale, also great Variety of Provisions.[6]

Travelers as a rule remarked the apparent fertility and prosperity of the kingdom of Whydah prior to the Dahomean conquest. It was densely populated and intensively farmed, and Europeans marveled at the industry of the Hweda (people of Whydah) in producing two harvests each year and husbanding abundant livestock. Provisions at Whydah were said to be the best and the least expensive along the African coast. By the end of the seventeenth century, the French and English had also built mud-walled fortified establishments at Glehwe, three miles from the sea and the site of the modern city of Whydah. Fon slaves would have passed through Glehwe, and possibly remained there in stockades as their sale was negotiated and enough slaves for a full cargo were assembled, a process that could take several months.

The degradation and terror that slaves must have felt as they reached the sea are easily imagined from the traders' accounts. Stripped of all clothing by their sellers, men and women alike squatted to preserve some semblance of modesty. They typically received cloth again only when they had boarded a ship. Slaves were examined by ships' doctors, who checked teeth, eyes, genitals, and general physical appearance, rejecting people estimated to be more than thirty-five years old, along with those who were lame or diseased, smallpox in particular being endemic. Once se-lected, slaves were branded on the chest or shoulder with a mark indicat-ing the trading company or ship, "the place being anointed with a little palm oil, which caus'd but little pain, the mark being usually well in four or five days, appearing very plain and white after," according to one slaver's claim.[7]

Men fetched a higher price than women. Just after the turn of the eighteenth century, products that had been produced by slave labor in Brazil—tobacco and gold—were beginning to be introduced as trade items, in addition to the cowry shells, metals, cloth, and firearms regu-larly traded in the seventeenth century. Tobacco would become a staple of the trade for more than a century. Treated with molasses to keep it from drying out and rotting, the tobacco shipped to the West African coast was of the lowest quality—so poor that it was not permitted to be imported into Portugal.

Scholarly statistics describe gender differences in the Atlantic trade, with men bought in significantly higher numbers than women. The male-to-female proportion shipped out of Whydah by French traders in the second decade of the eighteenth century, for example, has been esti-mated at 1.8 to 1.0.[8] But the neat averages disappear at the level of indi-vidual slave captains, who felt pressure to load cargoes regardless of gen-der. Once slaves were purchased, traders incurred costs by having to maintain them, albeit meanly. Life along the coast was known to be dan-gerous to the health of Europeans, and delays could reduce a ship's crew to dangerously low numbers. Malaria, not yet identified, was only one of a number of deadly fevers, and mosquitoes were so persistent that Englishmen in the Glehwe factory took opium or laudanum to sleep through incessant nightly bombardments. Holding slaves on board, the alternative to suffering ashore, was also a problem: again and again, slav-ers talk of rebellion and suicide by drowning on the part of slaves who expected to be eaten by the whites. In short, traders filled their ships as quickly as possible with whatever healthy humans were available—men, women, and children.

The final march for departing Fon slaves was the three-mile road from Glehwe to the sea. Passing over sand ridges, it dipped three times into streams that were muddy depressions in January to March but that could be neck-deep in water in May through July. Dahomean slaves arriving at the beach would have been hard-pressed even to see the European ships, which moored as far as two miles offshore. The surf between the ships and Whydah beach was legendary; it broke three times, over two sandbars and then the shore itself. So treacherous were the waves that Whydah fishermen never went to sea and fished only in the lagoons. Canoemen had to be imported from the Gold Coast, some one hundred miles to the west, to ferry goods to shore and human cargoes to the ships. William Bosman wrote after visits in 1697 and 1699 that "this Port is so incomodious and dangerous; by reason of the horrible Burnings in the Sea, that we cannot land here without running a great Risque; but in April, May, June and July, the Sea burns so violently, that according to the Proverb, he ought to have two Lives who ventures."[9] Canoes capsized nearly daily except in the relatively calm period at the end of the dry season. The hapless victims of upset boats were often torn apart by the sharks that literally patrolled the area and that were said by some to follow ships all the way to Barbados.

Notwithstanding the dangers, Whydah was a central slaving port, a site of the forced emigration at its height of as many as 15,000 persons annually. In all, the two-hundred-mile-long strip of West African beach that included Whydah and became known as the Slave Coast saw the export of Africans grow from a little more than 10,000 in the decade of the 1640s to peaks of more than 150,000 in each of the first two decades of the eighteenth century. The total number of persons who left the Slave Coast up to 1850 was estimated by Patrick Manning at nearly two million persons, nearly one-fifth of the entire volume of the Atlantic trade. Slave-trade statistics do not tell us how many Fon were among these numbers. However, Gbe-speaking peoples constituted the vast majority up to the turn of the nineteenth century.[10]

We have little information about what early Dahomeans knew of the conditions of the overseas slave trade, or of their attitudes toward it. There is no way to know, either, if all the Fon slaves at the turn of the eighteenth century were captives of war or if some were being sold into the trade by other Dahomeans, perhaps even by the monarchy itself. We know that Fon persons were trading slaves through several coastal ports by the 1710s. Europeans claimed that in Whydah, the king, who received women as wives from families within the kingdom, sometimes sold women of his own household to make up cargoes—something that was done by the king of Dahomey later in the eighteenth century. As early as 1727, sale into the overseas trade was used by the Dahomean monarchy to dispose of politically troublesome persons, including women of the palace organization. We also know with certainty that at least some of the original inhabitants of Wawe, the area from which Dahomey grew, were sold into the trade. Known as Gedevi (children of Gede), they left their traces in the Western Hemisphere: they established their vodun, Gede (Ghede), in Haiti, to guard the territory between the worlds of the living and the dead.[11]

Contemporary written accounts before the 1720s are preoccupied with the mechanics of the slave trade. Oral traditions that describe the same period in contrast speak only of the founding of Dahomey and its early wars. All agree that the kingdom began in Wawe, now a village approximately midway between Abomey and Cana. Details of the myth that describes the origins of the royal family were apparently guarded until the twentieth century by the royal lineage as part of the secret history of Dahomey. The myth tells the story of a line descended from the mating of a princess of the royal family of Tado, in what is now Togo, with a leopard. The princess's leopardlike son, Agasu, became the *tohwiyo* (mythical founder) of the clan of the Agasuvi (children of Agasu). Migrating from Tado, the Agasuvi settled in Allada, where they became the ruling lineage and hence took the name Alladahonu (people from Allada). After a succession dispute, three Agasuvi brothers separated. One remained to rule in Allada, a second went southeast to found the kingdom of Porto Novo, and the third traveled north to found Dahomey. Scholars have pointed out a number of problems with this myth as history: that a kinship link between the dynasties of Dahomey and Allada is unlikely, since the founding of Porto Novo and Dahomey were separated by some one hundred years, and neither the ruling line of Allada nor that of Porto Novo looked to Agasu as a tohwiyo. On the other hand, some scholars have taken the myth literally, using it to argue that the rulers of Dahomey were part of a diaspora of Yoruba-speaking peoples that began in Ife, Nigeria, and moved successively to Ketu and Tado. What is never in dispute, however, is the belief that the ruling dynasty came from somewhere outside the founding center of Wawe. The myth and its meaning will become important to our story during the reign of Agaja. Meanwhile, the likely scenario for the founding of Dahomey, which in fact does not contradict the oral traditions, is that a relatively small band of strangers settled in Wawe and came to control it. Given the banditry and fluctuating warfare among tiny polities in the region, Le Hérissé's description, which parallels other sources, seems apt: "One sees them first as an outlaw horde that settles among foreign tribes, forming alliances and then, under cover of these and using both force and trickery, spreading out like a stain of oil from the spot where they had landed." [12]

Table 1. Kings and Kpojito (reign-mates) of Dahomey

Dates	King	Kpojito
	Wegbaja	
	Akaba	
c. 1716–1740	Agaja	Adonon
1740–1774	Tegbesu	Hwanjile
1774–1789	Kpengla	Chai
1789–1797	Agonglo	Senume
1797–1818	Adandozan	Kentobasin
1818–1858	Gezo	Agontime
1858–1889	Glele	Zoyindi
1889–1894	Behanzin	Kamlin
1894–1900	Agoliagbo	Kanai

Dates in this table are the traditional order. See note 3 for a different view.

An etymology for the name Dahomey was published as early as 1789 by Robert Norris. Dan (Da, in Norris) was a king of Abomey defeated by Dakodonu (Tacoodonou), who then made good a threat by cutting open Dan's stomach and building his palace on the dead king's belly (*ho* = stomach; *me* = in; i.e., in the stomach of Dan). The story was repeated regularly during the next two hundred years, though the conquering king was sometimes said to have been Wegbaja or Akaba instead of Dakodonu, and Dan was occasionally called Agrim. False etymologies are common in Dahomean history, and the closely related term *honme* (*ho*, *hon* = portal or entrance, particularly to a palace; *me* = in), meaning royal palace, appears in other place-names, for example, at Ajahome (Aja royal palace), the site of a royal residence set up west of the Coufo River during the time of Tegbesu. Honme is even used to refer to the central palace in Abomey. Danhome, in the stomach of Dan, could well have originated as a pun on Danhonme, the royal palace of Dan. Even if the etymology is false, the story is important, because it conveys the bellicose spirit that typified Dahomey from its earliest days and that was deliberately directed toward potential enemies. In similar fashion, Agaja bragged to a European visitor in 1728 that his grandfather (Dakodonu) conquered 2 countries, his father (Wegbaja) 18, and his brother (Akaba) 42, while he himself had conquered 209, a comment that simultaneously underlines Dahomean militarism and emphasizes the small scale of political entities in the area.[13]

Interlopers from elsewhere, and people who had gained control by force, the founders of Dahomey would have needed to establish their authority and legitimacy. In a world where wealth and prestige were linked to the numbers of individuals under a person's control, the royal clan would have tried to increase its dependents as rapidly as possible. Slaves and wives, both of which were costly to acquire, were an obvious means to building larger numbers quickly. Raids would have yielded both, along with the hostility of peoples in the path of the Dahomeans. Evidence from the coast suggests that kings sometimes commandeered women from their subjects without compensating them with bridewealth, as patrilineal custom demanded, a practice that probably was the same in Dahomey, where in fact it occurred in later periods. The king's household would have grown to outnumber those of other prominent persons in the area. By 1724, Bulfinch Lamb would estimate the number of king's wives at more than two thousand.[14] The organization of the king's household during this period probably began to take on the forms that would be noted by later travelers. Descriptions of the palace of the kings of Whydah, for example, correspond to later evidence from Abomey: that the wives of the king cultivated fields and had the right to make and sell goods on their own accounts, that entry into the palace was strictly controlled, that people were forced to get out of the wives' paths when the women left the palace, and that new kings inherited the wives of their father. There is even evidence from Whydah that wives of the king were involved in administrative matters. Bosman reported at the end of the seventeenth century that the king's wives carried out the destruction of property of important persons who had been found guilty of offenses against the state. Nearly thirty years later, the Chevalier des Marchais similarly reported about Whydah that "when they [the king's wives] arrive at the house of the person that they are to chastise, they announce the will of the King to him and then immediately begin to strip, break or burn everything that they find. One cannot oppose them: apart from it being a state crime to obstruct the execution of the orders of the King, it is an unpardonable offense to touch a wife of the Prince." [15]

The Authority of Princesses: The Succession Struggle between Hangbe and Agaja ～

While the organization of the ahosi, the wives of the king, was beginning to take form, certain women ahovi, children of the royal line, were making a significant impact on the kingdom's history. It is probably not by coincidence that women of the royal lineage were prominent in the early years of the kingdom. Few in number and strangers to the Abomey plateau, the Alladahonu, or royal lineage, would not initially have had allies among the ruling lineages that they were displacing, nor would they have felt free to trust the loyalty of persons from lineages who came under their control. They would have had reason to enlist all the members of their lineage in the effort to establish their own hegemony

The organization of the Alladahonu lineage differed structurally from that of other patrilineages of the Abomey plateau, the difference being that the royal lineage affiliated the children of all of its members to itself. In other words, in contrast to usual patrilineal practice, children born of princesses, women of the royal family, became members of the Alladahonu rather than members of their fathers' lines. That difference had important implications for the autonomy of princesses, for their involvement in lineage decisions, and for their ability to participate in the politics of the kingdom. Depending upon the ideological vision of the monarchy at any given time, those implications were in turn perceived as negative or positive. The affiliation of children of daughters of the Alladahonu may have been deliberately devised in the early days of the kingdom to permit the more rapid growth of the lineage, or it may have been the continuation of a pattern derived from a matrilineal past.

The affiliation of their children to the Alladahonu freed the sexuality of princesses and made them socially male in patrilineal Fon society. The husbands of princesses had no reason, and no right, to try to control their sexuality, since the paternity of their children was irrelevant to their lineage affiliation. Princesses were autonomous within the households of their husbands, having separate quarters and bringing a large entourage of retainers with them. Because princesses did not bear children for another lineage, they were never forced to balance loyalties between the lineage of their birth and that of their marriage. They were thus free to take a more direct role in Alladahonu affairs. A princess was socially male, a person in control of her own sexuality, parent to children who were members of her own lineage, and head of an entourage that was effectively an independent household under her control.

Among the daughters of each king, the woman acknowledged as the most senior was known as *na daho* (*na* = honorific for princess; *daho* = large, great). Though she was usually termed the "oldest daughter" in European languages, the na daho was not necessarily the firstborn, but rather someone senior who was considered to have appropriate leadership capabilities. Paul Mercier has described patterns of authority and power of the "oldest daughter" in lineages in the broad region that included Dahomey, the Yoruba-speaking areas, and the kingdom of Benin.

The oldest daughter was central to lineage decisions, particularly if she was in fact older than the male head of the lineage. She installed new lineage heads and, in the interval between the death of one head and the installation of his successor, she served as regent. These patterns are consistent with evidence from the Dahomean royal family. There, the na daho had authority over all the sisters and daughters of the reigning king, supervising their marriages and mediating their marital disputes. The various na daho become visible from time to time in Dahomean history, particularly at moments of succession when, as the oldest child of a deceased monarch yet ineligible for the throne herself, na daho might use her authority to mediate between rival princes or to promote the claims of a would-be king.[16]

Princesses were associated with the affairs of state in the early eighteenth century in two capacities: as wife-ambassadors to neighboring kings and as senior sisters with authority at periods of succession. Marriage among Gbe-speaking peoples was conceived as an alliance between lineages that ideally was cemented through the exchange of wives, with a woman of each lineage becoming a wife to the other. Wives, as representatives of their line in the lineage of their husbands, played a central role in determining the nature of continued contacts between the lineages. The same principle held true at the level of ruling lineages. Snelgrave reported that, fearing an invasion by Oyo cavalry in early 1730, the king of Dahomey sent "one of his handsomest daughters" to the king of Oyo as part of his peace offerings. Once terms had been negotiated, as "a Confirmation of the Peace, the King of J-oe sent . . . one of his Daughters to the King of Dahome for a Wife; and she was received with great Joy by the King and his People."[17] Dahomean oral tradition similarly speaks of Na Geze, a princess married to Houffon, the king of Whydah at the time of the Dahomean invasion of that kingdom. As we will see shortly, legend credits Na Geze with helping the Dahomeans under Agaja defeat Whydah. Meanwhile, one of the most famous and important princesses of the Alladahonu lineage, Na Hangbe, played a central part in the succession struggle leading to the reign of Agaja. As senior sister to Agaja at the death of his brother and predecessor, Akaba, she used her authority to promote a candidate for king and may have served as regent during the interregnum between Akaba and Ajaga. Her story is set in the second decade of the eighteenth century.

Oral traditions and accounts of travelers begin to converge toward the end of the decade of the 1710s. At the beginning of 1718, word reached Europeans in Whydah of "a Battle between two Kings of Foay." The reference was very likely to the succession struggle between Agaja and a prince remembered in Abomey as Agbo Sassa.[18] Agaja was brother to his predecessor, Akaba, and Agbo Sassa was Akaba's son. Agbo Sassa was supported by Agaja's powerful sister, Na Hangbe, the twin sister of Akaba. Oral tradition further claims that Agaja was originally named Dosu, the name for the child born following twins. The implication is that all three—Akaba, Hangbe, and Agaja—were born of the same mother.

Twentieth-century oral accounts about Hangbe's era have several common refrains: that Akaba died suddenly and prematurely, leaving his son Agbo Sassa still a minor; that Hangbe became regent because she was a twin of Akaba, and each one of a pair of twins must be treated equally; that Hangbe ruled for three months or three years; and that she had an army that ultimately was defeated by Agaja. Variations of the story speak of the assassination of Hangbe's son, followed by her public abdication and cursing of the people of Dahomey. For good measure, one account even adds that she predicted the conquest of Dahomey by whites.[19]

What is the historical reality behind all this? Hangbe is not recognized in Dahomean king lists and is not mentioned in any written account before the twentieth century. Burton, however, heard of Agbo Sassa (Abosasa) during his 1863 visit, and notes that he "stirred up a useless war," though Burton mistakenly believes that Agbo Sassa was disputing the throne with Akaba, rather than Agaja. Akinjogbin argues that although Hangbe and Akaba were twins, Hangbe certainly never reigned, and that to avoid confusion of whether her children or those of Akaba should succeed, the "kingmakers" elected Agaja. Because Hangbe is not mentioned by precolonial travelers, Law argues that her story "is probably a later invention, devised to provide a mythical origin" for women warriors in Dahomey. He cites an article about her to prove that Agaja was named regent. However, the article claims that Agaja became regent only *after* Hangbe ruled as regent. Finally, Law acknowledges that the 1718 report refers to a civil war between Agaja and "a rival claimant to the throne," whom he identifies with the name Mbogela—a name that Skertchly, and no other source, recorded in the nineteenth century.[20]

There is no reason to doubt the existence of Hangbe. Her descendants today live in a compound adjacent to the central palace in Abomey. As of the early 1970s, they could name seven descendants who in succession over the years had assumed her identity through positional succession. Following Agaja's accesssion to the throne, they say, Hangbe and her household remained in the area of Abomey. Agbo Sassa, however, moved or fled north to Mahi country, from which his descendants returned to settle in Abomey only in the twentieth century. Hangbe's descendants credit Gezo, who reigned from 1818 to 1858, with acting as her benefactor, effectively reconstituting her house sometime in the mid–nineteenth century.[21]

As twin sister to Akaba, Hangbe would have been na daho. There is a sense in the traditions that Akaba died precipitately, possibly in the course of warfare; one account claims that he "disappeared," and another that he died of poison.[22] Several claim that Hangbe continued warfare begun in the Weme valley under Akaba. Her family even provides the name of her general. With the king having died unexpectedly, and without a clearly designated successor (or one who had the resources ready to take control), it would have been normal for Hangbe, as na daho, to have played a prominent role in the interregnum and to have served as regent. She would not in any sense have been considered to have been king, and hence there would have been no reason to make her part of the official king list. Later in the eighteenth century, travelers spoke of lapses of time as long as eighteen months between the death of one king and the public announcement of his death. Grand Customs, the ceremonial cycle that marked the final funeral for one king and the installation of his successor, typically took place as long as two years following the announcement of the death of the king, ostensibly to allow the successor king to make ceremonial preparations. Later patterns of the eighteenth century suggest that those preparations included the suppression of rivals for the throne. Ironically, Law's argument that the beginning of Agaja's reign, and hence Akaba's death, occurred in 1716 even lends credence to the accounts that Hangbe "reigned" for three years, since it indicates that there was no confirmed successor from 1716 to 1718. Hangbe, however, promoted the candidacy of the losing prince, and suffered the classic fate of the vanquished, being banished from the history constructed by the victor.[23]

Two other points offer intriguing but undocumented possibilities about Hangbe. The first has to do with the suggestion that Hangbe's and Akaba's sons each had a claim to the throne. Later Dahomeans asserted not only that kings had to be born of royal fathers, but that their mothers were always drawn from the ranks of common women. The killing of Hangbe's son, which her descendants say was done to prevent him from claiming the throne, suggests that things at one time may have been more fluid. Scholars have observed that the Alladahonu trace their royal blood matrilineally, because in their myth of origins, royal blood is derived from the princess of Tado, not the leopard with whom she mated. Nevertheless, by promoting Agbo Sassa and not her own child, Hangbe herself was supporting the principle of access to the kingship through the male line alone. Finally, the argument that Hangbe was entitled to rule by virtue of being a twin is most probably an anachronism drawn from later twinning practices. Hangbe's authority was based on her status as eldest sister, not as twin to Akaba. The emphasis on her as twin could well be related to the reign of Gezo, her benefactor, who in order to legitimize his own rule placed ceremonial emphasis on many forms of doubling.[24]

The Conquest of Allada and Whydah ∼

Outsiders' accounts and oral records agree that the major accomplishment of the period of the reign of Agaja was the conquest of Allada and Whydah, which brought Dahomey into direct contact with the coast and the European trade. Audaciously expansionist, Dahomey more than doubled its land area in a period of three years (1724–27), despite a devastating cavalry attack by the empire of Oyo in 1726. Apart from the usual reference to an imperative to expand, oral traditions say virtually nothing of the motives of the Dahomean monarchy for its conquest to the coast. In contrast, European slavers and twentieth-century scholars have debated motive at great length. John Atkins, who visited Whydah in 1721 as physician to a slave-trading expedition, argues that "this Prince (of Dahomey) was probably incited to the Conquest from the generous Motive of redeeming his own, and the neigboring Country People from those cruel Wars, and Slavery that was continually imposed on them." Writing more than two hundred years later, I. A. Akinjogbin draws on Atkins to argue that Agaja wanted first to destroy the existing political system in the area and, second, "to restrict and eventually stop the slave trade . . . and to substitute other 'legitimate' items of trade between Europe and the new kingdom of Dahomey." Though the possibility that an African monarch tried to put an end to the slave trade is obviously attractive in the twentieth century, historians who have closely considered the evidence from Dahomey suggest, as did the eighteenth-century slave traders, that Dahomey's motive was a desire to trade directly with Europe, and that the kingdom was willing to provide the product most desired by European traders, human beings. Akinjogbin's thesis therefore is not likely. However, both Atkins's idea that Dahomey wanted to stop raids on its own people *and* the argument that the Dahomeans were seeking direct overseas commerce in slaves are conceivable. In the political atmosphere of the early eighteenth century, with tiny states warring and selling captives, and where the choice was trading or being traded, military expansion and conquest would have allowed Dahomey to attack and stop potential raiders of its population and, by selling captives, to acquire the means to strengthen its state further.[25]

If oral sources are silent on the question of motives for the conquest to the coast, they are deeply interested in the mechanics of conquest, and of the defeat of Whydah in particular. The Whydah story merits close attention, because it provides insights into patterns of African oral interpretation that contrast with Western interpretive modes of history. Those contrasts in turn have implications for our understanding of the conduct and meaning of warfare in Dahomey. The difference between the two interpretive modes lies in the answers provided to explain the taking of Savi, the capital of Whydah, by the Dahomeans in 1727. First, we need to outline the "facts" of the taking of Allada and Whydah as they are generally accepted by twentieth-century historians.

The Dahomeans had been growing continually stronger in the first two decades of the eighteenth century, warring with some success in the Weme valley in the 1710s. Their objective may have been to secure a trade route east of Allada to outlets to the sea east of Lake Nokoue, an objective that apparently was successful. Following the succession struggle that brought Agaja to power around 1716–18, the Dahomeans became involved in Allada politics. In 1724, they attacked Allada in a bloody, three-day battle ostensibly fought in favor of a claimant to the throne. In the end, however, Agaja took effective control over the kingdom of Allada. Defeated elements from Allada and the Weme area then appealed to Oyo, which in 1726 attacked Dahomey with cavalry and destroyed its army. Agaja, who had fled with his entourage, sent tribute to Oyo to buy peace and the right to occupy Allada. In the meantime, Agaja is said to have tried to negotiate with Houffon, the king of Whydah, requesting permission for Dahomean traders to trade directly at Whydah. By refusing Agaja's request, Houffon conveniently provided a casus belli. From their base in Allada, the Dahomeans attacked and burned towns on the northern edges of Whydah control, despite opposition from a Whydah force described as more than ten times larger (three thousand Dahomeans versus forty thousand Hwedas). Arriving at the river that separated them from Savi on March 6, 1727, the Dahomeans halted. On March 9, when a small party of Dahomeans crossed the river, Whydah resistance collapsed, the king fled, and the city fell without opposition. The Dahomeans went on to devastate the kingdom, killing an estimated five thousand persons and taking ten thousand to eleven thousand prisoner.[26]

The mystery, of course, is why the Whydah defenses collapsed so precipitately and Savi was taken so easily, something that apparently surprised even the Dahomean victors at the time. Akinjogbin and Law provide explanations from a Western explanatory mode. They stress first that Whydah had been weakened by its internal divisions—and indeed, European correspondence for nearly two decades prior to the conquest chronicles various machinations at the court of Houffon. Law adds "treachery" (by people in Whydah) and "guile" (by Dahomeans) to his explanation, noting in the first instance that some of the Whydah chiefs may have gone over to Agaja's side even before the Dahomeans arrived. Law's evidence for guile is drawn from the oral account published by Le Hérissé, which argues, first, that Na Geze, the daughter of Agaja who was married to Houffon, poured water on the Whydah gunpowder the night before the attack and, second, that Agaja put the Hweda off their guard by publicly announcing that he was going to Allada to perform religious ceremonies. Law finds Agaja's ruse-by-departure credible (his presence at Allada is confirmed in contemporary European accounts), but Na Geze's actions "no more than a traditional stereotype." Akinjogbin, in contrast, gives credence to the Na Geze story and, in addition, finds another explanation for the Dahomean victory: the lack of defensive action by the European traders at Savi. He quotes Snelgrave to argue that the Dahomeans neutralized possible European intervention by promising to make the trade more attractive, should they prevail.[27]

Neither Akinjogbin nor Law provides details of the oral traditions about Na Geze. Her full story follows the classic lines of myth, in that it purports to explain a historical event—the unexpected capture of Savi. Like many myths, it is recounted in the form of a dramatic tale. And like myths, even as it describes details of events that almost certainly never happened, it resonates with the truths of popular conceptions and offers insights about history. The following summary of the myth is drawn from Gavoy's rendition of 1913.

Agaja gave Na Geze to Houffon in marriage as a sign of friendship and alliance between the two kings. Known also by the name Awliponuwe (meaning young girl, go and see), Na Geze acted as a spy, learning the key to Houffon's strengths in order to defeat him. Agaja had bought flintlock guns through Whydah. However, the Hwedas had removed the hammer, which forced the Dahomeans to fire them by having a second soldier stand next to the gunman and light the powder by hand. Na Geze charmed Houffon into explaining why Agaja's guns worked so badly and convinced him to give her access to the storehouse where the hammers were stored. She then visited her father, returning with a large number of servants and forty young women (forty and forty-one being numbers that were associated both with royalty and with ideas of perfection or completenesss). Since this entourage was too great to be easily accommodated, Na Geze announced that she was sending all the male servants home. They returned to Agaja with the missing hammers. Having repaired his guns, Agaja then complained to Houffon who, in an expression of defiance, confiscated Na Geze's people, giving the forty women to his chiefs and the remaining servants to his warriors. Agaja then demanded and received compensation for Houffon's seizure of Na Geze's retainers. Next, Na Geze received a large quantity of food and palm wine from her father so that she could entertain the Hweda. The ensuing party left the king and chiefs drunk, and Na Geze's servants went off to wet the king's and chiefs' gunpowder. The Dahomeans were then able to attack and win.[28]

There is a final explanatory story about Savi that is not mentioned by either Law or Akinjogbin. Snelgrave says that the people of Whydah relied solely on their principal deity, a python, to protect their capital. Rather than setting a guard at the riverbank, the Hweda "only went every Morning and Evening to the River side, to offer Sacrifice to their principal God, which was a particular harmless Snake they adored, and prayed to on this occasion, to keep their Enemies from coming over the river." Snelgrave continues that "there is a constant Tradition amongst them, whenever any Calamity threatens their Country, by imploring the Snake's Assistance, they are always delivered from it." He reports that "the Pass of the River being . . . wholly left to the Care of the Snakes, whom the Enemy little feared; and they having observed for several Days, that the *Whidaws* kept no set Guard there, it encouraged the King of *Dahomè*'s General to send two hundred of his Soldiers to ford the River: Which having done without Opposition . . . they marched towards the Town. . . . The Outguards . . . fled into the Town, reporting, that all the *Dahome* Army was got over the River: Which soon reaching the King's Ear, he immediately fled, with all his People, making no Resistance." Having failed to protect Whydah, the snakes suffered along with the general population, being killed and eaten by the Dahomeans. Snelgrave comments that "it is very strange, / the Conquerors should so far contemn the Gods of this Country, since they are so barbarous and savage themselves, as to offer human Sacrifices whenever they gain a Victory."[29]

Obviously, both Law and Akinjogbin work in a Western interpretive mode, accepting evidence that they perceive as reasonable by Western historical standards. Those standards offer a range of acceptable explanations for victory in warfare: better strategy or tactics, greater firepower, more technologically advanced weaponry, greater numbers of combatants, disunity or treason in enemy ranks, surprise, advantages of terrain, unexpected changes in weather, and sheer good luck. In addition, they allow for victory gained as a result of certain beliefs within the ranks of the winning combatants: that the winners were fighting for families or homelands, that defeat would mean death, or that God or rightness was on their side.

The Dahomean explanatory mode, in contrast, seems little concerned with typical Western explanatory factors. Rather, victory is more often explained by certain patterns, two of which are particularly important. The first argues that success is won by learning the source of an enemy's strength and neutralizing it. It applies both to material and to supernatural or spiritual power. The second pattern argues that victory is won by outsmarting the enemy through some kind of ruse. In both, fighting simply confirms an outcome already foreordained. Obviously, the Na Geze legend includes both patterns. Na Geze learns the source of Houffon's strength—properly working firearms—and neutralizes it by sending the flintlock hammers to Agaja and wetting the gunpowder. At the same time, she employs a classic ruse, getting the enemy drunk, to complete the preparations for the battle, which of course is irrelevant, the outcome having already been assured. The Na Geze myth is typical, too, in personalizing the strength of the enemy, focusing on the interpersonal relations of Na Geze, Houffon, and Agaja.

But what of snakes and rivers as explanation? Snelgrave arrived in Whydah three weeks after the conquest of the kingdom. What he collected was not a myth embellished by years of retelling but the kind of tale that would have reached twentieth-century Europeans through the whispers of their African servants and that would have been dismissed by them as superstitious kitchen gossip. Snelgrave, however, lived in a pre-Enlightenment world that was willing to consider alternative belief systems, and he accepts the snake story as one of several explanatory factors. In fact, it fits the patterns of the Dahomean explanatory mode, arguing that the strength of Whydah was contained in its national vodun, its supernatural protector. Certainly, the setting—with the Dahomeans stopping north of the river—is replete with factors inexplicable in "rational" terms. The river that forced the Dahomean army to halt was hardly a major physical obstacle. Called "a pretty deep and rapid river" by an eighteenth-century source,[30] the river in the twentieth century was a small stream that was part of the network of channels making up the lagoon area of the coast. Early March, the period of the attack, is the end of the dry season, when the stream would have been at the lowest level of the year; indeed, in the end the Dahomeans simply walked across it. Having easily defeated Whydah armies before, and seeing no defenses at the stream, why would they have hesitated for several days? Did the Hweda truly believe that their god would protect them? And if so, did the Dahomeans stop because they feared the power of that same god? In that case, why would any Dahomeans have dared to cross the river—and discover the fatal weakness of Whydah's divine defense? Snelgrave's description of the Dahomeans killing and eating pythons tends to substantiate the possibility that both sides believed in the efficacy of supernatural protection. According to him, the Dahomeans held up captured pythons, taunted them by saying, "If you are Gods, speak and save your selves," and then beheaded and broiled them. In later years, Dahomey would show extreme respect for the protector gods of any enemy locality, sending royal spies to neutralize them before attacks and often reestablishing in Dahomey the enemy vodun that were believed to be powerful. The python cult, though it was brought back to Abomey by the conquerors and though it did remain the central vodun of Whydah, never became a prominent deity on the Abomey plateau. The python's relative lack of popularity may have been associated with its failure in Dahomean eyes to protect Whydah from attack.

Both the Na Geze legend and Snelgrave's snake account remind us that there is one final crucial explanatory factor for understanding Dahomean warfare, and more broadly for understanding the actions of people generally in Dahomean history. In the same way that the beliefs of Western soldiers can be considered a factor in the outcome of war, the beliefs of the Dahomeans and their enemies are central to understanding historic warfare in the Dahomey gap. In short, people act on their beliefs, not on the "reality" that historians create in hindsight. Dahomey was without question a militaristic state, and Dahomean soldiers fought, killed, and died in battle; nevertheless, their approach to warfare, their understanding of enemy strengths and weaknesses, their desire to fight, and their willingness to die—all these were related to realities that Dahomeans perceived and that may not be shared by twentieth-century individuals. As in other areas of their lives, Dahomeans were quick to adopt European technologies for warfare, but they adapted those European means to Dahomean beliefs and Dahomean ends. At this distance, we cannot know precisely what the two sides in fact believed in 1727. But we can know that both sides acted on their beliefs and that it is very possible that Snelgrave learned something about what people believed.

The fact that Snelgrave did not record (and presumably did not hear) the legend of Na Geze suggests that her story was created at a later point in Dahomean history. Nevertheless, it, too, tells us something about what Dahomeans believed at some later point in their history. That had to do with the role and behavior of princesses in the homes of their husbands: that a princess was loyal to her father and not her husband, that she would report her husband's secrets to her father, and that she would betray her husband to promote the interests of her father. By the nineteenth century, when Dahomean notables were offered princesses as wives, daughters of the king were widely believed to be royal spies. And men favored by the king would consider that his gift of a princess-bride was a dubious honor at best.

Customs, Court, and the Palace in the Early 1700s ᨆ

Dahomey's rapid expansion signaled the beginning of a period of disruption and difficulty for the monarchy. The sudden military conquest of states covering a land area larger than the Abomey plateau raised major problems of control. Moreover, the victory over Whydah was not definitive: Houffon, the Whydah king, had escaped to the west and he would return more than once to try to retake his kingdom. The Abomey plateau had been overrun by Oyo horsemen and remained vulnerable, and the king and his entourage were forced to flee nearly every dry season. Work began on a deep ditch that would enclose the city of Abomey and serve as a first defense. Forty years later, it was described as a "wide and deep ditch" punctuated in four places by wooden bridges with guard houses.[31] Nevertheless, by 1730 the court had moved to Allada, where it would remain until Agaja's death in 1740, and even there peace was elusive, Dahomey alternately showing its strength and then being forced to retreat. When Oyo attacked the Dahomeans, the Hweda would throw off Dahomean control. Once peace with Oyo was regained (or once the rains forced the Oyo horsemen to retreat), Dahomey would move to reestablish control over the coast. In the newly conquered areas the habits of banditry appeared to die slowly, and if European accounts are to be believed, the Dahomeans did little more than devastate the lands of Allada and Whydah that they had conquered. In fact, contemporary sources suggest that administrative roughness and a scarcity of discipline characterized the Dahomean state organization in the first third of the eighteenth century. In particular, the European sources make clear that the Dahomeans lacked sophistication in dealing with the culture of interaction between African and European that had evolved on the coast. Trade terms negotiated with the king were sometimes not honored by Dahomean traders at the coast; the Dahomeans broke promises, occasionally imprisoned traders, and even executed one, a director of the English fort by the name of Testefol, who tried to help the Hweda regain control over their territory. Supplies of slaves were intermittent and when Europeans complained of these problems of the trade to the king of Dahomey, he argued that he had no control over his subordinates.

Despite the pressures on the Dahomean monarchy and the negative reports from European traders, there are signs during the reign of Agaja that Dahomey had begun to establish the elaborate ceremonial life and administrative control that characterized the state by the nineteenth century. By the mid-1720s, Europeans were beginning to record eyewitness accounts of the Dahomean court. The records of two English visitors, Bulfinch Lamb and William Snelgrave, are particularly rich. Lamb, in Allada at the time of the 1724 conquest, was captured by the Dahomeans and taken to Abomey, where he spent two years as an honored visitor/ prisoner. Snelgrave was received by the king in 1727 at a site that was probably the location of the Dahomean palace in modern Allada. Both suggest an impressive level of wealth, administrative organization, and social discipline.[32]

Both Lamb and Snelgrave witnessed ceremonial cycles of the kind that would later be called Annual Customs. Lamb wrote that the king was "obliged to go out at different times in the year, and strow great quantities of goods and money amongst the common people, and make sacrifices to . . . gods and forefathers, sometimes of slaves . . . sometimes of horses, other times of oxen, and other creatures." Snelgrave arrived in Allada just one month after the 1727 fall of Savi and at the end of a war against Toffo (or Tuffoe, north of Allada on a route to Abomey). He spent six days on a visit that is a prototype of the pattern of later Europeans' experience of Dahomean ceremonial cycles. Traveling by hammock, with two other traders and a Jakin official, he was greeted on arrival in Allada by a high Dahomean official. Once settled in his quarters, he received livestock and food provided for his sustenance and went off for an initial audience with the king. Snelgrave later watched military maneuvers and observed the payment of compensation by the king for captives and heads taken in war. He saw humans being sacrificed (later visitors often refused to watch), witnessed "ridiculous" rituals "which would be tedious for me to relate," and was told of other ceremonies to which he was not invited (e.g., the "King's Fetiche Day"). He learned that the king was also busy receiving ambassadors from "inland" countries. Finally, having negotiated his business with the king (agreeing to conditions of trade and prices of slaves), Snelgrave and his party were given gifts and departed.[33]

The accounts of both Lamb and Snelgrave touch on the central elements of state power—religious/ideological, military, and political/economic—and how they were reinforced through the ceremonial cycle. Snelgrave watched soldiers return from war with numerous prisoners and heads of enemy dead. The living were divided into two groups: those to be sacrificed to the king's "Guardian Angel" and those to be kept or sold. Snelgrave watched a person he presumed to be a priest lay his hand upon sacrifice victims' heads and speak "about two Minutes" before they were decapitated. Their blood, he was told, was "for the *Fetiche*, or God." When Snelgrave queried a Dahomean army officer about why sacrifices were made, he was told that after every conquest, a certain number of captives were sacrificed, "For they firmly believed, should this be omitted, no more Success would attend them." Moreover, some of the sacrifice victims were being sent to be, after death, servants to the twelve royal

wives who had been killed by the Tuffos and whose deaths had precipitated the war.[34]

Snelgrave, obviously, was seeing confirmed the central principles of
Dahomean religious belief: that there was mutual interdependence between the spirit and the visible worlds, with the blood of sacrifice victims
nourishing a "Guardian Angel" who would reciprocate by ensuring future victories. The "priest" was likely imparting a message, for persons
sacrificed were normally instructed to perform one of two services after
death: to carry messages to the world of the dead or to staff households
of deceased individuals. At the same time, their blood provided nourishment for the deities. But there was more, because the act of sacrifice was
also a political act. In a society where wealth was measured in terms of
the numbers of dependents under a person's control, human sacrifice
signaled the greatest possible expenditure of wealth. It also signaled military power and an implicit threat to Dahomey's neighbors, for those who
were sacrificed were captives of war. Snelgrave's traveling companion, the
Jakin official, arrived at his tent at one point terrified at having seen
people going to be sacrificed. If Snelgrave is to be believed, the man's
greatest fear was that the Dahomeans would sacrifice him and eat his
body. Rumors of Dahomean cannibalism were believed by Snelgrave,
though he had no more direct evidence of cannibalism than the thousands of Africans who believed that Europeans ate slaves. Nevertheless,
the Dahomeans on their way to war would have found it useful to have
neighboring peoples believe that they were cannibals. That was very likely
the reason that messages of power were sent during this period through
the decoration of palace walls with the skulls of people killed in war or
sacrificed. But military power in Dahomey was not left just to the spirit-
world's protection, to rumors of cannibalism, or to the implicit threat of
execution: Snelgrave carefully notes that, not only were the Dahomean
soldiers armed with guns and swords, but that their public demonstrations indicated a discipline and order "well worth seeing even by us
Europeans."[35]

Finally, both Lamb and Snelgrave noticed (and participated in as recipients) the public presentation of gifts by the monarchy to the people.
Largesse was a central element of ceremonial cycles, with the kings—aided
at times by European visitors and members of the court—throwing cloth

and cowries to crowds of people. Snelgrave estimates that the king gave "at least two hundred Captives" to courtiers and officers during his visit. The gesture was quintessentially West African. It was the patron bestowing gifts on the client. It was the chief giving gifts to attract followers. It was also a reenactment of the relationship between the living and the dead, and, like that relationship, it expressed mutual interdependence, because the gift-giving was not simply from the monarchy to the people. Neither Snelgrave nor Lamb noticed what was without question a part of the ceremonial process: the contributions of the people to the monarch. Losers in war paid tribute to victors, clients and followers owed something to patrons and chiefs. The monarchy of Dahomey by the nineteenth century would have a system of taxation worthy of any twentieth-century industrialized government. It is clear that at least portions of it were in place in the 1720s, when even in Whydah, William Smith, who arrived there a month after the fall of Savi, learned that the "King of Dahomey . . . has now laid heavy Taxes upon [the people of Whydah]." [36]

Beyond their observations of the ceremonial cycle, Lamb and Snelgrave confirm that certain characteristics of the Dahomean palace organization were already in place by the 1720s. Lamb testifies that the king's palaces covered vast areas, that he had many of them, that his Abomey palace with two thousand wives was "as big as a small Town," and that it was governed competently by the king's wives. Eunuchs had been used in the palace in Allada and had been captured by the conquering Dahomeans, but for the time being they were not used in Dahomean palaces. [37] The daklo already was in evidence, distancing the king's male leaders from direct conversation with the monarch. Snelgrave wrote that "the principal Men of the Court and Army" never went nearer than twenty feet from the king. "Whatsoever they had to say to his Majesty, first kissing the Ground, they whispered into the Ear of an old Woman, who went to the king; and having received his answer, she returned with it to them." At Snelgrave's first audience, the king was attended by seven women who "had on their Arms, many large Manelloes, or Rings of Gold and of great Value, and round their Necks, and in their Hair, abundance of their Country Jewels, which are a sort of Beads of divers Colours." Three of the women shaded the king with umbrellas, which in Dahomey as elsewhere in West Africa were symbols of high rank. Of greater importance, though, were the four other women. They stood with muskets on their shoulders. Lamb similarly described armed wives of the king, attending his person and holding "guns, pistols, and sabre, &c." [38]

The arming of palace women with guns set Dahomey apart from its neighbors. There appears to have been no precedent for it, and it was a crucial step that led to Dahomey's nineteenth-century army of women. Women as fighters were not unheard-of in eighteenth-century West Africa. A Dutch visitor to Akwamu (in present-day Ghana) in 1703 came upon a village where "everyone had a sword in his hand, men as well as women." Olaudah Equiano, an Igbo kidnapped into the slave trade in the eighteenth century, remembered that in the interior of what is now Nigeria, both women and men farmed, fought, and were "trained in the arts of war." The king of Oyo was reported to have a force of five hundred wives armed with spears in the early nineteenth century. Women were not considered to be physically weak in Dahomey and were widely reported being involved in farming. Dahomean traditions linked farming to fighting by claiming that the main weapon of Dahomey, before firearms, was a club derived from a short-handled hoe. Bosman describes it, saying that in the 1690s it was the principal weapon in Whydah and Allada, "a sort of Club about a Yard long, and five or six inches thick, very round and even, except a Knot at the Bottom, the breadth of a Hand, and three Fingers thick." Given these cultural traditions, it is hardly surprising that Lamb reported that the guards for the palace entrances were "a robusk sort of women slaves" or that Snelgrave reported that the Dahomeans met a 1729 challenge from the Hweda by adding detachments of women to their forces. [39]

What may be unusual, then, is not that women might be seen as capable of fighting, but that they would have been armed with firearms. During the colonial period and later, as new European technologies were introduced into Africa, they typically became the preserve of men. Moreover, guns were relatively new in Dahomey in the 1720s. The explanation for the firearms of the palace women undoubtedly lies in the women's function as bodyguards to the king. Women were said to have been bodyguards as early as the reign of Wegbaja, though as the putative first king, many innovations are attributed (and possibly misattributed) to his reign. Whatever their beginnings, the presence of the king's female guard signaled that the monarchy was already conceiving of the palace organization as something beyond a polygynous household. Armed women continued to be present at audiences and visible at the palace gates. To assure personal loyalty, each king founded his own guard, though apparently without disbanding the guard established by his predecessors. And as we will see, the guards' members played prominent roles in virtually all succession struggles up to and including that of Gezo in 1818.[40]

Snelgrave and Lamb provide little evidence about court officials central to the monarchy at this period. Snelgrave, for example, identifies the official who greeted him at Allada only as "the principal person of [Agaja's] Court," with the title of "Great Captain." Prior to the 1740s, the only Dahomean office mentioned by name in contemporary sources is that of the migan (*mi* = our, *gan* = chief, director). Called the temigan or chémigan by most eighteenth-century writers, the migan was adviser to the king and also royal executioner, effectively a prime minister who remained central to the kings' administrations throughout the history of the kingdom. Oral traditions claim that the office predated the arrival of the Alladahonu on the Abomey plateau. As executioner, the migan performed ritual as well as judicial functions, since many of the people killed under his direction were sacrifices to the ancestors. Indeed, the "priest" that Snelgrave saw at Customs may have been the migan. Toward the end of the eighteenth century, Chenevert and Bulet would insist on the centrality of the migan's office by claiming that he alone of all Dahomeans could never be executed by the king, but could only be exiled.[41]

The usually reliable Le Hérissé claims that the officer commonly called second minister, the meu, was created under Agaja's successor, Tegbesu. However, the office may have existed earlier, for Norris was told that the meu and the migan had selected Tegbesu to be king at the time of the death of Agaja, which would indicate that the office existed during Agaja's reign. As the minister charged with the oversight of territories south of Allada, the meu was responsible for the reception of European visitors from the coast and hence was highly visible in the accounts of European travelers. Later descriptions of Dahomean offices typically link the migan and the meu as complements. The migan, associated with the right hand of the king, was responsible for commoners; the meu, linked to the king's left, had authority over members of the royal family.[42]

Several other major offices existed during the reign of Agaja. Le Hérissé says that the first yovogan (*yovo* = white person; *gan* = chief, director), an office that had existed both in Allada and Whydah, was appointed by Agaja. Law has shown that the title was not used by Dahomey until the time of Agaja's successor, though earlier there were individuals, most importantly an officer called the tegan, who were responsible for what became the functions of the yovogan—relations with the European traders and the governing of Whydah. Two military offices, the commander in chief, or gau, and the posu, a subordinate, are mentioned by writers in the 1730s, and quite possibly they existed prior to that period.[43]

Even when they are available, the names of offices tell us little of the individuals who filled them or of the extent of the power that they exercised. Observing Whydah in the 1720s, the French naval officer Chevalier des Marchais claimed preponderant powers for the great ministers in comparison with the king; however, he was examining a kingdom that was deeply divided and that had a weak king. The Dahomean kings, at least in this period, seem to have been wary of their ministers' power. The 1730s and 1740s, the last decade of Agaja's reign and the first of Tegbesu's, have been described as a period of "internal crisis" by Robin Law. Both kings were challenged by mutinous officers, at least some of whom were members of the royal family, and executions of various chiefs were relatively commonplace.[44]

Women's offices and powerful women are virtually invisible in this period, save for two examples. The first is that of Adonon, the king's reignmate, to be discussed below. Adonon's history was retained through the oral tradition and is not mentioned in contemporary European accounts. The second example, recorded by Snelgrave, is a frustratingly tantalizing hint that women were important at court. His story concerns an incident that took place sometime between April 15 and July 1, 1727. The king's agent offered two women to Snelgrave for sale, one about fifty years old and the other about twenty, with the stipulation that "I would not let them be redeemed by any one that should offer to do it." Snelgrave offered to take the younger only. The following day he was told by his

Dahomean translator that the older woman—the one he had refused to buy—had that day "been sacrificed to the Sea, by order of the great Captain. For she had highly offended the King," and since Snelgrave would not take her, "his Majesty had ordered her to be destroyed this way." When Snelgrave asked the translator what crimes the woman had committed, he replied hastily, "Did I think he knew the King's Secrets?" adding, "She had lived a long time in the Court, with good Repute till now." Later Snelgrave learned that, without the Dahomeans knowing of it, his own crew had saved the woman from drowning. When he questioned her, she would not divulge the reason for the king's displeasure, and he appears to have been satisfied with his translator's guess that "he suspected, it was on account of her assisting some of the King's Women in their Amours." Snelgrave noted that this woman was known by a number of the slaves on board and used her influence on behalf of the slave traders: "The female *Negroes*, who used always to be the most troublesome to us, on account of the noise and clamour they made, were kept in such Order and Decorum by this Woman, that I had never the like in any Voyage before."[45]

Some sources claim that royal blood was not allowed to be spilled and hence that problem ahovi (children of the king) were drowned at Whydah or sold overseas. Although that prohibition was not strictly practiced at the time of succession struggles, it is possible that the woman in this case was a member of the royal family. Her influence over the Fon slaves resonates with the na daho's influence over female members of the royal line. As might be expected, oral records provide no clues to the woman's identity. In the absence of any other information, we cannot say with certainty if she was a member of the royal lineage, let alone who she was. Nevertheless, the story confirms that women were influential at court, and that the identity of powerful women was known to persons outside the palace even at this relatively early date.[46]

Adonon and the Creation of the Office of Kpojito ∽

The establishment of the most important women's office in Dahomey, that of kpojito, appears to date to the reign of Agaja. Kpojito, commonly translated into European languages as "mother of the king" or "queen mother," means literally the one who whelped the leopard (*kpo* = leopard; *ji* = to engender; *to* = agent). Each king was doubled by a kpojito, a woman drawn from among his predecessor's wives. She had a separate court and entourage within the central Abomey palace and was forbidden all contacts with men. Dahomean and European sources are generally vague about the formal functions of her office. At least in the nineteenth century, the kpojito heard appeals in religious cases from the court of the ajaho, the minister of religion, with final appeal to the king himself. The kpojito is said to have acted as an intercessor with the king, giving refuge to Dahomean subjects and pleading on their behalf to the king. Reputed to be very wealthy, the kpojito was supported by tributary villages and plantations of slaves. After death, she was replaced by a female descendant in the family of her birth who controlled her estate. Like the kings, the kpojito became vodun and was honored as part of the annual cycle of ceremonies. Mid-nineteenth-century witnesses write that the spirit of Adonon, the "mother of Agaja," was given offerings first, and that the ceremonies for her were followed by those for the kpojito associated with the kings who came after Agaja.[47] This ceremonial primacy of Adonon, combined with the nature of the oral traditions about her, make it likely that the office of kpojito was established during the time of Agaja. Since the interpretation of Adonon that I offer here is based on the argument that the Alladahonu lineage needed to legitimize itself in the eyes of its subjects on the Abomey plateau, and since the rulers of Dahomey had little time to deal with problems on the plateau following the conquest of Allada and Whydah, I date the creation of the office of kpojito to the six-year window between Agaja's establishment of his rule in about 1718 and the attack on Whydah in 1724.

Adonon was from the town of Wassa, about fifteen miles southeast of Abomey. Her story is directly linked to the myth of the founding of the royal lineage through the mating of a leopard with a princess of the royal line of Tado. The Tado princess, the myth tells us, was named Aligbonon. Both she and her leopardlike son, Agasu, were considered tohwiyo, vodun-founders of the Alladahonu lineage. However, traditions also link Aligbonon to Adonon. Tado, the supposed home of Aligbonon, was west of the Abomey plateau in present-day Togo, but *tado* (or *sado*) is also a term that in contemporary Fongbe usage signifies simply place of origin. Wassa, the home village of Adonon, is also cited in oral tradition as the place of origin of Aligbonon, and in fact Aligbonon was a prominent vodun there. Some oral accounts say that Adonon was Aligbonon, or that Adonon became Aligbonon, and others that Aligbonon was given to Adonon "to guard." The phrasing is similar to that commonly used to describe the relationship of a priest to her vodun, suggesting that Adonon was a vodunon, or priest, of Aligbonon.[48]

Oral traditions in the twentieth century also claim that the Alladahonu lineage can be traced back in an unbroken line to the kings of Allada. As noted above, recent historians have questioned the Dahomean royal lineage's link to the royal family of Allada. Robin Law argues that the Allada connection was invented in the second half of the eighteenth century. In light of the conquest of Allada by Dahomey, a story of kinship with Allada was "part of an attempt to clothe the authority which Dahomey had acquired by force in a cloak of traditional dynastic legitimacy." The Dahomean ruling dynasty presumably used the name Alladahonu, meaning the people from Allada, in preference to Agasuvi (children of Agasu) to underline their claims to descent from Allada. Law also observes that the claim to origins in Tado (Togo) was actually an element of the myth of the Allada royal lineage that the Dahomey royal myth borrowed. These arguments support the suggestion that Aligbonon, the mother of Agasu, was more appropriately associated with the town of Wassa on the Abomey plateau.[49]

Apart from the fictions of origins in Tado and of descent from the Allada royal lineage, there is a curious inconsistency in the mythic genealogy of the Dahomey royal lineage. Dakodonu was supposedly a son of an Allada prince who migrated north and settled in Wawe. Having then established Dahomey, Dakodonu was followed by his son Wegbaja, who was recognized as the first king of the Dahomean dynasty. The myth does not explain why Dakodonu, who created the kingdom, was simply a chief, a "mere captain," to quote Burton, while Wegbaja was remembered as the first real king. Traditions collected in the Abomey area from families other than the Alladahonu provide a probable answer: that Dakodonu was not a member of the Alladahonu lineage.[50]

What do all of these complicated myths and countermyths have to do with the establishment of the office of kpojito? The answer lies with the problem of legitimacy. The Dahomean royal dynasty appears to have established itself and expanded across the Abomey plateau by force alone. Yet typically in Africa, there was believed to be a sacred link between the earth and the people who lived in a locality. In effect, the earth belonged to supernatural forces and humans enjoyed what were only usufructory rights to it, with responsibility for the maintenance of a sacred contract with the earth held by the lineage recognized as having first arrived. Invading lineages normally made some kind of ceremonial accommodation with these local religious authorities, variously called "earth priests" or "owners of the land," in order to legitimize their claims to rule. The Alladahonu, on the other hand, do not appear initially to have recognized these ritual authorities, which would have made them illegitimate rulers in the eyes of their subjects. The adoption of Dakodonu into the Alladahonu dynasty and the creation of the office of kpojito appear to have been related attempts to legitimize the ruling lineage and thus gain better control.[51]

There is evidence that Agasu, the leopard totem of the royal family, existed on the Abomey plateau prior to the arrival of the Alladahonu. A cult dedicated to *kpo*, the leopard, was associated with the Gedevi, the people acknowledged to have lived there before the Alladahonu arrived and who were sometimes also called *ainon*, owners of the earth. The chief priest for Agasu, the agasunon, was always a member of the lineage descended from Dakodonu, and Dakodonu is said in nonroyal traditions to have been a Gedevi. The agasunon enjoyed ritual precedence over the kings of Dahomey, having the right to use royal prerogatives such as sandals. Because he was senior to the king, the king himself was required to prostrate before the agasunon. Most importantly, the agasunon was involved in installation ceremonies for the kings, who ritually "purchased" the country from him. All this suggests that during the reign of Agaja, the Alladahonu legitimized their hegemony by making an accommodation that acknowledged the owners of the earth—the lineage of Dakodonu—and linked the royal lineage to a common West African symbol of royalty—the leopard.[52]

The myth of origin provided royal blood for the Alladahonu through a maternal link, the princess Aligbonon. It also tied each successive king to Aligbonon's son, Agasu, and hence to the supernatural strength of the leopard. The mythic founders of the dynasty, then, were a dyad—mother and son. The creation of the office of kpojito enshrined that dyad, recreating it with each generation as each king named one of his predecessor's wives to the position of "the one who whelped the leopard." Yet we have seen that Agasu, the leopard, is himself linked to the "owners of the earth," and to the lineage of Dakodonu. Aligbonon similarly was linked to the Abomey plateau in the pre-Alladahonu period. Her priest, Adonon, was a key to the integration of Dakodonu into the royal lineage, because she also tied Dakodonu to Wegbaja. Some traditions maintain that Adonon was a Gedevi, bethrothed to Dakodonu, who was then impregnated by Wegbaja. By patrilineal law, her child would have been considered to be the child of Dakodonu. Royal family myths claim that Dakodonu was a member of the Alladahonu lineage; nonroyal myths say that Wegbaja was the adopted son of Dakodonu. In either case, Wegbaja's act would have been incestuous, and Dakodonu is said to have disinherited Wegbaja as a result. The two were reconciled only after Wegbaja killed an enemy of Dakodonu's. However, Adonon's position as kpojito makes immaterial the question of whether or not Dakodonu and Wegbaja were members of the same patrilineage. As kpojito, she was the symbolic progenitor of the Alladahonu. Dakodonu thus became father of the Alladahonu dynasty, and Adonon, through marriage and incest, linked the Alladahonu to the previous owners of the land. Wife to one king, Adonon was simultaneously mother to another dynasty, which by patrilineal code was descended from her husband, Dakodonu.[53]

The myths, speaking through the idiom of kinship and marriage, legitimized the Alladahonu as rulers over their subjects on the Abomey plateau. But they may represent more than just a ritual justification of power relationships. They also hint of power sharing between the royal lineage and the people that they found on the Abomey plateau. Adonon, though priestess to a royal vodun, was herself a commoner. Each of her successors as kpojito was a commoner. The mother-son dyad then, symbolically joined royal and commoner and suggested that Dahomey was a kingdom based on a union of royal and commoner. Moreover, that union of royal and commoner was made real in the eighteenth century as the kings built a monarchy that included persons from commoner roots, to the virtual exclusion of members of the royal family. The union also symbolized the access of commoners to the wealth and power of the monarchy.

Adonon well illustrates the point. Descendants of Adonon say that she was a rich and influential woman—in a culture where wealth and power were closely related. They say, for example, that Adonon convinced Agaja to wage a war of revenge on Weme Jigbe, a town where a son of hers had previously been captured and killed. Her wealth is suggested by the four families in the area of Abomey today that trace their ancestry to her, a sign that she controlled large numbers of people. Moreover, there are still farms in and around Abomey that are managed in her name and from which the current Adonon, who inherited the estate through positional succession, derives income. Estates of well-to-do persons were a legacy that contributed greatly to the well-being of lineages, and, at least by the nineteenth century, lineages began offering promising daughters to the king in the hope that they would do well in the palace organization.[54]

The story of Adonon speaks, too, to the integration of peoples into the expanding kingdom of Dahomey. Adonon would have become an ahosi, a wife of the king, during one of the reigns prior to Agaja. She was also from a town that was likely conquered during those early days of the monarchy. The origins of many later kpojito followed the same pattern; they came from regions that were targets of expansion in the recent past. The pattern suggests two things. First, women of newly conquered areas were being brought into the palace organization, which is not surprising considering that younger captives of war were either kept as slaves or sold into the overseas trade. Secondly, and a factor that had great importance later in the eighteenth century, opportunities were being granted to those newly conquered women to become part of the monarchy—to join that small group of persons closest to the king who wielded a certain amount of power in his name.

The office of kpojito raises another question. The kpojito was the "one who whelped the leopard." Adonon, as kpojito, was in a sense Aligbonon,

4. The Kpojito Adonon, with attendant, in 1972. Author's field photo shows a descendant of Dahomey's first kpojito, Adonon (1716–1740), the reign-mate of King Agaja. Successive generations hold the title in perpetuity

the mother of the leopard, and Agaja similarly was Agasu, the leopard. But was she also, as the translations into European languages imply, the biological mother of Agaja? Twentieth-century oral accounts seem to suggest this was so, because they link her as "mother" also to the twin siblings of Agaja, Akaba and Hangbe. The reason is that Agaja was named Dosu, which is a name given to the child born to a woman after she gives birth to twins. When other kpojito and their replacements by positional succession appeared at court in later times, travelers without exception were told by Dahomeans that they were the mothers of the kings. But it is not clear that biological motherhood was being described.

The word *kpojito* was not recorded until after the fall of the kingdom. As a term, it does not imply biological motherhood, and many of the European visitors differentiate between a "real" mother and an office holder. Dalzel explained that "besides the King's real mother, there is always a nominal one, who holds this title, as a mark of honour and rank among the women." Burton, who knew the kpojito of Glele, passed along gossip about the identity of the king's biological mother: "The pure reddish-brown of his [Glele's] skin, . . . several shades lighter than the lightest to be seen at his Court, confirms the general report that his mother is a slave-girl from the northern Makhi: others whisper that she is a mulatto, from the French factory, Whydah." At the end of the nine-teenth century, members of a French mission to the court of Dahomey similarly spoke of the "false mother of the prince," while a French re-searcher in the twentieth century was told that the biological mother of the king, even if she were alive, would be replaced by the kpojito. Herskovits similarly learned in 1931 that "the King's official mother was . . . a woman chosen for this role."[55]

The problem of the kpojito is in part a semantic one. Kinship was classificatory in Dahomey, so that children in polygynous households recognized as mother not just the woman who gave birth to them but each of her co-wives. The kingship in principle passed from father to son (though in fact also from brother to brother). By definition, every wife of a king's father was his mother, so from a Dahomean perspective, the question of whether or not the kpojito, the "mother" of the king, gave birth to the man who reigned was irrelevant.

An office known as "mother of the king" or "queen mother" was not unique to Dahomey. To create the kpojito, the Dahomeans could have drawn on models from their coastal neighbors to the south, the Akan areas to the west, Yoruba-speaking groups to the east, or Edo-speaking peoples of the empire of Benin even further east. In short, a high female office was typical of kingdoms across a broad stretch of coastal Africa. The particular form that the office of kpojito took, however, differed from neighboring models and may have been consciously manipulated by the Dahomeans to serve their own needs. The presence of a "mother of the king" is mentioned by visitors to Whydah and Jakin in the early eighteenth century. A plan of the Savi palace of King Houffon of Whydah drawn in the 1720s shows a central entrance room to the interior courtyard flanked by rooms of comparable size dedicated respectively to the king and to the "Mother of the King." Having slaves and revenues of her own, this woman, who was required to remain celibate, was said to receive many gifts from people who had need of her protection. Among the Akan, the queen mother, or *asantehema*, was a matrilineal relative of the king, or *asantehene*: a biological sister, mother, or sister's daughter. Like the "Mother of the King" at Whydah and the kpojito of Dahomey, she had a separate court. The asantehema had the authority to act as a kind of check on male power, interfering in judicial proceedings, giving pardons, or mitigating sentences imposed by the asantehene, and even advising or admonishing him and his courtiers. Influential in naming new chiefs, she nominated candidates for asantehene and played a central role in their enstoolments.[56]

Kingdoms to the east had a different model for the senior female position—a woman not of the king's lineage. There, the woman who birthed the king was acknowledged to have been the mother; but a biological mother created a ritual problem, particularly in kingdoms like Oyo and Benin, where the male ruler was believed to be divine. The king could not prostrate before any person, yet a child was always required to subordinate himself before his mother. What would happen if a divine king, who ranked higher than any other mortal in his realm, met his mother? In Benin, the oba, once enthroned, could never again see his mother. She remained in a palace outside the capital city with a court and courtiers, from where she was said to have had some influence on the politics of the kingdom. In Oyo, there was an important woman's office called the iya oba, which means literally the mother (*iya*) of the king (*oba*). In earlier times, the iya oba was indeed the biological mother of the *alafin*, or king, and in at least two instances, mothers reigned as regents for sons who succeeded as minors. At a later point, however, the biological mother was required to die when her son was installed, and thenceforth the iya oba was appointed from among palace women.[57]

As we have seen in the case of the agasunon, the problem of ritual ranking existed in Dahomey, too. There, it would have involved at least three persons, each of whom was senior to the monarch. They were the agasunon, the biological mother of the king, and—in the nineteenth century—the diviner of Fa who told the king his destiny. I have found no eyewitness accounts of the king prostrating to anyone in public; nevertheless, Dahomeans readily described what was supposed to have happened when they met, or at least when the king met the agasunon: "When the Agasunno appears in person before the monarch the latter must remove his sandals, prostrate himself before the church, kiss the ground, and throw a little dust upon his forehead, whilst all the courtiers take a sand bath, and white men stand up and bow." Interestingly, in the case of the "mother of the king," we have an eyewitness account of a meeting between the king and the kpojito, and it suggests that the problem of ritual ranking did not exist between them. The English traveler John Duncan in 1845 saw the reigning kpojito, the aged Agontime, prostrate before the reigning monarch, Gezo.[58] That elderly woman kneeling with forehead lowered to the earth is wordless evidence, and perhaps the strongest proof, that the holder of the office of kpojito was not normally the biological mother of the king. Yet descendants of the very next king, Glele, today insist that Glele's kpojito was in fact the biological mother of that king. The story of this exception that proves the rule will be told in chapter 6.⌇

3
The Age of Tegbesu and Hwanjile

Si men egbe don (a woman will not go to war for nothing).

J. A. Skertchly, transcription of a praise-name for Tegbesu

Succession: The Palace, the Monarchy, and the Struggle for Power ⟋

King Agaja died in early 1740. The succession was disputed, as it had been when Agaja came to power more than twenty years earlier, and as it would be at the death of every subsequent Dahomean king. Succession struggles were crucial moments in Dahomean history, when the monarchy was recreated, not just with a new king but with the appointment of numerous new officers, male and female. A new king was formally and finally enthroned only on the occasion of Grand Customs, which took place more than a year after the death of the king's predecessor and constituted his final funeral. During the interregnum, the would-be king and his supporters worked to consolidate control, to defeat and eliminate competing claims to the throne, and to demonstrate that the monarchy could command visible and supernatural sources of power. In effect, authority followed the demonstration of power. It did not precede it. Disputed successions, then, may be seen not as a violation of order, but rather as part of the process for recreating authority at the state's center. The enthronement or enstoolment of a new king was an acknowledgment of the material and supernatural control that a prince and his entourage could demonstrate, rather than a recognition of a prince's right to rule. Tegbesu was a case in point.[1]

A series of oral traditions justify Tegbesu's accession. The scene of the first tradition is an invasion of Dahomey by Oyo. Agaja and his court flee west with the Dahomean army; the enemy is close behind. The Dahomeans reach the banks of the Mono River, but are unable to cross the flooded waterway. Desperate, they confer about what to do. The gau (war chief) suggests that they fight to the end; when defeat is at hand, they will regroup near their stores of gunpowder and blow themselves up. The assembled chiefs and ministers concur. Then the five sons of Agaja are asked their opinion. Four agree with the suicide plan. The fifth and youngest is Avissou, who will later become Tegbesu. He suggests that they walk upstream in chest-deep water to a thick copse where they can easily hide. The plan works. The Oyo army arrives, sees footprints on the river-bank, and assumes that the Dahomeans have chosen to drown rather than fight.[2]

More frequently related are versions of a story of a sojourn of Teg-besu in Oyo. Dahomey negotiates a settlement with Oyo, agreeing to pay an annual tribute: forty-one young men (*forty-one* meaning "a full amount"); forty-one young women; forty-one guns, and so on—barrels of powder, bales of cloth, baskets of coral, and various domestic animals. As a guarantee and sign of good faith, a son of Agaja is demanded. Only Hwanjile, the mother of Tegbesu, will allow her son to be sent as a hos-tage to the enemy capital. There, he again demonstrates his unusual powers, but this time with the help of Hwanjile. Supplying her son with a red cloth and a protective charm, Hwanjile makes it possible for Tegbesu to refuse to speak, to eat, to wash, or to work in the fields, yet to remain clean and healthy. Tegbesu's obvious supernatural protection brings him to the attention of the king of Oyo, who sends him home. The young man returns with a variety of innovations: Oyo-style clothing, umbrellas, and the gods Heviosso and Sakpata.[3]

Having been twice a savior of Dahomey, Tegbesu is told by Agaja that he is the one Agaja wishes to succeed him. However, another brother is vidaho, the designated heir. Upon Agaja's death, Tegbesu's brothers plot to kill him. Tegbesu is helped by Landiga, a man he later names migan (prime minister). Needing to reach the central palace in order to be named king, Tegbesu is trapped in his own residence, his enemies block-ing the door. Landiga then taps on a wall with his left hand, and another way out opens. Tegbesu reaches the palace and is made king while his enemies wait at his door. But opposition does not end with Tegbesu's arrival at the palace. As part of the enstoolment ceremonies, the king must wear a certain tunic; laced with thorns and stinging medicines by his brothers, this garment is placed over Tegbesu's shoulders. The king endures and pronounces a strong name for himself in recognition: the buffalo who is dressed is impossible to undress.[4]

A final story about opposition to Tegbesu centers on another of Agaja's wives, not Hwanjile—this one is in charge of the storehouses of the treasures of the king. Prior to the death of Agaja, she sends a gift of very fine coral to Oyo with a request for intervention at the time of the succession. She promises that, should her son Agidisu become king, Oyo will always receive the finest coral from Dahomey. Agaja learns of her deception and imprisons her. Agidisu then moves to Allada, where he receives the support of several chiefs. Once enthroned at Abomey, Tegbesu defeats Agidisu. Vowing never again to permit a woman who has given birth to a son to be guardian of the royal treasure, Tegbesu entrusts the storehouse key to a male officer who lives in the household of the meu.[5]

What are we to make of these stories of the rise of Tegbesu to power? They are clearly self-serving, designed to celebrate the virtues and supernatural abilities of Tegbesu and those who surrounded him. They purport to demonstrate the clarity of the king's vision, how he alone could outwit Oyo when everyone else had given up, how he could live as a hostage among his enemies yet neither work for nor be dependent upon them, and how he could overcome the dangerous medicines of his evil brothers. They show that Tegbesu's own abilities were enhanced by allies endowed with supernatural powers. Though suffused with mythic elements, these tales of power and magic nevertheless are placed in historically plausible settings. Oyo invaded Dahomey in 1726, 1728, and 1729, and was involved in indecisive warfare with Dahomey in 1730–32. The Dahomeans typically abandoned Abomey with the arrival of the Oyo cavalry, fleeing south or west, and, at least in 1729, they fled across a river. Tribute was negotiated and paid in 1727, and a major settlement, that could well have included the handing over of a Dahomean prince as hostage, was made in 1730. Judging from the appearance of Oyo cultural and court influences during the mid–eighteenth century, it is very possible that Tegbesu spent time there as a young man.[6]

The oral traditions' evidence of a major succession struggle, or more accurately a series of struggles, is corroborated by contemporary European sources. Three names are mentioned as princes who opposed Tegbesu: Agidisu, Zingah, and Tokpa. Zingah was possibly a son of Agaja who had earlier defected with four thousand men from the Dahomean army during a campaign against the Mahi. He may also have been the same person called Agidisu by the oral tradition. Robin Law, referring to Agidisu's being based in Allada and Tegbesu's being in Abomey, hypothesizes that in effect the two cities represented competing power centers. In any event, Agidisu, Zingah, or Agidisu/Zingah were defeated militarily. Zingah's punishment was recorded by Norris. Because Alladahonu blood could not be spilled, Zingah was sewn into a hammock, carried to Whydah, and thrown into the sea. Tokpa's opposition to Tegbesu is less clear, but it resulted in his name being cursed. Like everyone else in Dahomey, a prince received his name from an ancestor, a *joto*, whose reincarnation in the infant was learned through divination. Following Tegbesu's curse, no prince whose *joto* was Tokpa could ever be permitted to reign. Norris describes what may have been a final show of opposition to Tegbesu's accession, a rebellion led by the meu, the king's second minister, some time after Zingah's challenge. The meu's army was defeated by a force under the gau, the war commander.[7] The role of Oyo in all of these battles is unclear. Law is willing to accept the possibility that Oyo supported Agidisu against Tegbesu, and that Tegbesu's accession thus signaled Dahomean hostility toward a powerful neighbor. Arguing the opposite position from essentially the same evidence, Pogla Glélé suggests that the story of Agidisu's mother masks the reality that Tegbesu himself was imposed on Dahomey by Oyo. Tegbesu was chosen because, having spent some of his youth in Oyo, he would be more receptive to Oyo influence.[8]

How, in fact, was Tegbesu chosen to be king? Visitors to Dahomey, like twentieth-century historians, looking for principles of orderly selection, arrange evidence about successions into a series of rules for an undisputed transfer of power. First, they claim that the king had to be the oldest son of the previous king, and some insist that the throne was inherited through primogeniture. Virtually all then add a caveat: that the oldest son was chosen only if he was judged capable of ruling. Archibald Dalzel, for example, says "the King's eldest son is the heir apparent; though, for reasons of state, the Ministers, after the King's death, may alter the order of succession." Writing at the turn of the nineteenth century, John M'Leod similarly points to an eldest son, but of a favorite wife, "provided there exists no particular reason for setting him aside." There is a certain vagueness about what qualities might make an elder son ineligible. Examples tend to focus on ritual handicaps—that the son had a minor physical deformity or that he had received the name of an ancestor who had been cursed, such as Tokpa.[9]

The use of the term "oldest son" is a semantic problem comparable to that of the use of the terms "oldest daughter" or "mother of the king." When heirs were named, they received the title vidaho (*vi* = child; *daho* = great, important), a term that was probably translated by Daho-means into European languages as "oldest son." According to Dahomean social principles, the firstborn always outranked all other members of any family; in that sense, the elder always in principle had to be the lineage head, and a firstborn prince would be king. Yet Dahomeans reserved the right to allow someone else, someone also of an appropriately mature age but not necessarily the firstborn, to be head of a lineage, or to be king. In short, a prince who was recognized as ruler was by definition, but not necessarily by years, the oldest. He would be called "oldest son" even if he had brothers born before him.[10]

During the nineteenth century, heirs would be named and publicly acknowledged. However, in the eighteenth the expected lines of succession were far less clear. Writing about Dahomey at the time of Tegbesu's death, Chenevert and Bulet claim that "all the children of the king are reared during early childhood in the harem. The women who have the right to give heirs to the throne compete to have their children adopted. An appanage [grant of land and income] is given to the child that the king selects; he and all his brothers remain far from the court. And those who are responsible for taking care of him guard the secret at the risk of their heads."[11]

European visitors consistently claim there was a second rule leading to orderly succession: that the person named king had to be a son born either after his father had been named heir apparent or after he had been enthroned. Certainly, the length of the reigns of most Dahomean kings would have allowed sons born after their investiture to have reached adulthood before their fathers' deaths. Of the eight kings whose reign dates are known, five reigned for more than twenty years. Of the other three, Kpengla ruled for fifteen, Agonglo had his reign cut short at nine years by assassination, and Behanzin was deposed by the French after four. Despite the short length of Agonglo's reign, his son Adandozan may well have been born after his father was confirmed king in 1789. Although Adandozan ceased being ruler in 1818 (regents apparently ruling for him until 1804), the king lived into the 1860s. Even Akaba, whose exact reign dates are not known, appears to fit the pattern. According to tradition, Akaba was of an advanced age when he reached the throne—old enough to have fathered children who were already adults or near-adults. Yet at his death, there was no potential heir old enough to be named king, apparently because his reign was too short for a child to grow to maturity. At least four Dahomean kings were said to have been brothers of their predecessors: Agaja, Kpengla, Gezo, and Agoliagbo (the latter being named after Behanzin was deposed). Nevertheless, all could have been born according to the norm; that is, after their father was recognized as heir or king.[12]

Writers about Dahomey also suggest that the number of wives whose sons were seen as potential kings was relatively small. An observer near the end of Tegbesu's reign, for example, says that the heir had to come from among the sons born to his "six great wives, who alone can give rulers to the kingdom." Le Hérissé, whose information was based on nineteenth-century practices, says that the vidaho was given ten to twenty women with whom he was supposed to create his potential successors.[13] Such a norm would explain why the oral traditions about Tegbesu imply that Agaja had only five sons. We have no demographic information for the royal family in this period, but it would be hard to believe that Agaja, who was in power for at least twenty-two years and had sexual access to hundreds of women, would have fathered so few male children. What is likely, then, is that there was a grouping of sons, born to a select group of women, who were seen as potential heirs to the throne. However, we have no way of knowing with certainty if the Dahomean kings who actually ruled came from that select group.

To sum up, normative thinking on Dahomey insists on the rights of the first son born after his father's succession or acknowledgment as heir. A closer look at the eighteenth-century evidence, however, makes clear that an acceptable king could be one of several princes. How, then, was it decided which of the several potential heirs would become king? Was there in fact an individual or a body with the authority to name a king?

One striking feature of the eighteenth-century descriptions of the selection of the king is that there is no consensus on precisely *who* had the authority to choose a new king. One source speaks of a "Council of Ministers" that gave the nod to Tegbesu. Another claims that even if there were an heir apparent, at the death of a king the migan and meu had the right to select the new monarch.[14] Other observers of eighteenth-century court life argue that the choice of heir was the king's decision. Once the king was dead, however, the women within the palace were key players: "Often [the death of the king] is kept secret from the public for some time by the women who during this sort of interregnum sometimes make changes in the last wishes of the dead king. The women are the trustees of his last intentions and have the right to proclaim the new king. It thus can happen that the one who was chosen by the king loses the profits because the mother of his brothers has plotted and formed a party. From that arise divisions and civil wars."[15] The lack of a recognized body of authorized kingmakers tends to confirm that it was not so much that the king was chosen, but that a prince and his supporters effectively took control and then were acknowledged. Contemporary sources make clear that control over the palace was a key to control over the kingdom. Writing about Whydah, for example, William Bosman says, "[F]or the eldest Son no sooner hears of the King's Death, than he immediately makes his interest amongst his Friends, to take Possession of the late King's Court and Wives; and succeeding happily in these Particulars, he need not doubt the remainder; for the Commonalty will not easily consent that after that he shall be driven from the Throne." The pattern was the same in Dahomey. The oral traditions about Tegbesu say that he hurried with Migan Landiga to the palace when he heard of his father's death. Kpengla and Adandozan are similarly associated with haste to reach the palace at the time of their predecessors' deaths. At the end of the nineteenth century, an ally present when Glele died sent word to Behanzin to come to the palace and, while awaiting his arrival, beheaded a servant girl at the scene to keep the news from being spread to others.[16]

The rush to the palace brings up another important point raised by the oral traditions about Tegbesu: that a prince made a bid for power in conjunction with other powerful persons, including women within the palace. A would-be king arrived at the palace with allies, normally armed retainers, and he typically was assisted by women on the inside. Speaking symbolically, the oral traditions name two individuals who helped Tegbesu: Landiga, whose left hand—the hand associated with ritual power—opened an escape hole in a wall, and Hwanjile, whose magical skills helped Tegbesu overcome danger and opposition. They also speak of a rival male-female alliance—the one that included Agidisu and the unnamed female keeper of the king's treasury.

There were a number of ways that women within the palace could aid or oppose a would-be king. First, attempts were made to keep the death of the king secret until his successor had taken control of the palace. But princes did not reside in the palace, and a prince who wished to be king needed contacts there to let him know that the king had died and hence that he should make his move. Eighteenth-century sources claim that the king's sons were kept away from court and were deliberately excluded from participation in politics. Pommegorge writes that "these young princes are absolutely nothing in the country of their father, which they see rarely. They are given no rank as long as the king lives. They are carefully kept away from knowledge of the affairs of the country; and they are kept in poverty, so that they are not able to form any party." Accounts scattered through the history of the kingdoms of Dahomey, Whydah, and Porto Novo insist that princes were brought up in humble circumstances in the households of commoners and that they were unaware of their status. King Houffon of Whydah, for example, was said to have been guarding the pigs of his foster family when courtiers arrived to make him king. As late as the accession of Gezo (1818), traditions insist that the king had been a simple farmer called from his fields to serve his people as king.[17]

These accounts of the lowly state of future kings were part of the mythic aura of kingship—that a ruler learned to understand his people, and to make friends with commoners who would later serve him as officials, by living among his people and sharing their experiences. Despite this ideological vision of king as everyman, it is obvious that Dahomean princes were aware of their status. We know, for example, that certain sons of Agaja and Tegbesu were provided with estates for their support. We know that as early as the reign of Agonglo, the sons with potential claims to the throne were educated in the household of the meu. Nevertheless, eighteenth-century princes do not appear to have been included in deliberations at court and they were not treated as high-ranking persons. Pommegorge describes a meal hosted by the king and eaten with a minister of state. The king's sons sat on the ground at the foot of the table, eating morsels that the guests tossed from their plates. A modest status, however, would not have precluded ambitious princes from preparing their bids for the kingship. For success, they would have needed strong allies, both inside and outside the palace.[18]

Beyond providing crucial intelligence, most importantly the news of the death of the king, women in the palace might have been able to muster armed female guards to take physical control. Female contacts within the palace might even have been able to hurry the demise of the reigning monarch. But tales of assassination move us ahead of our story and need to wait until the reign of Agonglo. Details of precisely what happened at the time of successions are still few at the accession of Tegbesu. They do suggest, however, that coalitions of persons made bids to control the monarchy. And they are the first records that directly implicate palace women in attempts to place specific individuals on the throne.

Who were the women who worked with princes to win control over the monarchy? Two—Hwanjile, and the mother of Agidisu—are noted by name at the accession of Tegbesu. Hwanjile was a foreigner to Dahomey, an Aja woman who was probably brought into the palace as a captive of war. We do not know precisely what position she held in the palace of Tegbesu's predecessor, Agaja. Traditions tell us two important details about the mother of Agidisu: that she was keeper of the royal treasury and that she wanted the kingship for her biological son. The first detail indicates that she ranked high within the palace; in common households, for example, it was always the head, or first, wife who controlled access to the storehouses. Traditions say that Tegbesu afterward vowed never to trust a woman who had given birth to a son, thus setting out an ideological position that appears to have been followed as policy, at least in the nineteenth century. During that period, we have a handful of cases where we know personal data about women within the palace. Those women in the highest offices and closest to the king did *not* have living male children.[19] In the eighteenth century, unfortunately, a dearth of corroborating evidence leaves us unable to evaluate fully the tradition of the mother of Agidisu. Indeed, it is not even clear if the story of the mother of Agidisu is based on a historic incident or if it is perhaps a formulaic statement about women's character, a myth like that of Na Geze, that expresses a later perspective on the relationship of princes to their biological mothers.

Despite the difficulties of distinguishing what can be taken literally, what emerges from these records is a pattern that would continue until the abolition of the kingdom by the French: powerful women within the palace would ally themselves with ambitious princes to build coalitions aimed at taking over the throne. No king was confirmed in office without being challenged. Oral traditions often retrospectively "legitimize" the struggle for control by claiming, as they do in the case of Tegbesu, that the preceding king had preferred the winner as his successor.[20] But something more seems to be operating in these accounts, something that is different from the distortion of history to conceal a usurping king. Dahomeans do not seem to have considered bids for control by factions other than those of a designated heir to be illegitimate. For example, the oral accounts of the accessions of the nineteenth-century kings Glele and Behanzin, both of whom were official heirs challenged by their brothers, do not emphasize the legitimacy of their own claims to the throne; nor do they condemn their opponents as illegitimate. Rather, like the traditions surrounding Tegbesu, they stress the abilities of the victors to overcome their enemies. In short, they point to a demonstration of power as a fundamental legitimizing act. They hint that a king was not named to power, but rather that he used power to demonstrate his legitimacy, proving himself the most capable heir in the line of the Alladahonu. The initial hurdle for a new king and his allies, then, was demonstrating an

ability to use power by gaining control of the center of the kingdom—
the palace. A second question, the legitimacy of the dynasty itself, continued to be disputed in the early days of Tegbesu's reign.

The Kpojito Hwanjile ⟿

Hwanjile was from Aja country to the west of Abomey. Traditions vary
about the means by which she entered the palace of Abomey. Some say
that she was a war captive; others assert that she was a trader who met
a wife of Agaja (or met Agaja himself) in a market and that she was
recruited to the palace because of her beauty. Some traditions justify and
legitimize her position by claiming that she was a good friend of Adonon,
the kpojito of Agaja, and that Adonon was responsible for marrying her
to Agaja. Other factors in Hwanjile's past are perhaps more revealing: that
she had already had two children before she arrived in the palace of Agaja
and that she was knowledgable about various vodun. In his treatment of
Dahomean religion, Bernard Maupoil comments that Hwanjile was "a
powerful woman, expert in making charms and a great psychologist."[21]
Fully adult and a priest when she became an ahosi (king's wife), Hwanjile
made good use of her experience, skills, and knowledge. Oral traditions,
as noted above, represent the young Tegbesu as a protégé of Hwanjile.
She became kpojito on the installation of the king and, "strong as a
man," she then worked to stabilize the monarchy.[22] We know that the
first Hwanjile died before the end of Tegbesu's reign, though Hwanjile,
in the form of replacements through positional succession, played a central role in a later succession struggle and she today continues to be an
important authority in the life of the area that once was the kingdom of
Dahomey. On a chance visit to her compound in the early 1970s, I found
her presiding over a family council of individuals resident in Whydah;
led by Tegbesu's yovogan, they had come to an audience with her in
Abomey to settle some land and lineage problems.

   The accession of Tegbesu and his ability to take control over the
Dahomean government confirmed his legitimacy as the heir of the Alladahonu lineage. Contemporary European sources and oral traditions,
however, indicate that the legitimacy of the dynasty itself was still being
disputed, despite the accommodations previously made with local "own-

ers of the earth." There is evidence from the 1730s and 1740s of unrest in the territories nominally under Dahomean control. Although European records point to problems of trust and command at the levels of officers and ministers of state, oral traditions point to unrest at a popular level that was expressed through religious institutions.

Followers of vodun were organized into local congregations, each of which was headed by a male-female pair of *vodunon* (*non* = owner, guardian, mother). The individual chapter houses in turn kept in touch with congregations in other localities. Because they were extrafamilial, and because they linked persons across broad geographic spans, the vodun represented a potential political threat to the monarchy. Maupoil, for example, comments that "the monarchy of Abomey was aware of the danger that was associated with powerful congregations of priests in close contact with the faithful that they advised and influenced. Their mastery of sacred amulets reinforced this influence, which was more than ready to deviate to the political level." Melville and Frances Herskovits collected oral traditions that argue specifically that religious institutions in the eighteenth century were perceived by the monarchy as threats to its authority. The Herskovitses were told that under Agaja there had been "many plots against the monarchy instigated by the Sagbata [Sakpata] gods and by the gods of the rivers and the silk-cotton trees. . . . So many of the *voduno* and their followers were sold into slavery." Tegbesu, upon achieving power, was faced with "the disaffection of the people, who were being swayed by the priesthoods of the autochthonous gods to resist the monarch." [23]

Hwanjile is credited with resolving the unrest by reordering the hierarchy of the vodun to more closely reflect the dynasty's interests and more effectively control the followers of the popular gods. There is evidence of strong monarchical efforts to encourage and control religious life during this period. Different traditions credit Hwanjile specifically with bringing numerous vodun to Abomey.[24] Oral traditions agree that her most important achievement was to import from Aja country a pair of creator vodun, Mawu and Lisa, and to set them up as supreme over the Fon pantheon of gods. Because Mawu and Lisa ranked highest in the hierarchy of the vodun, all other gods were subordinate to them, and

their priest, Hwanjile, became effective director of religious life in Dahomey. Crucial administrative decisions about the management of all the
vodun came under her jurisdiction: the confirmation in office of new
vodunon, the resolution of religious disputes, the approval of dates for
ceremonies, and the making of decisions about when and where vodun
might be installed. In addition, there appear to have been efforts to control the activities of the vodun through making them financially dependent on the monarchy. Chenevert and Bulet, writing after the end of
Tegbesu's reign, report that priests and their chapter houses were maintained by the monarchy through grants of land. Moreover, the king
covered expenses to support ceremonies that, to judge from twentieth-
century patterns, would have constituted a considerable financial subsidy.[25] In practical terms, then, by the end of Tegbesu's reign in 1774, the
monarchy controlled the vodun and their followers through direct regulation and financial support of chapter houses.

A number of other religious innovations also date to the mid–
eighteenth century. Two of these would have important ramifications
long after the deaths of Tegbesu and Hwanjile: the establishment of the
cult of the tohosu, which was dedicated to vodun of the royal family, and
the encouragement of vodun who could foretell the future. Apart from
the kings and kpojito, the first human-born creatures to be honored as
deities were the tohosu of the royal family. Tohosu (*to* = river, lake,
marsh; *hosu*, or *ahosu* = ruler, king) were said to appear on earth as
anomalous births, children born with missing or deformed limbs or with
teeth, hair, or other abnormalities that were interpreted as visible signs
of their nature. Powerful and dangerous beings, they were returned by
the Dahomeans to the waters from which they were believed to have
come. The active worship of tohosu was dated to the time of Tegbesu and
was associated with Zumadunu, a tohosu fathered by Akaba said to have
been born with six eyes and a beard, and who walked and talked at birth.
Various legends tell of problems—drought, fire, famine—that persisted
while the kings ignored the collective body of tohosu. The troubles ended
only when the royal lineage agreed to worship them. Beginning with
Akaba and Zumadunu, each king was linked to at least one major tohosu.
The worship of the tohosu, who were ranked hierarchically under their

firstborn, Zumadunu, was ultimately directed by a priest named Mivede. Zumadunu's temple in Abomey, and hence the headquarters for the to-hosu, was placed adjacent to but behind the temples of Mawu and Lisa. In the eighteenth century, like all other vodun, the tohosu and their priests were subordinate to Hwanjile's direction. Though far from central to religious life in Tegbesu's time, the tohosu were the harbingers of religious changes that would begin to focus attention and religious control specifically on the royal lineage.[26]

The second religious innovation with long-term implications had to do with vodun who could foretell the future, and specifically with divination. Spirit mediumship and various forms of divination appear to have existed from earlier times. They were a necessary part of faith in vodun, because humanity, which regularly sent prayers and sacrifices to the world of the shadows, needed mechanisms to receive messages and to interpret signs of the vodun. The system of divination known as Fa, or Ifa, among Yoruba-speaking peoples, was brought to the Abomey plateau during the reign of Agaja, though there is evidence that Fa was known in Allada and Whydah in earlier times. Maupoil records a legend that Fa was introduced by two Yoruba diviners who arrived in Abomey near the beginning of Agaja's reign. Tegbesu was the first king to be initiated in the forest of Fa and to receive his *kpoli*, the sacred object containing his sign, and the key to learning the details of his destiny. As a religious and conceptual system, Fa differed dramatically from the practices of vodun in Dahomey. It was individualistic, based on a process by which a person working privately through a diviner sought to understand his personal fate within the cosmos. And Fa and its practice were gendered male.[27]

Though within a hundred years Fa would become central to divining in Dahomey, during the period of Tegbesu it was clearly seen as only one of a number of vodun that could be utilized to learn the unknown. Indeed, the Herskovitses suggest that Fa itself was encouraged by the monarchy to compete with and discredit the *bokanto* (*bokan* = amulet, charm; *to* = father), diviners associated with the indigenous people of the Abomey plateau. Tegbesu is said to have made war on the Baribas in order to capture Muslim diviners. Hwanjile, too, is credited with importing the vodun Bagbo, who reputedly could foretell the future, from the area of Savalu in Mahi country. Traditions are specific on Bagbo's role as a competing divination system, for "two safeguards are better than one, and the monarchy might have an interest in setting diviners at variance with each other." We do not know specifically if spirit mediumship was suppressed at this time, but the Herskovitses collected a tradition that hints that it may have been, and it did not exist as a public phenomenon in later periods. Describing efforts to reduce the influence of the bokanto, people told Herskovits, "In early times, when the gods came into the heads of *vodunon*, and even *vodunsi*, they would prophesy. But the kings did not want this. A man or a woman in any village in Dahomey might then rule in the name of a god."[28]

The worship of vodun associated with the royal family and the practice of Fa divination would dramatically alter the monarchy in the nineteenth century. For the moment, however, it was Mawu and Lisa who embodied and symbolized the political control over religious life that the Dahomean monarchy achieved during the period of Tegbesu. The two deities reinforced and elaborated an ideological vision of power relationships at the center of the state of Dahomey. Mawu (female) and Lisa (male) were gendered deities associated with acts of creation, but they do not appear otherwise to have been linked as husband and wife. Though brought from an area west of Dahomey, Mawu and Lisa were originally linked to Yoruba-speaking cultures to the east. In Yoruba thought, Mawu (Yeye Mowo) was wife of the creator god Obatala; Lisa (Oshala), in his Yoruba incarnation, had been the deity that molds human beings out of clay. The Herskovitses found Mawu and Lisa described variously as twins or as an androgynous mother and son. In either case, they were a pair with contrasting attributes: female/male, moon/sun, night/day, coolness/heat, older/younger, west/east. The joining of Mawu and Lisa was reminiscent of the ideological message established in the previous reign through the pairing of Aligbonon with Agasu and Kpojito Adonon with King Agaja: that power and authority derive from a male-female pair with contrasting attributes. It is significant that in neither case was the pair a husband and wife, a relationship in which the female was considered to be dependent and subordinate. Moreover, Aligbonon/Agasu, Adonon/Agaja, and Hwanjile/Tegbesu paired individuals from royal and commoner lineages. Though royalty had initially resided in the female, Aligbonon, and the Alladahonu traced their royal blood matrilineally to her, with the creation of the kpojito and king dyad, royalty was derived from the male, following patrilineal succession. Drawing on the ideological images at the end of the nineteenth century, Maurice Glélé argues that the king and kpojito formed the central ideological unity—man and woman, royal and commoner—upon which the state was based. Glélé could be speaking directly to the challenges of the reign of Tegbesu and to the solutions found by Hwanjile when he asserts: "Thus an equilibrium, a counterweight, was established and continually strived for at the very heart of the monarchy's conception of power. The power of the king was limited in its very essence, on the one hand, by other princes who could on the basis of their origin claim the throne. It was limited on the other hand, at the level of the people, by the commoners from whom his mother had come and whom he could neither deny nor forget." [29]

Ministers, Traders, and the Monarchy ∾

The ideological vision of balanced power centers that is expressed by Maurice Glélé was a reality of the monarchy in the second half of the eighteenth century. It was perhaps most vividly illustrated by the pairing of Tegbesu and Hwanjile, who appear to have been perceived as corulers. But it was reflected, too, in more than the two power centers that they represented, because the proliferation of state offices was beginning to create pockets of power and wealth among the commoners who were being drawn into the kingdom's government. By the 1750s, we can see the dynamics of inside-outside tensions that contrasted the palace and its focus on the interests of the royal lineage, on the one hand, with the outside and its focus on the interests of common lineages, on the other. Yet the tensions were far more complex than the binary model implied by inside/outside or royal/commoner. Because of the centrality of the lineage in social life, individuals involved in the state always had divided loyalties. Faithful service to the king offered rich rewards, but one's material and spiritual past and future were tied up with the lineage. The tug of those loyalties can be imagined most easily for women within the palace, who were pledged to serve the king yet who stood to enrich themselves and their lineages if they managed their resources and opportunities well. Officials outside the palace similarly worked simultaneously for the state and for their own interests.

The concern of the dynasty for divided loyalties was reflected in relations of the kings with their courtiers. In the early days of the kingdom, as the Alladahonu established themselves on the Abomey plateau, they probably relied heavily on members of their own lineage for positions of greatest responsibility and only gradually began to trust people outside the royal lineage. The conquest of the territories of Allada and Whydah more than doubled the size of the kingdom and necessitated dramatic changes in the administration of the kingdom. Pressures were exacerbated by external attacks—usually alternating between the Oyo cavalry and the exiled leadership of Whydah—that were nearly constant from the 1720s until 1748. In that year, a settlement with Oyo by which Dahomey agreed to pay permanent annual tribute brought relative peace to Dahomey, though Whydah would continue to be a problem. The struggle to order the vodun and their followers reflected a response to one form of popular opposition during these troubled decades. It was paralleled by strife internal to the workings of the state as the dynasty coped with how and to whom to entrust greater administrative power. Reports from the last decade of Agaja's reign suggest that the 1730s were characterized by tensions between the kings and their appointed officials. Law describes a "campaign of terror" during the first two decades of Tegbesu's reign, when executions of high-ranking male officials were frequent and often appeared to have been based on little more than vague suspicions of disloyalty. Nine of the ten yovogan who held office between 1743 and 1763 were executed. Contemporary Europeans recorded tales of intrigue worthy of the most imaginative fiction. Norris, for example, wrote of Shampo, a military officer of Tegbesu's, who "was the darling of the soldiers, and every tongue was busy in his praise: such merit could not fail to excite a tyrant's jealousy. Ahadee [Tegbesu] from that moment determined to cut him off. Shampo had a sister in the king's house, who, by some means, got intimation of the king's design: she could have no interview with her brother, for the king's women are forbidden to hold discourse with any man; but as she was at liberty to send provisions for his table, from the royal mansion, she concealed a knife and a cord, with a noose on the end of it, among the victuals." Shampo got the point and fled the country, taking "a considerable part of the army" with him.[30]

By the end of Tegbesu's reign, stories of arbitrary dismissal and execution were less frequent and the offices of state were being used to integrate nonroyal men and women into the kingdom's government. In retrospect, Dahomeans claimed that the kings deliberately excluded persons who were of royal blood from the kingdom's administration, on grounds that royalty would have pursued their own ambitions, whereas commoners were grateful and faithful after being elevated to high office.[31]

Service to the monarchy was handsomely rewarded, particularly at the highest levels. Among the men who were part of the closest circle of the monarchy were what I will call ministers of state. Their number varied over time but does not seem ever to have exceeded seven. Beyond this circle were dozens of high officers variously referred to as chiefs, or caboceers, from the Portuguese *cabeceiro*, or headman. In addition, titled women within the palace and certain of the brothers and sisters of each king enjoyed the kind of privileges and rewards that I describe below.

Scholars have debated two related points—whether or not there was a landed or a commercial aristocracy and whether or not offices were hereditary. Obviously, if there had been a nobility and if offices had been hereditary, the power of the king and his close supporters would have been severely limited. I argue that, apart from the royal lineage, Dahomey did not have an aristocratic or noble class, though it did develop social cleavages based on wealth. Offices were not hereditary, which meant that each succession opened the way for a new set of persons to make up the monarchy—that cluster of persons around the king who exercised power with him and in his name.

The evidence about offices and their occupants can be confusing. Norris, for example, is sometimes cited as evidence that offices were inherited and that the kings were forced to deal with a hereditary noble class. Norris describes the revolt of the meu against Tegbesu and his death in battle fighting the king's forces. He then comments that "the king seems to have harboured no vindictive resentment against Mayhou's [the meu's] family, for he soon after advanced his younger brother into his office." But Norris himself contradicts those who would interpret this as being evidence of a hereditary class. He describes the major ministers of state, including the meu, saying "these are the principal personages of the kingdom; to which offices they have no hereditary claim."[32]

Le Hérissé understood and described the system, though his description may seem contradictory at first glance. "The duties of the grand chiefs or caboceers that were bestowed on Dahomeans who were not members of the royal family formed them into a distinguishable class in society, a sort of nobility. They [the duties] were not hereditary; nevertheless the title-holders transmitted the name that they had carried as great chiefs to the oldest of their sons. These then became *zinkponon, owners of the stool*." The distinction in essence is one between title and function. The title of any office, once conferred, became part of the estate of the titleholder and was passed down in perpetuity to his or her descendants. However, the functions of given offices were not inherited, and each king appointed new officers with the same titles, who were generally not members of the lineage of the previous holders of that office and title. When Agaja's meu died fighting Tegbesu, for example, someone among his descendants needed to be confirmed to replace him as *zinkponon*, holder of the stool (or title) and director of the dead man's estate. By law, the entire estate of the deceased meu reverted to the king, who then could have returned all or only portions of the estate to the heir apparent. Unfortunately, Norris does not record how much of the estate was returned to the family in the meu's case, though he does make clear that an heir within the dead meu's lineage was confirmed as titleholder. Heirs were probably nominated by lineages, though they were subject to formal approval and appointment by the king. Meanwhile, though, Tegbesu had appointed a different man, Sahenni, to be meu and to perform the functions of that office during his reign. Only one lineage is remembered in Abomey as having provided numerous ministers to the kings, that of the migan for Agaja, Amossugá. Two of his sons were migan and meu for Agonglo. Later descendants served as migan and sogan for Gezo, and another descendant was meu to Glele.[33]

A small group of officers, the gbonugan daho (*gbonu* = outside; *gan* = chief, director; *daho* = great, important), held what were considered to be the central ministerial positions outside the palace. Sources number these offices at between five and seven, depending upon the

period of the kingdom's history. At least three, the migan (prime minister), meu (second minister), and yovogan (chief for the Europeans),
consistently appear in lists of major officers from the 1740s to the abolition of the kingdom. Visitors during Tegbesu's reign claim that at that
period there were five principal ministers: the migan (sometimes, in
other sources, spelled Tamegah), meu (Mayhou), yovogan (Eubigah),
gau (Agaow), and ajaho (Jahou, or Diaou). We met the first four in the
preceding chapter. The fifth, the ajaho, occupied a politically sensitive
office said to have had a variety of functions: chief of the secret police,
superintendent of the palace, and, in the nineteenth century, minister of
religion. In effect, the ajaho was a gatekeeper who had authority over the
boundaries between the inside and the outside. He controlled access to
the palace, deciding who could be presented in audience to the king.
Described in 1776 as the head of the eunuchs (though it is not clear if he
was one himself), the ajaho was also charged with the guard of the palace
and the supervision of the royal drummers. By the 1790s, the ajaho was
identified as the head of the *legede*, who were the king's informers. In
mid–nineteenth century, he would be described as a minister of religion,
and the person to whom all commoner men who operated outside the
palace on behalf of the monarchy reported. These five highest officials
of the king enjoyed special prerogatives at court. Norris reports that he
and the ministers viewed public ceremonies "seated on stools, placed on
leopard's skins, at the king's gate, and sheltered under large umbrellas
from the sun." The prestige of major male officeholders was further enhanced by their very public exchange of daughters with the kings.[34]

Once a cluster of high-ranking officials had been appointed by a given
king, they formed an administration that remained intact even after the
king's death. For example, after Tegbesu died, his direct descendants became a sublineage of the royal line under the direction of a senior son of
the dead king. The son's title was vigan (*vi* = child; *gan* = chief, director),
or head of the children. Since the vigan were always confirmed in office
after their fathers' deaths, we can assume that the men who became vigan
for the various kings were close allies of the new kings. In the case of
Tegbesu, the vigan's personal name was Agessi Voyon. His sublineage was
(and is) headquartered in Tegbesu's palace in the Agblome quarter of

Abomey, and it is from there that Vigan Agessi Voyon manages Tegbesu family affairs in perpetuity. His court includes the titleholders from the ministers and other high officers appointed by Tegbesu and the dozen or so most prominent sons and daughters of Tegbesu, who are also zinkponon, holders of titles or stools.

High male officials were drawn into alliances with the king that were described through an idiom of marriage. The suffix -*si* in Fongbe means wife. A husband was *asu* and a wife *asi*. The oldest daughter of the king married the migan and became na migansi. The king was *ahosu* and everyone else in the palace—whether eunuch or woman, servant or sexual partner of the king—was ahosi. Initiates into congregations of vodun were vodunsi. Royal serfs bound to the land were *glesi* (*gle* = cultivated field). Merchants were *ahisi* (*ahi* − market). In short, -*si* meant wife but it also meant dependent. It was applied to virtually any situation where a subordinate owed service and loyalty to a superior, and where a superior had reciprocal responsibilities to the subordinate. It was used for links that otherwise would be called client-patron, though it was not limited to strictly human relationships. Dahomeans perceived of these relations in terms that were fully gendered. Typical was the history of an ancestor recounted by the head of the family of Tegbesu's meu: "Meu Sahenni was from Lissezoume [about five miles south of Abomey]. Tegbesu went there and saw him. He was a very handsome man, and had a beautiful neck. Tegbesu went home and asked his father if he could have a wife. Agaja gave him the bridewealth and he went back, gave the bridewealth to the young man's family, and brought him back to Abomey. He gave him the house where Meu Sahenni's descendants still live. His name at first was Kognon [*ko* = neck; *gnon* = good]. When Tegbesu reached the throne, he called Kognon and gave him a tunic to wear [e.g., made him a minister]." [35] The gendered language marked certain legal realities. Meu Sahenni's status was comparable to that of a palace woman and he was called ahosi. He owed service and loyalty to the king, though he was expected to amass resources that would be considered his own and his lineage's property. However, as in any marriage in patrilineal Fon society, Sahenni's children fell under the legal control of the husband, the king. The marriages of the minister's children, for example, would have to be formally approved by Tegbesu, or after the king's death by his vigan, Agessi Voyon. Though they were not considered to be members of the royal family (ahovi), Sahenni and his descendants were part of the permanent cluster of people around the children of Tegbesu. He was a zinkponon, owner of a stool, and enjoyed prestige as a powerful and wealthy individual, one involved in the affairs of the descendants of Tegbesu in perpetuity. At the same time, he would have been respected by his own lineage and been an influential member there. Yet the movement of talented and ambitious men from their lineages into permanent service to the king had to have had weakening effects on the potential political strength of lineages. In short, the legal ties to the monarchy helped consolidate state power and undermine that of independent lineages.³⁶

The oral account says that Tegbesu provided a place for Sahenni to live—a parallel to a man's responsibility to provide housing for a wife. Typically, men brought to Abomey to serve as ahosi would be settled with their own wives and other dependents in the quarter of Abomey reserved for retainers of that particular king. As Abomey and the kingdom grew, the royal emplacements and the palaces that served as their cores were built farther and farther from the center of the capital city. High-ranking officials—male and female—and certain siblings of the king were also granted wealth-generating resources of land and labor. In addition to receiving a compound site near Abomey, an official might be given one or more villages or plantations to provide income, along with slaves and/or wives to work the rural lands. For example, the testimony of a descendant of Hwanjile and resident of a village called Agbagnizon (Agbanlizun), some ten miles south-southwest of Abomey, provides some sense of how dependent villages operated. Hwanjile gave birth to Gudu, the patron of the village, before she entered the palace of Dahomey.

> When Tegbesu became king, he looked for a place for Gudu and found Agbanlizun, the antelope forest [*agbanlin* = antelope; *zun* = forest]. Gudu appointed someone who is called Gudu Zogo to look after his house in Agbanlizun. Gudu Zogo is father of all the children of Gudu who live in Agbanlizun. When ceremonies are to be held, they are cleared with Gudu Zogo. Legal disputes are settled by Gudu. Gudu has five wives. The people of Agbanlizun sent him girls

as wives. Before, people gave contributions to Gudu, such as maize, oil, etc. This continued into the colonial era when the *chef de canton* (district administrator) demanded, in the name of the French, twenty-five kilograms of palm nuts and maize from everyone. The people carried their tax to the market where the representative of the chef de canton collected it.[37]

The emphasis on oil products reflects the late nineteenth century, and the comments on the colonial period provide insights into how the French learned to adapt their own administration to previous practices. As the account makes clear, dependent villages, which were used to supply their patrons in Abomey, were important sources of provisions at times of ceremonies and warfare, when their patrons were effectively taxed. Men in villages such as these were also summoned to serve with the Dahomean army under their patrons. The implications of the system, too, provide insights into what has been described as the royal dictum: to make Dahomey ever larger. The ideal was more than an ideological rallying point; given the ever-growing body of royal dependents whose needs had to be supplied by the monarchy, expansion was also a practical political imperative.

In addition to control over villages, certain top officials had jurisdiction over provinces and could draw portions of tax revenues from them. Tegbesu gave the migan, for example, responsibility for oversight of the old kingdom of Allada. The governor of Allada, the aplogan, became his subordinate at the head of a hierarchy of offices in that province. In similar fashion, the meu, as overseer of Whydah, had authority over the yovogan and his subordinates. Both officials received a portion of all taxes collected in their respective areas. The migan and meu also managed prisons. Not only did they receive the benefits of any labor performed by prisoners, but all children born of women prisoners became their dependents.[38]

At least some high officials at this period had another lucrative source of income—the slave trade. Le Hérissé says that Agaja, to commemorate the conquest of the coast, organized a celebration in Allada during which he presented the migan and the gau each with a slave that he authorized them to sell, an apparent signal that these ministers would henceforth be

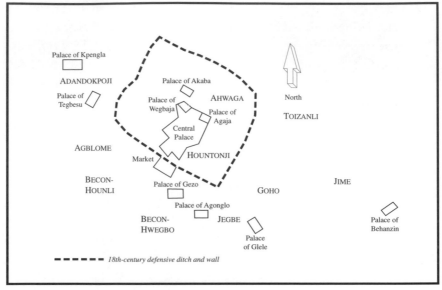

5. Center of Abomey showing quarters associated with the kings

permitted to trade in slaves. On the other hand, the evidence of contemporary European traders suggests that Agaja attempted to make the trade a personal monopoly, and wives of the king, possibly trading on his account, were known to have traveled back and forth between the coast and the Abomey plateau in the late 1720s. In any case, at the latest under Tegbesu, certain Dahomean individuals were permitted to trade. The monarchy controlled the traffic in two ways: by allowing Dahomeans to trade only with the permission of the king or a designated official, and by refusing, at least in principle, to allow the sale of persons born in Dahomey.[39]

By the 1760s, two sets of official traders were visible at Whydah. The first were four or five merchants who worked exclusively for the king. The second were private traders (*ahisinon*, meaning suppliers to merchants), who sold on commission or on their own accounts and who were supervised by the state. The ahisinon traded slaves on behalf of persons authorized by the king to trade, probably high officials of the reigning king plus holders of titles, or zinkponon, both royal and commoner, of previous reigns. In addition, the private traders handled the trade for suppliers beyond Dahomey. Among the richest private traders in the late eighteenth century was a woman named Paussie, whose name was recorded only because she ran afoul of Kpengla and was executed. Unfortunately, we have no other references to gender among the ahisinon, though women within the palace organization were described trading along with the king's male traders in the slave market of Whydah in the 1770s.[40] Whether they were effectively "king's traders," trading on the king's account, or whether they were trading for prominent women within the palace is not known. The proportion of the slaves supplied by sellers other than the king was at times very large. Two recent scholars, one using two sample cargoes and the other a traveler's estimate, suggest, respectively, that the king's portion of the trade in the late eighteenth century was as little as 10 percent and in the 1840s as low as 38 percent. Nevertheless, the greatest single trader was always the king.[41]

Where did prominent Dahomeans acquire slaves to trade? There were three possible sources. First, the king made gifts of slaves to courtiers as a reward for service to the monarchy; second, there was an active trade in slaves from areas further into the interior, so persons authorized to trade could buy and sell as middlemen; third, evidence suggests that at least some wealthy Dahomeans traded their own war captives. However, there is controversy about this last point: some scholars have argued that all war captives were owned by the king. The controversy is important, because it relates to the monarchy's later motives for expanding the armed forces of women.

In the eighteenth century, a standing army of the king was apparently drawn from the villages controlled directly by the king and hence made up of soldiers who were his direct dependents. In addition, titled officials, male and female, provided fighters from among the people dependent upon them. Dalzel describes the system as follows. "The King of Dahomy maintains a considerable standing army, commanded by an *Agaow*, or general, with several other subordinate military officers, who must hold themselves in readiness to take the field upon all occasions at the command of the Sovereign. The payment of these troops chiefly depends on the success of the expeditions in which they are engaged. On extraordinary occasions, all the males able to bear arms, are obliged to repair to the general's standard; every *Caboceer* marching at the head of his own people." Trophies of war were living captives and the heads of enemies, both of which were brought back to Dahomey. There are two eyewitness accounts of payments made directly by the king to soldiers in exchange for the persons or heads of enemies captured or killed in war. On the basis of this evidence, some scholars have argued that all war captives were "purchased" by the king.[42]

However, a mid-nineteenth-century account by John Duncan argues that the king had access only to the captives taken by his own soldiers. Duncan quotes Gezo as saying that "although he supposed many white men believed he sold the greater part of the slaves sent from that country, he could assure me it was not the case; but the cabeceers, whose soldiers captured them, were always considered to be the owners of slaves taken in war." Clearly, the king in the 1840s had reason to dissemble with a European who was pressing him to end the trade. As Law points out, "the king on this occasion was evidently concerned to minimize the extent of his own involvement in the slave trade, in order to evade British pressure for its abolition." Yet if Gezo wanted to argue that he profited little from the trade, it is odd that he would admit to benefits by adding that "the cabeceers always pay a nominal duty upon all slaves taken in war when sold." Also, apparently in response to prodding by Duncan, Gezo admitted that "all prisoners taken by his wives, or female soldiers, were his property." The implications of this conversation are twofold. First, as Dalzel implied, there were two groups of war captives, those taken by the king's forces and those captured by the soldiers of the king's major officials. Second, the passage suggests that no individual soldier in fact "owned" a person taken in combat, but rather that ownership lay with the patron of the soldier, the person upon whom the soldier was dependent. The suggestion that the king "purchased" captives, then, is distorting in the same way as is the suggestion that the payment of bridewealth meant that a man purchased a wife.[43]

Nevertheless, it is clear that something of value was given publicly by the king to soldiers at the time that they presented their captives and enemy heads at court. Snelgrave in 1727 and Burton in 1864 witnessed such payments. The Snelgrave occasion was a war of revenge following a raid by the Tuffos. It was not a full-scale war, but rather one in which "the King sent part of his Army against them," and hence all of the soldiers involved could have been the king's. On their return from war, the soldiers turned all captives and enemy heads over to the king and in turn received twenty shillings each for men, ten shillings for women, boys, and girls, and five shillings for heads of dead enemies. At this period of time, the price of a male slave at Whydah was £15, or fifteen times the amount the king "paid" for a male captive.[44]

Obviously, the sums offered were nominal, and did not represent the value of a male slave. These symbolic sums for captives and for the heads of those killed in fact sound very much like another documented payment of the kings, the small sums given to ahosi or dependents when those persons had performed a service on behalf of the king. Commoner wives typically were given a gift when they assisted their husband with a productive activity, a principle that was followed within the palace. For example, women within the palace pierced and strung cowries to be used as the king's currency. Each woman was permitted to keep one of the forty cowries meant for each string, which left the strings one short.[45] In a parallel fashion, the soldiers who were dependents of the king were warring for the king, not for themselves. As the king's dependents, or ahosi, the product of their work was the king's, and he acknowledged the value of their service by rewarding them with nominal sums.[46]

The slave trade enriched the king and favored courtiers. It also created and enriched a commercial elite at Whydah that would remain peripheral to the monarchy's control. Europeans and Africans had traded along the Slave Coast for 150 years prior to the Dahomean conquest of Whydah and had developed a trading culture that was foreign to the Dahomeans. Beginning with Agaja, each eighteenth-century king struggled to understand the coastal culture and to involve Dahomey in it in ways that maximized the kingdom's interests. The results could never have been wholly satisfactory from the monarchy's perspective; one senses a great distance between Abomey and the coast, both psychologically and culturally. Though technically a part of the kingdom from the 1720s, people at the coast spoke always of "going to Dahomey" when they traveled to the Abomey plateau, and Abomeans as late as the twentieth century used a term of contempt, *kogudonu* (person from beyond the ko marsh), to describe people from the coast. During Tegbesu's reign, the Dahomeans colonized Whydah, settling three new quarters of the city with people from the Abomey plateau;[47] the distance between Abomey and Whydah nevertheless remained great, and was underlined by the persistence of autonomous entrepreneurs and officials at the coast who, though appointed by the monarchy and subject to royal control, represented an economic independence with political overtones that was not known among royal appointees on the Abomey plateau. From Abomey's perspective, then, Whydah in particular was not only something alien, but an entity that could not be wholly controlled. Throughout the history of the kingdom, the relations between the kings and prominent coastal individuals reflected the tension of that incipient independence.

Evidence from the mid–eighteenth century suggests the difficulties of control over the coastal trade that were experienced by the Dahomean monarchy. In Agaja's day, the negotiation of prices and customs payments appears to have been done directly with the king. Snelgrave, for example, made his trip to Allada specifically to arrange the terms of trade. We know little of the officials at the coast appointed initially by Agaja, except that they included translators and collectors of customs who were responsible for organizing and supervising the trade. Snelgrave, however, who was trying to fill his ship through Jakin, found that neither the governor of Jakin nor the king's traders were willing to honor the terms he had negotiated with the king. Agaja appointed officials at Whydah to supervise the trade and the traders, and to trade on the king's behalf. Their broad responsibilities would have made them wealthy and powerful—and vulnerable to royal displeasure.[48]

Tegbesu clearly made attempts to ensure that the officials at Whydah would be loyal to the monarchy, though it is not clear that he appointed persons who knew either Whydah or the trade. Norris provides a telling but uncorroborated account of an official appointed to an office called the *tegan*, obviously a forerunner of that of yovogan. Mistaking the word *tegan* for a personal name, Norris calls the official Tanga. He reports that the official was a eunuch who had been in Tegbesu's service for a long time. The tegan, however, clearly overstepped the bounds of usual intercourse with the Europeans, offending them in ways that are not specified by the contemporary sources. At one point, he forcibly prevented the governors of the European forts from traveling to Abomey to complain about his behavior. Norris claims that the tegan wanted to make himself king of Whydah, which Norris found incomprehensible, since "the post which he already possessed was a very honorable one, and his opulence so considerable, that it amply afforded him the gratification of every desire, except that of insatiable ambition." After the tegan attempted to take the English fort, Tegbesu turned against him and eventually he was killed while resisting the Dahomean army. The tegan appears to have served as a bitter lesson for Tegbesu. Shortly after, and possibly in the aftermath of this incident, Tegbesu ordered all the official traders executed and replaced with traders selected by the migan and the meu. These traders or their successors would have been the "four or five traders" who worked for the king and who were described for the 1760s, along with the independent private traders (ahisinon) who acted as agents for other sellers. Meanwhile, the office of yovogan appeared. Governor of Whydah and supervisor of the trade, the yovogan apparently traded on his own account, but not on behalf of the king.[49]

At the latest by the time of Tegbesu, then, the kings were working closely with trusted persons of common birth. We can recognize five top male ministers close to Tegbesu in a relationship that was to continue in perpetuity. Decendants of these ministers in subsequent generations held prestigious titles and sometimes served other kings in other capacities, but it is clear that the functions of ministerial office were not hereditary. The ministers' relationship to the king was gendered female. Other major retainers of the kings were similarly linked to specific kings as the administration of the kingdom and the court life became increasingly complex. Wealth for the king's officials was gained through service to the king, though it was never inalienable and power could be revoked. The death of a zinkponon, or titleholder, technically returned the entire estate to the king. The practice—a crucial element of state power—permitted the monarchy to keep a portion of an estate as tax revenue and to control the choice of any titleholder's heir. A crime by the zinkponon could mean the confiscation of the entire estate and the reduction of family members to servile status. Those individuals closest to a king, then, had, in the politics of the kingdom, perhaps the greatest wealth and prestige both to gain and to risk. Their wealth, however, was always far less than the riches controlled by the palace in the name of the king. And even though it is not apparent in the mid–eighteenth century, the wealth of the king would increasingly be rivaled by the commercial interests that were based on the coast and particularly in Whydah.

The Impact of Oyo ⌇

The young Tegbesu was said to have been a hostage in Oyo and to have returned home with ideas for innovations in Dahomey. There are a number of characteristics similar to Oyo that appear in European accounts of Dahomey during Tegbesu's reign. However, deciding which were imported from Oyo can be difficult.

Oyo and Dahomey were both part of a coastal cultural universe that stretched from present-day Ghana nearly to the Niger River, one in which broad similarities—in kinship structures, social organization, spiritual concepts, and ruling practices—can be discerned. Some Oyo-like institutions that seem to appear in Dahomey in Tegbesu's time were known also in neighboring kingdoms such as Allada or Whydah and could have been drawn from them. Also, there is the possibility that cultural characteristics that first appear in the written records during the reign of Tegbesu in fact existed previously and were simply not noted by earlier observers. The problem of demonstrating Oyo influence, then, is not just to show that an institution or practice existed during Tegbesu's time; it is also necessary to demonstrate that it did *not* exist prior to that time and that there was some rationale for it having been imported by Dahomey's fourth king.

Oyo had a system of government in which the power of the king, or alafin, was balanced by the oyo mesi, a seven-person grouping of the heads of prominent lineages that acted as a check on the alafin's power. The oyo mesi selected the alafin and tended to have ritual and religious forms of authority, rather than secular functions in the administration of the state. Relations between the oyo mesi and the alafin were in turn mediated by the priestly leaders of the Ogboni cult of the earth. If the oyo mesi lacked confidence in the king, and if their lack of confidence was confirmed ritually, they could demand his suicide. The potential misuse of the oyo mesi's power, however, was checked not only by the Ogboni but also by the requirement that one member of the oyo mesi die with the king.

In contrast, there were no constitutional checks on the Dahomean

kings' power, and none was imported from Oyo, though by mid–
eighteenth century the kings were in effect sharing power with officials
drawn from commoner lineages. Indeed, the probable innovations of
Tegbesu are as telling in what was *not* adopted from Oyo as in what was.
For example, no Dahomean official independent of the king ever had the
authority to determine if he continued to enjoy the support of his ancestors or the right to demand his suicide. Failed kings in Dahomey were
deposed only through the extralegal means of assassination and coup.
The ritual authority over the earth, in the form of Dakodonu and his
family, had been co-opted by the monarchy during the reign of Agaja,
though other earth-deities would become problematic for later kings.
Other religious authorities were subordinated by the monarchy through
Hwanjile's administrative control over Mawu and Lisa, under whom were
ranked all the other vodun. The new institutions that appeared in mid-
eighteenth-century Dahomey can all be linked to the monarchy's efforts
to centralize control and exercise power efficiently and effectively. Innovations from Oyo were directed to two related goals: (1) the mystification
of the king and his entourage, and (2) the centralization of the administration of the kingdom, in large part through the more creative use of
eunuchs and slaves.

Oral traditions collected among Tegbesu's descendants say that he
brought three cultural innovations back from Oyo: umbrellas, the gods
Heviosso and Sakpata, and Oyo-style clothing. In fact, these were among
the least likely imports. Umbrellas were a widespread symbol of high
rank throughout the Slave Coast and were specifically noted at the court
of Agaja in the 1720s. Parallels to Heviosso and Sakpata existed in Oyo;
they were Shango, the god of thunder, and Shoponna, or Obaluiaye,
the god associated with smallpox. However, traditions associated with
Heviosso claim that this vodun was brought to Dahomey during the
period of Tegbesu, but from the town of Hévié (south of Allada), where
Heviosso had previously been established. Sakpata's origins are linked to
Mahi country to the north, and Sakpata's entry into Dahomey is associated with the reign of Agaja. Clothing at every historical period in Dahomey was diverse at court, and included styles from the Muslim north,
the Akan west, the Yoruba-speaking east, and Europe (the latter coming
from the south, via the coastal ports). Early accounts of the kingdom

note a predilection on the part of the kings for European fabrics and accessories. The Yoruba *agbada*, a gown that later became an emblem of ministerial rank in Dahomey, could have been imported in Tegbesu's time. Chenevert and Bulet report that court dress for men was "like a surplice without sleeves," which could be a description of an agbada.[50]

Another element indirectly associated with attire—the public appearance of the king—changed at least in part during Tegbesu's reign. In Oyo, as elsewhere in Yorubaland, the king, or alafin, was surrounded by ritual restrictions associated with his divine nature. The alafin appeared publicly outside the palace only three times a year, to participate in sacred festivals. The face of the alafin, said to be so radiant that human eyes could not gaze upon it, was hidden behind a veil of strings of beads hanging from his beaded crown. Some of the trappings of Yoruba divine monarchy seem to have been practiced beginning in Tegbesu's time, apparently to distance and mystify the kingship, although the well-being of Dahomey was never associated with the health of the king. Tegbesu's predecessor, Agaja, was described as regularly moving about the kingdom, in explicit contrast not only to the rulers of Oyo but also of Allada and Whydah. Agaja accompanied his troops to war and seems to have been relatively accessible. Tegbesu, in contrast, was isolated from public view. Pommegorge says that he appeared in public only once a year, for four or five minutes, during one particular ceremony at Customs. The rest of the time, if he did leave the palace, it was in a closed hammock.[51] Neither Tegbesu nor any other Dahomean king was recorded as wearing a beaded crown. However, Norris describes a woman at court in 1772 who was "too sacred to be seen" and was shielded from his view by "targets of leather, covered with red and blue taffata, with which they encompassed her," a description that evokes the effect of the veils of beads over the faces of Yoruba-speaking kings.[52] Why would palace women wear garb meant for a divine king? From time to time in Dahomey, there are accounts of the kings honoring trusted retainers by transferring ritual restrictions to them rather than undergoing the inconvenience of observing the restrictions themselves. Such may have been the case with the secluded wife.[53]

There were three categories of palace official in Oyo: eunuchs, *ilari* (scar-head, in Yoruba), and titled officers. Highest in rank were the eunuchs, who guarded the king's wives and children. Among them were three central officials who were responsible respectively for judicial decisions, for supervision of the shrine of Shango, and for collection of revenues and other administrative duties. Eunuchs had not been present at Agaja's court, but they were very visible during Tegbesu's reign, and in capacities that paralleled their use in Oyo. Armed women had served as palace guards in Dahomey at least since the 1720s; in 1772, Norris found eunuchs along with armed women guards at the gates of the Abomey palace. Some worked within the palace, and those who were in close attendance on the king wore women's dress. At least by the end of the century and probably dating from Tegbesu's reign, eunuchs also served as legede. Legede would accompany ambassadors, ministers, and other officials outside the presence of the king to ensure that they conveyed messages to and from the king with accuracy. At least on some occasions, they acted as interpreters between Europeans and the king. The term *legede* came down into modern Fongbe with strong negative connotations, suggesting a tattletale or informer. A description of legede in 1797 marks the first mention of what would become descriptions of multiple layers of extra eyes and ears placed around the officials of the king to ensure their loyalty.[54]

Tegbesu also appointed eunuchs to two very sensitive and powerful ministries: the tegan (later, yovogan) of Whydah and the ajaho. As we saw above, the tegan of Whydah proved to be a poor choice. The eunuch ajaho may not have been entirely successful, either. Although he remained technically responsible for the eunuchs within the palace, over time the ajaho became better known for two other roles: appointments secretary for the king, controlling who was allowed into the audience courtyards, and supervisor of the legede, hence "chief of the king's secret police." By the mid–nineteenth century, sources cite the tononu, an important officer in the interior of the palace, as the head of the eunuchs. Indeed, even Tegbesu's enthusiasm for eunuchs may have diminished over time; by the 1760s, only twelve boys were being castrated each year to join their ranks.[55] Nevertheless, eunuchs are cited as important players in palace politics in the 1790s. Eunuchs would continue to be involved in the court until the French conquest, but they were less prominent in later reigns, and I have no evidence that any later yovogan or ajaho was a eunuch. Legede, too, do not appear to have been eunuchs in the nineteenth century.

The title *ilari* (scar-head) was a reference to the initiation of a group of Oyo royal slaves whose heads were shaved and incisions made on them rubbed with empowering medicines. After their initiation, ilari wore a distinctive hairstyle, with alternate sides of the head being shaved at intervals. There were hundreds of ilari in Oyo—male and female. They worked as the king's bodyguard, as messengers, as highly-placed servants, and as tax collectors.[56] Although they had existed in the kingdom of Whydah earlier in the century, ilari were first mentioned as messengers of the Dahomean king only after Tegbesu came to power, in January 1746. Following that date, Europeans often spoke of the "half-heads," who were called either the generic *wensagon*, meaning messenger, or *lali*, a term obviously derived from the Yoruba. Pommegorge describes one who arrived in the company of the Yovogan to deliver the king's greetings to a new commander of the French fort. "He [the yovogan] brings with him the messenger of the king, who has half his head shaved, the other half with all his hair, a sash, like our bodyguards, except that it is composed of fourteen or fifteen rows of human teeth, threaded one against the other, and for clothing, only a kind of short silk skirt twenty to twenty-four inches long; it is placed on the hips and reaches to the bottom of the knees."[57]

An element of the structure of ilari in Oyo may have served as inspiration for the male-female doubling of offices in Dahomey that would become prominent at court in the nineteenth century. The Reverend Samuel Johnson, an African with Oyo roots who collected oral traditions in New Oyo, writes that "every male Ilari has a female counterpart who is called his companion. The Ilaris themselves by courtesy call them their 'mother.' They are both created at one and the same time and they are supposed to seek each other's interest, although there must be no intimacy between them; the female Ilaris being denizens of the King's harem." In fact, not just the ilari, but all male palace officials had court mothers in Oyo. In Dahomey, descendants of Tegbesu claim that there were female counterparts to the gbonugan daho (ministers of state) during their ancestor's reign. These palace women were identified by the suffix *-non*, which like *-si* was a gendered suffix. Translated as mother and used to indicate biological motherhood, *-non* was also used more broadly to signal ownership or the holding of a charge or responsibility. For example, the mother of a girl named Hwefa was called Hwefanon. The head of a congregation of vodun was a vodunon. A seller of maize or corn (*gbade*) was *gbadenon*. The head of a household (*hwe*) was *hwenon*. In Tegbesu's time, the counterpart to the meu was the meunon, a woman whose personal name was Naye Yeme and whose zinkponon (titleholder) still lives in Abomey. The title meunon was normally translated "mother of the meu" in European languages.[58]

The third category of Oyo officials were titled officers. Titled officials were known in kingdoms throughout the Slave Coast. However, at least one office, that of sogan (*so* = horse; *gan* = chief, director), the "master of the horse," may have been adapted from Oyo during Tegbesu's time. In Oyo, the olokun esin, or master of the horse (literally, the chief holder of the bridle of the king's horse) was one of the most important of the high-ranking officials. He supervised the royal stables and was required to die with the king. The master of the horse and his assistants also followed the army to organize the gathering of fodder for the horses.[59] The evidence for an Oyo connection for the Dahomean office of sogan is far from conclusive. There had also been a master of the horse in Allada and the office could have been introduced into Dahomey from there well before Tegbesu, though there is no mention of it prior to Tegbesu's reign. My suspicion that the sogan was introduced from Oyo is based on the fact that it was an anomaly for Dahomey. A master of the horse in Oyo, a horse-riding culture, was a major position. In Dahomey, horses were rare, and the Dahomeans never developed the regular use of them, either as cavalry or as domestic animals. Horses were sometimes presented to officials as gifts of the king, but riding was ceremonial. In fact, the largest number of horses ever noted at court at one time was seen by Norris, who on one day in 1772 saw seven horses waiting to be sacrificed and the heads of thirty-two others that had been killed in earlier ceremonies.[60]

In Dahomey, the sogan in mid-eighteenth century was said to have two functions: responsibility for the care of "criminals" and supervision of the plantations that provisioned the palace. The sogan was later described as a military officer of high rank, but he was nevertheless left behind with the baggage and camp followers during a war in 1775. At the end of the eighteenth century, the sogan was said to be responsible for receiving war captives and accounting for them to the meu. In addition, he distributed the horsemeat from equine sacrifices. And by the late nineteenth century, the sogan was described as a minor official responsible for providing wood and water for the palace, but also with responsibility for supervision of the captives who were to work the royal plantations.[61] There are several possible explanations for this seeming multiplicity of functions over time. First, some of the Europeans who recorded these various responsibilities could have misunderstood their Dahomean sources; or we may be looking at different ways of describing related functions. The "criminals" in the sogan's care could have been war captives, for example, who were put to work on royal plantations; supervising the plantations that provisioned the palace and providing wood and water would seem to be related functions, and remaining behind during warfare similarly suggests provisioning responsibilities. Alternatively, the functions of the sogan could have been changing over time. We have no way of knowing precisely what were the responsibilities of the sogan at any given time, and most particularly at the moment that the office was created in Dahomey. One point that the eighteenth-century sources make clear, however, is that during that period the sogan ranked among the highest officials of state; that he was, in fact, a minister of state.

The fact that a master of the horse had virtually nothing to do with horses—or at least with living horses—hints that the position may have been created in Dahomey only because of its importance as an office in Oyo. The master of the horse died with the king in Oyo, which meant that he was one of a handful of officials, male and female, who worked very closely with the person of the alafin, who were required to commit suicide when the king died and in whom the king had absolute trust.

Dalzel relates a story about a Dahomean sogan that provides an ideal model for such loyal behavior. During the Grand Customs for Tegbesu in 1775, the yovogan was accused in a whisper campaign of disrespect for the king. Kpengla very nearly beheaded him and the man was saved from sudden public execution only by the intercession of the migan. The sogan then gave a speech in which he swore to commit suicide at the least hint of any disloyalty, rather than be subject to similar allegations. When the sogan was later captured in war, the king ransomed him, but the sogan refused to return; rather, he reminded people of his previous speech and committed suicide.[62] The sogan may have been an important official from Tegbesu's perspective, then, not because of the monarchy's need for a caretaker for horses, but because of the king's need for people who could be trusted. An official who knew that he or she would die on the day of the death of the king would without question be interested in promoting the well-being of the monarch and his administration. Although some wives were reportedly required to die when the kings of Allada and Whydah died, it is very likely that specific offices within the palace became associated with a requirement of death during the reign of Tegbesu.

There is a final Oyo-linked characteristic of the courts of Tegbesu and the kings who followed him in the fifty years after his death; that was the increased importance of the town of Cana, some seven and one-half miles southeast of Abomey. Cana is mentioned in early written accounts of Dahomey. It was sited centrally in the small area of the Abomey plateau that oral traditions link to the religious and political beginnings of what became Dahomey. As early as the 1730s, the Dahomeans were reported to be performing ceremonies there. Its location would have made it a logical stopping point in the trade route from Oyo to Allada and the coast, and there were Yoruba-speaking settlers in Cana from early in the recorded history of Dahomey.

The centrality of Cana after the mid–eighteenth century was very possibly the result of Oyo exactions rather than Dahomean choice, because Norris reports that the 1748 settlement with Oyo required that tribute be paid to Oyo each November in Cana, and visitors to the town told of seeing Oyo ambassadors there. By the early 1770s, Cana was beginning to rival Abomey in size, with an estimated population of fifteen thousand. Abomey's was twenty-four thousand. There are suggestions in the sources that Cana had become the effective seat of government by this period. From Tegbesu to Gezo, each king built a royal palace in Cana, and Norris testifies that Tegbesu frequently resided there. Hwanjile, his powerful kpojito, was buried at Cana, and Dalzel describes Cana as the place where the king "generally resides," though he would go to Abomey to perform Customs. Agonglo, arranging ceremonies for Kpengla, had slaves sacrificed in his path so that he "would walk in blood, all the way from Calmina [Cana] to Abomey, to see his father." Contemporary Europeans speak without comment of meetings with the kings at Cana, which suggests that it was an accepted center of government.[63]

Cana's importance would decline in the first half of the nineteenth century, when Dahomey was no longer subject to Oyo. By midcentury, travelers began to describe Cana as the old capital—the capital when Dahomey was a tributary state of Oyo. So important had been Cana's position that at least one visitor believed that Abomey itself had been founded after the accession of Gezo in c. 1818. As of the 1840s, Cana was visited by the court only once a year, when upon the return from annual warfare the king would spend a month there to perform ceremonies in honor of the royal ancestors and then continue to Abomey to celebrate Customs there.[64]

Oyo, then, clearly had an impact on Dahomey at the level of state organization and functioning. The Oyo empire was administered through the use of male and female slaves, of eunuchs, and of a number of female officials within the palace. Possibly following the Oyo model, Tegbesu entrusted high office to eunuchs, though with mixed success. In the meantime, slaves and women within the palace organization were proving their worth to the monarchy. Women slaves in particular, in the form of young captives, were growing up in a palace organization that channeled their talents and energies and offered them rich material rewards for loyal service. The latter part of the eighteenth century would prove to be the high period of women's power in the court of the kings of Dahomey.〜

4
The Struggle to Maintain the State

The people of the country are hospitable. They gladly offer you lodging
and refreshments. . . . Roads are safe, to the point that you can travel
at night as well as during the day.

P. Labarthe, describing Dahomey in 1803

The Reigns of Kpengla, Agonglo, and Adandozan ⁓

Tegbesu's was a long and vigorous reign. During his more than thirty
years in power, the Dahomean monarchy consolidated its domination of
the Abomey plateau heartland and much of the territory it had conquered. It established a kind of Pax Dahomiensis. Order, discipline, and
relative affluence were characteristics of the civil populace as observed by
Europeans of the period. The monarchy succeeded in accommodating
Oyo, negotiating a tributary status that gave the kingdom reasonable security on its eastern boundaries and freed it to deal with neighbors to the
north, west, and south. Internal opposition to the monarchy and the
royal family ended, at least for the time being, and there were few signs
by 1770 that the legitimacy of the regime was still being questioned. The
integration of captive peoples, particularly women into the palace organization, was producing a vigor that enriched the kingdom culturally as
well as socially. Accounts of Dahomean history tend to name as two of
the more important monarchs Agaja and Gezo: Agaja is praised for expansion to the coast and Gezo for administrative innovations. However,
without the consolidations of Tegbesu's period, Agaja's triumph over
Whydah and Allada might have been lost. And many of the so-called
innovations of Gezo were in fact the innovations of Tegbesu, present in
Dahomey in the mid–eighteenth century and ready to be enlarged and

119

elaborated in the nineteenth. In retrospect, the reign of Tegbesu takes on the glow of a golden age.

The final years of Tegbesu's reign, however, were characterized by decline. As the king aged and his health began to fail, a certain lassitude set in politically and economically, as if Tegbesu were in fact a divine king whose kingdom reflected his physical state. Chenevert and Bulet argue that, in his later years, Tegbesu "neglected all sorts of business: this negligence passed to his ministers, and there was disorder in finances, in the troops, in commerce." The army by the early 1770s was said to include only three thousand men. As late as a decade after Tegbesu's death, a French visitor claimed that the Dahomeans could muster only eight thousand to ten thousand soldiers.[1] By the time Kpengla came to power, Weme was independent and allied with the former rulers of Allada against Dahomey. The Allada ruling line had established itself east of the Weme River under the protection of Oyo, and it ultimately consolidated its rule in the trading center of Porto Novo. The Hweda were regularly raiding Whydah beach, and African traders, particularly those from Oyo, avoided the kingdom and took their slaves to ports further east. Supplies of slaves and trade revenues at Whydah dropped and the monarchy was forced to begin selling Dahomeans. Dahomey had begun a long period of economic stagnation that was related to the decline of the overseas slave trade.

Slaves would continue to be virtually the sole overseas export of Dahomey throughout the reigns of Kpengla, Agonglo, and Adandozan. Wars between European nations, international recession, and changing policies among the various overseas buyers over the decades from 1774 to 1818 created variations in the levels of trade that masked the progression of the slave trade toward its inevitable end, something that can be seen clearly only in retrospect. Each of the three kings tried various remedies to make trade thrive. But the overseas trade represented an integration of the kingdom into a larger economic system whose fluctuations were beyond the ability of the Dahomeans to control. The experience of the monarchy under Kpengla typified the position of Dahomey. Early in Kpengla's reign, the monarchy tried to improve the military and capture larger numbers of slaves to sell. When that did not bring a return of prosperity, they made the situation worse by trying to monopolize the trade, fixing prices, and forcing traders to sell slaves to the monarchy at less than market prices. Traders avoided Dahomey, and Porto Novo, some forty-five miles to the southeast, flourished. In the end, the slave trade revived slightly only after changes over which Dahomey had no control: the resumption of European interest in slaving following the American War of Independence and the relative decline in the attractiveness of Porto Novo when Oyo, weakened and sliding into permanent decline, could no longer protect it from Dahomean raids.[2]

After Kpengla's death in 1789, Agonglo and Adandozan faced even more serious, long-term threats to the health of the slave trade. The French abolished the trade in 1794, then relegalized it in 1802. The English abolished the trade in 1807 and began the process of suppression that ultimately led a string of envoys to Abomey to try to negotiate its end. By the first decade of the nineteenth century, all three European trading forts at Whydah—English, French, and Portuguese—had been closed. Another revival of the trade and some improvement in the economic situation began only after 1810, when an Anglo-Portuguese treaty was signed allowing the slave trade to continue out of Whydah. Even that legal loophole was closed by 1815, after which all trade from along the Slave Coast technically was prohibited and the slave trade became clandestine.

Was Dahomey wholly dependent upon the slave trade? Having enjoyed a certain prosperity and strength in the mid–eighteenth century as a result of the trade, could the kingdom have survived without overseas trade—in slaves or any other commodity? With the kingdom suffering depopulation, keeping slaves in-country would have offered increased economic productivity. Overseas imports, one can argue, were luxury items: cloth and other manufactured goods, tobacco, cowries, alcohol, and firearms. Making an abolitionist argument in the 1780s, Pruneau de Pommegorge comments with reference to Dahomean imports: "The country produces everything that is essentially necessary to life." Pommegorge was correct in asserting that Dahomey produced all that was necessary for subsistence, but he missed a central point: that Dahomey's was far from a subsistence economy. For example, domestic surplus had for years supported the state through taxation and tribute payments. Accounts from Allada and Whydah prior to the Dahomean conquest describe a number of taxes, all of which existed later in Dahomey (along with additional levies). There were taxes on sales in the markets, on entries into the kingdom and the crossing of rivers, on agricultural production, on inheritance, annually on all adult men, and on cash incomes. Collection of market taxes and travel tolls was done locally with the collectors and their superiors retaining a portion before sending the remainder to Abomey. The greatest public payment of taxes was at the time of Customs, as Norris reports, when ministers and governors of provinces came with gifts, and African traders and heads of families brought "a quantity of cowries, proportioned to their circumstances: each of them endeavours to make his present (which is in fact a tax) as respectable as he can." Law points out that Norris may have been witnessing the payment of taxes on traders' cash incomes. Norris could in addition have been watching the taxing of all adult males. We cannot be sure, and the point is an important one, since a portion of taxes collected outside the palace was retained by the collector. Taxes brought to the palace would have gone directly into the royal treasury.[3]

In addition to taxes on individuals and their activities, tribute was received from states dominated by Dahomey. Payments in kind made by prominent persons who had been given control over villages or plantations were also effectively tribute. They included foodstuffs and other provisions that were an essential part of the maintenance of the palace population and the preparations for Customs. On a lower social level, labor power was extracted from the common people. The Dahomean monarchy required villages to provide young men for the standing army and family heads to offer young women for the palace organization. Unfortunately, we do not know how often such human tribute was demanded in this period. Chenevert and Bulet say that labor for public works was required on the part of people who lived reasonably near transportation routes. In 1779, for example, the Dahomean chiefs mustered their subjects to broaden to thirty feet the road that ran from Abomey to the beach at Whydah. However, Dalzel insists that the king paid the laborers involved in such public works.[4]

The system of domestic taxation and tribute underlined the nature of Dahomey as a state with a fully monetarized economy. The cowries that served as its currency were the single largest import of the overseas trade. The Dahomean money supply, then, was inextricably linked into the overseas trade. But cowries were only the most numerous of a number of imports. The others were luxury goods and war matériel. There were enormous profits made from the sale of slaves in the name of the king, and prominent individuals in Dahomey were licensed to sell in their own names as well. In exchange, those who traded received commodities and manufactured goods that were highly valued: a wide variety of textiles, guns and powder, beads, tobacco, alcohol, and metals that included iron, brass, copper, silver, and gold. There is evidence that the monarchy attempted at times to monopolize or at least to control the distribution of guns, powder, and iron bars (which could be made into shot). In addition, certain luxury items such as coral beads, gold, and silver were monopolized, or at any rate hoarded. Were the king and the other members of the monarchy, then, just merchant capitalists greedy to maximize material profits?

The trade goods that Dahomey acquired from overseas were more than luxury items to be used for the personal indulgence of a ruling elite. They were tied to the political economy in the sense that they provided a means by which the monarchy and powerful persons in the kingdom solidified their patronage. The truest wealth in Dahomey was not in material goods, but in control over dependents and followers: kinspeople, wives, slaves, and pawns. Though legal statuses were technically inflexible, many dependent individuals had a certain amount of latitude in the way that they became attached to patrons. Kinship was a basis for social relations, yet kinship was flexible and fluid. A titleholder (zinkponon) perceived as powerful could attract poor kinspeople as followers. Individuals, including women, involved in marital negotiations often had some say in the determination of marriage alliances. Marriage as a social idiom linked individuals of either sex in patron-client relationships. Oath taking also re-formed alliances and ties of obligation, so that individuals had some ability to transfer their support from one patron to another. The slave trade reinforced the system, because it permitted the monarchy and other powerful individuals to create wealth through the trade and the manipulation of human beings and imported goods. The king, ministers, prominent members of the royal family, male titleholders, caboceers, and titled women could trade slaves or use their dependents to gain captives. Some slaves would be retained and others exchanged for the luxury goods that were material signs of their owners' wealth and that would in turn attract more followers and dependents. The most obvious means for demonstrating one's control over resources was to flaunt and distribute them. In effect, by giving away people and goods, wealthy men and women could attract additional people, who then helped to produce more people and goods.

Within this system, the king and his apparent wealth were paramount. The king was the largest single slave trader, the person in whose name duties and fees were extracted at Whydah, the individual to whom all Dahomeans owed taxes, tribute, and indeed their very lives. In principle, all Dahomeans were dependents of the king. His wealth and that of the state were synonymous, because the king ruled in the name of the dynasty. In addition to direct revenues from trade, the terms of trade at Whydah themselves enhanced royal revenues. The king's representative received first a payment in goods for the right to trade, its amount depending upon the size of the slave ship. An additional customs payment was required for each slave sold. Overseas slave traders were forced to purchase the king's slaves first, and at a price higher than the prices paid for other slaves. The total returned to the king from the sale of the king's slaves and the terms of trade is not known, but it has to have been impressive. Akinjogbin estimates that revenues in 1750 from the export of the king's slaves alone were between $605,000 and $800,000 in 1960s U.S. dollars.[5] A British visitor in the 1840s believed that the king's revenues from the slave trade, including the sale of his own slaves (based on the export of eight thousand slaves, of which three thousand were the king's), was $300,000 annually (in nineteenth-century dollars).[6]

Not only did the king, or the state, have access to the greatest means of acquiring material wealth, the monarchy held the trump cards in ensuring that the king's revenues always outstripped those of any Dahomean individual. With the backing of its military power, the monarchy, in the king's name, could control the level of accumulation of any individual. Important and influential men and women in Dahomey enlarged their personal resources yet had to be careful not to exceed the wealth of the king, or appear even to begin to rival his position, because the king held the ultimate sanction. That sanction might be exercised in two ways: the king could opt to keep large portions of the estate of a deceased individual, or a person could be accused of crimes against the state and stripped of both dependents and material wealth.

The king's generosity—and hence his power and affluence—was most visible at the time of Customs, when he offered gifts to those who supported him: to the royal ancestors upon whom the kingdom depended for its well-being, and to the loyal subjects who worked to help Dahomey reach its destiny. The bulk of the material wealth distributed at Customs was in trade goods, but supplemented with locally manufactured items, foodstuffs, and, most importantly, the most valuable possession of all, human beings. The size of royal largesse toward any individual was in direct proportion to the importance of the recipient. The poorest of the royal subjects were the people that Europeans typically described scrambling for cloth, cowries, tobacco, and beads thrown from a platform where the king, a group of palace women, the ministers of state, and European visitors were seated. Food and alcoholic drink were provided regularly during Customs to large numbers of people. Dalzel, for example, describes food and locally brewed beer that had been prepared within the palace being carried in procession by palace women and distributed "not only among the more distinguished guests, but even without the camp, where the vulgar partake plentifully." Higher-ranking persons were also given cloth and captives. Norris recounts that the governors of towns and provinces received a gift, "generally a large cotton cloth, manufactured in the Eyo [Oyo] country, of excellent workmanship, which they afterwards wear for an upper garment." European visitors and their entourages were lodged and boarded at royal expense from the moment they left the coast. They also received gifts, the most valuable being at the point of departure from Abomey, when they were usually given locally made cotton cloth and one or two female slaves. Dalzel argues that the value of what was received by the European traders far outweighed their own annual gifts of silk, brandy, and other items, which Dalzel valued at £50. Ministers of state were formally appointed at the time of Customs, and presumably it was at that time that they were given gifts of control over people, villages, and plantations.[7]

Palace women were bestowed as wives during the same period. Poorer people paid a form of bridewealth in exchange for women who were probably war captives. Higher-ranking individuals received women as outright gifts. Theoretically, the highest-ranking royal honor was the ennobling of a commoner by marriage with a princess. Princesses were presented publicly to their husbands at Customs and sent off from the palace with a generous dowry of servants and goods. The formal ties between king and ministers, for example, were cemented through marriage. The king's elder daughter (i.e., the one recognized as most senior, the na daho) became a wife of the migan. Her first junior sister married the meu. In exchange, daughters of ranking officials entered the palace; we do not have specific evidence of precisely where they were placed in the hierarchy, except for a nineteenth-century observation that indicates that social hierarchy was preserved within the palace.[8]

The granting of gifts and the public displays of royal generosity were supplemented by ostentatious parades of the wealth of the monarchy, and particularly the unique precious items that were derived from the overseas trade. The lengthy processions of the king's wealth, viewed with contempt by generations of bored European visitors, were material demonstrations of the king's status, visible signs that the royal ancestors continued to favor the dynasty and abundant evidence of the continued prosperity of the kingdom. Processions of the king's wealth in the late eighteenth century were described by Pommegorge: "He [the king] has all that he possesses in his houses brought out through a door and carried on the head of . . . women, as in a procession, one after the other. These riches consist of baskets of coral, of fabric of gold or silk, or of silver, of bundles of silk and cotton cloth, of some vases of silver, and generally of all that he owns." Norris similarly said of the 1772 Customs that "there was a display of the king's furniture and trinkets, most of the women carrying something or other of his; some of them fine swords; others silver-mounted guns; above a hundred of them held either gold, or silver-

6. *Public Procession of the King's Women,* from Archibald Dalzel, *The History of Dahomy* (London, 1793)

headed canes, in their hands; and that none might be unprovided, some carried a candlestick, and others a lamp, perhaps fifty at least of each, with many other articles; which were all held up for the gaping multitude to admire."[9]

Popular belief held that the king kept a length of every pattern and color of every different fabric brought through Whydah. In fact, mid-nineteenth-century visitors saw an enormous strip of patchwork cloth, said to have been created during the reign of Gezo. Its size was estimated at four hundred to six hundred yards long by two to three yards wide. Twentieth-century descendants of the monarchy similarly claimed that a princess, Na Agbanukwen, appeared annually during Customs wearing a wrapper that included a length of cloth from every different fabric ever imported. A visitor in 1871 said of the cloth that "the pieces are not of uniform size, varying from a square foot to a full-sized piece, three feet by nine. The various kinds of cloth, such as denhams, chintzes, silks, ventopullams, velvets, &c., are arranged hap-hazard, and are of every hue and design that can be imagined. Reds, blues, greens, yellows, browns, blacks, and whites are mingled indiscriminately; while striped, checked, plaid, and figured patterns add to the medley." [10]

Following Dahomean social norms, European traders brought gifts when they came for audiences with the kings, who in turn did not hesitate to order special items of European manufacture. In 1772, for example, Norris presented Tegbesu with a chamber organ and a sedan chair of red morocco leather. A tiny sample of the accumulated gifts of Europeans as seen in 1850 included—along with hundreds of other items of European manufacture—two glass chandeliers, a four-poster bed with crimson silk damask curtains, chariots and coaches, a rocking chair, and a toilet table with drawers and mirror. The grand procession of the king's wealth that year would involve 6,500 persons and innumerable objects of European and African manufacture. All of the riches of the monarchy— cowries, trade goods, gifts, and provisions—were stored in the palaces of the king. It is little wonder, then, that the position of keeper of the stores would have been one of great responsibility and power. And it is little wonder that the story of the mother of Tegbesu's rival, who offered the treasures of the king to Oyo, would have spoken volumes to Dahomeans about the powers of women within the palace and women's potential for involvement in the state. [11]

The luxury goods imported as a result of the overseas trade were an underpinning of the system of patronage by which coalitions formed and competed for power. Dahomey's famous dictum, that each king make the kingdom always greater, was an economic as well as territorial dictate. The monarchy—that is the kings and their immediate followers—could ill afford to be perceived as less prosperous or less strong than their predecessors. A reduction in the quantity of such sumptuous goods threatened a reduction in the numbers of followers and supporters of the king. In effect, participation in the slave trade had drawn Dahomey into an international commercial network from which it could withdraw only at the cost of the possible destruction of its social and political system.

To what extent were the Dahomeans aware of this relationship to a changing world economy? Did they fully understand the importance of the slave trade to their own political economy? Later, the kings would argue, as had Pommegorge, that they had lived without European goods in the past and could do so again. Yet when it finally became clear that the slave trade was no longer viable, they focussed their energies not on cutting off contacts with Europe, but on controlling an alternative commodity for which Europe offered a market—palm oil. In the late eighteenth century, however, neither Dahomeans nor Europeans appeared to be thinking of alternative trades. Norris notes that there were a good many oil palms in the vicinity of Allada and that "large quantities" of oil were exported for use in British wool processing and soap manufacturing. Chenevert and Bulet devote some comments to the processing of palm oil. However, neither suggests that oil might become an important product in the export trade. Indeed, the Frenchmen discuss instead the trade possibilities for Dahomean textiles made of raffia and cotton. The raffia was used in Europe for women's summer underskirts and the cotton for tablecloths and bedspreads. Both raffia and cotton textiles, however, were contraband materials in prerevolutionary France.[12]

The Military in the Late Eighteenth Century

Dahomey expanded through war, and the fruits of conquest were human. Conquered people enhanced the king's and the kingdom's wealth. With conquered people came control over the land that they occupied and the vodun who owned and protected it. Defeated villages and towns could become permanently subordinant to the monarchy, available to be granted as gifts to high-ranking persons. They could be farmed indefinitely for agricultural products, for manufactured goods like pottery or agricultural implements, and for labor power for the military and palace organizations. War victories brought the immediate reward of human heads and living captives who could be gratefully sacrificed to the royal ancestors, sold into the overseas slave trade, or absorbed into Dahomean households. In this sense, warfare was a basis for Dahomean prosperity.

From early on, Dahomean military strength was feared by neighboring peoples and respected by Europeans at the coast. As early as 1733, for example, a European reported that the troops of Dahomey "have thrown such terror into the spirits of all the blacks that the simple rumor of their approach makes people drop everything and flee." European traders appeared to take to heart Bulfinch Lamb's praise of Agaja, the "greatest warrior in this Part of the World," who "in Time, will subdue most of the countries round him." [13] Following the 1729 killing of the English factor Testefol, who had openly assisted the Hweda and shown contempt for Dahomey, the directors of the trading forts at Whydah never openly supported the exiled Hweda in their quest to retake control of their kingdom. Rather, their "neutrality"—to the point of not cooperating with an occupation by the Hweda in 1743—was a tacit endorsement of Dahomean control and an effective support for the Dahomean armed forces. Nineteenth-century visitors and twentieth-century scholars have similarly expressed respect, and even admiration, for the Dahomean military. Robin Law goes so far as to argue that "Dahomey differed from its predecessors in being an essentially military state, whose institutions and ideology were permeated by a military ethos beyond anything which had existed in [Allada or Whydah]. War was, in effect, the principal purpose of the Dahomian state." [14] However, there are curious inconsistencies in interpretations of Dahomey as a nation of unrelieved militarism. Europeans admired the army for its European-style discipline and its relatively modern arms. Locally, the legends of the Dahomean army consistently stressed its invincibility. Yet the Dahomean armed forces were beaten ignominiously, and more than once, when they faced foes of roughly equal strength. For nearly one hundred years they remained subordinate to Oyo, being forced into humiliating retreats from Oyo cavalry and prevented from fully consolidating their control over their major conquests: Weme, Allada, and Whydah.

Why, then, did Dahomey have a reputation for military success? Why do so many scholars stress militarism in Dahomey? What was the key to the kingdom's victories, and why did military prowess seem to fail Dahomey so oddly and so often? I believe that Dahomey was neither a military state nor a state with warring as its raison d'être. A military spirit was part of a larger pattern of ritual and political strategies to promote the well-being of the state. As in all other areas of cultural life, the Dahomeans freely adopted war technologies, particularly from Europe, and they incorporated new weaponry and other innovations. However, their military genius lay not in their borrowings from other cultures; rather it lay in their understanding and subversion of African rules of war. Throughout their history, the Dahomeans remained wedded to fighting strategies and tactics that were rooted in Gbe culture. They showed little or no interest in altering those fundamental approaches to war, but they were adept at modifying elements of Gbe warfare to give themselves advantages.

The rules of war of the Slave Coast included shared beliefs about what behaviors and circumstances would lead to victory, and what natural and supernatural forces could protect individuals and communities from harm. In chapter 2, we looked at the myth of Na Geze and found two patterns that were believed to lead to victory: discovering the source of the strength of an enemy force and neutralizing it, and using a ruse to make an enemy vulnerable. Enemies' powers were said to be neutralized through the use of spies, known as *agbajigbeto* (*agbaji* = verandah, reception room; *gbeto* = hunter—literally, hunters in the reception area). Agbajigbeto were sent to enemy territory to seek out the roots of enemy power and dismantle it. Created during the reign of Agaja, they were regularly cited as a crucial element of Dahomean military strategy.

There is an important contrast between the description of these Dahomean spies given by European primary sources, on the one hand, and that given by a major Dahomean source, Paul Hazoumé, on the other. Le Hérissé explains that the agbajigbeto were sent in the guise of merchants to live and make friends in enemy territory, even going so far as to swear oaths of loyalty to enemy individuals. They would study the roads of the area, learn the numbers of warriors and the habits of the people, and then return to Dahomey to convey all of this strategic information to the king. Herskovits echoes Le Hérissé's description, saying that the royal spies "brought back information concerning the nature of the terrain, the number of people to be encountered and, if possible, something of the defensive tactics of the enemy." Hazoumé, in contrast, records oral descriptions that stress two other points. First, they speak of the strength of the oath sworn between the spies and a representative of the Dahomean monarchy: the targeted territories were the places of origin of the spies, the home towns where "they had passed a good part of their lives," but where they arrived as strangers who were not even recognized by family and former neighbors; in effect, Hazoumé's oral traditions stress the strength of an oath that cemented loyalty to Dahomey; the spies were so changed by the oath, so far removed from older ties of kin and place, that no one at home could recognize them. Second, the oral traditions that Hazoumé records emphasize the actions taken by spies to destroy the power of protective gods and other forces. Then, "the victory of the Dahomeans no longer depended upon the bravery of the army, for the god no longer protected the city." Spies, say Hazoumé's traditions, would try to link themselves as "brothers" to the enemy through swearing oaths in order to learn the supernatural strengths of the town. Then, they would go out at night to bury charms that would bring discord among the enemy or generate calamities that would leave them weak and exhausted. They would feed the city's protector deities substances that were incompatible with their natures, unleashing divine anger that caused bloody internal battles and burned whole sections of town. They would also—and this is clearly secondary—note the locations of the households of kings and important leaders, the placement of gates to the city, the organization of the enemy army, and they would draw a map.[15]

Spies were not the only means to rework the balance of power to Dahomey's favor. In the eighteenth century, there is also evidence that rituals, and particularly divination, were used to guide military decision making. Following indecisive warfare over Whydah beach in the 1740s, for example, the Dahomeans withdrew closer to Whydah town on the advice of priests who had divined the reasons for their inability to control the beach. In 1784, the gau, commander in chief of the army, left his forces encamped near Badagry to go "a considerable way down the river" for three days to perform ceremonies.[16] The spies, the divination, and the ceremonies were all directed to the same goal: to know the sources of power of the enemy and to make it ineffective. The Dahomeans, and doubtless other Gbe-speaking states, would have worked always to reassure soldiers going to war that the power of the enemy had already been destroyed.

Stories about ruses appear frequently in accounts of war on the Slave Coast. They take several forms. In one, an enemy is lured into complacency by alcohol or other distractions. An account of the first war between Dahomey and Oyo, for example, claims that the Dahomeans retreated leaving "Liquor as Bait for the Enemy," and returned later to rout the drunken horsemen. A less common ruse pattern to lull enemies into complacency involved breaking negotiated arrangements with enemies. In 1778, the Dahomean army was lured into a swampy area and attacked by a much smaller force from Epe (a port southwest of Porto Novo). Surrounded, the Dahomeans offered to resolve the situation through single combat, but when their champion was killed, they attacked the Epe army and defeated it.[17]

Another very common form of ruse story tends to be taken literally by scholars. It claims that the Dahomeans would march away from the target they intended to attack, and then would turn back and strike. Dalzel, for example, says that in 1789 the Dahomeans announced that they would attack the Popos to the southwest, when in fact they intended to move on Ketu to the northeast. Whether or not either kind of ruse story ever described actual events is questionable, and in a sense irrelevant. When the Dahomeans arrived at the gates of Ketu in 1789, for example, the Ketu were securely behind their walls, daring the Dahomeans to come through the gate. Nevertheless, the Dahomeans won through a ruse, feigning retreat and drawing the Ketu outside. All of the ruse stories establish the same principle: that a successful army attacks unexpectedly. As such, they underline beliefs about what kinds of military behaviors lead to victory. In fact, Dahomean forces regularly tried to attack by surprise, and they were at times surprised by others.[18]

Both Europeans and Africans—with the obvious exception of Oyo—believed in the invulnerability of the Dahomean forces; or at least they behaved as if they did. Pommegorge writes of Dahomean indomitability despite evidence to the contrary, including his own knowledge that Dahomey paid tribute each year to Oyo to avoid being attacked. He asserts that the army had never been defeated in war or even beaten in battle, adding that the army "is viewed by neighboring peoples as invincible, it makes all those who have to defend themselves tremble; they even claim that if this army were defeated, if only one person remained to come with the news, he would have his head cut off on the spot. If this law is barbarous and worthy of the sovereign who made it, it certainly maintains the spirit of bravery of this army, and spreads terror among the neighbors that the Dahomeans ceaselessly pillage; but since they are not able always to succeed, the king is obliged to pillage or steal from his own subjects." Pommegorge, then, acknowledges the mixed successes of the Dahomean armed forces, even as he insists that they are without equal. Indeed, soldiers did often act as if they dared not return defeated; we know, however, that they sometimes were beaten and that defeated Dahomean soldiers lived to fight other wars. Such traditions would have been reinforced by stories like the one Norris relates of a 1753 incident when a Dahomean army was destroyed at the coast. The twenty-four survivors sent back to tell the tale were sacrificed by Tegbesu to tell their comrades how much they had angered their king. Similarly, there is evidence of a tradition of suicide by army leaders who failed in battle. And European descriptions of warfare, most of which were told to them secondhand by Africans, consistently note a reckless daring and obstinate persistence in the behavior of Dahomean soldiers. "Fear," Robert Norris says, "never enters into the mind of a Dahoman; cowardice is no part of his composition." [19]

Images of Dahomean military power were consciously and consistently nurtured by war songs and belligerent public boasting and underlined by the thousands of skulls that decorated the palace walls in the eighteenth century. Parades of armed forces were a central element of Customs and a regular event of life at court. We do not know precisely how parade maneuvers affected enemy perceptions of Dahomey, but they certainly made strong impressions on European visitors, who often expressed their admiration in proportion to the degree to which the army approached European military norms. Snelgrave, for example, notes that the soldiers marched "in a much more regular Order than I had ever seen before [in Africa]" and that they were organized into companies with "their proper Colours, and Officers." By the late eighteenth century, women soldiers were included in these displays, prompting Dalzel to observe that "the singularity of this institution never fails to attract the particular attention of the Europeans, when . . . they are presented with the unusual spectacle of a *review* of female troops." Pommegorge counts four or five distinct corps of women, probably representing guard companies for past kings, each of which included from twenty-four to one hundred young women, whose ages he estimates at no more than sixteen to seventeen years of age. Noting that their leaders had the same titles as the male war leaders, he reports that the women soldiers were "each one well armed with a small musketoon and a small short sword for which the scabbard is ordinarily of crimson velvet; their only clothing is a little wrapper of silk around the hips, which comes down to their knees. Thus armed and with two or three flags of silk, these women with their commanders march slowly in rows of four each." Women armed with muskets had first been seen by Europeans in 1727. They represented a Dahomean innovation on an old principle of warfare, that everyone in a community would be called out to fight in time of war. Yet the parades of armed women at court projected an image of Dahomey as dramatically different, as breaking from tradition, as building a military that was beyond imagination—and beyond defeat.[20]

Like the armies of other states in the area, the Dahomeans engaged in two kinds of warfare: direct attacks against entire villages or towns on the one hand, and fights against armed forces representing other states on the other. Early accounts of warfare along the Slave Coast suggest that the resources of an entire attacked community would be mustered to defend it. Ritual powers and protections—deities and war charms—were kept "well-fed" and were invoked to protect the community. Men, women, and probably older children used whatever arms were available—machetes, clubs, spears, hoes—to fight against attackers. Armies that went off to fight on behalf of a state also appear to have included large proportions of communities. Sources often claim that the entire population, or at the very least all the adult males, would go to war.[21] Their described numbers were extraordinarily, even unbelievably, large. Europeans recorded estimates of armies, most of which they never saw, that for Whydah alone ranged from twenty thousand to two-hundred thousand in the late seventeenth to early eighteenth centuries. Bulfinch Lamb claimed that Agaja could field a force of five-hundred thousand

men in the mid-1720s.[22] Tegbesu supposedly sent fifty thousand men to
relieve the occupation of Whydah in 1743. Casualty rates are similarly
enormous: Allada was said to have lost fifty thousand persons when attacked and defeated by Dahomey, with an additional eight thousand
captured.

We have no way to judge the accuracy of these figures. What the accounts imply, however, and what the African informants who provided
these numbers probably meant, was that armies were ideally of an overwhelming size. Moreover, the larger side would invariably be the victor.
When two armies met, people asserted, the side that was smaller and
hence weaker would retreat or flee. Describing warfare in the kingdom of
Whydah, Marchais additionally says that two armies that were of a similar
size would not engage, but wait for a future moment of less equal odds.
Presumably reflecting accounts from Dahomeans, Norris's descriptions
of war consistently stress the idea that the larger force will win. The Dahomeans successfully beseiged a Mahi stronghold because of "the bravery
of the Dahomans, and their superior numbers." An invading force from
Oyo that defeated the Dahomeans was "an irresistible army . . . advancing
with an incredible multitude." In 1743 at Whydah, the Dahomeans were
beaten because they were "destitute of leaders, and overpowered by
numbers."[23]

Snelgrave provides a specific example of action taken on the principle
that larger armies by definition dominate the field. The setting was the
retaking of Whydah by an alliance of the Hweda in league with neighboring Popo forces in late 1729. Since Agaja was unable to match the
invading force with an army of male soldiers of greater size, "he ordered
a great number of Women to be armed like Soldiers, and appointed Officers to each Company, with Colours, Drums and Umbrellas. . . . Then
ordering the Army to march, the Women Soldiers were placed in the
Rear, to prevent Discovery." The two armies met and the combined
Hweda-Popo force, "much surprized to see such Numbers of Dahomè
Soldiers," divided over whether to fight or run. In the end, they did both,
and lost.[24]

Snelgrave's is the first European record of the use of Dahomean women
in offensive warfare, and his account has been used both to prove and to

disprove the claim that a standing army of women existed in Dahomey in the eighteenth century. Hélène d'Almeida-Topor, who has written a book-length study of Dahomey's women soldiers, sees Snelgrave's account as confirmation of some oral traditions that claim regular female troops existed prior to the nineteenth century. Law, on the other hand, maintains that because Snelgrave says that the women were enlisted only because the Dahomean army was short of regular soldiers, "the female forces were a form of bluff rather than a serious reinforcement." Since armed women were already being used by Agaja as a personal guard, it seems reasonable to suppose that he would have used this force, and possibly other women from his entourage, to enlarge Dahomean army numbers when needed. The idea would have been in keeping with the principle that an entire population, male and female, would fight to defend its home. In the case of Agaja, however, this was an attacking rather than a defensive force, and in that difference lay a significant departure from the usual practice of war in the area.[25]

An incident that occurred fifty years later repeated the pattern, but in this case the despatching of the king's female bodyguard to war was part of a response based on the principle that an entire community responds to attack. When Oyo in 1781 demanded extra numbers of women as part of the Dahomean tribute, Kpengla sent his army to capture women in the neighboring area of Agoonah. The force being badly beaten, Dalzel writes, and the news

> being brought to the King of Dahomy at mid-day, he immediately got up, girt on his cartouch-box, shouldered his firelock, and marched towards Agoonah, at the head of eight hundred armed women.
>
> The whole country was in motion, men, women, and children. The King's big mother, who never dies, though she is sometimes put to death, fell down lifeless, before she got a league from Calmina [Cana]: many were trodden to death, and not a few expired from excessive fatigue, and the extreme heat of a vertical sun.

The eight hundred women would have been the palace guard, and "the King's big mother" was obviously the kpojito. The principle is clear. Kpengla was interpreting the defeat of his forces as an attack on Dahomey

7. *Armed Women with the King at their head, going to War,* from Archibald Dalzel, *The History of Dahomy* (London, 1793)

and was literally calling upon the entire community to defend the nation. However, this force, rather than simply defending a homeland from attack, went on the offensive. The principle that everyone respond was invoked, but defense was defined as a retaliatory attack. As in the case of the Hweda and Popo, the law of overwhelming numbers worked, because "on the approach of this uncommon army, the people fled." [26]

These two accounts are the only evidence found yet in European records of Dahomean women being used for offensive warfare outside the palace in the eighteenth century. European documents assert that women within the palace organization were armed and trained for fighting and that their organization and leadership paralleled that of the male military. Whether or not they were a regular part of the armed forces on campaign, however, is not clear. Later, in the nineteenth century, we know that the comparable palace guard of women went to war, but was held in reserve while other forces, including female soldiers, attacked. In 1849, Frederick Forbes would be told that Kpengla had created the army of women; however, we have no confirming eyewitness accounts from eighteenth-century Europeans, who rarely saw the Dahomean army on campaign. They typically describe forces in terms of numbers of men, though the use of the term *men* would have been standard usage rather than a comment on gender based on actual observation. The oral traditions cited by d'Almeida-Topor purport to describe women soldiers at war in the early 1700s. They were collected in the 1970s in the Weme region by Amélie Degbelo, but they are difficult to accept because they are not corroborated elsewhere and they were drawn from persons who were well versed in later myths about fighting women. An oral account given to me in 1972 by a descendant of Tegbesu fits the written evidence of women and men facing enemies together, but this, too, cannot be called conclusive. Tegbesu's descendant says that after Gezo took power, the women "were separated and no longer fought with the men," thus implying that in an earlier period women and men had fought together. In the absence of evidence that either proves or disproves the regular presence of female troops in the eighteenth century, we can only argue that it is clear that the idea of women fighting was very much a part of the Dahomean worldview, that trained military women were part of the palace organization, and that if a standing army of women did not exist in the eighteenth century, it was a very short step in the nineteenth to establish one.[27]

Initially, Dahomean soldiers in the eighteenth century seem to have been recruited in the same manner as fighters in Allada and Whydah. Detachments of fighters were provided by officials and chiefs. They joined the king's troops to create a massed army led by a war chief or general appointed by the king. The king's troops in Dahomey, however, were more visibly a trained force—noted as such in the 1720s by Snelgrave and called a standing army by Dalzel late in the century. Chenevert and Bulet see Dahomean society as divided into three classes: militia, merchants, and laborers. The military class, they argue, earned their own keep when not at war—a subtle but telling distinction that contrasts with the idea of people occasionally being called up from earning their own keep in order to make war. The Dahomean king appears to have provided arms and ammunition, which is less often noted in other states in the region. Nevertheless, it is hard to sustain the argument that Dahomey in the eighteenth century was a military state. Snelgrave suggests that the army was composed mainly of slaves. The gau, or commander in chief, was only one of five ministers of state and was not the most important of them. Military service was not a prerequisite for ministerial rank. The kings are sometimes described as going to war, but after the time of Agaja accounts argue that they normally remained behind their armies and did not lead them into battle. The Dahomeans, then, did not dramatically change the methods of mustering armies, but they appear to have made the king's own troops more professional, including giving them a sense of Dahomean invulnerability.[28]

The principle that a larger force would always prevail was a central precept of warfare in the Gbe region. The Dahomeans appear to have believed it and practiced it whenever possible. Paradoxically, however, they were also not afraid to violate it, and are regularly recorded as having attacked, or resisted, forces that outnumbered them. Part of their myth of invulnerability, then, lay with this violation of the norms of war. For example, "though inferior in numbers," the Dahomeans stood against Oyo on one occasion. Dalzel recounts a story of the sogan single-handedly resisting an attack by an enemy force that broke through the Dahomean front lines in 1775.[29] One of the few detailed eyewitness accounts of battle tells of the resistance of Dahomeans when the Hweda, allied with the Popo, attempted to retake Whydah in 1763. Written by Pommegorge, it tells of a surprise attack by eight thousand to nine thousand Hweda and Popo that was met by a Dahomean force one-tenth the size. When half of the Dahomeans were cut down by the initial gun volley, Pommegorge himself gave the wounded refuge in the French fort, while the remainder stayed outside in the fort's protective ditch. The attackers stopped, apparently to deliberate their next action, and in the interim a Dahomean war captain with thirty men led a sudden attack on the leaders of the enemy forces. Fighting with swords, they decapitated the commanding general and killed numbers of other high officers before being cut down themselves. The final scene, before the Hweda and Popo troops departed on hearing rumors of the approach of the regular Dahomean army, was the request by the wounded yovogan that a gate of the fort be opened to allow a contingent of the Dahomeans to go on the attack.[30] In short, the Dahomeans had a professional soldier's willingness to fight, if necessary, despite unfavorable odds.

The Dahomeans in the eighteenth century appeared to embrace various European concepts and components of warfare, as did many of their neighbors. A French clerk by the name of Etienne Gallot, who arrived in Whydah in 1725 and who claimed to have taught the Dahomeans how to dig trenches and build fortifications, was only the first of many foreign military advisers. As noted above, the Dahomeans formed their troops into organizational ranks and paraded with a discipline that traders associated with European armies, though they did not yet wear distinctive uniforms. Most importantly, the Dahomeans quickly and enthusiastically adopted firearms, even though the quality of imported arms was poor. However, European observers did not seem to notice that the Dahomeans were adapting the trappings of European warfare to an unchanged model of combat.[31]

Describing warfare on the coast in the 1720s, Marchais says that attacks were heralded by the overpowering noise of shouts, drums, gongs, and gunfire. There followed volleys of arrows, spears, and clubs, and then the real fighting, hand-to-hand combat with no quarter given. It was only when one side turned to flee that soldiers concentrated on capturing and securing prisoners. Once the chase for captives ended, the victors returned to the battlefield, stripped the dead (and presumably the seriously wounded) of clothing and arms, and cut off their heads. The account is telling, Marchais arguing that the goal of war was taking captives. Guns for Marchais were part of the preliminaries, an element of the terrifying uproar designed to drive an enemy to flight. Victory required a closing with the enemy and an ability to run down and physically restrain enemy soldiers.

The use of guns by Dahomey became increasingly sophisticated and by midcentury guns were clearly an essential and deadly first thrust at enemy forces. Nevertheless, the capture of enemies and the collection of heads remained the central goal of war. Troops marched in order on parade, but an attack in the manner of eighteenth-century Europe, with long, orderly rows of infantry, was contrary to the point. Dahomeans wished to create a melee that would panic an enemy. Chenevert and Bulet, contemptuously describing Dahomean attacks, underscore the gulf between European and African concepts of attack: "The militia has neither discipline nor tactics, they go into fire like flocks of sheep; they only skirmish while making a dreadful din with ridiculous contortions and frightful howls accompanied by drums, goat horns, whistles and gongs."[32]

The Dahomeans used firearms, but firearms did not prompt them to rethink their approach to war. Twenty-five cannon were brought to Abomey in the wake of the capture of Allada. In the mid-1720s Agaja reportedly had them fired each market day (every fourth day), but they do not appear to have been used, for example, when the Dahomeans tried to defend Abomey against Oyo early in Tegbesu's reign.[33] The Dahomean response to cavalry was similar. In the history of warfare in Europe, foot soldiers in medieval times developed strategies for meeting and defeating horsemen; once firearms became available, reasonably well-disciplined infantry could nearly always overcome cavalry. An account of the first meeting of Dahomean soldiers and Oyo cavalry says that initially the sound of firearms frightened the horses. However, when the engagement ended after four days, the Dahomeans were "still much afraid of a second Invasion, an Army of Horses being very terrible to them."[34] For the most part, the Dahomean army fled from Oyo cavalry. In effect, firearms did not prompt the Dahomeans to rethink how cavalry might be met or to rework the classic pattern of deafening attack, close combat, and the capture of prisoners.

The Palace in the Late Eighteenth Century ～

As Dahomey expanded, the palace became a principal vehicle for the centralization of the kingdom. It was enlarged by two means: by incorporating war captives and by drafting young women from Dahomean families. As such, the palace was a cross section of the peoples who made up Dahomey, and because most ahosi (king's wives) were permitted to keep in touch with their home areas and kinspeople, the palace functioned literally as a vehicle of political and social integration. It also proved to be an important avenue for the introduction of foreign cultural innovations. The palace was already relatively large by 1724, when Bulfinch Lamb estimated its population at two thousand. Fifty years later, Norris claimed that it included three thousand to four thousand women. Like the kings of Dahomey, kings in neighboring states were known for having vast numbers of wives; scholars have even suggested that the incidence of large polygynous institutions was characteristic of the Slave Coast.[35] However, the Dahomeans developed the king's household into an institution that went beyond the norms of the region and that ultimately used ahosi for a unique range of administrative and cultural activities— economic, military, political, and religious. In Dahomey, women carried out functions that were performed elsewhere by eunuchs, male slaves, male members of palace associations, and male retainers selected from commoner lineages. Why were women used for responsibilities that were the purview of men in other African societies? I believe that the palace became a singular institution through the convergence of a number of social and demographic factors: gender variations in kinship and social structures, general population levels, gender patterns in the overseas slave trade, and women's demonstrated abilities.

The palace was in one sense simply a polygynous household writ large. Fon culture was patrilineal and patrilocal. Marriages were alliances between lineages, not individuals, and the individuals who carried out the terms of those alliances, who represented their lineages in physical unions, did not in theory have the right to name their terms or their partners. Ideally, bridewealth was paid by the lineage of the husband to the lineage of the wife, and certain services (brideservice) were performed for the woman's parents by the husband. Upon marriage, a woman moved into the compound of her husband's family. Her behavior and treatment there were central factors determining the nature and quality of future relations between the two lineages. Twentieth-century Dahomeans described an ideal marriage as one in which the wife moved at a very young age into the household of the lineage of her marriage, sometimes even before a specific partner had been chosen for her. She would then be trained by her husband's family and be given to a young man of the family when she reached an appropriate age.[36] Because hierachies among wives were based on the date of arrival in a lineage, rather than on age, a woman married as a child had a greater possibility of enjoying the fruits of seniority. If, for example, she was the first woman married to the person who later became head of the household, she would become head wife, with authority over all other wives. Also, girls more often than boys were used as pawns. As such, they represented security for a debt and moved into the household of a lender; their work in that household was a form of interest. Later, if a pawn could not be redeemed, she became a wife in the lender's lineage. In short, girl-children in Fon culture were socialized to serve a lineage other than that of their birth. Women learned to divide their loyalties, remaining in touch with their own lineages, which had the responsibility of protecting their interests, and often moving back to their birth homes when they were beyond their child-rearing years. These principles made recruitment of women to the palace and to the service of the king a more attractive option than the recruitment of men. The use of the idiom of marriage to describe the links between the kings and their male retainers underscored the qualities of loyalty and service that the palace required.

If the behavioral expectations that surrounded women's role in marriage were a rationale for building the palace organization with women, an even more ideal recruit was a woman slave. Slaves by definition had no kinspeople and no lineages to protect them or to interfere with their master's demands. In theory, their loyalties were undivided. A woman slave thus represented the perfect ahosi—a person socialized to serve the lineage and who in addition lacked kin obligations and protections. Popular traditions argue that all of the kpojito of Dahomey, those women who epitomized the ideals of service and the rewards of success, had been slaves. In reality, one can argue that all the women within the palace, whether they originated in Dahomey, arrived as captives of war, or were persons sold or pawned into service, were in a sense slaves. The distinction between them and women married into other lineages lay in their lack of the right to terminate membership in the palace organization. Divorce was possible, and probably common, in Fon marriages. Assuming that her lineage agreed with her position, a woman mistreated by her husband or his family might leave a bad marriage—and her lineage would not be required to return the bridewealth; a woman who found a man that she preferred to her husband could marry him, provided she replaced the original bridewealth with her own or her new spouse's resources. However, a woman within the palace—whether slave or free—could do neither. No one divorced the king. It is little wonder that twentieth-century Dahomeans typically spoke of all ahosi as slaves, and that travelers used terms like *stolen* and *kidnapped* in describing women's entry into the palace. There is no evidence that any woman in Dahomey ever became an ahosi willingly. Marchais claims that girls in Whydah sometimes jumped into wells rather than enter the palace of the king.[37] The same story—with the same means of suicide—was told of the Dahomey palace as late as the 1970s.

Once inside the palace, however, most women appear to have accepted their situation. Neither fully slave nor fully free, ahosi were nevertheless part of a complex hierarchic organization in which some might achieve a good deal of material success and wield a great deal of power. An esprit, an elitism, a sense of participation at the pivot of power in the kingdom, seems to have pervaded the palace atmosphere. Women there had opportunities for gain—for material wealth, including control over many dependents, and for the exercise of power. Even legal slave status did not erase regional ties or cancel kinship for palace women. Traditions make clear that at least some slave women within the palace, and particularly those who were high in rank, maintained contact with the towns and villages of their birth. Some moved kinsmen to Abomey and established estates that they bequeathed to relatives in the lineages of their birth. Others, like the Kpojito Hwanjile, imported specific cultural traditions that included new gods. Some bore children and some of the children visited their mothers' home areas; some nineteenth-century princes, for example, learned to be diviners of Fa in the lineages of their Yoruba mothers. In sum, the legal status of ahosi was ambiguous. Sentenced to the palace for life, some clearly languished there as in a prison. However, many others found the palace a place of opportunity. Ambitious women may have found the exercise of power and the possibility of material gain a prime motivating force.[38]

The growth of the palace may also have been linked to serious depopulation of Gbe-speaking areas as a result of the slave trade; the population of the region declined steadily from 1700 to 1850. Moreover, the demographics of the overseas slave trade, with male slaves purchased in higher proportions than women, created a shortage of men. Patrick Manning calculates an overall average sex ratio of seventy adult men for one hundred women in Gbe-speaking areas, a ratio that fell as low as from fifty to sixty-five men for one hundred women in areas where trading was concentrated. Wegbaja, Dahomey's first king, is credited with establishing a precept that no Dahomean could be sold out of the country, and Dahomeans were defined as any person born in Dahomey no matter what the legal status of either parent. Nevertheless, there were so few slaves available from outside the kingdom in the later years of Tegbesu's reign that the king was said to have allowed the selling of Dahomeans, and presumably more men than women, which would have further exacerbated the gender imbalance in Dahomey. Male slaves, obviously, were not available in large numbers to fill the ranks of the king's retainers. Such shortages of manpower—literally, *man* power—in the late eighteenth century would have proved an incentive to women's activities being enlarged.[39]

The scarcity of male labor is perhaps reflected in patterns for the division of labor by sex in Fon society. Certain ritual and leadership positions required gender pairing. Institutions like lineages and congregations of vodun were headed by a man and a woman. Their functions were described as different yet complementary, which suggests a conception of functions appropriate to each gender. By the late eighteenth century, we begin to see evidence of a similar pairing in numerous offices of state. Productive work undertaken by individuals, however, was another matter. It is difficult to find occupations or tasks that were not done by women, either inside or outside the palace. Women tended and harvested crops, processed food and palm oil, brewed beer, traded, worked as porters, and made pots, baskets, and mats. They cooked, cleaned, and reared children. Women do not appear to have built houses, cleared land for farming, cut palm nuts, or worked at certain artisanal occupations such as smithing or woodcarving. Writing in the mid–nineteenth century, W. Winwood Reade scornfully asserts that "in Africa the sphere of woman is slavery," yet sums up the broad range of Dahomean women's work with Victorian eloquence: "She is also employed in diplomatic missions and in commercial enterprise. She is shepherd, agriculturalist, warrior, trader, embassadress, and sometimes queen. In this practical country one meets with admirable illustrations of the axiom of Plato . . . that, 'So far as her nature is concerned, the woman is admissible to all pursuits as well as the man.' " [40]

Women's presumed malleability can be seen in the differentiation that Dahomeans made between the utility of female as opposed to male slaves. Young female captives were integrated into the palace organization and reared into service and loyalty to the king. The range of functions that they might perform as part of the palace was broad, including everything from military to medical services. There was no comparable institution for the socialization of those male captives who were not sold into the overseas trade. The royal farms during the eighteenth century were described as being worked by women. Beginning with the reign of Tegbesu, a few male slaves were castrated each year to join the ranks of the eunuchs and to work as part of the palace. Yet the very practice of castration in itself makes a point—that male slaves had to be transformed into something other than "men" to be useful to the monarchy. The major use for young male captives was integration into the standing army of men. Snelgrave appears to be referring to male captives when he comments that "the King allowed every common Soldier a Boy at the publick charge, in order to be trained up in Hardships from their youth; and that the greatest part of the present Army consisted of Soldiers, bred up in this manner, and under this Establishment." [41]

Women in the palace initially were needed for performing the same kinds of services that they performed in common polygynous households; however, the scale of their work on behalf of the king went far beyond the common norm. There were thousands of people to be fed at the time of Customs, processions to be organized, and dances and songs to be rehearsed; there were enormous storage requirements to be met for the goods acquired through the overseas trade and for the provisions brought to the palace from throughout the kingdom; and, at least in the nineteenth century, census records were kept by the palace. [42] There were royal palaces of the kings in Allada, Cana, Ajahome, and, by the nineteenth century, in Zagnanado, plus resting establishments along the route between Whydah and Abomey. All housed palace women and functioned as administrative centers. Over time, palace industries were founded, all of which were managed by women. In short, the process of the palace moving from the household of the king to a complex institution that supported the state and managed many of its functions was a gradual one, and was the product of Dahomean pragmatism. Men were relatively few, and they were socialized to promote the interests of their own kin. Women were more readily available, and they were socialized to serve persons other than their kinspeople.

Even in popular thought, there was a sense of the value of a woman that pervades accounts of Fon culture. Like water on the Abomey plateau, women were described by men as scarce, and hence valuable commodities. Vincent Kinhwe, a guide to the Abomey museum and lifelong student of Fon life, provided a popular etymology of the word for woman, *gnonnu*. "*Gnon* means 'to know' and *nu* means 'to drink'; thus *gnonnu* literally means 'to know how to drink.' A woman, like water, is a precious commodity and men must know that they can't take too much of it. A man must not abuse a woman because a woman doesn't belong to him. Women are for everyone. If you take a wife today she's for you, but when you die she'll go to another. Use a woman with moderation. Know that you can't drink the full bottle; you must conserve some of the contents." [43]

The idea of a scarcity of women, despite a gender imbalance in which women far outnumbered men, was not simply because their services were considered to be so valuable. Polygyny, at the level of the palace as well as of lesser officials, more than offset the numerical gender imbalance in the overall population. Polygyny denied women to lower-ranking and younger men and emphasized the power of the higher-ranking men and women who headed large polygynous households. Norris argues that not only did the king monopolize thousands of women but that his "principal men" had from one hundred to four hundred wives each; lower-ranking officials had from twelve to twenty each. Perhaps more telling than Norris's guesses at the numbers of dependents in the households of major officials were policies that appear to have been designed to provide access to women, if for no more than sexual services, for those men who were otherwise outside the system. [44]

Prostitution was described in the kingdom of Whydah as early as the 1690s. There, Bosman reports, special houses existed where women received men for a set price of 3 cowries. He notes that "'tis customary for some of the most considerable and rich Negroe ladies, when lying upon their Death-bed, to buy some foreign female slaves whom they donate to the Community for this use." Norris describes a system that is strikingly similar, though in Dahomey it was the king who provided the women who were literally sex slaves. In this case they were part of the palace organization, "ladies of pleasure, ordered to be such by royal authority." He says that "in every town there is a certain number of women, proportioned to its size, who are to be obliging to every customer that offers: the price of their favors is regulated, and very moderate." Moderate is an understatement. In Bosman's day, when sex in Whydah cost 3 cowries, the price of a chicken was 96 cowries. In the 1710s, sex in Whydah cost 5 cowries, and in the 1720s, chickens sold there for 160 cowries each. By the mid–nineteenth century, a royal prostitute's price was 20 cowries, when a chicken cost 280. The price of sex, in contrast to chickens, was set by the monarchy and not by market forces. Norris notes that royal prostitutes in the late eighteenth century in fact earned their livings through breeding chickens and brewing beer. He saw them at Customs, and says that they were paying a heavy tax to the king. The "tax" was probably simply the king's due, from which they would have subtracted their portions, as was customary when an ahosi performed an economic service on behalf of the king.[45]

The palace also made women available as wives for low-ranking men— people whom Norris calls "the servants of chiefs." In the 1770s, for a bridewealth payment to the palace of five heads of cowries (20,000 cowries), a small fraction of the price for a woman slave, they received a woman as wife. These women would likely have been war captives rather than women drawn from the Dahomean population. Norris comments that "I have known the king's wives, who are the agents in this business, hand out in malicious sport, the man's mother to him, whom he must maintain afterwards; and wait, content, till his circumstances enable him to try his luck on some future occasion." Norris appears to have misunderstood, because "mother" in this context has to have meant an older woman, not a biological kinswoman. A man of low rank or a slave who won the release of his own mother from the palace would have been pleased. However, he would have been justifiably distressed to receive an older woman, a "mother," someone unable to provide either productive labor or the reproductive service of bearing children.[46]

The existence of state-sponsored prostitution and of arrangements for acquiring wives is a commentary on power relations within the kingdom. Low-ranking men were deprived of access to resources, and specifically women, with which to build their lineages and their own positions in Dahomean society. The monarchy in a sense acknowledged the implicit threat of their powerlessness by providing sexual services and women at low cost. The Portuguese priest Pires, who visited Dahomey in 1797, provides an additional example of the monarchy responding to a population with few resources. He reports that when market sellers refused to sell tobacco in tiny quantities, the king arranged for its sale in quantities worth five cowries.[47]

We have little information for the eighteenth century on the organization of the palace. Marchais claims that there were three classes of women within the palace of the kings of Whydah: the youngest and prettiest, the older women no longer able to "serve the pleasures of the prince," and the women brought into the palace as servants.[48] The evidence about Dahomey, even when the palace is first described, suggests more complicated arrangements that were not focused solely on the sexual and physical needs of the king. In polygynous households, the wife first married was normally considered the manager of all the wives who followed her and was responsible for maintaining order and seeing that household tasks were done. The story of the mother of Tegbesu's rival, who kept the keys to the royal storehouses, typifies that model, and the story of her fall makes the point that the Dahomey palace was not organized in the same manner as common households. Although sources at various times cite certain "favorites" of the king, there is no indication that any single woman stood at the apex of the palace organization; rather, several functional groupings of high-ranking women emerge.

The kpojito represented a series of power centers separate from that of the palace organization yet housed within the palace walls. Each kpojito maintained her own court with her own retainers and slaves. Pires, who was in Abomey at the end of the reign of Agonglo in 1797, says that the most important woman within the palace was the naie dada, which from the context appears to be a reference to Agonglo's kpojito, Senume. Naie (*naye*) was an honorific applied to women within the palace; *dada* was an honorific for the king. The implied meaning of the term, then, is the woman king. This "woman king" is described as being the equivalent of the king, having among other powers the right to order capital punishment.[49] Nevertheless, the kpojito, if that was in fact the woman being described as naie dada, was not a wife of the king; she represented the generation of his mother and, as a parallel officer to the king, she would not have had administrative control over his dependents in the manner of a first wife.

Descriptions of the palace in the eighteenth century also speak of multiple "favorites" of the kings. For example, six "favorites" of Tegbesu, each sheltered by an umbrella and followed by a train of seventy women retainers, paraded past Norris in 1772. It is tempting to link those six with the six women who were buried alive with Tegbesu in 1774. In a likely reference to the reign of Tegbesu, six was further cited by Chenevert and Bulet as the number of women whose sons were eligible for the throne. Keeping the women who were the biological mothers of potential kings as a separate group, highly honored yet required to die with the king, fits with other evidence for succession in Tegbesu's time.[50] However, neither Norris nor any other source links them, and we are thus left with intriguing but only circumstantial evidence.

Another important grouping within the palace was that of the women named to offices parallel to those of leading male officials. By the end of the century, European travelers began to notice that each male office had a corresponding female office within the palace, a practice that began with Tegbesu.[51] There are, then, several categories of women who clearly were high-ranking in the eighteenth century. No single simple hierarchy among them emerges from the sources.

If the organizational structures remained obscure, the impact of palace women's participation in policy making and politics was evident. Complaints about women are a measure of their effectiveness. At the beginning of his reign (1789), Agonglo indirectly acknowledged women's skills in assisting outsiders needing intercession at the level of the monarchy. He announced that "he had adopted Ahadee's [Tegbesu's] principles of governing . . . that he would hear no complaints but through his Caboceers; and threatened to punish with instant death, the least whisper to his women: a crime that had been too common in [his predecessor Kpengla's] time." Women within the palace organization intervened to assist those on the outside, providing information, mitigating punishments, and improving chances for favorable responses to requests to the king. Pires notes that women were involved in commercial as well as political dealings. Though we can seldom distinguish the issues involved, we have examples of women's actions, many of which were in favor of relatives. We have already seen the example of Shampo, who fled Dahomey when his sister in the palace signaled danger. Dalzel describes a complicated instance of court intrigue that took place in 1775 when the meu sought vengeance on the yovogan for a family dispute and eventually had him disgraced and executed. Although several of the yovogan's subordinates were killed when they refused to turn against him, one, who had a sister in the palace, survived because of her intercession.[52]

Major policies were credited at times to the influence of women. Nearly thirty years of warfare with Mahi began, if Norris's account is to be believed, because a "favorite" wife of Tegbesu, who was herself Mahi, had convinced the king to create a kingship in Mahi country for her brother. The Mahi wars ended temporarily during the reign of Kpengla, when the kpojito was another Mahi woman, Chai. Dalzel believes that the Mahi sought peace and agreed to assist the Dahomeans on grounds that they were kin to Kpengla. During the reign of Kpengla, 150 men from the area of Cana were sold into the slave trade after being accused of being lovers of palace women; only later was it discovered that most were innocent. Women were also said to use their power against people they considered to be enemies. The Kpojito Hwanjile left as part of her legacy the adoption of crucifixion on large trees as a form of execution. First used against an Aja enemy of Hwanjile's, crucifixion became a ceremonial tradition, with each succeeding king using it to execute at least one person.[53]

By the late eighteenth century, observers began to talk more frequently of political parties, or blocs. As in the case of the accession of Tegbesu, women were typically cited as central to these parties, which influenced politics through councils of state and were also involved in succession struggles. Pires was told that the most important voices in state deliberations were those of the palace women, followed by the eunuchs, and then ministers such as the migan and meu. Political blocs, according to him, would be formed around a combination of women, eunuchs, and ministers. Decisions of the councils of state were said to be subject to inordinate influence by palace women, who were believed to be able to even scores with anyone who disagreed with them. The transitions between kings, and the succession struggles that accompanied them, were key moments in the life of the kingdom—windows on the struggles of parties and factions to capture the monarchy.[54]

Successions and Political Instability ∽

Norris visited Tegbesu in December 1773, five months before the king's death. Old and sick, Tegbesu received the European in his private courtyard. Norris describes his sleeping area, a detached room whose floor was paved with the skulls of enemy kings and other important persons. He assumes that the king gained "the savage gratification of trampling on the heads of his enemies, when he pleased." Had he asked, Norris might also have been told of the immense power concentrated in that room and available to nurture and strengthen its occupant as he slept. In any event, Tegbesu died as king, apparently of old age. None of his three immediate successors enjoyed that privilege, which was perhaps a testament to the growing political instability of Dahomey and the increasing inability of monarchies to maintain their followers and control rival interests.[55]

There was a period of one to two years between the death of one king and the formal beginning of the reign of his successor. During that period, several distinct processes were completed: (1) the dead king was buried after a brief period of mourning; (2) the contesting political coalitions fought through their differences until one was able to take and hold control; and (3) a long period of preparation culminated in Grand Customs, the final funeral of the preceding king and the formal installation of the new monarch. Eighteenth-century European accounts provide some information on interregnums at Whydah but scant information about the process in Dahomey. When Dahomean successions are described, it tends to be from long distance and specifically from Whydah, and writers appear to incorporate material from Whydah traditions with stories reported to them about Dahomey. Successive events are telescoped and condensed into narrow time frames, and the European sources sometimes contradict each other. On only one occasion— the death of Agonglo in 1797—did a European in Abomey at the moment of the death of a Dahomean monarch record his observations. The account, by Vicente Ferreira Pires, is invaluable, though not without flaws. Pires had arrived on the coast less than a month before the death of the king and had been in Abomey fewer than ten days when Agonglo was assassinated. Ill with fever at key moments, Pires patched together his account from information he heard in the weeks afterwards. Most of his informants were outsiders to Abomey: Brazilian sailors captured in wars at the coast, mixed-race individuals who happened to be in Abomey, and Africans who may or may not have been Dahomeans. Nevertheless, retrospective sources from the twentieth century confirm much of Pires's general information on royal deaths and burials.

The order of events of successions was not set. Evidence suggests strongly that the death of the king was kept secret as long as possible: the persons in attendance on the king would have tried to control the news in order to assure that a candidate of their choice took power. The new monarchy was sometimes in command by the time that word of the king's death was leaked; for example, the successors to Agaja and Tegbesu were in effective power by the time the kings' deaths became known. At least by the late eighteenth century, the migan was centrally involved at the death of a king. When a king was clearly ill and dying, for example, he was in close attendance. In the nineteenth century, the migan acted as regent during the period until a claim to the throne was acknowledged. Whether or not a successor was able to take control immediately, no one could openly say that the king had died, even when it became apparent outside the palace that something was terribly wrong. Rather, euphemisms were employed: *zan ku,* night has fallen, and *Dada yi Allada*, the king has gone to Allada, were two of the more common ones. Describing

Kpengla's death from the vantage point of the European trading forts, Dalzel speaks of a month-long absence of royal messengers arriving in Whydah, creating an eerie silence in which "every countenance betrayed a secret which the tongue durst not reveal." Then, says Dalzel, word came that Kpengla had died of smallpox. In 1797, Pires was told that Agonglo was ill with smallpox. When a few days later a prince made an assault on the palace, it became clear to him that the king had died.[56]

The association of smallpox with the deaths of Dahomean kings tends to be taken literally by historians, who attribute it as a cause of death. Outbreaks of smallpox were common in the area, and at least three kings were reported to have had pockmarks on their faces. Smallpox was specifically associated with the death of three kings—Kpengla, Agonglo, and Gezo. However, it is not at all certain that any of these monarchs actually died of the disease. No epidemics of smallpox were reported at the time of any of their deaths. Kpengla and Gezo were both away at war just prior to their deaths. In the case of Gezo, there are credible traditions that claim that the king was killed early in 1858 on his way back from war. Moreover, Gezo was described by more than one visitor as pockmarked and hence possibly immune to smallpox. We also know that smallpox was not the cause of death of Agonglo. He was poisoned through a plot led by Dogan, one of his brothers, who conspired with a "black woman who was kin to the king" to kill Agonglo.[57]

If, then, the disease of smallpox did not cause the demise of Dahomean monarchs, why was it named in conjunction with their deaths? Smallpox was associated with the popular vodun Sakpata or Sagbata, a name often translated from Fongbe into European languages as "smallpox." Sakpata in fact was a series of deities associated with the earth that were said to have been imported into Dahomey during the reign of Agaja. Sakpata earth deities controlled the fertility of the soil, offering to those who respected them the fullness of harvests, the fruit of the earth itself. Myths collected by Herskovits speak of Sakpata and Heviosso (the vodun associated with thunder) as siblings who ranked highest among the "children" or dependents of Mawu and Lisa. Sakpata controlled the earth and Heviosso fire and water, so the two were forced to cooperate to provide for humankind. Heviosso punished those who showed no respect by hurling thunderbolts; Sakpata punished by having the grains that people ate erupt on their skins in the form of rashes, the most dangerous of which was smallpox.[58]

The essence of both Sakpata and Heviosso was also known in Yoruba city-states. In Yorubaland, Heviosso, known there as Shango, came to be associated with kingly power in Oyo where the vodun effectively under-girded royal authority. In Dahomey, it was Sakpata who was associated with kingly power. However, Sakpata did not complement the ruling dynasty, but opposed it, mimicking the authority of the kings and express-ing hostility toward the royal lineage. Because the vodun's name was dangerous to invoke, Sakpata was referred to as *Ainon*, owner of the earth, *Aihosu*, king of the earth, or even *Ahosu*, king. Like the king of Dahomey, Sakpata inflicted capital punishment—the king's penalty—but in the form of smallpox. And like the Alladahonu rulers, Sakpata the earth king claimed the body and possessions of those people he had pun-ished—the victims of smallpox. Herskovits claims that shrines to Sakpata were built outside of Abomey because "two kings cannot rule in the same city."[59]

Herskovits believes that the Dahomean kings were simply fearful of the disease of smallpox and for that reason opposed the gods associated with it. Yet the associations of Sakpata with claims to kingly status suggest something more—a challenge to the legitimacy of the dynasty. During the reign of Agaja, the Alladahonu had been challenged by the ritual au-thority vested in the "owners of the earth," the lineage acknowledged as the first-arrived on the land and that held a sacred covenant with the earth. The royal lineage effectively co-opted these owners of the earth, bringing them into the monarchy through making one of their members, Dakodonu, the fictive father of the dynasty, and through permanently empowering one of their line through the office of the agasunon. Nev-ertheless, opposition to the ruling dynasty continued into the reign of Tegbesu. There it was checked through Hwanjile's establishment of a new order of vodun. In the reigns that followed Tegbesu, voices of popular opposition appear to have coalesced around Sakpata, the earth itself, where they continued to echo the old question of legitimacy.

Did Sakpata, then, represent literally a form of political opposition?

Did opponents of the Alladahonu organize through the congregations of vodun, and were kings killed by priests of Sakpata, as some have claimed? Did the followers of Sakpata spread smallpox to gain political advantage? There is some evidence that variolation—inoculation through deliberate infection with the live virus—was practiced through Sakpata worship, probably most often on the sakpatasi, or adepts of the vodun. There is no evidence, however, that attempts were made by Sakpata priests to protect the general population through variolation or, more to the point, to spread the disease for political ends.[60]

By the end of the eighteenth century, the royal dynasty was far beyond being easily dislodged. Struggles occurred within it, but it was never seriously threatened from outside. Its own position and its own conception of its power were expressed through the growing importance that it placed on the tohosu, the monstrous and dangerous royal spirit children headed by the tohosu child of Akaba, Zumadunu. By the nineteenth century, it is clear that Sakpata had come to represent one of the few voices of opposition to the monarchy, and there is evidence of attempts to control if not suppress its worship. Le Hérissé was told at the turn of the twentieth century that the cult of Sakpata was formally outlawed during the reigns of Gezo and Glele, and women who had been pledged to Sakpata were not taken as members of the palace organization. A contradictory story was collected by Pierre Verger, whose oral history claims that the priests of Sakpata became very important in Dahomey during Agonglo's reign because of a major smallpox epidemic; in response, Adandozan drove them away from Dahomey when he took power in 1797, Gezo later bringing the vodun back to Abomey. Verger recorded a series of songs supposedly sung on Sakpata's return. The singers were priests possessed respectively by Da Zodji, a Sakpata deity, and by Zumadunu, the chief of the tohosu. Whether the song texts express a historical event is unknown; however, they convey Dahomeans' perspectives on the ranking of the gods. In their dueling sentiments the voice of Sakpata prods and challenges; Zumadunu insists on his primacy, his identity with the leopard of the royal family. In the end, Sakpata relents, "Zomadonu, no one can make war against you." Like the disease with which it was associated, Sakpata was an irritant and a danger, a threat to the well-being of the kingdom, but neither Sakpata nor its ultimate sanction, smallpox, had the power to destroy the dynasty.[61]

Smallpox, then, was a euphemism when used in conjunction with the king's health. To say that the king was suffering from smallpox was a way of invoking associations of challenge to the monarchy, of danger and disorder. In the cases of Kpengla, Agonglo, and Gezo, it drew attention to deaths that were caused by malevolent forces. Shoponna, the deity of smallpox among the Yoruba, was associated with heat, and with destructive revelations that brought danger and death. As such, the god was constrained to live away from towns, in the deep forest, where its revelatory qualities could be controlled and concealed. In Dahomey, Sakpata similarly was a vodun of the country, of the bush. Dancing and drumming—activities associated with burials—were forbidden when Shoponna came to town, and when people died from smallpox. Saying that the king had smallpox was to warn of heat, confusion, and chaos. It announced the temporary loss of order and peace. As such, it paralleled processes described by several observers of Whydah prior to the Dahomean conquest. There, a kind of ritual anarchy at the death of a king was said to exist until the naming of his successor. Bosman wrote, "On occasion of the King's Death; which is no sooner publickly known than every Person falls a stealing to as great a value of his Neighbour's Goods as he can possibly come at . . . as tho' the Death of the King put an end to all manner of Reason and Justice." In the mid-1720s, another visitor to Whydah described what might be called a liminal state in the period following the announcement of the death of the king, when order was temporarily suspended.

> Laws, the police, and justice seem to have died with the King. Those who have enemies use this period of time to get vengeance and commit all sorts of excesses. . . . Everything is in terrible disorder, but this period of troubles lasts only five days from the time that the King has been declared dead. It takes five days to go get the Prince who will fill the Throne and allow him to get possession of the Palace. They fire a number of cannon shots to warn the people that there is a King, and soon all disorder ceases, calm and good order

reappear; trade begins again, the markets open, and everyone goes about their business with the same peace and security as before.[62]

In contrast to Whydah, both ritual disorder and real disorder were reported for Dahomey at the time of the death of the king. The ritual disorder was related to the burial of the king and was related to a three-day suspension of normal daily activity; the real had to do with the struggles of competing factions to win the monarchy. When the king died outside the Abomey palace, which happened in the cases of both Kpengla and Agonglo, the body had to be returned for burial. Pires says that Agonglo was moved in secret from Cana to Abomey on the night of Dogan's abortive attack. Once in the Abomey central palace, the body was washed, the hair shaved, and the nails clipped. Then the king was dressed as if alive. Agonglo's body was placed in a coffin, prepared long in advance, of clay moistened with the blood of human sacrifice. Located in an underground tomb reached by a narrow ramp, the coffin was surrounded by foodstuffs, silk cloths, and rich furnishings of silver and gold. A living guard of eighty women and fifty men was sent into the tomb to accompany the king on his journey to the world of the dead and to serve him there. Pires remarks that the legs of the king's entourage were broken to keep the attendants from leaving. The entrance was not sealed for three days and during that period others were said to enter the tomb to accompany the king on his journey to Kutome. Outside, the three days were days of formal mourning and suspended activity, when no one could wear new clothes, laugh, or show signs of pleasure. Pires's account of three days of cessation of everyday activity was echoed ninety years later, during the three-day period of public mourning for Glele, when it was similarly reported that no one could build a fire, go to market, draw water, wash, eat, or sit on a chair. Everyone shaved his or her head and covered the forehead, shoulders, and chest with clay. It was only with the closing of the tomb that normal activities resumed.[63]

The burial period might be preceded, interrupted, or followed by the active struggles of claimants to the throne. The three succession struggles —for Kpengla, Agonglo, and Adandozan—that followed Tegbesu's reign were among the bloodiest in the history of the kingdom. Tegbesu had named an heir, a vidaho, early in his reign; nevertheless, there was a dispute at his death. There are two historical controversies about the transition to Kpengla. The first has to do with whether Kpengla was the sole vidaho or heir apparent named; the second is whether Kpengla was the son or the brother of Tegbesu. European accounts contradict each other on the identity of the vidaho. The director of the French fort at Whydah claimed in 1774 that Kpengla was a son of Tegbesu and that he had been named heir by 1751. However, Norris tells of a vidaho named Jupera who died while returning from warfare in Mahi country in 1764 or 1765, so there had to have been at least one change of vidaho. Norris met a vidaho, the future Kpengla, in 1772, two years before the death of Tegbesu. Yet another prince alleged to have been vidaho was Ajokpalo, a senior son among the children of Tegbesu who continues through positional succession to be active in Abomey. Royal family members explain that Ajokpalo was vidaho, but that he was set aside because "his ideas were not good," and he was unbecomingly anxious to replace Tegbesu. Dunglas collected traditions that claim that Ajokpalo was deposed as vidaho, effectively for reasons of character: he was vain and arrogant. More, they charge that he was illegitimate. The proof for illegitimacy? The traditions claim that Tegbesu was impotent.[64]

Impotence serves nicely not only to discredit Ajokpalo, but also to justify succession from brother to brother. We in fact have no direct evidence that Kpengla was a brother rather than a son of Tegbesu; however, the actual kin relationship is of little importance, despite the emphasis placed on it by several historians.[65] Indeed, brothers of deceased kings were named as competitors for the throne following the reigns of both Kpengla and Agonglo. What was significant for Kpengla was that he had the requisite support—an appropriately large party, or coalition—to win and consolidate power. Norris's report on this sucession seems to indicate a battle for control of the palace: "A horrid scene commences in the palace, the moment the king expires; which continues until *Tamegah* [migan] and *Mayhou* [meu] have announced that event to his successor, and till he takes possession of it: this he loses no time in doing, that he may put an end to the mischief going on there. The wives of the deceased begin, with breaking and destroying the furniture of the house, the gold and silver ornaments and utensils, the coral, and in short, every thing of value that belonged either to themselves, or to the late king, and then *murder one another.*[66] By the time Kpengla's followers had overpowered those of Ajokpalo, 285 women were dead. Like Akaba's sister Hangbe some sixty years before, Ajokpalo had a large enough following so that he could not be executed. He continues to rank today second only to the vigan (chief of the children) of Tegbesu, even though Abomey is rife with stories of his bad character.

There were four claimants to the throne when Kpengla died fifteen years later, two of whom were brothers of the king. Agonglo, a son, was the winner. Dalzel seems to make an odd distinction about events at the time of Kpengla's death—or he does not realize that his account is internally inconsistent. He reports that 595 women were killed in two and a half days within the palace and that Agonglo "rushed into the palace, and put a stop to the carnage among the women." On the other hand, he asserts that the migan had arranged a peaceful transition so "the struggle for the succession was not so violent as to occasion the loss of any lives." It is not at all clear what Dalzel believed was the meaning of nearly three days of killing among the female retainers of the king.[67]

Pires's account of the succession following the death of Agonglo, which is virtually day by day, provides a sense of the complexity of the ritual and political drama that took place at royal transitions. There were two distinct battles within the palace, providing insights into who was involved in the struggles, and how. The first battle took place after the poisoning of Agonglo by a woman of the palace. Dogan had promised that, if the plot worked, "he would marry her and she would become Queen"—an apparent reference to the office of kpojito. In the small hours of the morning of May 1, 1797, Dogan and a party of three hundred armed retainers attacked the palace. Pires reports that the migan and meu were inside the palace, attending to the king's death. They had a warning gong sounded and distributed arms "to the king's family." Given the restrictions on access to the interior, "the king's family" must have been no more than the king's guard of women, a handful of male officials, and some siblings of the king. Dogan and his followers, caught between armed resistance in the palace and people arriving from the exterior, were defeated. Pires's account was later corroborated by the director of the French fort at Whydah, who implicated the Kpojito Hwanjile in the plot: the king "was assassinated . . . by one of his wives, named Nai-Ouangerie, who intended to promote one of her relatives." [68]

Dogan's abortive revolt was the initial engagement. Later, a second fight occurred between two of the four sons of Agonglo who apparently were technically eligible to succeed. Pires was told that the elder of the four, Anibabel, had earlier been excluded from consideration because he had a deformed foot, a blemish that oral traditions claim was a hammer toe. The second, who became king as Adandozan, was vidaho. Adandozan was relatively young at the time, and he and his followers do not appear to have been fully prepared to seize power, because Pires's account implies that fighting and political maneuvering were being done on his behalf, possibly in part by persons associated with Agonglo. Perhaps it was Adandozan's youth that led Anibabel to make a move to win the throne. He and his followers attacked the assembled court on the day of Agonglo's burial. Pires reports that four hundred of Anibabel's followers were captured and fifty other people died before the coup attempt was put down. In the aftermath, the remaining brothers of Adandozan, the two younger ones, were killed to prevent further uprisings and there was fairly widespread killing and imprisonment of suspected opposition members. Princesses of the royal line were apparently also implicated, because Pires describes the killing of women of the king's family. The royal women were tied up out of doors, fed salty food, and denied water until they expired. A total of nine hundred prisoners were taken by the victors in the two battles; some three hundred of them became slaves who were parceled out among the followers of the new king and another six hundred, including a woman named Agontime who would later become kpojito to Adandozan's successor, were sent to Whydah to be sold into the overseas slave trade.[69]

The ritual mourning and burial were thus intermixed with the ongoing struggles of candidates for the kingship. This blending of the religious and the political was reflected in the human sacrifices made at the time of burial. Traditions about who was buried with the king are highly contradictory. Dahomean sources insist that it was a great honor to accompany the king in death. Labarthe's 1803 synthesis of information about Dahomey is typical: "[A] crowd of wives of the king comes forward to solicit the honor of being buried in the tomb in order to serve the dead king. They choose 24 of them; the women who are not called to take part in this barbaric ceremony sigh and complain about the injustice that they believe was done to them." Yet the legs of those so honored had to be broken to keep them in the tomb. In Whydah, the Chevalier des Marchais observed, women were tricked into entering the king's tomb, then trapped there and left to die, while male servants fled or hid, returning only after they were sure that the tomb had been closed. An earlier visitor to Whydah, Jean Barbot, commented that "at the moment of the death of kings all the courtiers can be heard expressing a wish to be able to die with him. But I am convinced that, in reality, they withdraw the offer as soon as they can."

There seem to have been similar sentiments in Dahomey. Human sacrifice later would become a major issue in Dahomey's relations with Europe, and particularly with England. Travelers of the eighteenth century suggest that, in pragmatic Dahomey, a sufficiency of royal servants was a relatively small number, particularly when they had to be drawn from among palace inhabitants and other royal retainers in the capital. The aged Tegbesu, for example, instructed his survivors to send him only a few servants—his musicians and some other persons.[70] The 285 women who in fact died in the fighting after Tegbesu's death were those buried with the king to serve as his entourage. Only the six additional women discussed above, the six "favorites" who may have been mothers of potential heirs, augmented their ranks. At least some of the sacrificial requirements at the death of the king, then, were conveniently filled by the losers in succession struggles.

In addition to personal servants to the dead king, whose positions could have been filled by virtually anyone, there may have been specific officers required to die when the king died. A smattering of suggestions—including Dalzel's ambiguous comment that the king's "Big Mother" was sometimes put to death—hint that, as in Oyo, there were some important individuals who were expected to die with the king. Testimony from the late nineteenth century argues that individuals closest to the person of the king and those most trusted by him were required to die at his death. In a perverse way, the requirement to die with the king would have been a measure of an individual's influence with the king and possibly her or his power at court. With the greatest opportunities to inflict harm, those in the most intimate contact had every reason to keep the king in good health. Ellis names persons close to the king, including the kposi (literally, wife of the leopard), the women associated with the sacred totem of the dynasty. Skertchly reports that the male and female heads of the palace eunuchs normally died, though in the transition from Gezo to Glele, both remained alive. A mid–nineteenth century visitor was told that "before, it was the custom that when a king died, the cabeceers had to accompany him," a practice that was abolished by Gezo. Le Hérissé claims that many persons would offer to be sacrificed but be refused by the new king. They would later claim that the king had "bought back their life," an idiom that perhaps expressed a sense of obligation and loyalty to the new king. Pires says that the entrance to the king's tomb was not sealed for three days so that in addition to those required to die with the king, men and women who wished to accompany him might enter. The open entrance left indeterminate the actual numbers, if any, of persons whose devotion led them willingly to join the king in death. It also made unchallengeable the belief that many volunteered to travel to the world of the dead with their sovereign.[71]

Grand Customs, the final funeral of the dead king and the formal installation of his successor, took place only after the new king was fully in place and opposition to the new monarchy had been crushed. Described as a ceremonial cycle more elaborate than the annual honoring of the ancestral kings and kpojito, Grand Customs was always delayed until preparations were complete: quantities of trade goods acquired, sacrificial victims captured, foodstuffs gathered and processed, and musicians and dancers trained. To some extent, the exterior relations of the kingdom would have had to have been relatively peaceful, because the cycle required the attention of the court over a prolonged period of time. One year seems to have been the minimum time for the consolidation of the new monarchy's position and the ceremonial preparations. Tegbesu, for example, died in May 1774 and the Grand Customs that confirmed Kpengla took place a year later, in June 1775. Kpengla died in April 1789.

Nearly two years passed before the enstoolment ceremonies for Agonglo in January through March 1791.

Pires describes one of the ceremonies associated with the installation of the new king, a process that he would not have seen but rather have been told about, presumably from the accounts of people who had witnessed the installation of Agonglo six years before. The remains of the deceased king were exhumed. The king then appeared publicly holding the skull of his predecessor in his left hand and a ceremonial knife in his right, to demonstrate that he had been ruling in the name of his father. Dropping the skull and machete, the new king took up his own sceptre, or *récade*, indicating that henceforth he would be ruler in his own name. Later accounts note that kings typically proclaimed a personal praise-name, or "strong name," at the time of their installation. Given the severity and length of struggles between the various parties to successions, it is little wonder that most of these allegorical names refer to the obstacles that had stood in the way of the king, and to the special powers or characteristics of the man who had successfully overcome them. The strong names were said to have been sung daily around the palace and they ultimately became the personal names by which each king was remembered. Kpengla, for example, was associated with the phrase: *sinmê kpén gla ma djè avivo*—the stone in the water does not fear the cold. Agaja's strong name was *naki dja agadja, ma'gnon zô dô*—one cannot put branches still on the tree in the fire. Once formally installed, the king reigned until his death. But even this rule of state was violated on one occasion in the history of Dahomey. The exception to the rule was Adandozan, who was deposed by supporters of Gezo. The deposition of Adandozan, rather than the chronology of passing years, marked the real beginning of the nineteenth century in Dahomey.[72]

5

The Implications of Cultural and Commercial Change

His Dahoman Majesty, King Gézo, is about forty-eight years of age, good-looking, . . . his appearance commanding, and his countenance intellectual, though stern in the extreme. That he is proud there can be no doubt, for he treads the earth as if it were honoured by its burden.

Frederick E. Forbes, 1849

Gezo's Coup d'État ∽

The Portuguese priest Pires believed that Agonglo was assassinated because he planned to be baptized and make Christianity the state religion. Pires and a second priest had come to Abomey, not because the king had requested religious instruction, but in response to a Dahomean commercial embassy despatched to Lisbon in 1795. The Dahomean ambassadors had been sent to request improvements in trade relations, including the granting of exclusive trading rights between Whydah and the Brazilian port of Bahia, and to complain of the poor administration of the director of the Portuguese fort in Whydah. As such, their mission followed in the steps of a similar embassy sent in 1750 during the reign of Tegbesu.[1]

The heir to the Portuguese throne replied in a letter, and his devout mother, the reigning monarch, sent the two priests to try to convert Agonglo to Roman Catholicism. The priests had been received by the king a week before he died and he had indicated a willingness to be baptized. We have no way of knowing if Agonglo in fact intended to be baptized. Perhaps more importantly, we have no way of knowing what he believed baptism meant. Similarly, we cannot know if Dogan, whose name was associated with the plot to kill Agonglo, was prompted to act by the possibility that the king would adopt Christianity, or whether the assassination of Agonglo when Pires was present was simply a co-incidence.

Pires's self-promoting account of Agonglo's great enthusiasm for Catholicism is suspect. Nevertheless, there is a smattering of circumstantial evidence that suggests that the Christian god may have been a factor in Agonglo's demise. The god of Christianity was known within the palace by Agonglo's time, and the Dahomeans appear to have respected its power. It is also clear that they conceived of the Christian god as a deity that acted in ways comparable to any other vodun. Chenevert and Bulet, for example, comment that "in general, they respect each others fetishes [gods], and they have reverence for the ceremonies of the whites, that they also call our fetishes."[2]

Ironically, given its exclusively male priesthood, the veneration of the god of Christianity was promoted in the palace of Dahomey by women, as was characteristic of Dahomean vodun. By the 1790s there were at least two women within the palace organization who were practicing Christians. The first was an Afro-Dutch woman named Sophie, who had been married to the director of the French fort, Joseph Ollivier Montaguère, and who had borne him two sons before he returned to France. When European traders left Whydah, their estates were inherited by the king in the same way that the estates of other prominent Dahomeans passed through the hands of the monarchy on their death. As part of Ollivier's estate, Sophie had been brought to Abomey, where she was retained and made an ahosi by Kpengla. Subsequently inherited by Agonglo, with whom she had a third son, Sophie maintained a Roman Catholic shrine in the palace. The second woman, the wife of the interpreter who accompanied the Dahomean embassy to Portugal, was residing during his absence in the palace under the sponsorship of the woman that Pires calls the naie dada, who was probably Agonglo's kpojito, Senume. Pires recounts two occasions when the interpreter's wife was believed to have successfully invoked the powers of the god of Christianity. Once, during a severe thunderstorm, she prayed until the storm abated, and Agonglo was said to have commented in response that "true witchcraft came from the white people." At another point, the naie dada appealed to the interpreter's wife after having unsuccessfully consulted with "all" the vodun priests to produce a suitable husband for her daughter. The woman gave the naie dada an image of Saint Anthony and told her to pray. On the following day, the king announced that arrangements had been made for the marriage of the daughter to a caboceer, and in gratitude the naie dada began to send money weekly to the chapel of the Portuguese fort in Whydah for the saying of masses.[3]

The respect enjoyed by the god of Christianity could easily have been interpreted as a threat by certain powerful persons in Abomey. The Kpojito Hwanjile was named as a principal in the plot against Agonglo. Hwanjile, as director of the shrines to Mawu and Lisa, the supreme creator deities of the Fon pantheon, was the earthly authority over all the vodun and their followers. In explaining their deity to Dahomeans, the Europeans typically stressed that their god also was a creator and supreme deity. As such, the Christian god was directly comparable to Mawu and Lisa. Capuchin missionaries in Allada in the mid–seventeenth century, for example, used the name Lisa to translate *God* into Fongbe. By the nineteenth century, Mawu was the name commonly used. Was there some expectation, then, that Agonglo would install the Christian god as the paramount vodun of Dahomey, replacing Mawu and Lisa at the head of the Fon pantheon? Did Hwanjile and others anticipate that a European, or perhaps an Afro-European woman, would replace Hwanjile as director of religious life in the kingdom?

We will never know with certainty if the perceived influence of the Christian deity was in fact a motive in the plot against Agonglo. However, the presence of two followers of the Christian god within the palace organization is indicative of the growth of a particular form of European cultural influence by the end of the eighteenth century. That cultural influence was sparked by European commercial visitors in residence along the coast. The European traders had had varying relationships of cordiality with Dahomeans and the monarchy. Individuals like the Frenchmen Pruneau de Pommegorge and Ollivier Montaguère, the Englishmen Archibald Dalzel and Lionel Abson, and the Portuguese João Basilio lived relatively long periods of time in Whydah. Several spoke Fongbe, married Dahomean women, fathered children, and functioned comfortably in Dahomean culture. Nevertheless, their sojourns were temporary; they lived within the confines of foreign enclaves, the European forts, as representatives of European-based governments and trading companies. When their tours of duty ended, the families that they had established remained in Dahomey.

By the turn of the nineteenth century, another community in Whydah was replacing in influence the European society spawned by the old European forts. It was made up of a cultural and racial mix: descendants of the earlier European traders and their African wives, Africans who had had close relationships with the forts, and persons who had come to West Africa from Brazil and other Portuguese territories. The latter included West Africans who had been taken to Brazil as slaves and won their manumission, descendants of Brazilian slaves, and individuals of European extraction, many of whom were adventurers trying their luck at commerce in slaves. Settled along the coast from Little Popo (Anecho) to Lagos, these racially and culturally mixed communities became culture brokers between Africa and Europe. What they had in common was experience in the Western Hemisphere, the knowledge of European languages, and a particular affinity for Portuguese-Brazilian or lusophone culture. Portuguese was their acknowledged lingua franca and Roman Catholicism their religion. Dubbed the Aguda (Ajuda) by the Dahomeans, from a probable Portuguese corruption of Hweda, members of this mixed lusophonic community were commonly called Brazilians by speakers of European languages, though we will here call them Afro-Brazilians to stress their role as cultural and racial intermediaries. In effect, towns like Whydah became colonial enclaves, cultural outposts of Brazil that were informal colonies of a colony.

Like expatriates in other settings, the Afro-Brazilians nurtured and preserved their lusophone culture. Some sent their children to be educated in Bahia; others cherished plans to return to Brazil, sometimes even as they lay on their deathbeds in Whydah. So predominant was the Brazilian-Portuguese influence in Dahomey in the nineteenth century that families like the descendants of Ollivier changed their name to d'Oliveira. Yet the Afro-Brazilians differed from the older generations of European traders in their full acknowledgment of the Dahomean state as the civil authority over their lives. They participated on Dahomean terms in the life of the kingdom, developing links of friendship and marriage with members of the monarchy, and involving themselves in the kingdom's politics. At the same time, the Afro-Brazilians maintained their connections with European culture, and particularly the cultures of Brazil and Portugal. As mediators between and participants in both European and African cultures, the Afro-Brazilian community over the nineteenth century was enormously influential, though never wholly united about its objectives, particularly as European interests toward the end of the century turned to the creation of colonies on African soil.

The spirit of the Afro-Brazilian community is perhaps best exemplified by its most famous member, Francisco Félix de Souza. Born of a Portuguese father and Native American mother, de Souza arrived on the West African coast about 1800. After failing in trade at Badagry, he moved to Whydah, where he became bookkeeper and secretary to the Portuguese fort which at that period was commanded by his brother. Within a few years he had become an independent slave trader based at Little Popo. As his trading successes and wealth grew, de Souza eventually had commercial dealings with Dahomey's King Adandozan, who at one point imprisoned him in Abomey. De Souza emerged from prison as a friend of Adandozan's brother Gakpe, the future Gezo.[4]

Later, during Gezo's reign (1818–58), the friendship between the king and de Souza continued. Under the sobriquet of "the Chacha," he was appointed governor of Whydah by Gezo and wielded power that overshadowed that of the yovogan. Granted a large tract of land that became the "Brazilian" quarter of Whydah, de Souza and his polygynous household were the center of a community that grew substantially, particularly in the mid-1830s through immigration from Bahia. De Souza was described by European visitors as being completely "Africanized"; nevertheless, he graciously received and charmed European visitors, briefing them on Dahomey and its mores. De Souza would discuss the pros and cons of the slave trade with missionaries and government representatives bent on its destruction. Meanwhile, he continued his own trade in slaves and maintained his control over the availability of slaves to other traders involved in the clandestine commerce. De Souza was very consciously a cultural intermediary, advising Europeans about the king and Dahomean

politics and policies, and advising the monarchy about European interests. He is generally credited with encouraging the Dahomeans to develop palm oil as an export crop. On his death in 1849, the chacha was
replaced by a son. Though his descendants continued to be prominent
in the politics of the kingdom and, later, the French colony of Dahomey,
his successors never wielded power comparable to that of the dynasty
founder.[5]

De Souza's rise to prominence as an official of the king of Dahomey was
directly related to his role in supporting the coup d'état of Gezo against
Adandozan. Little is known of the events leading up to Adandozan's fall.
Even the date of the coup is uncertain; most authorities quote 1818, but it
may have happened as early as 1817 or as late as 1820. Oral traditions are
not helpful in providing motives. As in the cases of losers in succession
struggles, they paint Adandozan with the brush of evil character, calling
him a tyrant and despot who had usurped the stool from the rightful
heir, Gezo. Many names of the putative members of the coalition that
destooled Adandozan have been retained, both in oral traditions and in
the accounts of later nineteenth-century visitors. De Souza's role was central in setting the stage. Hazoumé claims that during the time that the
slave trader was imprisoned in Abomey, de Souza, Gezo, and a third
member of the coastal trading community, Dosso-Yovo, swore an oath of
friendship and vowed to destool Adandozan. According to d'Oliveira
family traditions, Nicola d'Oliveira, the son of Sophie, was involved in
freeing de Souza. Nicola was able to contact his mother, who was resident
in the Abomey palace and who ultimately arranged de Souza's escape.
Gezo himself is credited with providing a sixty-person escort to help the
Brazilian reach Little Popo safely. Upon regaining the coast, de Souza
sent the prince gifts—rum, tobacco, and cloth—and opened lucrative
slave-trading links with Gezo. Gezo in turn built a following through the
distribution of his profits from trading in slaves—trade goods and arms.
Hazoumé, in describing Gezo's growing entourage, provides a lively description of the process by which ambitious persons gained dependents
in Dahomey. According to Hazoumé, admirers of a new garment of one
of Gezo's people, a wrapper, were told, "I received this cloth from Gapé
(Gezo). You can have similar ones, our prince is so generous." Hazoumé

continues, "Soon Gapé saw even his enemies come forward; all came to receive pretty cloth, to drink good rum, and to fill their pipes with tobacco, things that one didn't get from Adandozan."[6]

Beyond the Afro-Brazilian community, Gezo was said to have been allied with a number of his brothers and sisters: the princes Tometin and Adukonu (both said to have been brothers by the same mother as Adandozan), Gansé, Atakin-So-Nou, Oundanoucou, Gnimavo, Atinkpasso, Linpehoun, and Toffa, among others, plus his sisters Sinkutin, Sàvà, and Nagban. Dunglas indicates that several of Adandozan's ministers, including the migan, the meu, and the ajaho, were supporters of Gezo. A descendant of Dosso-Yovo included the names Binazon, Baku (possibly meaning Atindebaku, who was migan), Voglosu (Adandozan's meu), Adjéhunou, Adjumanwessu, six hundred other followers, two hundred families of Bahia, and the kings of Savalou, Ketu, and Save.[7] It is unclear if the personal names given by Dosso-Yovo were members of the royal family, and it is difficult generally to judge the accuracy of these lists. Many of these individuals were later named to high office under Gezo, which gives their claims credibility; on the other hand, there is a tendency for people to wish to have their ancestral names associated with the winning side, which could account particularly for the "200 families of Bahia." What is notable about the lists of names of conspirators is that, apart from the role purportedly played by Sophie in freeing de Souza, no woman of the palace organization was remembered as having been part of the coalition. Palace women would be remembered, however, as having been involved in fighting at the time of the coup and particularly in providing opposition to the coalition around Gezo.

Maurice Ahanhanzo Glélé, drawing on royal family traditions collected in the 1960s, provides a series of possible motives for the deposing of Adandozan. He says that Adandozan for economic reasons had failed to perform ceremonies in honor of the royal ancestors, and the royal family split over what to do about it. Meanwhile, the common people were transferring their allegiance from the Alladahonu dynasty to a commoner-chief named Josu, who was from Munyon, a village about four miles north of Abomey. Precipitating the coup was Adandozan's decision to sacrifice one of his own sisters, Sinkutin, as a messenger to the ancestors. The king reasoned that if he wished to have someone plead his case before the ancestors, it would be better to have a member of the royal family, someone who could recognize the ancestors and speak well on the king's behalf, rather than an anonymous prisoner of war. With the royal family aroused and divided against itself, civil war ensued within the palace: Adandozan was neutralized and Gezo became regent for Adandozan's son Dakpo. Gezo then tried to unite the royal family factions around the metaphor of a perforated pot, saying "in the time of our ancestors, Dahomey was like a normal pot and was able to contain and retain water. But now we, the descendants of Agonglo, by our quarrels and disputes have transformed it into a pot pierced with holes that is no longer able to hold water. If each one of us, with his and her fingers, comes to fill the holes of the pot, it will once again hold water and Dahomey will be saved."[8]

Dunglas provides a slightly different account but one not wholly inconsistent with Glélé's version. In Dunglas, Josu of Munyon and Adandozan were close friends. The king had given a daughter in marriage to the commoner and began to suggest that he would make Josu his heir. People began to gather around Josu and treat him like an important personage, which offended members of the royal family and high-ranking officials in Abomey and prompted them to act.[9]

Dunglas also provides a romantic description of the court scene as Adandozan was destooled: Adandozan and his assembled courtiers suddenly hear in the distance the solemn sounds of Dogba, the great war drum. Stunned, Adandozan looks to the spot where the sacred drum normally stands in close proximity to the king; it has disappeared. The slow rumble of Dogba draws nearer and the entire assembly sits, frozen into immobility. A royal procession enters the court with Gezo in the place of the king. Adandozan's migan, Atindebaku, his voice choking with emotion, announces, "Two suns cannot shine at the same time." He approaches Adandozan, removes the royal sandals, the sign of kingship, and declares, "You are no longer king. You can no longer occupy the seat of Wegbaja."[10] The reality, including traditions recorded by this same Dunglas, appears to have been less gentle, as will be apparent below.

There is evidence that the destooling of Adandozan was not sufficient to confirm Gezo in power and that at some point fighting broke out. Glélé says that Gezo ruled as regent for Dakpo, the heir of Adandozan, for about twenty years. Then, when Gezo decided to name his own son as vidaho, Adandozan's son set the palace on fire and was killed. It was only then that Gezo fully assumed the role of king. In his novel *Doguicimi*, Paul Hazoumé similarly speaks of a fire set by sons of Adandozan. In this account, the situation was saved by a wife of Gezo named Yêpommê Avognondé, whose shouts and firing of a gun alerted others of the attack. Thomas Birch Freeman, who visited Abomey in the 1840s, was also told about a revolt within the palace some time after Adandozan had been removed from power, and Bernard Maupoil, in the 1930s, collected traditions telling of the burning of the palace by sons of Adandozan. Dunglas himself describes violence that took place after the destooling of Adandozan. He notes that several sons of Adandozan were executed "in the repression that followed" Gezo's coup, and that Adandozan's vidaho, Dakpo, was shot by Na Bekonsi, the na daho, who was a sister of Gezo and Adandozan. Dakpo's "mother," a woman named Dohoue, is recalled through a song that describes her being dragged by the neck through the streets of Abomey, while people called out to cut her into pieces and burn her. Finally, Dunglas mentions in passing that a bodyguard of women was killed in its entirety in a section of the palace called Aligo when they attempted to resist Gezo's followers.[11]

We will never know exactly what happened when Adandozan was deposed, but one thing is certain—and difficult to explain. The deposed king was allowed to live. Visitors in the mid–nineteenth century learned what was an open secret around Abomey: that Adandozan remained alive in one of the palaces. Though one source reported that he died in the late 1840s, more reliable ones indicate that Adandozan outlived Gezo himself, dying in the early 1860s. By that time, his surviving descendants and followers, who resided in the Becon-Hwegbo quarter of Abomey, no longer associated themselves with his name; rather, they were part of a grouping of royal descendants that included the children of Agonglo and that was called *bahanyan*, or disorder. All the events of Adandozan's twenty-one year reign were completely ignored in the songs of the *kpanligan*, the court heralds and praise-singers. Thus Adandozan suffered a bizarre punishment that was perhaps worse than assassination—to watch history be reworked as though he had never lived.

Though we do not know what happened at the time of Gezo's accession, nor precisely why Adandozan was deposed, there are certain themes that emerge from the traditions about the coup and the changes made after it. First, most of the accounts point to a fundamental loss of support as a reason for Adandozan's fall. The de Souza traditions emphasize the size of Gezo's following in implicit contrast to a lesser number of dependents for Adandozan. Glélé argues that to continue to rule, the king had to retain the support of his followers and adhere to accepted rules of behavior for a Dahomean king: "the king thus has power, but he must respect the laws of the kingdom. Exclusive holder of all powers, he [the king] was not able to exercise them all alone; that is why he was assisted by numerous dignitaries who constituted, with him, the central power, and formed the territorial and provincial administration." [12] In short, Glélé suggests that Adandozan tried to rule without a monarchy—without the dependents and supporters who enhanced his power as they shared it. The traditions about de Souza clearly show Gezo building and utilizing his followers, creating a coalition that at the appropriate moment became a monarchy.

Second, the traditions about Josu of Munyon hint at tensions between royalty and commoner. Taken literally, the idea that a commoner from a village north of Abomey would aspire to replace a dynastic heir is absurd. What, then, are the royal oral records suggesting? They seem to speak of commoner arrogance, of the idea that a common man given privilege and wealth overreaches his limits. In earlier times, intimations of popular unrest were expressed in terms of religious friction. The Kpojito Hwanjile, for example, was said to have reordered the hierarchy of the gods the better to co-opt priestly leadership and control the followers of the "popular" vodun. The Josu of Munyon traditions are of a slightly different nature, suggesting less general unrest among the people and more the dangers of permitting a person of nonroyal lineage to acquire too much power. In that sense, the Josu tradition rationalizes and justifies Gezo's appointment of members of the royal family to central positions in his monarchy.

Glélé also mentions a third theme—a split in the royal family, with the deposition crisis precipitated by the king's decision to sacrifice his sister. In a sense, a split in the royal family was not extraordinary: there is abundant evidence for royal conflict earlier in the history of the dynasty, particularly at moments of succession. The interesting point about this case is the resolution of the crisis, with the deposed king surviving. That resolution suggests two things: that the factions were balanced in terms of relative strength, and that the palace organization was effective in its protection of the person of the reigning monarch. Gezo's supporters clearly were unable to arrange to kill Adandozan, but at the same time the king's supporters were not strong enough to maintain him in power. The fact of the survival of the king also provides evidence that Gezo may well have been appointed as regent, so that he initially reigned as a prince, not king—a distinction that would later be enshrined in ritual. Finally, the story of the threatened sacrifice of the king's sister may on the one hand be read as a myth justifying Adandozan's deposition by emphasizing his evil character. On the other hand, the idea of sacrificing a person of relatively great importance fit Dahomean concepts of sacrifice. As we shall see, similar thinking would inspire Behanzin to take the life of his own kpojito some seventy-five years later.

Another important theme in Gezo's rise was the nature of his support. The composition of the coalition that brought Gezo to power marked a dramatic departure from previous succession struggles. The central moving forces were of two kinds: de Souza (and to a lesser extent the Afro-Brazilian community); and the siblings of Gezo. The prominent role played by a major slave trader suggests economic motives as a factor, or at least that the commercial community hoped for improved trading opportunities with a new king. Along with the traditions about Josu of Munyon, the centrality of Gezo's siblings suggests a degree of class conflict, or more specifically, continued rivalry between royalty and commoners. Tensions between royalty and commoners in the eighteenth century had been acknowledged and resolved through ritual accommodations and institutional structures that included the office of kpojito. Male commoners, including several ministers of Adandozan, were said to have been involved in deposing Adandozan, but in roles that appear to have been secondary to those of the members of the royal family. Women commoners within the palace organization were notably absent as allies of Gezo, which suggests both that they were loyal to the ruling monarchy and that they may have been a crucial factor in Adandozan's physical survival.

As noted above, de Souza was generously rewarded once Gezo came to power, and he continued throughout the remainder of his life to play the role of powerful confidant and adviser to the king. Though Europeans and Afro-Europeans had been advisors and long-term visitors to the courts of the Dahomean kings in the past, none, prior to Gezo, was known to have been directly involved in a succession dispute. Siblings of would-be kings, on the other hand, had been involved in the past, and the siblings of Gezo who were involved in bringing him to power received rich rewards. Departing from previous practice, Gezo named them to ministerial and other high offices simultaneously with persons of common birth. Atindebaku, for example, the migan of Adandozan, continued as migan, but Gansé, Gezo's brother, was also named to the position. Adandozan's meu, Voglosu, who along with Atindebaku was named as a conspirator, was meu under Gezo. But Tometin, Gezo's brother, was also meu. The greater role of persons of royal blood and specifically of siblings of the king in prominent positions in the kingdom became a characteristic of the nineteenth-century state.

Accounts of the organization of the state that are based on royal family perspectives after the fall of the kingdom stress that as a matter of principle ministers and other high officials were always drawn from among common people. Le Hérissé, for example, was told in the early 1900s that the kings never named members of their family to positions of responsibility, but rather showered them with riches and kept them in the vicinity of Abomey in a "domesticité dorée," a gilded cage. Clearly following royal family interpretations, Le Hérissé insists that when in a few cases siblings of Gezo became ministers, such positions were simply honorific and the royal family members who held them were merely assistants to the major figures. Glélé similarly stresses the point that the kings, with a few exceptions, always chose ministers from among commoners, noting "when it happened that the king named princes as ministers, the true holder of the office was always the dignitary drawn from among the people. The *anato* (commoners), knowing that they owed everything to the king, remained loyal and very faithful to him; they succeeded through their zeal, their ardor in service to the king, to rise in society, to hold the highest responsibilities and to constitute a kind of nobility of function that was generally more natural than the princes who were kept away from power." The argument that members of the royal family were simply honorary ministers with no real role was not strictly true, even during the reign of Gezo. As late as the visit of Forbes in 1849, the commoner migan and meu were recognized as the officeholders, while Gansé and Tometin, the princely migan and meu, were listed simply as royal brothers. Nevertheless, we have evidence suggesting that Gezo's brothers played more than a nominal role. The commoner migan, Atindebaku, was despatched on a mission abroad that kept him out of Dahomey for a number of years, which presumably meant that Prince Gansé functioned as migan at the very least for that period of time. The greater closeness of siblings of the king to active participation in the monarchy foreshadowed changes to be made during the reign of Glele.[13]

After the destoolment of Adandozan, commoner women, too, within the palace began to experience changes. In the past and for the future, coalitions that reached for control over Dahomey included women of the palace organization. If any were involved in assisting the forces of Gezo, however, they were not acknowledged in the aftermath of the successful coup. Gezo's choice of a kpojito was indicative. In the past, kings had recognized the involvement of powerful women in succession struggles by naming them kpojito; although traditions about her are contradictory on important points, all agree that Gezo's kpojito, Agontime, was *not* directly involved in the events that made Gezo king.

The Kpojito Agontime ∼

Agontime was a wife of Agonglo, having been brought to Abomey from Tendji, a town about nine miles to the northeast, where her mother's family resided. Agontime is said to have been involved on the losing side in the succession struggle at the death of Agonglo in 1797, and she was one of the persons sold into the overseas trade in the aftermath. She is said to have been later brought back at Gezo's direction. What precisely was her relationship to Gezo? Most sources simply say that she was his "mother," an answer that, as we have seen, can be anthropologically correct but biologically misleading. D'Oliveira family traditions say that Agontime was a wet nurse to Gezo, but we have no corroborating evidence for any direct relationship between the two.[14]

People were occasionally redeemed from slavery in the Western Hemisphere. A prince taken to Brazil during Tegbesu's reign, for example, was redeemed by Kpengla and competed against Agonglo for the royal stool. Gezo is known to have sent delegations to the Western Hemisphere, at least two of which are remembered as having been sent in search of Agontime; Dosso-Yovo and Migan Atindebaku led the searches. Traditions vary about the circumstances. Most versions agree that the Dahomean ambassadors spent three years on the first trip; however, they disagree on the sites visited, naming variously Brazil, Cuba, or elsewhere in the Antilles. Most accounts of Agontime claim that she returned after the second trip, though two important authorities, Hazoumé and Glélé, claim that she was never found. In any event, a kpojito was enstooled relatively early in Gezo's reign, possibly at the time of his own formal enstoolment. One source links her appearance in Abomey with a Dahomean victory over Oyo in 1823; another claims that she spent twenty-four years in "Ame'ika," which would date a return to Dahomey to around 1821. She took the name Agontime from the praise-phrase *Agossi yovo gboje agontime*, which translated literally means, the monkey has come from the country of the whites and is now in a field of pineapples. Its meaning contrasts Agontime's degrading past with the riches of her present.[15]

Pierre Verger has published an essay that hypothesizes that Agontime lived in the Western Hemisphere in Saõ Luis de Maranhaõ in northeastern Brazil. There, in a temple known locally as the House of the Minas (Mina being a term for coastal peoples in the area of Whydah), a number of old Dahomean deities were honored in the twentieth century. Along with numerous popular vodun they included Nesuhwe, deified members of the royal family—but only royal individuals who had lived prior to the reign of Agonglo. Though he has no evidence that links her specifically with the site, Verger argues that it was Agontime who established the worship of these deities that are fixed in time by their association with the reigns before Agonglo.[16]

The image of Agontime as a powerful priest, skilled in the means to venerate the vodun, links her to the traditions of the great kpojito of the eighteenth century, Adonon and Hwanjile. But while superficially resembling that older model, Agontime does not approach it in fact. First, she is not remembered by her descendants as having been a priest.[17] In addition, she was not a member of the coalition that sought power in Gezo's name, and she was not highly visible, as were individuals like de Souza or Tometin, in the politics of the kingdom during his reign. Unlike Hwanjile, there are no traditions of activism in organizing religious life associated with Gezo's kpojito.

The lack of agreement on whether or not Agontime really returned from the Western Hemisphere is telling, because in the political realities of Gezo's time, her return was irrelevant. She was fixed as a symbolic rather than real figure in Dahomean history. As an individual sold out of Dahomey at the time of Adandozan's succession, she was an emblem of opposition to the king who was later deposed by Gezo and his supporters. She can also be seen as a symbol of the interests of Gezo's monarchy in working closely with Brazilians to encourage overseas trade. The delegations ostensibly sent to search for her in the Western Hemisphere appear to have had other, or at least additional, charges. A governor of the Portuguese fort in Whydah in the late nineteenth century, who interviewed Dosso-Yovo when he was a very old man, claimed that the mission had been despatched as a formal diplomatic mission to meet with the Portuguese King Don João VI in Rio de Janeiro.[18] Another informant, a direct descendant of Dosso-Yovo, testified in the 1970s that his ancestor had been involved in encouraging the migration of two hundred Bahian families to Whydah.[19] The search for Agontime, then, may be seen as part of the expression of interest by the Gezo monarchy in continuing contacts with the Western Hemisphere, and specifically with Brazil.

Though Agontime was in several senses a symbol of the monarchy's interests and directions, she was nevertheless a real person with real family ties. One tradition claims that she was the younger sister of Blé, the man who founded the Yemadje lineage of appliqué makers to the kings. Immediately following Agontime's marriage to Agonglo, the king is said to have sent for Blé, marrying him as an ahosi, and setting him up in a workshop in Abomey with eight wives and eight young apprentices.[20] Significantly, these traditions about the family connections of the kpojito are a departure from earlier ones. In the cases of Adonon and Hwanjile, traditions show the kpojito promoting her own children to positions of prominence (Hwanjile) or responding to slights by her lineage by effective retribution (Adonon). In the case of Agontime and of the kpojito of Glele who followed her, traditions stress the importance of siblings and lineage connections, implying that those connections were what raised the women to importance in the first instance. Agontime, according to Verger's tradition, was a younger sister to an artisan who was very important in the reign of Gezo. In similar fashion, Glele's kpojito was said to have been a younger sister to a chief diviner and advisor to Glele. The impression is given that the women were prominent at court because they were from important families, rather than suggesting the earlier pattern, that their families became important because of the prominence of the kpojito.

The traditions about Gezo's coup and his kpojito also hint ominously of changing popular perceptions of the kpojito and her authority. Visiting some thirty years after Gezo's coup, the English naval commander Frederick Forbes heard a story that purported to explain the deposition of Adandozan. When a candidate for the stool of Jena (a town to the east of Abomey but otherwise not identifiable) fled for protection to Dahomey, Adandozan refused to assist him because his "mother" was from Jena, the implication being that Adandozan's kpojito did not support the would-be chief. At that, "already disgusted with the cruelties of their monarch, [the Dahomean people], with one consent, called his next brother, Gezo, to the throne."[21] Earlier kpojito had been known for protecting their homelands and for advancing or punishing local individuals and kinspeople. Now, in mid–nineteenth century, Forbes was hearing that the interests of the state, or of the Dahomean people, were not to be outweighed by the interests of the Kpojito. The growing hostility to female power as embodied by the Kpojito would continue in the reign of Glele.

Innovations of the Age of Gezo ⟷

Both oral traditions and twentieth-century interpretive histories tend to focus on the age of Gezo as one of remarkable reform, innovation, and accomplishment. Herskovits is typical, introducing Gezo by saying, "With the accession of Gezo . . . the fortunes of the Aladaxonu dynasty rose." Recording oral traditions of the royal family, Le Hérissé asserts that Gezo was second only to Wegbaja in achievements, because "Wegbaja (Oouègbadja) founded Dahomey; Gezo made it free." [22] European accounts, particularly numerous in the English popular press in the 1840–75 period, also contribute to the impression of the centrality of Gezo in the history of Dahomey. By the weight of their numbers and details alone, they give the impression of a kingdom dramatically changed from the eighteenth century and enhance the reputation of Gezo as an innovator. A series of significant political, economic, and cultural changes did take place during the era of Gezo. But it is not clear that Dahomey by the end of the reign of Gezo was that different an entity, and some of the changes may have been in the eyes of the European beholders.

Why, then, is Gezo's reign remembered as so central to the history of Dahomey? A number of factors have conspired to distort, and possibly augment, the importance of the era of Gezo. First, the reign of Gezo appears in oral tradition to have been one of extraordinary length. Adandozan, Gezo's immediate predecessor, was in power for twenty-one years, but his removal from formal histories of the kingdom meant that changes that occurred during the two decades prior to Gezo's coup were attributed to Gezo's reign. In that sense, the period of Gezo looms particularly large in the history of Dahomey for good reason. More than sixty years of Dahomean history—out of a recorded lifetime of the kingdom of fewer than two hundred years—are associated with this king alone. Moreover, the discrediting of Adandozan in the oral history of the kingdom of necessity marks his successor as dramatically different. Gezo becomes the good and noble king who corrected the evils of his despotic predecessor.

The oral descriptions of the kingdom's history that were recorded in the twentieth century were drawn mainly from the siblings and children of Glele, a son of Gezo. As such, they depict Gezo as an illustrious innovator who set the stage for Glele. Gezo and Glele together represent the pinnacles of the glories of Dahomey, glories that are seen as all the more lustrous given the French conquest in the 1890s and the divisions in the royal family that it sparked. From the perspective of the Glele oral traditions, historical time is divided into three periods: a far-distant past at the founding of the kingdom and reign of Wegbaja; a middle-distant past of developments after Wegbaja; and the specifics of the reign of Glele. With the exception of Agaja's conquests to the coast, most major developments of the history of the kingdom are collapsed into the middle period, which is described effectively as the reign of Gezo.

The perceptions of outsiders also had changed significantly by the time of the period of Gezo. As commercial travelers, eighteenth-century European visitors had been concerned with political and economic details that might affect their relationships with the monarchy of Dahomey. By the 1840s, the European political and intellectual climate, particularly in the British homeland of the majority of midcentury visitors, had changed. Imbued with the humanitarian spirit of the first half of the nineteenth century, travelers were obsessed with the need to understand Dahomey in order to reform it, and in particular to end what the British considered to be the dual evils of the slave trade and human sacrifice. Augmenting their humanitarian concerns was the spirit of inquiry associated with the growing interest in scientific exploration. Mid-nineteenth-century visitors thus were insatiably curious about Dahomey and its culture, determined to make observations and record as many details as possible.

Finally, the Dahomean monarchy in the age of Gezo welcomed, indeed courted, contacts with Europeans. Suffering from extreme losses of revenue with the decline in the slave trade, the monarchy was concerned to negotiate, if not a resumption of the slave trade, at least the substitution of other sources of revenue through cooperation with European nations.

But the interest characteristic of the forty years of Gezo's reign went far beyond simple economics, and appears to have been motivated by a genuine interest in European culture and technology and a sincere curiosity about how Dahomey might benefit from the adoption of European ways. That attitude in turn is reflected in the comments of European visitors, who on the whole responded warmly to Gezo and his court and filled their accounts with admiration for the king and with comments on his importance and his accomplishments.

All of these factors work together to enhance and augment the impression of the reign of Gezo as a period of extraordinary vigor in Dahomean history. The problem with the rich historical material on the reign of Gezo, then, is to distinguish when a source is simply fleshing out our understanding of systems in place at an earlier date, and when a traveler or an oral tradition is describing something that in fact did not exist before—that was indeed an innovation of the period of Gezo. Given these interpretive precautions, the period of Gezo is notable for five major changes: the ending of the tributary relationship with Oyo, commemorated in Le Hérissé's reference to Gezo "freeing" Dahomey, and the development of rivalry with the Egba Yoruba city-state of Abeokuta; the cultural impact of the settlement in Dahomey of large numbers of Yoruba-speaking slaves; the replacement of slaves by palm oil as the major commodity of overseas trade; the growth of the palace organization and development of Dahomey's army of women; and the dramatic expansion in ceremonial and court life, that involved factors as seemingly disparate as increased militarism and the invention of ritual. The first change had little to do with initiatives of Gezo's monarchy, but was effectively under way by the time he came to power. The latter four, which are all related to each other, were policy directions taken during the time of Gezo, and can be seen at least in part as responses to continued challenges to the economic viability of the kingdom.

Freedom from Oyo and Rivalry with Abeokuta

The empire of Oyo had begun to collapse at its center even before the turn of the nineteenth century. The 1790s saw the deposition of an unpopular alafin, or king, and the beginnings of provincial rebellions that would culminate by 1817 in a revolt by Muslims inspired by the Fulani jihad to the north. Dahomey had shown resistance to the weakening Oyo as early as the reign of Kpengla and appears to have refused to pay tribute at least at one point during the reign of his successor, Agonglo, thus provoking another Oyo invasion to reestablish the tributary relationship. Resistance to Oyo appears to have continued in the following reign, because a visitor just after the turn of the nineteenth century reported that Adandozan had been "irregular" in paying tribute to Oyo.[23]

The final break came shortly after the deposition of Adandozan from the stool of Dahomey. Facing an Oyo further weakened by the Muslim revolt, Dahomey provoked war in 1823, possibly by refusing to pay tribute. Defeating Oyo forces in two separate engagements, the Dahomeans by the mid-1820s had effectively ended their tributary status. The reality was not so much that Dahomey had grown strong as that Oyo had begun to disintegrate. Indeed, the first two decades of Gezo's reign roughly coincided with a period of intense internal warfare in Yorubaland, which culminated in the sacking of the capital city of Oyo in 1837. During those years, the constant fighting in the area that had been the empire of Oyo created thousands of refugees. These displaced persons flooded southwards, establishing new cities that in turn forced the restructuring of relationships among states all the way to the coast. Other victims of the unrest became captives to be sold abroad, and coastal slave markets were swamped with Yoruba-speaking slaves.

For Dahomey, the changed military-political relationship meant that for the immediate future, areas to the east, northeast, and southeast of Abomey that had formerly been protected by Oyo would be vulnerable to Dahomean attack. Moreover, freed from the threat of incursions from Oyo on the Abomey plateau, the Dahomeans could turn their attention to enemies elsewhere. Early in the reign of Gezo, wars were waged in Mahi country to the north and in Gbe-speaking and Akan-speaking areas to the southwest. With the Yoruba kingdoms of Ketu and Sabe to the east relatively strong, the Dahomeans then turned their attention to the southeast, where the Egbado Yoruba area was politically fragmented and lay vulnerable to raids. By that time, they found that a new rival, Abeokuta, had begun to establish its interests in precisely the same area.

Abeokuta had been forged by Egba Yoruba who had been driven

southwards from their homelands with the disintegration of Oyo. Many Egba had settled temporarily in the new city of Ibadan, but had ultimately moved westward to an easily defended site on the Ogun River. The Abeokutans looked to the west and south for land and access to the sea, seeing Egbadoland as their natural corridor, and Badagry, to the east of Porto Novo, their port. An important feature of the development of Abeokuta during the period of Gezo was the arrival there of numbers of Egba Yoruba who had been sold into the overseas trade. Liberated from slave ships by the British and landed in Sierra Leone, many acquired European trade skills and converted to Christianity before deciding to return to Yorubaland. Having made their way inland from Badagry to Abeokuta, these returnees paved the way for the arrival of British missionaries in the 1840s. The missionaries in turn assisted the Egba in their political and military struggles, particularly with Dahomey, by providing ammunition and obtaining military advisors when Dahomey threatened.

By the 1840s, Abeokuta had become a major rival and dominant preoccupation of the Dahomean monarchy. A series of nearly-annual military encounters between Dahomey and the Egba, including an ambush of the Dahomean army in 1844 that led to the capture of royal regalia, turned Abeokuta into an archenemy. Dahomey would eventually attack the fortified city of Abeokuta directly on two occasions, in 1851 and 1864, and both times it would be badly beaten. Meanwhile, though, the deluge of slave-victims of the breakup of Oyo and the constant warfare against the Egba and other Yoruba-speaking peoples were yielding a massive population of captives, too large to be absorbed into Fon culture. Their presence in Dahomey was to have a deep and lasting impact on the kingdom.

Yoruba Cultural Influence

Yoruba culture, through tributary contacts with Oyo, had had an impact on Dahomey in the mid–eighteenth century during the reign of Tegbesu. At that period, Oyo influence was felt at the highest levels of the state, as the monarchy created offices and organizational structures that appear to have been inspired by familiarity with the court of Oyo. In contrast, during the reign of Gezo, Yoruba influence was widely diffused throughout

Fon society, directly affecting even remote areas of the Abomey plateau and working its way upward to the highest decision-making levels of the monarchy. It was carried by the thousands of Yoruba-speaking captives sold or captured into slavery in the chaos of the collapse of the Oyo empire.

The Yoruba migration into Dahomey was not only related to the decline of Oyo but also to changes in the overseas trade that were beyond the control of the monarchy. By the time Gezo came to power, the slave trade had been officially abandoned by the major European slaving powers, though the illegal trade flourished. Over the four decades of Gezo's reign, the British were systematically attempting to suppress the slave trade by other states, setting up an antislavery squadron on the West African coast to capture and free cargoes of slaves and entering into treaties with other European nations in hopes of stopping the trade. Ultimately, they began sending envoys to heads of African governments to the same end. By the 1840s, Dahomey began to be visited by a stream of emissaries with treaties and proposals for the ending of the export of slaves and the replacement of the slave trade with "legitimate commerce," which in the case of Dahomey would prove to be trade in oil-palm products.

The Dahomeans resisted stopping the overseas slave trade. Nevertheless, despite occasional spurts of strength, it in fact declined steeply in volume during the first half of the nineteenth century. Meanwhile, the civil chaos in Yorubaland and Dahomey's own wars against her neighbors continued to yield large numbers of captives. With the overseas trade no longer a viable outlet for the bulk of the prisoners, larger numbers of captives were settled in the kingdom.

Captives had been settled in earlier periods in and around Abomey. Families, even entire villages, can today recount the circumstances of their resettlement on the Abomey plateau under particular monarchs. Some, like the Akan-speaking village of brass casters at Hoja, less than four miles from the center of Abomey, maintained a distinct artisan tradition, along with vestiges of the language and culture of their areas of origin. Like Dahomeans of Fon origin, they owed tribute in goods and services to a court official, usually a member of the monarchy; otherwise, their communities were effectively self-governing. Many other captives were integrated into Fon society as individuals, placed as wives or slaves in farming villages or urban households, where they adapted themselves to the language and culture of the dominant society.

Because of its massive volume, the new Yoruba influx into Dahomey was of a different nature, heralding dramatic changes in Fon culture itself. Initially, large numbers of Yoruba-speaking captives were retained near the coast by Afro-Brazilian traders expanding their operations into palm-oil production. By the 1840s, communities of Yoruba-speaking captives were also visible on the Abomey plateau. In rural areas, they were concentrated in plantations that ultimately became known for the cultivation of oil palms. In Abomey itself, they became the nucleus of a quarter of the city that has maintained an identity as an enclave of Yoruba culture up to the present day. Many more Yoruba-speaking persons were integrated into Dahomean families, where they began to have a dramatic impact as culture brokers.

Initially, the settlement of Yoruba captives on plantations may have been intended to be temporary, to employ slaves until they might be sent to Whydah for shipment overseas. Over time, and possibly as the commercial production of palm oil developed, the plantations became a permanent part of the Dahomean cultural landscape. The first such plantation on the Abomey plateau that was mentioned in European sources was Lefu Lefu, named for an Egba village attacked by the Dahomeans in 1843. The old and weak were killed after the attack, and probably some of the less firm were brought back for use as royal sacrifices. Healthy young people of both sexes, however, were settled near the road between Cana and Abomey on a plantation "under the direction of a Dahoman cabooceer." Frederick Forbes heard of the plantation in 1849 and described it glowingly as a place for cultivation of palms and corn, "justly remarkable for the superiority of its cultivation and the industry of its denizens." [24]

Forbes's enthusiasm for Lefu Lefu was likely prompted by his desire to see Dahomey replace the slave trade with commerce in palm products, because other such plantations were less appealing. To the southwest of the city, along the east bank of the Coufo River, was the most infamous of the plantations, Afomai. With a name that meant literally "no foot (i.e., person) is allowed there," Afomai was forbidden to Dahomeans and became popularly dreaded as a place where no one went willingly and from which few returned. The numbers of plantations continued to grow through the second half of the nineteenth century. Le Hérissé was able to collect the names of six slave camps a decade after the fall of the kingdom. At the time of the French conquest in 1892, much of the territory to the southeast of Abomey was farmed by slaves, who resided during the dry season at Goho, an area on the outskirts of the city. And Afomai was still in operation, being worked by some one thousand slaves.[25]

In urban Dahomey, skilled Yoruba-speaking artisans became prominent during the reign of Gezo. It is not clear whether they settled voluntarily as refugees from the constant warfare in the wake of Oyo's end, or whether they were part of the captive population taken by Dahomean armies. Earlier monarchies had patronized artisans, including Yoruba-speaking persons, settling them with gifts of wives and slaves, usually in the section of Abomey developed for the descendants and courtiers of their king. Among others in the period, the Yemadje family of appliqué artisans, who arrived during the reign of Agonglo, flourished under the patronage of Gezo. Appliqué artistry was not mentioned by eighteenth-century visitors at court, but it was prominent by the 1840s as decoration for umbrellas, tents, and army uniforms.

The monarchy of Gezo became known for the expanded scale at which it recruited artisans to the capital and for its characteristic use of the idiom of marriage to describe that recruitment, making the newly settled artisans ahosi, technically wives of the king. Indeed, a large portion of the population of Becon Hounli, the quarter settled by retainers of Gezo, today claims to descend from ancestors who were brought through the payment of "bridewealth" by that king. The Azali section of Abomey includes some of the quarter's most prominent smiths, who appear to have promoted the fortunes of the Yoruba god of iron, Ogun, renamed Gu in Dahomey. Gu was associated with the growing militarism of Dahomey during the period of Gezo and was honored through his commemoration in a famous iron sculpture of a god in human form, his hat bristling with the iron implements associated with the power of metal. The statue of Gu, which was taken by the French in the 1890s and ultimately made its way to the collection of Paris's Musée de l'Homme, is said to have been crafted by the founder of a prominent Yoruba-speaking lineage, a smith named Akati. Akati in fact is an example of the upward mobility of these same Yoruba-speaking Abomeans. Said to have originally been sent to Afomai, where he smelted iron, he (or a descendant) was brought to Azali to practice smithing. An Akati ultimately became a member of the monarchy of Gezo, serving as gau, minister of war, before he died in the 1851 assault on the walls of Abeokuta.[26]

Other Yoruba ritual and spiritual traditions began to flourish, in part through the agency of women who had been absorbed into Dahomean families as wives. Large numbers of girls and young women captured in war were incorporated into the palace organization. Many of the younger ones, dubbed *sudofi*, "brought up here," were trained to become members of the palace guard or standing army of women. Others became the gift-wives for princes, princesses, officials of the king, or other high-ranking persons. By their large numbers, those Yoruba-speaking wives and mothers to Dahomean children were in a position to influence the next generation with their cultural traditions, and specifically the sons and daughters of Gezo who came to constitute, nearly exclusively, the monarchy of Glele. For example, the presence of the secret societies Oro and Egungun are dated by Abomeans to the period of Gezo. Egungun, which may be the first masking society to have been permitted in Dahomey, was renamed Kutito (from ghost, or literally dead one from the other world). Its twentieth-century costuming—narrow-band loom strips of appliquéed fabric accompanied by drums suspended from the shoulder—link it to Oyo traditions. Even prominent Afro-Brazilian families in Whydah note a transformation of their Luso-Catholic culture during this period, adopting Kutito and Oro, as well as numerous Yoruba deities, thanks to women brought into families as slave-wives.[27]

Diviners of Fa (Ifa in Yorubaland) were also becoming more prominent in this period. Though Fa had been known in Dahomey since the 1720s, it came slowly to prominence at the level of the monarchy. Tegbesu had been the first king to receive his *kpoli*, that is to begin the process of knowing his destiny. By the time of Gezo, there were an estimated dozen *bokonon*, or diviners, in the service of the king. During Glele's reign, when bokonon became the chief personal advisers to the king, selected children of the king himself were being sent to Yorubaland to train as diviners in the families of their mothers.

Along with the existence of distinct settlements of Yoruba-speakers, there is some suggestion of social tensions between the newcomers and the Fon. Ironically, then, even while Fon culture was being transformed by Yoruba institutions, there appears to have been a distancing of individual Yoruba-speakers from those who considered themselves to be true Dahomeans. Twentieth-century oral traditions, which were based on nineteenth-century realities, describe three legal statuses in Dahomean society: the *ahovi*, the children or descendants of the kings; the *anato*, free commoners; and the *kannumon*, or slaves. Though rank might change over the life of an individual, a person's legal status remained ahovi, anato, or kannumon. In fact, there were variations within each category that worked to disadvantage some individuals. Children born of kannumon were normally considered to be anato; however, some kannumon had become slaves in perpetuity. For example, *glesi* (literally, wife or dependent of cultivated land) were persons attached to landholdings in a manner comparable to European serfs; they were part of the estates granted by the kings to members of the royal family and to kpojito. Particularly associated with oil-palm cultivation, glesi kept a portion of their harvests, giving the remainder to their patron. *Gandoba* were slave-women controlled by the palace. Granted to male and female retainers of the king, gandoba would be married to a man of their owner's choice. Their male children became members of their owner's line; female children returned to the palace as gandoba. Evidence from the Dosso-Yovo family of Whydah similarly indicates that slave status could bring status disadvantage over more than one generation. Children of Yoruba captives granted to the family were made into soldiers, a practice that was common also in other prominent Whydah families. Each of these families had a war chief of Yoruba slave origins to lead their family army when it was called up for war.[28]

Ethnic tensions are suggested, too, in traditions of the Hountondji smiths, who clearly saw themselves as rivals to the Yoruba newcomers. Oral traditions of the Hountondji stress the antiquity of their roots in Dahomey, arguing that they were brought from Allada at the behest of

King Agaja, shortly after the conquest of that city-state in 1724, in order to be the preeminent makers of weapons for the Alladahonu. Embroidering a myth associated with the conquest of Whydah, a myth that almost certainly dates to a much later period than the 1720s, the Hountondji claim that they were involved in saving the day when the Dahomeans attacked the Hweda of Whydah. The myth is that of the princess, Na Geze (chapter 2, pp. 59–60), who helped her father Agaja in his attack on Whydah by learning why guns purchased from the Europeans at the coast failed to work. Na Geze arranged to steal the hammers that had been removed by the Hwedas to keep the flintlocks from operating properly. In the Hountondji version, it was Hountondji smiths who reset those hammers. Certainly by the nineteenth century, and probably before, the Hountondji smiths had become better known as the leading silversmiths and jewelers to the kings. Nevertheless, the Hountondji insist on their importance as makers of royal weaponry and as the most important of the smithing lineages of the capital.

The inability of Dahomey fully to absorb so many of the new Yoruba immigrants presented a real danger to the kingdom's security. From the 1840s, Dahomey looked mainly to the Yoruba-speaking east for targets of war. Many of the new captives in Dahomey would have had friends and relatives in areas marked for war. The existence of distinctive and large communities of Yoruba peoples, many of whom had been marginalized within the Dahomean social system, left the kingdom vulnerable to reactions and revolt. In 1855, a traveler reported that a conspiracy had been uncovered: the Egbas were about to attack with the assistance of people enslaved at Whydah and other Yoruba slaves owned by "natives in other parts of the country."[29] Whether the danger was real or imagined, the panic that ensued underlined the problem of keeping large numbers of a potentially hostile population marginalized within the kingdom. The Yoruba influx of the nineteenth century, then, appears to have increased certain social tensions, even as it enriched Fon culture.

The Trade in Palm Products

Although the slave trade had technically been made illegal on an international level by the time Gezo took power, the demand for slaves in the

United States, Cuba, and Brazil continued until the effective abolition of slavery in the Western Hemisphere, between 1860 and 1890. At the same time, schemes for the purchase of slaves through thinly disguised requests for "indentured" workers or "free laborers" were proposed and enthusiastically accepted from time to time up until the consolidation of colonial control in the mid-1890s. The French in the late 1850s, for example, competed against U.S. and Spanish American slave traders to obtain "free emigrants" to be transported to French possessions. The Portuguese in the late 1880s took several thousand "indentured laborers" to São Tomé, and the Germans in the early 1890s helped to arm King Behanzin against the French by trading guns and ammunition for "laborers" to work in their colony of Cameroon.

From the perspective of the kingdom, then, the overseas slave trade in the nineteenth century became a less and less viable source of income, but it did not end definitively. By midcentury, there were periods when no buyers arrived along the coast, but the demand for persons to be shipped overseas continued to revive right up to the conquest of the kingdom by the French. The monarchy went to relatively great lengths to ensure that avenues remained open to permit the export of slaves as opportunities arose. Thus it would prove an ironic twist, and perhaps a form of poetic justice, that in early 1894 the last captives taken off Dahomean shores for involuntary transport to the Western Hemisphere were Behanzin and the vestiges of his court: five wives, a son, the prince who was his best friend, and several servants.

Intent upon stamping out the overseas slave trade, British policy ignored the ramifications of what continued to be an active internal commerce in slaves. Thus the British encouraged the palm-oil trade, a supposedly "legitimate" product for overseas trade, but one that of necessity had to be produced, at least in part, by slave labor. In Dahomey the development of production in labor-intensive palm products provided a substitute outlet for the captives taken in war and the slaves traded into Dahomey.

By the 1840s, factors had begun to set up shop in Whydah and elsewhere along the coast to encourage the export of palm-oil products. Palm oil had been a subsidiary product in the overseas trade since the late eighteenth century. Its development as a product of commercial agriculture and major export occurred relatively quickly between 1840 and 1860. Afro-Brazilian slave traders appear initially to have cultivated coastal plantations of palm trees and staffed them with slaves awaiting transport overseas. Francisco Félix de Souza is generally credited with influencing the monarchy to encourage oil products in the early 1840s through a series of administrative decrees that effectively promoted palm oil as a commercial crop. For example, undergrowth was to be cleared from around young trees, which enlarged their yield and protected them when fields were burned before the planting of other crops. The felling of trees for palm wine was prohibited, and oil palms were declared sacred and hence protected from destruction. Despite the administrative interest in promoting the oil trade, the monarchy showed little interest initially in commercial agriculture for itself, leaving palm-oil production to the Afro-Brazilians, to the Saros (freed slaves returned from Sierra Leone), and to small Dahomean producers. It was only in the 1850s that the monarchy moved definitively to begin to produce palm oil for the export trade. By the end of that decade, the production and trade in palm products was such that the quantity of palm oil exported from Dahomey was as high as it would be in the 1890s.[30]

Twentieth-century historians agree that the transition from slave to palm products meant an effective lessening of the economic strength of the monarchy. In comparison with the overseas slave trade, the trade in oil-palm products had distinct economic disadvantages for the Abomey monarchy. First, since most slaves were "produced" through warfare, the slave trade required the organization of large raiding parties with access to firearms, which made it relatively easy for a state to monitor, tax, and control. In contrast, the production of palm oil was rather democratic, suited not only to large plantations but also to small producers who could and did bring their produce directly to Atlantic ports like Whydah, and who might avoid attempts by a state to expropriate a portion of the product of their labor. There is for example evidence for Porto Novo of the inability of chiefs and other would-be middlemen to control the collection and sale of the oil to coastal shippers.[31]

Slaves could be marched to the coast, thus incurring only the cost of their maintenance before sale. Large-scale production of palm oil, on the other hand, required carriers, whose loads were limited to five-gallon clay containers and who had to be maintained during a roundtrip journey to a port. The commercial production of palm products thus favored producers located near the coast, or at least near a navigable waterway, giving a great advantage to the coastal communities that the monarchy had long distrusted. And unlike slaves, who metaphorically could be plucked like ripe fruit from their home villages, albeit with the use of force, palm oil was produced through means that were highly labor-intensive. Two historians, Patrick Manning and John Reid, have independently calculated the implications of the intensity of labor required to produce and transport oil in Dahomey. Manning estimates that the production of a ton of oil required some 315 workdays of processing from seventeen tons of palm fruit bunches (roughly ten tons of fruit). One ton of kernels, produced by cracking open the nuts after the oil had been extracted from the fruit, required an additional 167 workdays. Reid reckons that portage of a ton of oil from the Abomey area to the coast would have involved another 420 workdays. He suggests that the production of two thousand tons of oil from the Abomey region would have involved the full-time work of about ten thousand slaves during the six months of the year when oil was usually harvested and processed. Taking a dramatic midcentury inflation of the cowry currency into account, he calculates that by the 1860s a ton of palm oil produced in the Abomey area by slave labor and transported to Whydah would have incurred production costs of £18 7s. 6d. and been sold for £22 10s.[32] Even under the best conditions, profit margins from the sale of palm products could not begin to approach the levels of the slave trade, and it is no wonder that the monarchy showed little enthusiasm for commercial agriculture.

Not only was the palm-oil trade far less profitable than the slave trade, but Dahomey's continued interest in warring and raiding for slaves in the late nineteenth century may have interfered with commercial agriculture. Where attacks were made, warfare disrupted trade routes, the argument goes. War also drew people away from home during the dry season, November through March, the usual period for palm-oil harvesting and processing, though the fruit can be harvested year-round. Elsewhere, and in the twentieth-century colony of Dahomey, palm-oil processing was a dry-season complement to the growing of food crops; in that sense,

warring for the slave trade did disrupt the entire farming cycle. Nevertheless, the question of whether or not the two trades were mutually exclusive is debatable. Certainly in the early years, the Afro-Brazilians
found the slave and oil trades to be complementary, because together
they permitted slaves to be usefully employed until an opportunity to slip
them off shore and into the clandestine trade might arise.[33] From the
monarchy's perspective, a similar complementarity is evident. Slaves
could be kept on plantations and, in the brief periods when slave trading
revived, they could be sent to Whydah and other embarkation points.
Certainly warfare at times did interrupt trade routes and prevent oil from
being carried to the coast, most notably when war was waged south of
the Lama swamp. But as the century passed, that sometimes became the
point—to interfere with the processing and sale of oil by others. Processing of oil during the rainy season did in fact put extra labor burdens
on Dahomean farmers and, as we shall see, had an impact on the division
of labor by gender. But there may have been other rationales for it. For
example, rainy-season processing would have eased the difficulty of making palm oil on the Abomey plateau. With no rivers, lakes, or natural
sources of ground water, there were and continue to be serious shortages
of water during the dry season. Since large amounts of water were required for the processing of palm oil, it made sense to process oil between
the end of March and September, when water was far more plentiful
around Abomey.

Despite the difficulties of production and transport, by midcentury
the monarchy had begun to establish palm plantations on the Abomey
plateau. Slave villages for agricultural production had been established
regularly in Dahomey for more than a hundred years, but presumably
preserved the division of labor by gender that obtained more broadly in
farming in the region. Large-scale production of oil-palm products, however, had labor requirements that may have necessitated a change in gender roles required of slaves controlled by the monarchy. Male captives
possibly were being forced to process palm oil, something that was considered to be women's work and was viewed with contempt by Yoruba-
speaking men. This characteristic of palm-oil production—that it was
considered to be women's work—was to have important social and economic implications for nineteenth-century Dahomey.[34]

Typically, men climbed the palm trees and cut the bunches of red fruit. Women did virtually everything else to produce palm oil: carry the clusters of fruit to a processing point, boil them in water, trample the fruit to remove the nuts from the oil-bearing pericarp, separate the nuts and fiber from the trampled pulp and squeeze the oil out of the pulp, skim the oil off the top of the water and then extract even more oil from the pulp. The collected oil had to be boiled to separate out impurities and residual water. Finally, the nuts were dried and cracked to remove the palm kernels, which were also exportable, though they were not initially a part of the trade.[35]

But the processing of palm oil was far from the sum total of women's work in Dahomey. Besides the cooking, cleaning, child care, gathering of firewood, and fetching of water that were usual home-centered tasks for women, they were centrally involved in agriculture. Accounts of the gender division of labor in farming are reasonably consistent from the late seventeenth to the twentieth century. Men were instrumental in clearing fields and planting; women tended the crops and harvested. Hoeing appears to have been women's work in the precolonial period, but was done only by men by the early twentieth century.[36] In addition, women were cited as traders in markets from the earliest records, and by mid–nineteenth century were also frequently seen working as long-distance porters. Obviously, not every woman worked at all these occupations. It is unlikely, for example, that women who hired out as porters also processed palm oil for sale. It is not clear if market women were selling only oil and other products made by themselves and their dependents, or whether they were urban-based, full-time traders acting as middlemen between producers and exporters.

Nevertheless, given the labor intensity of palm-oil production, combined with the expectations of women's work in other areas, the introduction of the export trade in palm products has to have heralded a massive increase in demand for the labor of women. Moreover, that demand for increased women's labor came at the end of two hundred years of overall decline in population in the area of Dahomey. The new situation had significant gender implications. Because palm products could be manufactured on a small scale, women who had processed palm oil for domestic consumption prior to the opening of the trade may have seen it as a new source of cash income. They could expand their own personal production, because women—married or single, free or slave—had the right to amass personal wealth outside the control of the person on whom they depended. Indeed, travelers at midcentury testified to numbers of women selling small quantities of oil to European factors.[37] At another level, the trade had implications, and opportunities, for entre-preneurial women who might be able to mobilize the labor of other women—women who owned many female slaves, or women who were head wives in large households. Yet even women with extra resources had obligations to the person—husband or lineage head—upon whom they depended. Thus it did not necessarily follow that the production of palm oil would make women as a category more powerful, or even necessarily more wealthy. With a reduced population, and with women's work a key to success, the question became one of who controlled large numbers of women and their labor. A woman or man who could control the labor of women, or the labor of male slaves who could be forced to do women's work, could become a major player in the trade in oil products. That presumably was the impetus, along with the insecurity of markets for slaves at the coast, that prompted the establishment of plantations of slave laborers—female and male—on the Abomey plateau.

The Growth of the Palace and Development of the Army of Women

From the perspective of the monarchy, women by mid–nineteenth century had become more important, not because they could become allies or partners in the building of a state but because their labor could enrich those who controlled it, just as the slaves captured in the eighteenth century enriched those who sold them. Moreover, because the oil trade was less easily controlled than the slave trade, the talents of entrepreneurial women who might become independently wealthy through the trade needed to be channeled into the support of the monarchy. By the 1840s, the story of Dahomey becomes one more fully concerned with attempts by the monarchy to control access to women, and to monopolize both their talents and their labor. Those attempts were manifest at the level of the palace organization. Perhaps an indication of the success of the monarchy in controlling the best of Dahomey's women and channeling their energies to its uses was provided during my field experience as I searched for stories of prominent women in the kingdom. I found that virtually all of the women remembered in the region of Abomey for their importance or riches were either ahosi or princesses; conversely, people along the coast would describe independent wealthy women, and particularly women involved in the palm-oil trade, women of Mina and Yoruba origins who carried on their work in the nineteenth century in areas peripheral to the core of the kingdom.

Estimates of the population of Dahomey were always highly speculative, and estimates of the numbers of women within the palace organization, hidden from public view by massive mud walls, were even more subject to question. Nevertheless, there appears to have been a dramatic growth in the size of the palace population during the nineteenth century. A 1724 visitor claimed there were "at least" two thousand women in the palace, an estimate that was increased to between three thousand and four thousand by the turn of the nineteenth century. By mid–nineteenth century, some five thousand to six thousand women were said to inhabit the palace. A French mission to Dahomey in 1889 estimated the Abomey palace population at seven thousand to eight thousand. Those figures were echoed by Le Hérissé, who lived in Abomey shortly after the fall of the kingdom and insisted that a figure of more than eight thousand persons in the palace in the second half of the nineteenth century was not the least exaggerated.[38] If population estimates of 150,000 to 200,000 for the kingdom as a whole are correct for the late nineteenth century, then the palace organization may have included fully 4 to 5 percent of the entire population of the kingdom.

Many of the inhabitants of the expanded palace were Yoruba captives. But the recruitment of Dahomean women into the king's service also appears to have become significantly more systematic in the nineteenth century. Writing in the 1760s, Pommegorge had claimed that each commoner family was required to offer a daughter as tribute to the king. A century later, visitors were told that the Gezo monarchy had required "every Dahoman of note" to present his daughters, and that they then placed them in the palace in accordance with the class structure of the kingdom. The king "selected the most promising of the children of the upper ten [percent], and created them officers, while the lower orders were dubbed soldiers, and the children of slave parents became the slaves of the Amazons within the palace." During Glele's reign, a court official, the kpakpa, traveled around the countryside to visit villages at three-year intervals and select girls for service to the monarchy. An account provided by a contemporary Abomean family hints that the visits were not welcome: "The king's representatives came and took daughters. The whole family would be assembled and the head of the family would be asked three times in succession, are there more children in the house? After hearing a negative reply three times, the king's people took a drink prepared by the ajaho [minister of religion] and gave it to a chicken. If the chicken crowed, no children were hidden; if the chicken died, a search would be made and the girls hidden would be taken." The head of another family, based in Zagnanado on the eastern frontier of nineteenth-century Dahomey, recalled the traditional means of greeting royalty—kneeling and throwing the dirt of the courtyard over one's head and shoulders. For him, rather than receiving bridewealth in return for losing a daughter to Abomey, one received "dust on your head." [39]

In 1850 Forbes was told, but did not believe, that Gezo no longer permitted women to be sacrifice victims. Twenty years later, Skertchly noted that, although women were sometimes presented along with the men slated for sacrifice, he "never heard of a woman being decapitated as an offering." He learned that one of the six major laws of Dahomey was that women were not to leave the country, which indicates both the relative importance and the scarcity of women in the late Dahomean state. [40] The transition toward more confiscatory means of drawing women into the service of the monarchy paralleled other administrative changes that would make the monarchy an increasingly repressive government as the century wore on.

Meanwhile, though, the activities of the ahosi women residents of the various palaces of Dahomey were becoming more visible to visitors. Of all the king's women, travelers would spill the most ink over the women soldiers. The king's female bodyguard and palace troops had existed for nearly a century prior to Gezo's reign, and his coup had been resisted by the female palace guard. In the aftermath, the monarchy was faced with a classic decision: whether to suppress the palace troops that had opposed the coup or to reform it into a force loyal to the new regime. Gezo's monarchy chose the latter course, but then did far more than simply work to ensure the loyalty of the palace corps; rather, they added to the palace guard an elite standing army of women that was better equipped, disciplined, and trained than that of the men. By the 1840s, Freeman reported that Dahomey's women soldiers "excell in martial appearance any body of native troops I have ever seen." John Duncan echoed the sentiment, calling them "all well armed, and generally fine strong healthy women, and doubtless capable of enduring great fatigue . . . their appearance is more martial than the generality of the men; and if undertaking a campaign, I should prefer the females to the male soldiers of this country." [41]

A certain uniformity of dress for the palace guard had been noted by late-eighteenth-century visitors. Now both the women's army and the men's, appeared in uniforms. "They wear a blue and white striped cotton surtout, the stripes about one and a half inch wide, of stout native manufacture, *without sleeves*, leaving freedom for the arms. The skirt or tunic reaches as low as the kilt of the Highlanders. A pair of short trowsers is worn underneath, reaching two inches below the knee. The cartouche-box [cartridge belt], or *agbwadya*, forms a girdle, and keeps all their dress snug and close." [42] The wearing of pants gave the soldiers freedom of movement, and was as unusual for Dahomean women as below-the-knee shorts would have been for European women of the day. The tunic top most likely was drawn from Yoruba culture, but was tailored to avoid bulkiness that could hamper movement. Companies were distinguished by emblems appliquéd to caps worn by the women. Three midcentury insignia, for example, were a crocodile, a cross, and a crown. These were parade uniforms. In the field, the fighting women wore shorts and tunics of brown fabric, presumably manufactured of locally grown and woven cotton. Their bodies were adorned with protective charms, "necklaces, projecting *glorias* of brown monkey skins, quantities of fetish beads, talismans and other decorations." [43]

The infantry were the most numerous of the women soldiers. Best armed of any Dahomean troops, the women soldiers used their firearms in the European manner, aiming and shooting from the shoulder, while at least some of the male troops continued to fire from the hip. A visitor in the early 1860s watched a demonstration of shooting at targets, and was particularly impressed when "the King's body-guard of Amazons distinguished themselves by their good shots." The women's infantry were described as carrying a variety of arms: Danish muskets and short swords in the 1840s; carbines, trade guns, and short sabers in the 1850s; and Tower muskets, also known as the Brown Bess, in the 1860s. Like those of other African armies of the nineteenth century, the Dahomean firearms were often of lesser quality than those of European armies, and the Dahomeans were aware of their deficiencies. After hearing complaints by the crown prince, Hahansu (Ahanhanzo), about the quality of imported guns, a visitor in 1871 admitted dryly that "the trade guns of which he spoke are Birmingham manufactured articles . . . but as they can be purchased retail for seven shillings and sixpence, their finish is not the acme of perfection." [44] Moreover, the arms sold in Africa were at best the weapons of the previous generation of European armies, and at worst, guns that were long obsolete in Europe. The Brown Bess, for example, went out of service among British forces between 1839 and 1848. Nevertheless, by late in the century, women sharpshooters would be able to threaten invading French troops.

Beyond the infantry, there were additional specialized corps, each of which was distinguished by unusual arms or functions and made public appearances without fail on ceremonial occasions in Abomey. Most striking were the women soldiers dubbed "razor women" by visitors. They carried a weapon, said to have been designed by a brother of Gezo, that was modeled on the straight-edged razor of nineteenth-century Europe, with a blade described by visitors in lengths ranging from eighteen inches to more than three feet. Like the razor on which it was based, the blade snapped into a wooden carrying cover. The whole apparatus weighed more than twenty pounds and prompted Burton to comment with characteristic sarcasm that "the terror which they inspire may render them useful." A company of archers paraded regularly, too. A visitor in the mid-1850s claimed that they were chosen from "among the young virgin daughters of the best families of the kingdom." Observers believed they were not used in combat. Burton claimed that the archers were used in the field only as scouts, porters, and carriers of the wounded, and Skertchly, visiting eight years later, reported that they were mainly a "show corps."[45]

Visitors at midcentury also reported seeing women armed with blunderbusses, a weapon that had been popular in the eighteenth century in Europe. Blunderbusses had a fearsome reputation in their day because of the erroneous belief that the belled muzzle would scatter shot in all directions, a belief that was likely sold along with the weapons to African purchasers. Blunderbusses were designed to be fired at close range; as such they were suited to the Dahomean style of warfare. Moreover, their wide bores made them easy to reload quickly. Even though they were impossible to aim accurately because of the shortness of the muzzle, more than one writer has commented on the powerful psychological impact of staring into the gaping maw of a blunderbuss muzzle, an impact that was presumably not lost on the Dahomeans and their enemies. But in Europe, the blunderbuss, like the other arms used by the Dahomean infantry, had given way to more accurate and effective arms, in this case by the 1840s.

Much was also made of the company of elephant hunters, who were reportedly particularly husky women. Le Hérissé offers what must have been a commonly repeated story, that the corps of women warriors had evolved from palace women who were elephant hunters during the reign of Wegbaja. The story is unlikely, since elephants had been absent from areas south of the Abomey plateau in the seventeenth century and had reappeared only at the end of the eighteenth, as the human population declined. In Gezo's day, elephant hunting was done during the dry season in the Lama swampland by women hunters "under the charge of a eunuch, but immediately under the command of an amazon officer." The meat was consumed during ceremonies in Abomey and the skulls and bones were salvaged for ritual purposes. The tusks made their way to Europe through Whydah. Forbes reported in 1850 that the hunters targeted the youngest elephants, which may explain why a dozen years later all the elephants had been hunted out of Dahomey proper. By the 1870s, the few remaining elephants in the hills of Mahi country to the north were in the process of being decimated by the Dahomean hunters.[46]

Although large numbers of the palace population had as their occupation that of professional soldier, there is no way to estimate their numbers precisely. Nineteenth-century observers tended to refer to the entire palace population as "amazons." Moreover, a ceremonial fiction played out during Customs held that everyone in the population of the nation was a warrior, which further confuses the issue of who actually fought. In the mid-1840s, the female troops were said to number five thousand to six thousand, prior to Dahomey's disastrous 1851 attack on the Yoruba city of Abeokuta, when they lost from one thousand to two thousand. In the early 1860s, an epidemic of smallpox and the second fruitless attack on Abeokuta again thinned the ranks of the women's army, and estimates of their numbers for the remainder of the reign of Glele range from fifteen hundred to three thousand. Part of the difficulty of knowing the numbers of ahosi in the standing army lies in the manner by which the armed forces were assembled for war, the old system having been preserved: the king's standing army continued to be supplemented by contingents offered by chiefs, officials, and other prominent individuals. Now, though, both the standing army and the forces called up for war included women along with men.[47]

By fully incorporating women into both the standing and draft forces, the Dahomeans had gone full circle. Warfare and weaponry, tradition maintained, had originated with farmers who used their hoe handles to fight enemies who surprised them in their fields. In ancient times, entire communities—men and women—had risen up to defend their lands and their lives. In like manner, by mid–nineteenth century, the entire nation of Dahomey rose up annually for war. The idea of farmers abandoning their fields when called to war was enshrined in a weapon paraded by women soldiers in the 1870s—red-colored guns with brass hoes fixed like bayonets to their muzzles.[48]

There were ironies in the use of farming and fighting metaphors. Farming, and particularly the labor-intensive work of weeding, harvesting, and processing agricultural produce, was women's work. The war songs of the women soldiers played on farming imagery, contrasting the drudgery of farm work with the glories of soldiering. Two war songs that have been preserved underline the women soldiers' freedom from farm labor:

> We are digging up, turning over, plowing up our spirit. Let the men harvest the manioc!
> We are digging up, turning over, plowing up our spirit. Let the men harvest the manioc!
> Until our mouth opens to swallow the calabash, the bloody way will remain bloody.
> We are digging up, turning over, plowing up our spirit. Let the men harvest the manioc! [49]

> Men, men, stay!
> Let the men stay at home!
> Let them grow maize
> and cultivate palm trees. . . .
> We, we will go to war.
> We march, our swords forward!
> They form around the kingdom
> a high, high rampart,
> As high as the mountain of the Mahis.
> We are going to plow the entrails of the enemy. [50]

Gezo, possibly using intentional irony, extended the metaphor in his arguments with British envoys who sought a Dahomean commitment to the end of the slave trade. On more than one occasion the king pleaded that "my people are a military people, male and female. . . . I cannot send my women to cultivate the soil, it would kill them." [51]

To be a woman soldier circa 1850 was a position of some prestige, yet paradoxically one that many women would have tried to avoid. Many if not most women soldiers were captives, indicating that Dahomean girls as a rule managed to avoid their ranks. Rumor had it that Dahomean men would offer recalcitrant wives to the king for his army; other soldiers were said to have been convicted criminals. Myths swirled around the women warriors and continued to grow long after their companies were disbanded. Their sexuality was said to have been strictly controlled through required celibacy, prompting more than one male writer to link the women's ferocity to their lack of sexual fulfillment.[52] Recently, it has even been claimed that they underwent clitoridectomy, presumably to control their sexual desire.[53] Le Hérissé's research, carried out shortly after the end of the kingdom, led him to conclude more reasonably that "we don't believe that anyone should give credibility to certain descriptions that show us amazons bound to virginity or forced to submit to cutting off the right breast. We have not obtained any oral information from the natives corroborating these facts. On the contrary, we have met several former warriors who . . . seem to have preserved from their old occupation only an undisputed fighting spirit that gets applied mainly to their husbands." In fact, though the soldiers did not normally become physical wives of the king, Glele is known to have fathered children by warriors.[54]

There was complicity on the part of the monarchy in the myth-making, in the distancing of the women warriors from ideals of female behavior, and in the emphases on the women's ferocity and bloodthirstiness. We have to assume that the effort was a deliberate attempt to strike fear in potential enemies—a *dual* fear. It combined the threat of defeat and death in warfare with the added humiliation of being subdued by the hand of a woman. That such a popular (male) image of women existed by mid–nineteenth century speaks volumes to the changing perceptions of women and their place in Dahomean society. Publicly, the warrior songs of the women not only celebrated war but reflected and responded to that popular imagery. Contempt for the status of women suffuses two typical songs:

This war where we are going,
Since we are armed with our guns
We fear nothing.
We are marching together, we are marching like men
Thus we are going to our goal.
No one gives mustard

In place of an offering to a divinity.
Ogou Kploya—Ogun the destructor
We have already asked him to destroy
To destroy, to destroy
We are going to march like men.[55]

We march'd against Attahpahms as against men,
We came and found them women.
What we catch in the bush we never divide.[56]

Abeokutan myth has it that the Dahomean women warriors' participation in battle in 1851 provoked a backlash. When the only soldiers to scramble over the city walls were women, the Egba were unable to follow their tradition of decapitating the first enemy captured and cutting off his genitals. Furious at the insult, they fought all the harder.[57]

Some observers recognized that the women soldiers held high status within the palace, even though paradoxically large numbers of them were slaves by origin and legal status. Freeman said that they "are fully aware that their position is a most singular one; and they appear to glory in it." They resided in a separate section of the palace interior, with their meals prepared for them by their servants, numbered by Burton at "from one to 50 each." Their pride and their loyalty to the monarchy were legendary. A missionary stationed at Abeokuta published a story about the loyalty instilled in sudofi soldiers "brought up here." Following the 1851 attack on Abeokuta, the Egbas took their prisoners to Ketu, where they were to be redeemed by the Dahomeans. One of those prisoners was a Ketu girl captured as a child and reared to be a soldier. When her parents learned of her presence and tried to redeem her, she refused, saying "No, I will go back to my master."[58]

Exemplary service in the armed forces was rewarded at court with great pomp, and the monarchy made a point of introducing visitors to outstanding women soldiers. In the mid-1840s, John Duncan was presented to Adadimo, a young woman who had been promoted within the army for taking a male prisoner in each of the preceding two years. A later visitor was introduced to Wedje, an agbadjibeto (spy) during the reign of Glele. Her service had been so valuable that she was rewarded with a house and land to the southwest of Abomey; on her death, her spirit was added to those of the Nesuhwe, the cult of the royal dead. A young Yoruba-speaking soldier interviewed in the early twentieth century told of receiving cloth and cowries after killing a man in warfare; she had then been taken as a physical wife by Glele.[59]

These accounts of recognition through prowess in war raise questions about patterns of advancement within the palace in the late nineteenth century. Did women rise to high office through battlefield accomplishment? At midcentury, it appears, at least some women in high positions were directly active in the field of battle, but it is not clear if they had been placed in their positions initially because of valor in war. The meunon (female counterpart to the second minister) was killed in Dahomey's war against Atakpame in 1840; the miganon (female prime minister), on the other hand, was accused of having fled the field of battle with her troops.[60]

Another distinguished soldier and high-ranking palace official of the 1840s, a woman named Yewe, looms inordinately large in the British accounts. She was assigned to serve as "English mother," an officer responsible for the affairs of British visitors who was present when they appeared at royal audiences and who looked after their well-being. Freeman spoke glowingly of "Lady Yaway" and her hospitality. On his arrival in Cana, for example, Yewe provided twenty-five calabashes of food for his retainers and six large basins of "stews, hashes, roast fowls, yams" for Freeman himself. "Thus we were all regaled with a plentiful supply of fresh and wholesome food," a supply that continued throughout his stay and was accompanied by locally brewed beer "of excellent quality." When John Duncan arrived in Abomey in 1845, he was introduced to the same "mother," whose name he transcribed as Knawie, a woman who commanded a regiment of six hundred women. Duncan later explored areas north of Abomey under the protection of Gezo and was greeted outside one town by "bad fetish," a pot of magical substances left in the road. Later, the Dahomean army avenged the insult by attacking and "breaking" the town. Forbes learned that the key to victory in that engagement had been Yewe, the English mother. Burton never met the

English mother when he visited thirteen years later, though he was aware of the tradition, which may mean that Yewe had died by 1863 and had not yet been replaced.[61]

On the other hand, we know that others of the women officials did *not* gain their rank through warfare. For example, Glele's yovoganon was a Yoruba woman from Oyo named Miagbe (called Na Dudeagoa by Burton). She apparently was one of the first wives given to Glele as crown prince, for she is remembered for having produced his first official children, a set of twins who were followed by two additional sets, a mark of extraordinary distinction in Fon society. The first set were girls and were designated to become Migansi and Meusi, the prestigious princess-wives of the first ministers of the state.[62]

Whether soldiers or not, women within the palace appear more often in the nineteenth-century accounts than earlier, carrying out responsibilities for the palace and themselves. Travelers would typically first meet the king's women en route from Whydah to Abomey; ahosi staffed resting stops at regular intervals from Allada north to Abomey: Henvie, Akpwe (or Appey), Agrime, and Cana. They would meet visitors with the traditional offering of water and then provide meals. European travelers would be lodged in the homes of male officials.

Once in Abomey, visitors would complain bitterly of having to make way for processions of ahosi outside the palace walls, since men were required to turn their gaze away when women of the palace went about town. Forbes, for example, grumbled to his diary on June 6, 1850 that "the bells of the sable beauties are constantly warning man to run and hide himself. I was one morning near three quarters of an hour endeavouring to enter the Cumassee gate, from the constant succession of royal wives carrying food from one palace to the other. This morning, as we were leaving, we were desired not to go to the eastward, as 4000 of the king's wives (amazons, &c.) were gone forth to bathe."[63]

Toward the end of Gezo's reign, we find evidence that the ahosi had embarked on a variety of new and expanded activities that had numerous economic implications. First, some of their work was clearly meant to enhance the royal income, which had dropped so dangerously with the decline in the slave trade. Second, the work of the ahosi contributed to the continued, and enlarged, public royal prestige so evident in the later years of Gezo's reign. And third, the women's work provided income for the women themselves; like wives in common households, they were expected to earn their own keep.

Along with the development of the production of palm products on a commercial level, the monarchy by mid–nineteenth century had begun numerous industries staffed by female and slave labor. Palm-oil cultivation and processing was just one of many. Though plantations of palms on the Abomey plateau were associated with slave labor drawn from Yorubaland, the processing of oil later in the century appears to have been in the hands of the ahosi. For example, a visitor in the early 1870s was shown an old palace between Cana and Abomey that was being used as a palm-oil factory under the operation of the king's women. By this period, ahosi were involved in transporting oil to Whydah, where a portion of the yovogan's compound had been given over to the ahosi oil carriers. The ahosi porters would have returned with trade goods such as the cases of gin and sacks of salt described by a visitor of the 1880s.[64]

Pottery and dye industries late in Gezo's time were royal monopolies managed by the king's women. One group of women potters, for example, were "married" by the king and settled south of Abomey to found a village, Avali, near rich clay pits. Along with other pots, they apparently made the small pipe bowls that were symbols of high rank at court. At least one other pottery factory existed to the north of the city during the same period.[65]

As they had in earlier times, ahosi in the nineteenth century strung cowries; however, by the 1870s they were taking a much larger cut on their work. In the late eighteenth century, the women kept fifty cowries per head strung (each head being made up of fifty strings). By the 1870s they were keeping ten cowries per string, or five hundred cowries per head strung, a tenfold increase in profit.[66]

State-sponsored prostitution, too, which had existed since very early times in Dahomey, also continued. It was regularly described as inexpensive and widely available. Testimony from a family founded during the period of Gezo suggests that brothels directed by wives of the king were established, possibly for the first time, during that period. The descendants of a woman named Avloko, a wife of Gezo, say that she was sent to

Whydah by the king to set up an establishment with 333 female slaves. "If a stranger came and he needed a woman, he could come to her house and find one. If strangers came and gave money, she [Avloko] would send it to Gezo. The children born in her house belonged to her." The wealth of Avloko in persons enabled her to establish her household as a lineage. Her heirs were the children of the women granted to her by Gezo. Additional forms of prostitution also began to provide income and services for the monarchy. Visitors later in the century would complain that the king's women would seduce Europeans. When the women subsequently denounced them, the clients would be forced to pay large fines. The same process worked for hapless Dahomean men; rather than paying fines, though, the men would be forced to join the standing army.[67]

Thousands of military uniforms were woven, dyed, tailored, and appliquéd in Abomey during the nineteenth century. Men of the royal family appear to have done virtually all the work of weaving the local cotton into cloth, work that was the only manual occupation acceptable to male members of the Alladahonu lineage and one that continues to be monopolized by them. The dyehouses of the ahosi then created the indigo blues described by various visitors. Ahosi apparently also did much of the sewing and embroidery work. During the reign of Glele, for example, some 130 women of the royal sewing workshops were apprenticed to the Yemadje family specialists in appliqué.[68]

Royal women's work was essential to the ceremonial cycle, too, which was doubled in length late in the reign of Gezo. The Annual Customs presented enormous problems of organization. Food had to be collected and prepared to feed thousands of persons over several weeks; treasures had to be removed from storage and women organized for the long processions of the wealth of the king; hundreds of women had to train to dance and sing praises; others prepared offerings to the ancestors. Burton, visiting in the early 1860s, observed women singing the exploits of Gezo and Glele. "All is repeated 'by heart' and a tenacious memory is required. But the practice is hard. I rarely passed a palace when the king was out without hearing a loud singing lesson within."[69] Storage alone within the palace would have been a monumental task by the mid-nineteenth century. In addition to the fresh foodstuffs and currency that were collected as tax and tribute, and then partially distributed as part of the ceremonies, there was the vast royal treasury of gifts and imported goods that had accumulated over more than a century and that was brought out and paraded each year.

In addition to all these activities with their direct implications for the well-being of the monarchy, women in the palace, as noted earlier, worked for their own accounts. Indeed, one of the responsibilities of the monarch-husband was to provide dependents of the monarchy with opportunities to enrich themselves and their own followers. At the most modest level, a small market existed on the northwest side of the palace, where ahosi or small servant-children of the palace would sell prepared foods and handicrafts made by the women within the palace walls. Sagbadju Glele, for example, a son of Glele who became head of the royal family in the mid–twentieth century, testified that his mother, in addition to her required royal duty of preparing the king's food, also wove mats that she sold through the palace market. "Every woman in the palace had an occupation. Some of them prepared balls of *akasa* [cassava flour cooked with water], others fried yams into cakes, others were dyers of indigo. Little girls carried their products to the market to sell them. In the interior of the palace there was also a market where the women could come to do their own selling. Men were not allowed there."[70] The mother of Sagbadju Glele typified large numbers of ahosi in the nineteenth century in another sense: she was a Yoruba-speaking woman captured in warfare in Egbado country—specifically, at the conquest of Okeodan in 1848. Sagbadju himself was one of the sons of Glele who learned divination skills through training among his mother's kinsmen.

Other women ahosi operated at a more lucrative commercial level. High-ranking women granted control over villages and plantations were said to have their agents at Whydah who traded on their behalf. One such woman was a wife of Glele, Tondove, who was a daughter of the Nyawi, one of the five ahisinon, or principal trading families, of Whydah. The life story recounted by one of her retainers suggests the hierarchical patterns of interconnection and dependence among prominent individuals and families in late-nineteenth-century Dahomey. The informant was a Yoruba-speaking boy taken in war as a tiny child and granted to Tondove. When he reached an appropriate age, she gave him over to the care of

Nugbodohwe, one of Glele's diviners. Nugbodohwe placed the young man in a trading apprenticeship under one Adohun Agbanu, a merchant who bought and sold oil and palm nuts for Tondove. Other prominent ahosi were similarly remembered as having had agents who traded for their accounts. Such women, and others like them, were also involved in finance. Freeman learned in the 1840s that Dahomeans could get loans from the palace through the offices of wives of the king. Visesegan, the favorite wife of Glele, was one of the richest women in the kingdom in the 1880s. In addition to building her wealth through her trading agents, she had control over the profitable practice of issuing commercial licences on behalf of the monarchy.[71]

By mid–nineteenth century, then, the palace had expanded dramatically, incorporating literally thousands of Dahomean and foreign women. As an institution, it constituted a complex community that reflected and consciously replicated the relations of class, status, and ethnicity of the kingdom as a whole. Militarily, it contained the elite corps of fighters, as it publicly cultivated and celebrated a national spirit of aggression. Economically, it promoted the interests of the monarchy even as it enriched select individuals at its higher levels. And the palace also embodied the ceremonial and political core of Dahomey. In the words of one of the most astute students of Dahomean life, "the palace of the king was the pivot of political life. In this sense, the Abomey palace was a microcosm of the kingdom as a whole."[72] Nevertheless, as we shall see, the palace at the moment of its greatest prominence and visibility also masked patterns of growing exclusion from power for women and men of poorer classes.

The Expansion of the Ceremonial Cycle

By mid–nineteenth century, travelers and Dahomeans alike were complaining about the extraordinarily long periods of time that they and thousands of others spent in Cana and Abomey participating in Customs. There is little evidence of precisely what motives prompted the monarchy of Gezo to extend the ceremonial cycle. Nevertheless, whether intended to or not, the longer ceremonies had a number of effects that may have proved valuable for the needs of the ruling coalitions of the nineteenth century. First, they vividly demonstrated the devotion of the living toward the dead. If anything could underscore the prosperity of the visible world to the invisible, it was the long and lavish ceremonies held in honor of the ancestors. Those ceremonies were intended to ensure the primacy of the Alladahonu in Kutome and to reinforce and strengthen the royal ancestors' ability to support their living descendants. In face of the realities of economic decline, extravagant honoring of the ancestors and associated vodun celebrated a fiction that was designed to recreate prosperity.

Second, the extended ceremonial cycle kept large numbers of people occupied at court through long periods of time. A visitor to the court of Glele remarked that "people have no time for peaceful pursuits: war, war, war is alone thought of, and the King gives them no rest. Many of the chiefs complain of this, and seem heartily tired of it. . . . They have no time to themselves: there is always some 'custom' going on, and hence the country is in a state of desolation, and the population is gradually decreasing." Customs demanded the presence in Abomey or Cana of virtually all persons of significance in the kingdom. It thus offered the monarchy the possibility of greater control over political rivals. Courtiers staying in Abomey could be closely watched and manipulated. Moreover, economic rivals of the dynasty, those owners and managers of coastal plantations, were less able to get on with their work. As a French trader grumbled, the constant celebrations at the capital were ruinous to commerce, preventing people from processing palm oil.[73]

Third, Customs was a stage, a performance arena for the transmission of a variety of messages about the kingdom. Some were directed to the Dahomean citizenry itself, reminding them of the achievements of the kingdom, of its strength and invincibility. Others were meant to strike fear in the hearts of Dahomey's enemies and potential victims. Yet others were targeted to various European audiences. The Dahomeans understood and played to the differing concerns of the British, French, and Portuguese, using Customs as an opportunity to argue their positions and an excuse to prolong or cut short negotiations with various envoys.

During the era of Gezo, Customs was enlarged by the addition of at least two major ceremonial cycles: the so-called Oyo Customs, and the ceremonies performed in the name of Gezo before he was enstooled.

The Oyo Customs, which took place in Cana following the annual season of war, commemorated the freeing of Dahomey from the suzerainty of Oyo. They may have been instituted fairly early in the era of Gezo, shortly after the Dahomeans defeated Oyo in the early 1820s. They appear to have included a reenactment of the presentation of the tribute to Oyo that the Dahomeans were forced to make at Cana for more than seventy years. In Dahomey's Oyo Customs, the tribute-carriers were Yoruba-speaking captives who were killed and whose bodies were later propped up on scaffolding and left holding samples of the products that had formerly been sent to Oyo.

The ceremonies performed in the name of Gezo as prince are not specifically mentioned in visitors' accounts prior to 1856, including in the detailed descriptions of Forbes. However, six years after Forbes's 1850 visit to Abomey, Thomas Birch Freeman was present when the *ato* (platform) ceremonies were performed twice, the first time on behalf of the king and the second in the name of one Guarpay, "an imaginary personage called the King's brother." Burton later used the term "bush king" to refer to this double of the king, whose name he transcribed as Ga-kpwe. The name in fact is Gakpe, the name of Gezo before he was enstooled as king. Glele subsequently used the praise-name Addokpon for his imaginary self as prince. From the 1850s to the end of the kingdom, ceremonies were performed in the name of the king-as-king, in the name of the kpojito, then in the name of the king-as-prince, and finally in the name of the kpojito-as-ahosi. As Skertchly put it, "whatever is done for the king in public is thrice repeated; first for the Amazons, then for Addokpon, and thirdly, for Addokpon's Amazons." [74]

Scholars have debated the meaning of this innovation, which doubled the length of the central ceremonies that visitors had witnessed since the time of Agaja. Three major explanations for the king-as-prince have emerged, none of which is wholly satisfactory. Proposed by Burton and echoed by Skertchly, the first argues that, since it was beneath the dignity of the king to trade, the king-as-prince was created to allow the king to be involved in commerce, to "take all the onus of ignoble trade, leaving the true monarch to rule over his subjects and spend his revenues." Later scholars, acknowledging that kings had regularly traded in slaves, have argued that the problem was simply trade in agricultural products, presumably a demeaning occupation for a warrior king. Thus when Gezo made the decision to begin to provide oil to the European market, he had to create a fictional being to trade on his behalf.[75]

A second explanation, articulated first in 1954 by French scholar Paul Mercier, is based on the presumed importance of doubling and twinning in a Dahomean worldview. The king's double was an extension of the ideology that complements are necessary to achieve completeness—visible and invisible worlds, women and men, Mawu and Lisa, migan and meu, city king and bush king. Mercier argues that Gezo and Gakpe were a "dual monarchy," modeled on twins who ruled together, King Akaba and his sister Hangbe.[76] It is true that the house of Hangbe had been in eclipse during the one hundred years following Agaja's accession and that Gezo is credited with returning her descendants to respectability. However, Akaba and Hangbe had not ruled together, and in that sense were hardly a model for Gezo. Besides, the nineteenth-century kings were "doubled" by several other entities, including for example the kpojito and the royal vodun called tohosu. There would appear to be no particular reason to create this particular additional double for the king.

I have argued a third explanation, that the king-as-prince helped to legitimate Gezo's position. Gezo was his predecessor Adandozan's brother. Because Adandozan had performed the lavish Grand Customs for their father, Gezo was unable to undergo the normal full cycle of funerary/enstoolment ceremonies; instead, he demonstrated his legitimacy through reaffirming the devotion to the ancestors and loyalty to the dynasty that he had shown as a prince. By reminding Dahomey and the ancestors of his fealty and piety, he underscored the correctness of his position and effectively absolved himself of responsibility for his own coup d'état. But legitimacy as the motive for the creation of ceremonies for the king-as-prince, as Robin Law and John Reid have pointed out, is also problematic.[77] We have no record of ceremonies in the name of Gakpe being performed prior to 1856. Why would Gezo feel a need to invent these ceremonies only in the 1850s, after he had been in power for more than thirty years?

The first argument, that the kings could not trade in agricultural products, remains the leading explanation for the doubling of the major ceremonies of Customs by Gezo. Nevertheless, I find it unsatisfactory. Certainly, both Gezo and Glele repeatedly stressed to British envoys that Dahomey was in essence a military, not an agricultural, state. But that very insistence is troubling for two reasons. First, the kings do not appear to have protested that Dahomey was incapable of developing commercial agriculture to envoys of nations *other* than Britain. Second, there is no corroborating evidence retained in the oral traditions that suggests either that agriculture was a despised occupation or that the king could not trade in agricultural products. Only in European accounts, and specifically in statements of the kings made to British envoys at mid–nineteenth century, do we hear that Dahomey was a military nation whose people were not and could not be farmers. The numerous accounts left by French traders and missionaries of midcentury are oddly silent about the monarchy's attitude toward agriculture. Since many of those individuals were in Dahomey in order to promote commercial agriculture, one would expect them to have heard from the king that there were difficulties for Dahomean production of palm oil. And the oral memory of the kingdom normally confirms or complements strong evidence from European sources. We should expect to find some hint in oral traditions that it was inappropriate for the king to trade agricultural products. After all, there were a number of other prohibitions that surrounded the person of the king. In the nineteenth century, for example, he was not permitted to eat or drink in public. He could cross a body of water only on pain of death. And he could not be addressed by his name, but rather was greeted only with praise-names and honorifics.

Freeman, the first to witness ceremonies in the name of Gakpe, provides an extended description of the meaning of the king-as-prince that points the way to a possible resolution of the problem.

> Guarpay . . . is a kind of ideal representative of the genius of the nation. He takes the credit of all works of art which could not with propriety be attributed to the royal person. For instance, when I was in Dahomey in 1856, during a long day-interview with the late King, he showed me a neatly made blunderbuss, which he declared to be native manufacture, and it was so well executed that I was much surprised and interested. Not doubting the truthfulness of the

King's statement, I inquired by whose skills such an excellent article
had been produced, and the royal answer was "Guarpay made it."
From the manner in which the answer was given, I saw that there
was some mystery about this Mr. Guarpay but I concealed my curiosity until I could make further inquiry . . , and I . . . learnt
that . . . the king could not say, without derogation from his dignity,
"I made it."

Both Burton and Skertchly later confirmed that the palace of the king-as-
prince enjoyed monopolies over several industries: the weaving of cloth
for the king, the making of pipes and pottery, and the manufacture of
mats.[78] The functions of the king-as-prince, then, were broader than agriculture and the trade in palm oil. In theory, virtually all of the economic
activities of the palace organization were being credited to Gezo's Gakpe
and later to Glele's Addokpon. As Freeman stresses in citing the king's
"dignity," the king-as-prince set the king free of associations with the
mundane economic activities of production and distribution or sale. This
distancing of the person of the king from such workaday activities would
have contributed to his aura of mystery. It would have been in keeping
with the growing emphasis on the majesty of the person of the king. And
it also meant that the king could deny his own complicity in the clandestine trade in slaves.

    There are two possible cultural influences that could have been at work
in prompting the Dahomeans to create a mechanism that would distance
the king from common production. The first was the influence of Yoruba
culture, which, as we have seen, was having a particularly strong impact
on the Fon at this period. The divine kings of Yorubaland lived in seclu-
sion, so separate from worldly activities that they almost never appeared
in public. When they did, they were cloaked in mystery—their faces invisible, their words inaudible. The central symbol of the divine nature of
the Yoruba kings was their veil of beads. Though the Dahomean kings
were never seen by outsiders wearing such headgear, it is significant that
a beaded crown of obvious Yoruba influence was one of Glele's personal
possessions.[79]

    The second influence that may have helped to prompt the separation of the person of the king from economic activity was that of Europe, and Britain in particular. In the United Kingdom, the queen possessed great wealth, but never directly dirtied her hands in economic activities. Judging from descriptions of interactions between Dahomeans and Europeans, signals and quite possibly direct comments about the appropriateness of various activities to the dignity and majesty of a king were made by British visitors. For example, Gezo provided the explorer John Duncan with an ideal opening, asking that the Englishman "salute him as I would the Queen of England, for he was anxious to become acquainted with European manners and customs."[80] Travelers record in passing numerous incidents of Dahomean curiosity—questions about technical devices, medicine, foods, climate, clothing, social mores, and political systems.

Running through the formal and informal exchanges that were recorded are odd glimpses of Europe refracted and reflected by Dahomean cultural lenses. An emblematic incident was described by Forbes and his colleague Arthur Fanshawe, who arrived one morning at the audience room of the king, only to find themselves assisting a woman they knew as Mae-hae-pah, the head of the king's daklo (women who conveyed messages between outsiders and the king). "The old lady was very busy winding up eight Sam-Slick clocks! some upside down!! others on their sides, and one, by mistake, in its proper position." Forbes and Fanshawe assisted with the winding, setting times and arranging the clocks, and even carrying away for replacement a watch whose glass they had inadvertently broken. Like other travelers of the period, they clearly placed this incident in the category of technology misunderstood by the savage mind.[81] Yet the placing of numerous timepieces in the audience room of the king suggests more. European visitors detested the long hours that they waited for ceremonies to begin and most probably lectured the Dahomeans on the virtues of punctuality and the need to adhere to the discipline of clocks. Clocks in the audience room where they waited were a Dahomean response that, ironically, mirrored European travelers' own preoccupations, as visitors from industrializing nations where life rhythms and meanings associated with time had been changing dramatically over the preceding fifty years.

Whether or not it was inspired by Yoruba or British notions of the need to separate a proper monarch from commonplace economic activity, the creation of a king-as-prince had useful practical implications for the monarchy in negotiations with the British. From the 1840s to the 1870s, British contacts with Dahomey were mainly on an official level, as a series of governmental missions were sent with two related demands that remained constant: that Dahomey cease slave trading and that the kingdom stop human sacrifice. When the monarchy stressed the impossibility of doing either, the British offered to provide a temporary subsidy to replace the income lost in the abandonment of the slave trade. Two British missions at the end of the 1840s, including the one that Forbes accompanied, had as one of their goals the determination of the amount of income that the monarchy derived from the slave trade and the value of expenses incurred by the king during Customs. The British government made several subsidy offers to Gezo, none of which approached the estimates provided by the envoys.

Meanwhile, trade in palm-oil products, or "legitimate commerce," was growing along the coast. The most active European commercial presence was the French firm of Victor Régis, which set up shop in the old French slaving fort in Whydah in 1841. Régis agents were widely suspected of trading for slaves as well as oil, yet another indication of the relative compatibility between the two trades. A French envoy negotiated a treaty with Dahomey in 1851 that provided extremely favorable conditions for their trade and for the house of Régis in particular. Following the signing of Dahomey's treaty with France and the failure of British negotiations to stop the slave trade and to end human sacrifice, the British blockaded Whydah in September 1851. Within four months the Dahomeans agreed to stop the export of slaves, though Gezo refused to sign the full treaty that the British presented to him. When the Dahomeans continued to refuse to abolish human sacrifice, make peace with Abeokuta, or permit missionaries to settle in Abomey, the British finally relented and lifted the blockade in mid-1852.

Recent historians have argued that the period from 1852 to the death of the king in 1858 represented a significant policy change. They maintain that the monarchy was sincerely cooperating with the British, pushing hard to promote the production of palm oil as a substitute for the trade in slaves. They note that Gezo personally ceased to ship slaves overseas and that he prohibited their export from Whydah. They claim that he continued to reduce the numbers of victims sacrificed during ceremonies, a trend said to have begun in the 1840s. In response, a reactionary party led by the heir apparent, Badahun (who became Glele when enstooled), is said to have opposed the changes and worked for a return to slave trading and increased human sacrifice. By 1857, the policy of cooperation of Gezo had effectively failed, and the king relented and resumed trading slaves. With the death of Gezo in 1858 (which one historian argues was by political assassination rather than an enemy bullet), the conservative party triumphed and reversed the gestures of conciliation toward Britain.[82]

However, there are other possible interpretations of this key period in the 1850s. The monarchy of Dahomey had far more at risk than did Britain as it contemplated the British demands. The Dahomeans clearly felt the economic reality of the drop in income with the falling off of the slave trade. Their interest in a subsidy, which they stressed long after the British had decided against such a cash indemnity, corresponds to a constant thread of concern expressed about royal revenues. Indeed, as late as the 1870s, Glele was asking a British visitor if the mahogany grown near Abomey might be sold in England.[83] Certainly, there is evidence that the monarchy began to take palm-oil production seriously in the 1850s and actively embarked upon its cultivation and processing. Nevertheless, I would argue that throughout the years of negotiation with the British, the Dahomean position was constant: to look for alternatives to the slave trade, to negotiate, to encourage the British to pay a subsidy, and to trade in slaves to whatever extent was feasible. Why then did the monarchy of Gezo agree to a treaty in 1852 that committed the king to ending the slave trade? First, the king made clear the Dahomean interpretation of the terms of the treaty: that only the slave trade out of the port of Whydah was forbidden. Gezo argued in response to British protestations that he could control only goods shipped out of that port. Second, the king personally no longer traded slaves. Gezo, ever solicitous and cooperative to the British, could in all sincerity insist that he traded no slaves. Gakpe was another matter.

Traders along the coast in the 1850s noted the activities of a prince they variously called Garpuay, Gampé, and Guerpay, whose base of operations was an embarkation point called Prya Nova (New Beach, in Portuguese), seven to eight miles west of Whydah. This prince, whose name was known by contemporary Europeans to be a pseudonym for the king, solicited ships to visit the new port, ostensibly to purchase palm oil. In 1857, however, when the British intercepted a shipment of slaves there, the "incident . . . drove the King to fury and led to the punitive curtailment of all trade through ports under his sovereignty until the demanded recompense for the loss had been obtained from coastal traders."[84] Following that occasion, the king's name was linked once again with slave trading from Dahomey.

Gakpe, then, appears to have had multiple implications for the ritual and commercial life of Dahomey. By relieving Gezo of all responsibility for economic activities, he helped to recreate the kingship on the model of European and Yoruba rulers, further distancing and mystifying the person of the king. He allowed the king to commit himself personally to the abandonment of the slave trade, yet not risk losing potential income should buyers appear along the coast. He further lengthened the long ceremonial cycle, allowing the monarchy to keep important persons in Abomey where they could be more easily managed. Moreover, the longer ceremonies could also have been expected to impress the British, who had studied the monarchy's expenses for ritual in the late 1840s. In the 1850s the Dahomeans still hoped for a subsidy, and would have wanted to demonstrate to the British the need for a great deal of cash. Finally, Gakpe presented Dahomeans with reminders of their king before he was involved in the overthrow of Adandozan. As represented at midcentury, Gakpe was a law-abiding and peaceable man said to have been the real choice of his father to be king. Kept from power by the "evil" Adandozan, the noble king-as-prince busily pursued economic activities and supposedly agreed to become king only reluctantly, in response to abuses of power by his predecessor.~

6
The Decline of Dahomey

The cultivated lands in the interior of Dahomey are superb and equal the best of European farming.

Auguste Bouët, 1851, quoted by Nardin

The last chapter explored five major changes of the age of Gezo. At least three of those changes—the influx of Yoruba-speaking peoples, the growth of the palace population, and the expansion of the ceremonial life of the kingdom—were instituted by the monarchy of Gezo but continued into the reign of Glele. Indeed, many trends of the nineteenth-century state blend so continuously from one king's period to the next that they cannot be linked to a single monarchy. That is why I have chosen not to use dates to separate the chapters that treat the monarchies of Gezo and Glele. The theme of cultural and commercial change continues well beyond the end of the reign of Gezo, and decline begins long before Glele's enstoolment. In fact, the changing state policies of the nineteenth century in both kings' reigns can be linked to a broad tendency toward greater control from the center that became more and more prevalent in the life of the kingdom as the century progressed. The need for control in turn grew out of continuing political-economic crisis.

Dahomey at mid–nineteenth century seemed visibly at its height. In the previous three decades, it had thrown off imperial Oyo, conquered large areas of Mahi country, threatened enemies to the southwest and southeast, and absorbed thousands of Yoruba-speaking captives and slaves. It was making a transition from slaving to commercial agriculture, and European trading houses were competing for the red oil that promised future prosperity. The steady stream of European traders and diplomats called attention to the brilliantly colorful pageantry of Customs with their long public parades of the riches of the monarchy. Court officials, including palace women, appeared in lavish dress that was constantly changing, and women soldiers made astounding displays of military prowess. But Dahomey at mid–nineteenth century was also fully engaged in a spiral of decline. Within fewer than fifty years, the people of Dahomey would see the destruction of the palace as spatial entity and human institution. They would watch the abolition of the office of king and the effective dismantling of the monarchy. French imperialism would end the independence of the kingdom, but Dahomey would be weakened long before the arrival of the French and Senegalese soldiers who accomplished the task of conquest.

Even as the kingdom visibly gloried in its prosperity, the monarchy was losing a struggle to maintain standards of wealth from earlier eras. The dictum that each succeeding king was "to make Dahomey ever greater" rang hollow as the nineteenth-century monarchies struggled to keep even with, let alone surpass, the greatness of their predecessors. Power and growth were now inextricably tied to an international economy that no longer demanded the high-profit human commodity that had once helped the kingdom to prosper. With royal revenues dropping, and with economic opportunities increasing for Dahomeans who were not closely associated with the Abomey ruling elite, the monarchy responded with greater efforts to control the political life of the nation and to regulate the flow of economic resources. A kingdom that had been notable in the eighteenth century for order and discipline became one in the nineteenth in which the ruling authorities became obsessed with control: control over goods exported and imported, control over the production and distribution of crops and locally made goods of every kind, control over spiritual entities and religious institutions, control over the physical movement of people, and control over the actions of potential and imagined enemies. By the 1880s, the monarchy's obsession with control had become so oppressive that Dahomeans were literally moving away from the center, migrating toward territory that fell outside the effective jurisdiction of the ruling dynasty.

In the past, monarchies had been built of coalitions whose female and male members were drawn from the Alladahonu royal family, from common Dahomeans of the Abomey plateau, from peoples newly incorporated into the kingdom, and from slaves and captives. With the diminished resource base of the nineteenth century, the composition of monarchies began to change. The royal family turned inward, increasingly excluding nonroyals from the wealth that created and supported power. Even as early as the accession of Gezo, brothers and sisters of the king were being brought into the monarchy. The trend intensified in the second half of the century. With fewer resources, the Alladahonu chose to concentrate wealth in their own hands. As a son of Behanzin confided to me in the early 1970s, his father made a sister a minister "in order to make her rich."[1] Eventually, even the sisters of the ruling kings would find themselves shut out as the men of the royal family redefined power as something to be wielded only by men of royal blood.

Meanwhile, the ritual life of the kingdom flourished. The paradox of increasing opulence and lavish ceremonial during a period of constantly contracting resources was one rooted in Fon culture. The power and material success of the monarchy were attributable to the skillful use of both supernatural and human resources. Dahomey had risen through conquest and trade, but only because of a combination of divine support and human endeavor. The ceremonies called Customs, and indeed numerous other events of the ceremonial cycle, were occasions for prayers of thanks and supplication. Supernatural beings, the most central of whom were the royal ancestors, were offered sacrifices of all that was necessary for the good life in Kutome: food and drink, slaves and servants, trade goods and animals. And the living shared in the thanksgiving. Dependents and followers of the monarchy—the people of Dahomey—received gifts for use in the visible world: cowries, food, goods, wives, slaves, and land. The relationship was mutually reinforcing on all sides. The welfare of the kingdom and the dynasty was dependent on the support of both the visible and the invisible; and the well-being of both the gods and the people of Dahomey was dependent on the continued expenditure of wealth by the monarchy.

Unfortunately, the monarchy had less wealth to spend. The nineteenth century was an increasingly troubled period in Dahomey. The loss of income with the deterioration of the slave trade had been the beginning, and was arguably the root cause of decline. By the last decade of the age of Gezo, omens of various kinds were beginning to appear that for the monarchy signaled dissatisfaction on the part of the ancestors. Failures of policy and a loss of prosperity were followed over the years by defeats in warfare, by earthquake, and by premature and sudden deaths. Even the death of Gezo in 1858 would prove to be the fulfillment of a dark prophecy recorded by Forbes in 1850. Only one response offered relief: increased devotion as exemplified through more ritual and greater sacrifice. And ceremony, as we have already seen, also had secular implications.

The New Militarism ∿

European observers as early as the 1840s had remarked the centrality of ritual in Dahomey. Forbes charted the ceremonial calendar by month: war was made in December–January, followed by preliminary ceremonies at Cana. The major ceremonies, which included the parading of the king's wealth, those traditionally called Customs, began in March. May and June saw rituals that were specifically associated with trade, including the throwing of gifts to crowds. The highlight of July was the gunshot relay to and from Whydah, when soldiers stationed at intervals of about 250 yards all along the sixty-two miles from Abomey to the beach, taking their cues by ear, fired their guns in succession, the sound traveling to Whydah and back. Preparations for war took place in August and September, and a final round of ceremonies in honor of the ancestors of the king was reserved for the end of the year.[2]

In fact, the succession of ceremonies varied far more than Forbes realized, though certain portions of it were linked to the seasonal cycles of rainy and dry months. Judging from other accounts, the sole invariables by mid–nineteenth century were offerings to the royal ancestors, which came in December–January during the long dry season, and the annual war campaign, held immediately afterwards and completed before the beginning of the heavy rains in April. As in the Forbes list, May through July was typically busy with ceremonies, before a relatively quiet period in August–November.

One of the most striking aspects of the descriptions of the ceremonial life of mid–nineteenth century was the way in which it combined an alternating rhythm of war and ritual. War to a great extent had become ritualized, and ritual had become militarized. Forbes remarked in 1850 that "the time is . . . yearly divided in war and festival." Burton similarly said "the season of the Customs, which combine carnival, general muster, and lits de justice, seems to comprise the whole year, except the epoch of the annual slave-hunts, here dignified by the name of 'wars.'"[3] During Gezo's reign, war became quite literally an annual affair, undertaken only at a particular season, under particular conditions, and circumscribed by strict behavioral directives. Methods of warfare generally remained the same as before: the attempts to harness supernatural support, the techniques to neutralize the sources of enemies' power, the taking of war decisions based on a desire for vengeance, the use of ruses, and, toward the end of the century, a return to the use of foreign advisers. But there appears to have been an intensification of martial characteristics of the previous era—a heightened desire to impress upon the people of the kingdom, upon their supposed enemies, upon the European nations that sent representatives to Customs, and upon the ancestors themselves that Dahomey was at heart a militaristic state.

Performance was central to the ritualized militarism of the nineteenth century. Some elements had been visible in some form in the eighteenth—for example, the parading of armed women and the display of the skulls of sacrifice victims on the palace walls. By mid–nineteenth century, accounts often described items of personal royal regalia that were adorned with the crania of enemy chiefs and kings—possibly a telling symbol of the ideological move toward emphasis on the person of the king. Long sequences of belligerent song and dance began to be noted. And there were additional measures seemingly designed to terrorize. Following his 1871 visit, Skertchly described a group of four men who were said to eat the flesh of sacrifice victims:

> [W]hen the captives are beheaded they take one of the bodies and cut off pieces of flesh, which they rub with palm-oil, and roast over a fire kindled in the square before the platform. The human flesh is then skewered on the pointed sticks, and carried round the marketplace; after which the [men] parade before the State prisoners, and go through the action of eating the flesh. They chew the human meat before the terrified captives, but do not swallow it; and when

they have worked upon the fears of the poor wretches . . . they retire, and spitting out the chewed flesh, take strong medicine which acts as an emetic.[4]

The women's army was the embodiment of nineteenth-century militarism and symbol of a nation bent on exhibiting its war-making capabilities. Travelers had been witness to the parading of troops in the eighteenth century; in the nineteenth, visitors additionally watched sham battles and displays of the ferocity of the women warriors. Typical was the scene described by a French missionary in 1861. A mock fortified town had been built on a parade ground. The town was represented by a series of small buildings, which were protected behind a fifteen-foot-high houselike structure roofed with bushes bearing long, sharp thorns, which represented a walled rampart. Further outside stood a barrier of the same thorns, roughly six feet high and eighteen feet deep, which represented an exterior protective bank. "According to the programme, the barefooted female warriors were to surmount three times the heap of thorns which represented the curtain of the works, descend into the clear space which took the place of the ditch, escalade the house, which represented a citadel bristling with defences, and go and take the town simulated by the row of huts. They were to be twice repulsed by the enemy, but at the third assault they were to be victorious, and drag the prisoners to the king's feet in token of success. The first to surmount all the obstacles would receive from his hand the reward of bravery." The account goes on to describe the assault in detail. After approaching in a silent crouch, the women form a line of battle. The king gives them a rousing speech and sends them to the attack. "At a given signal, they throw themselves with indescribable fury upon the bank of thorns, cross it, leap upon the thorny house, retire from it as if driven back, and return three times to the charge—all this with such rapidity that the eye can scarcely follow them. They clamber over the thorny obstacles as lightly as a dancer vaults upon a floor, and that though their naked feet are pierced in all directions with the sharp thorns of the cactus."[5]

War was endlessly debated during the ceremonial cycles. A Dahomean historian has written that "war was not just a purely technical matter that was left to a simple victory of arms; nor was war a matter of mercenaries; rather, it was an essential activity in which all the constituent parts of the state took part." Targets of future campaigns were discussed, along with the leadership of the armed forces. Those said to have shown valor were honored, and cowards publicly humiliated. In the safety of Abomey, everyone was a soldier. Forbes noted during Customs in 1850 that "to-day the whole nation was military; mother, wife, daughter, minister, even the hunchbacks and dwarfs, were strutting by in all the pride of military array." One of Forbes's entourage expressed astonishment to his journal "when in the midst of the Amazons stood the Royal Mother, wives, female Ministers, all in uniform and armed each with a musket, sword and club and which each by her actions shewed she knew well to use."[6] Companies were named for prominent individuals, and there were specific companies made up of princes and princesses.

Eminent individuals "commanded" companies, but it is not clear that they necessarily led them in war, particularly late in the century. Nor is it clear that all the companies went into battle, and particularly the companies of members of the royal family. In the preceding chapter, we saw that some high-ranking women were active fighters, at least at mid-century. In the 1870s, Skertchly claimed that "the higher the rank the person holds in the military scale the higher his position in everything." He said that the migan was, in addition to being prime minister, a "field-marshal, and war captain-in-chief." Yet evidence suggests that Burton was more accurate in saying that the migan was commander "ex officio" of the army. Accounts of both attacks on Abeokuta credit the gau, not the migan, with leading the Dahomean forces. The two top-ranking professional military offices—those of the gau and the kpossu (posu)—had existed since at least the 1730s. Significantly, the gau, who in earlier eras had typically been listed among the five to seven most important ministers, by the 1850s was no longer described as a member of the gbonugan daho (great chiefs of the outside). Skertchly called the gau a subordinate of the migan. Designating the gau as the migan's "lieutenant," he described a debate about naming a new gau, with court officials debating the merits of the candidates' warrior skills.[7]

Descendants of Glele and Behanzin insisted that no important person ever went into battle; rather, they argued, when songs were sung of the exploits of particular princes or princesses, the reference was only to the soldiers sponsored by those individuals. Similarly, one of the best-remembered princesses of Behanzin's court was Jikada, a sister to the king who was appointed gaunon (female counterpart to the gau). One of her nephews testified that she did not go into battle; nor for that matter did any sons of Glele. "Only wives and slaves made war." [8] On the other hand, the king in the nineteenth century "went to war." Yet sources make clear that he remained distant from any fighting. At times, the Dahomeans' enemies overran emplacements, capturing regalia of the king and members of the court, and Gezo was mortally wounded en route from a war campaign. Nevertheless, the pattern of the nineteenth century suggests that male ministers and members of the royal family were ceremonial warriors only, following the armed forces to war and carefully remaining at what they expected to be a safe distance. In contrast, as we saw in the last chapter, certain prominent women of the palace were in fact field commanders.

What is suggested by the evidence is a gulf between the publicly expressed militarism of the court and the realities of warfare. The army-in-performance and the army-in-the-field were increasingly two very distinct and different entities. The Dahomean forces on campaign continued to adhere to the old Gbe principles of war, and particularly to formulas of behavior long believed to be efficacious. Ruses and dependence on supernatural support loom large in nineteenth-century accounts of actual warfare, just as they had in the eighteenth. Success was mixed with failure, as it had been in earlier eras. Mahi country to the north was gradually conquered in the 1820s and 1830s. Later in the century, the more common targets were Yoruba-speaking peoples to the east. Most often, successful war was made by surprise on large villages. The army was typically described as marching past its target then turning and making a surprise attack before dawn. With thousands of soldiers descending on sleeping villages whose total population may have been fewer than the Dahomean forces, victory was assured. It was a ruse that enabled the Dahomeans to win their most decisive victory in the late nineteenth century—the destruction of the Yoruba city of Ketu. After beseiging the city for three months in 1886, the Dahomeans convinced the Ketu war leaders to leave the protection of their walls to negotiate an honorable surrender, only to have their army take the emissaries captive and storm the city. Similarly, near the end of the campaign against the French, the Dahomeans pretended to want to negotiate peace in an attempt to lure the French into an ambush.[9]

Judging from accounts of war itself, only the women soldiers fulfilled in battle the promise they exhibited in ceremony. Forbes tells of an 1840 attack against Atakpame, whose inhabitants he calls the Attahpahms. By his account, the city had been forewarned and all fled, save "400 resolute men [who] kept the Dahomeans in check, killed many, put the males to the rout, and had it not been for a rally of the amazons, would have discomfited the Dahomean army." Occasionally, the Dahomeans were the victims of ruses. As their army approached Abeokuta in early March 1851, an Egba chief at Ishagga, some twelve miles from the enemy target, surrendered his town. Fooled by the surrender into believing that the town supported them, the Dahomeans followed the chief's "advice" and waited until daylight to cross the shallow Ogun River to attack the only section of the Abeokutan fortifications that had been reinforced. Twelve years later, the Dahomeans set out to avenge their earlier defeat at Abeokuta, but turned back within sight of the city when Glele dreamed that a royal spirit had warned him not to attack but to return the following year, when war would be made successfully. When they returned a year later, the Dahomean army went via a tortuously convoluted route, in the belief that a twenty-two-day indirect march to arrive at a city some 110 miles from Abomey would permit them to surprise the Egba. The exhausted and hungry Dahomean troops, estimated at ten thousand, were beaten back at the ramparts of Abeokuta and were then pursued and attacked for two days during their retreat. Their estimated losses were more than 2,200 dead to 50 killed on the Egba side. The only Dahomean soldiers to have broken through the city defenses were four women.[10]

If warfare itself had changed little, why did Dahomey become more militaristic at mid–nineteenth century? The answer, it seems, lay in the change to a commercial agricultural economy. Paradoxically, a cult of militarism was unnecessary while the monarchy was able to monopolize and channel the armed forces of the kingdom into the production of slaves. However, the production of palm products left the central monarchy at a distinct disadvantage; a rigidly organized central government was unnecessary for the cultivation of oil palms by individuals, and wealthy men and women controlling coastal plantations could more easily cultivate, process, and transport oil and kernels to ports of embarkation. In short, the celebration of militarism underscored what the monarchy of Dahomey had been uniquely equipped to do and denied the realities of changing economic and political orders that would increasingly be concentrated at the coast. Militarism set the ruling elite above other Dahomeans, emphasizing their distance from and disdain for work in agriculture. Ritualized militarism was a kind of performance-prayer, offered in order to create in Kutome a world that would then be reified in Gbetome, the visible world. In that invented world, as in the Dahomey of old, the kingdom would prosper through the conquest and capture of enemy populations. Implicitly, it included a vision of a return to a flourishing slave trade.

Burton expressed what he heard in Abomey when he noted that "agriculture is despised, because slaves are employed in it."[11] Yet contemporary members of the royal family point out that royal grants of land and slaves meant that every important person was a farmer, at least in the sense of a gentleman farmer whose wealth was linked to the product of his or her estate. Moreover, twentieth-century oral traditions about Gezo before he became king claim that he lived near Cana, spending his time in farming and hunting. Granted, these traditions may have been created at a point when commercial agriculture had become a more valued way of life for members of the royal family; nevertheless, sources dating back as far as the early eighteenth century insist that in Gbe-speaking areas, potential kings lived far from court on estates granted them by their father. As we will see below, these contradictory signals about agriculture may well have been associated with the midcentury representation of the kingdom to outsiders, and particularly to the British.

Ritual presented Dahomey as prosperous, rich, and militarily invincible. It gloried in the military victories of the past and in ceremonies designed to reorder present realities. Historians have been able to discern some of the internal struggles in Abomey over responses to the demands of European powers and the growth of imperialism. Militarism as a response was backward-looking. But in retrospect, it is apparent that modernizing and fully cooperating with agents of change could not have saved the kingdom in the long run.

Surveillance and the Palace ⌁

Europeans and Afro-Brazilians from the coast pronounced the expanded ceremonial cycle an onerous innovation harmful to the economic interests of themselves and the kingdom. Yet more ceremonies were but one of a number of changes toward increased centralization that Dahomeans must have found burdensome. In the second half of the nineteenth century, governmental dominance tightened and widened. Taxes increased, physical mobility decreased, and controls over virtually all aspects of life became the norm. Checks and counterchecks on anyone of substance seemed to multiply along with a sense of collective paranoia. Controls were administered through officials, both inside and outside the palace organization, who themselves were subject to new demands and extra surveillance. Along with closer control was a steady trend toward the consolidation of power and wealth in the hands of members of the royal lineage, and particularly the hands of princes.

Royal revenues were a first concern. If palm oil was to replace lost revenues from the slave trade, it had to be made to pay. The terms of trade remained highly favorable to the king and favored officials, the members of the monarchy. Beyond that, the concentration on palm-oil production in the 1850s prompted a series of new exactions: exporters paid the monarchy one gallon of palm oil for every eighteen that they sold to the European factors. An older, in-kind tax on all kinds of agricultural produce, the *kuzu*, was turned into an annual payment that had to be submitted in the form of palm oil. In a move apparently aimed at the prosperous coastal palm-oil producers, a new and powerful court officer, the tavisa, was named to collect the kuzu in the area of Whydah. The preoccupation with revenues generated by commercial agriculture led to attempts to control what was grown and where, not just to favor oil palms, but also to discourage or even forbid crops like shea butter, peanuts, coffee, sugarcane, tobacco, and rice.[12]

As in the past, small payments were exacted, again and again, on travelers and their goods. Customs houses were virtually everywhere, at the entrances and exits to towns, along the lagoons, and at gated roads. Skertchly described one such toll house.

> A quarter of an hour's walk through the plantations brought us to the Denum, a more imposing structure than any we had hitherto seen. The road was crossed by a fence of six-foot poles, crowned by a vigorous growth of shoots. In the centre was an opening about six feet wide, through which every traveller must pass. It is the custom for the caboceers, when sending any of their servants on a journey, to furnish them with a stick carved with the heraldic insignia of the owner and a number of cowries or other small articles denoting the number of persons this primitive passport allows to accompany the principal messenger. This permit is carefully scrutinized by the Denum keeper, and woe betide the unlucky wight who is detected in trying to pass without due authority.[13]

Tax "farmers" collected funds from all who passed such customs houses. They kept a portion and passed the rest of their revenues along to a caboceer or other official, who similarly kept some and passed the remainder along to the monarchy. Fees were collected at markets on everything sold. Collectors kept a portion and took the remainder to Abomey.

Earlier visitors had reported that every able-bodied person paid a personal tax annually. In the nineteenth century, the personal tax appears to have been proportionately heavier, and the expected total amount of personal tax was calculated through a census taken each year, the results of which were guarded in the palace at Abomey. Nevertheless, the sums paid were negotiated, at least quietly, and Le Hérissé was told that the royal coffers often did not get their due. As in the past, the estates of all deceased persons of any wealth were inherited by the king, who had the right to keep any portion of the goods. Even if nothing was retained, the state received other additional payments in cash and kind on the death of persons of any substance.[14]

The greater one's wealth, the greater was one's vulnerability in nineteenth-century Dahomey. Though fears of loss of control over the palm-oil trade may have prompted the close supervision of some individuals, the concern for control was generalized throughout society. Everywhere were people charged with watching others, informers whose job it was to bear witness to the relative honesty of others. No one was trusted, and offices became layered with levels of assistants responsible for checking on the behavior of others. The legede, the special messengers created at the end of the eighteenth century to assure proper delivery of messages between ambassadors, were commonly dubbed "secret police" in the nineteenth. By Burton's day, the ranks of the legede had been greatly expanded, and a legede—a "spy, or to use a more delicate term, 'second in command'"—was assigned to watch virtually every major official. Burton comments sourly that "if a captain is sent to prison, he must be accompanied by his Légédé, who prevents the wives sending food, and who is answerable for the sentence being carried out in its strictness." [15]

Two groups whose positions were synonymous with wealth and power were particularly susceptible to suspicion: the merchants at Whydah, both the Dahomeans and those who made up the Afro-Brazilian community, and the highest officials in the kingdom outside the palace, the gbonugan daho (literally, the great chiefs of the outside). The merchants found themselves subject to denunciations and to arbitrary policy decisions that could easily harm their commerce; the great chiefs, who had always before constituted the core of the monarchy, found that decision making and policy implementation during the reign of Glele as often as not were entrusted to others.

As palm oil grew to be the favored export and the item most productive of revenue for the monarchy, oil was literally treasured. Unlike slaves, whose bodies represented an indivisible commercial value and who would have been able to testify to irregularities in their treatment, small quantities of palm oil were relatively easy to pilfer. Penalties for theft were severe. Skertchly witnessed brutal floggings given to men convicted of having stolen "some of the King's palm oil." Higher on the social scale, the ahisinon, traders licensed by the palace, seem to have been a particular target of suspicion, whether justified or not. The "breaking" of a household for crimes against the monarchy is attested as early as the seventeenth century in Whydah. Individuals said to be guilty of crimes against the state had all their goods confiscated and their immediate family members dispersed as slaves by the monarchy. Such became the fate of certain nineteenth-century ahisinon. For example, a descendant of the Whydah-based family of Codjia told me of his ancestor being taken to Abomey during the time of Glele because some "tattlers" had reported that he was not sending all the money that he should to the king. The entire household and all moveable goods were carried off to Abomey, where the descendant's mother was given to the vidaho, Kondo, as a slave wife. She returned to Whydah only "after the war," that is, after the French conquest. According to Codjia's descendant, having one's house broken and being sent off to Abomey was a common occurrence for ahisinon in the nineteenth century. Forbes similarly spoke of the constraints on Isidore de Souza, the heir of the de Souza family and son of the original chacha, who was supervised by six superintendents of trade who reported directly to the king. They were seconded during the chacha's "hours of recreation" by "ladies of the blood royal," who also reported to the king. Burton described Isidore's successor, Chicou, as an official "surrounded by the cleverest spies and councilors." Moreover, by the early 1860s Glele had appointed a prince, Chyodotan, to a position as "assistant" to the yovogan of Whydah, one of the gbonugan daho and the kingdom's minister of commerce. Chyodotan overshadowed virtually everyone in Whydah, becoming the central figure along the coast who supervised trade and, as the imperial threat grew in the 1870s and 1880s, serving as a chief Dahomean envoy for negotiations with the European powers.[16]

The gbonugan daho typically included five to seven male officials, all of whom were effectively part of the monarchy. Their ranks from the mid–eighteenth century onward always included the migan, or prime minister, the meu, or second minister, the yovogan, chief for the whites, and the ajaho, variously called a minister of religion or chief of the secret police. Beyond those four central posts, sources differ as to which titled officials made up the ranks and how many were considered to be gbonugan daho, as opposed to lower-ranking chiefs and caboceers, at any given moment.[17] All sources do agree on three points about the nineteenth century, however. First, numerous persons—princess-wives, legede, princely and commoner assistants—were attached to the households of the gbonugan daho to oversee their performance; second, over time larger numbers of men of the royal family, and particularly brothers, sons, and grandsons of the nineteenth-century monarchs, were named to positions as gbonugan daho; and third, one of the most prominent of the gbonugan daho was the ajaho. The ajaho's prominence appears to have been related to his functions as the official who dealt with the boundaries between the inside and outside, and specifically with the flow of information to the king and monarchy. Supervisor of spies, both domestically (legede) and outside the kingdom (agbadjibeto), the ajaho also decided who might be present in audiences with the king and had overall responsibility for the eunuchs within the palace. In the nineteenth century, he became the official responsible for the formal supervision of religious activities, which, as we will see, became a cornerstone of efforts at control over the population.

European visitors regularly commented on their own experiences with royal surveillance. Duncan reported that a male ahosi was sent on an expedition north with him in 1845. Though the man's usual job was "to report, by private messenger to the King, any misconduct or neglect of the superior officers," in Duncan's case the ahosi was assigned to receive any complaints that the Englishman might have against his Dahomean escort or against any of the chiefs or caboceers in any towns through which he passed. Abomeans claim that servants offered by Glele to visitors were in fact eavesdroppers in the service of the monarchy who knew various European languages and collected intelligence. The oral memories are corroborated by written accounts of the late nineteenth century. A Frenchman who lived in Whydah in the late 1880s saw Chacha de Souza warn Europeans leaving for Abomey that "above all, what ever happens or what ever you see, not a word, not a comment between you in any language; if you want to chat, go into open fields, and even then beware!" [18]

Europeans appreciated the small private audiences that Gezo and Glele granted them as opportunities to speak more openly and frankly with the king. The French visitor Repin reported that Gezo received private visitors in the quarters of his favorite wife. A map sketched at the period shows the house of this unnamed wife adjacent to a palace gate that stood opposite the residence of the meu, where European visitors were normally lodged. Burton similarly met Glele in a private audience in the palace. The king "was attended by six of his Privy Council . . . also by five of his principal wives." We do not know where Burton was received in the palace, but we may speculate that it was in the house of Visesegan, Glele's favorite and most powerful wife, because we know that the king had a door cut into the wall behind his public reception room so that he might easily approach her quarters. Skertchly, too, met in private audiences with Glele and his heir. At his final audience, the king sat "under a long shed. . . . The English landlady [the "English mother" described in Chapter 5] and [the king's] Leopard-wives surrounded him, with a few Dahkros [daklo]." Interpretation in these private audiences was a crucial issue for both sides. Europeans were often concerned that they be able to hire an independent and trustworthy interpreter on the coast to travel to Abomey with them, and they insisted that he be the one used in conversations with the king. But the Dahomeans, too, took precautions. A grandson of Glele testified that "in the palace there was a woman who spoke French, another who spoke English. When a stranger came, the male interpreter would interpret, and the woman would sit beside the king as a check. If all was properly done, she would tell the king after their departure." [19]

The pattern of a palace woman present as listening ear and memory bank extended beyond private audiences with Europeans and beyond the interpretation of foreign languages; it was part of the general oversight characteristic of the late nineteenth century. Edouard Chaudoin, a French factor resident in Whydah in the 1880s commented, for example, that "the wives of the king play a considerable part in the politics of the country; they attend councils, and their opinions weigh heavily with the king. They are the ones who remind him of certain facts and whisper his speeches to him or his addresses to the chiefs and people." [20] The visibility of women in these roles at court and the belief that women were influential in matters of state raise interesting but difficult questions about women and their changing position in nineteenth-century Dahomey.

In the past, certain high-ranking ahosi and some women of the royal family had clearly been a part of the monarchy. Evidence from the eighteenth century shows that women in the palace were directly involved in succession struggles. Princesses had been deeply involved in building Dahomey and strengthening the royal lineage. Women were still visible and active in discussions of policy questions at mid–nineteenth century. Indeed, women's open participation in court discussion was so commonplace that Forbes, who came from a society where women might reign as head of state but not govern as members of Parliament, found it unremarkable. Freeman reported that judicial appeals from districts were heard in Abomey by a council that included "the two chief ministers of the state and the chief leaders of the Amazons. In all such cases, however, the latter are considered to have the greater influence: it being a leading feature of Dahomean polity that in the counsels of the King the female sex have the ascendant." An appellant would seek the king's ear through "the chief ladies of the court." Despite severe prohibitions for men to have contact with ahosi, such approaches to the palace could easily be made through the palace women's female relatives, who were allowed free access.[21]

Yet as time passed, women, both commoner and royal, more and more became the instruments of control over others and less and less an active part of the monarchy. Real power became concentrated elsewhere. Their changing position by the late nineteenth century is suggested by Gedegbe, one of Glele's chief diviners, who reminisced that the king received visitors in his audience room "surrounded by some of his wives. When an important matter was to be discussed, he made them leave." In early 1890, in the midst of Behanzin's first major crisis with the French, the king held a secret audience at 3:00 A.M. for eight Frenchmen who had been taken hostage. One later described the scene, noting the presence of "five very fine-looking black women attendants" and the royal council, "two rows of caboceers," kneeling on either side of the king.[22] The implication is that the council was exclusively male. Nevertheless, there is evidence of the importance of women as listeners, if not active participants, in state discussions.

An elaborate gendered system of dual offices, which claimed its origins in the reign of Tegbesu, was strikingly apparent to virtually all mid- and late-nineteenth-century visitors. Male-female pairs of officials ranged from the very highest offices of the kingdom down to relatively low-ranking positions. At the top, every member of the gbonugan daho was doubled by a woman within the palace. The man held the ministerial title and the woman within the palace had a comparable title with the suffix -*non*, meaning "person charged with responsibility for," or "mother of." Thus, the male prime minister was the migan; his female counterpart was the miganon. Similarly, the second highest-ranking officials were the meu and meunon; and the yovogan was doubled by the yovoganon. Sources agree that the female counterpart had to be present whenever the male minister appeared at court, and some have argued that these high-ranking women "were nearly equally important as the ministers."[23]

But beyond being present when her counterpart reported at court, it is not clear precisely what functions these female ministers performed. Their roles have been debated by scholars. Logically, there would seem to be a contradiction in appointing ahosi who were physically inside the palace to titled positions paralleling the gbonugan daho, who performed functions on the outside. Some have argued that the women officials in fact had little to do with their counterparts' functions; rather, they simply had corresponding responsibility within the palace for functions discharged outside by the male officials, who could not be permitted to have jurisdiction over women inside. Thus, as the migan was the chief executioner of the outside, the miganon was responsible for executing condemned criminals within the palace population. An alternative explanation supported by the preponderance of evidence is that the women officials provided a check or control over the male officials' activity. Indeed, women who were counterparts to the great chiefs of the outside, as well as a number of lower-ranking women counterparts to other male officials of the outside, appear to have performed both oversight and advocacy roles. For example, a grandson of Glele argued that the envoys of the yovogan carried goods and revenues to the palace, handing them over to the yovoganon, who was responsible for accounts and reports to the king.[24]

We have a relatively large amount of evidence about palace women's relationships with outsiders for lower-level offices. Forbes, for example, argued that every soldier was doubled: "[T]he same equivalent rank is carried down to the private in each brigade, male and female. These relationships in military rank are called father and mother; and, as will appear, the male soldier, when accused, appeals to his 'mother' to speak for him." He similarly describes Yewe, the "English mother" whom we met in chapter 5. However, while Forbes and other English-speaking visitors tended to see such women as little more than hostesses for foreigners, French agents attributed greater influence to them. A midcentury French trader claimed that the "European mothers" cared for the well-being of their charges but also acted as intermediaries with the king: "These mothers are generally very influential on the thinking of the king." Chaudoin similarly explained that each of the European commercial establishments at Whydah was represented at court by a woman, who "is responsible for defending the interests of her charge before the king when circumstances require it." [25]

Using the example of the yovogan, Melville Herskovits posits a complex system of checking and counterchecking by the women who paralleled the gbonugan daho within the palace. The "mother" of each male minister was responsible for hearing and remembering the reports of her counterpart as well as remembering the accounts of other individuals from the outside assigned to survey the minister's work. The "mothers" were in turn controlled by a body of women known as the kposi. Drawing on testimony describing the reign of Behanzin, Herskovits claims that there were twenty-four kposi divided into three groups of eight each. Eight were present whenever anyone reported anything before the king; they were the overall memories of the court and their word "was final when a statement was in dispute." Another eight kposi were responsible for remembering reports of the various chiefs, while the third group of eight was charged with remembering the accounts presented by priests. Herskovits's scheme is not directly corroborated elsewhere, though it resonates with the memories of an elderly Yoruba woman, a former palace slave, who was interviewed in Nigeria by the anthropologist William Bascom in 1951. She recalled three separate, very high-ranking groups of eight women each: the kposi, the hudohwe, and the hume. The most senior were the kposi, or great wives, followed by the other two and then by the lower ranks of palace women. [26]

Herskovits's description, even if not fully corroborated, certainly underscores other evidence that the women within the palace had some responsibility in the late nineteenth century for surveillance of the men who worked in the administration of the kingdom outside the palace. The Herskovits passage is significant too, for its suggestion of political roles for the kposi, who otherwise are seen in the literature as wholly holy women. It points to a possible understanding of the kposi as extensions of the entity of the king, the king himself being both man and mythical animal, a living person and an embodiment of the spirits of all the previous kings. Like other words incorporating the suffix -*si*, *kposi* indicates someone dependent upon, a subordinate to, or wife of Kpo. As we saw in chapter 2, *kpo* in Fongbe means leopard, and the sacred leopard Kpo had associations both with the ancestry of the intrusive Alladahonu ruling lineage and the people acknowledged as the original owners of the Abomey plateau. In the context of Dahomean religious life, then, the term *kposi* suggests adepts of a cult dedicated to the vodun Kpo.

The kposi are not mentioned in eighteenth-century sources, though that does not necessarily mean that they were not present within the palaces of earlier kings. Later sources, however, are consistent in drawing attention to their special rank. Le Hérissé, for example, says that the wives of the king were divided into two distinct categories, "the Kposi, wives of the leopard, and the Ahosi, wives of the king." He adds that the kposi "enjoyed a privileged position in the harem. They lived in the section reserved for the king, and had no other job than to surround their master, silent and attentive to his least desires." No one was permitted to speak to kposi, who were preceded everywhere they went, even in the palace, by servants who would cry, "Look out!" or "Move aside!" Simple ahosi passed kposi with lowered heads.[27]

Mid-nineteenth-century visitors saw kposi in processions and typically made two observations: that they numbered well under a dozen and that they were extraordinarily well-dressed. Forbes, for example, described six kposi of Gezo "dressed most magnificently in scarlet and gold tunics, slashed with green silk and satin, with sashes and handkerchiefs of silk, satin, and velvet of every colour; coral and bead necklaces, silver ornaments and wristbands." Burton and Skertchly each saw eight, rather than six, elderly women who were identified as Gezo's "leopard wives."

Both were impressed with the sight of the eight kposi of Glele, whom Skertchly called the king's favorite wives and Burton praised as "the youngest and fairest of the harem."[28] Distinguished by their finery and their distance from others, the kposi appeared at court "each under her own state umbrella of gorgeous hue. They were dressed in green and blue silk, richly embroidered with gold lace, and glittered in the sun in the profusion of their jewelry of silver and coral. All wore a string of silver ornaments round their heads, which contrasted well with their dark skins, and the royal coiffure of a turban-like tuft on the top of the head was combed and pomatumed to perfection."[29] Except for agreeing that they were separate, special, and sacred, there is no consensus among the written sources or the oral testimonies about the kposi's functions. Paul Hazoumé says they were the biological mothers of potential heirs; descendants in the royal family disagree. Herskovits says that they supervised the ahosi; descendants in the royal family again disagree. The segregation of the kposi from others and their sacred status, however, point the way to a possible interpretation of their importance, at least in the nineteenth century.

The kposi underwent an initiation process in the palace to become vodunsi of Kpo, and are described as having on occasion worn the beaded crowns associated with the Yoruba sacred monarchies. One descendant of Glele claimed that they became agasusi, initiated followers of the leopard-totem of the royal family, on the death of the king who had made them kposi. Symbolically, as adepts of the leopard that linked the ancestry of the royal lineage with the original owners of the land of Dahomey, the kposi represented the dual character of the social covenant that legitimized Alladahonu rule. However, the kposi's separation from contact with virtually all persons but the king had political implications, too. Though they were dedicated ritually to a sacred being who embodied the royal/commoner and intruder/landowner accommodation that legitimized the dynasty, they in fact were women absolutely under the control of only one person, the man who represented one-half of that equation— the king—and they were said by at least one source to have had to die with him.[30] In contrast to the pairing of the king and kpojito that embodied the ethos of the eighteenth century, and that also symbolized the fundamental social contract, the closeness of the kposi to the person of the king and the access that he alone had to them suggests a shift toward emphasis on the king and his personal power. The prominence of the kposi, who unquestionably were in close public and private attendance on the king, can be read as an extension of the aura of mystery that increasingly surrounded the person of the monarch. At the same time, the kposi offered very real and practical possibilities for playing the role that Herskovits attributes to them. Silent yet present, indissolubly tied to the king himself and loyal to him alone, the kposi were extensions of his intelligence and consciousness, and they were very likely aids to his thinking and decision making. Yet their lack of autonomy and recognized authority hint at significant changes in the ability of women to exercise autonomous power in the kingdom, in changed conceptions of appropriate gender roles, and in controls over women in Dahomey.

Daughters of the king and other princesses are also linked to nineteenth-century efforts to control the people of Dahomey, and particularly to control individuals of high rank. We saw in chapter 2 that princesses in the early years of the kingdom were prominent politically, participating directly in events that established their lineage's preeminence on the Abomey plateau. Children born of princesses became members of the royal family, and marriages between siblings who were not born of the same mother were allowed within the royal lineage. Both of these deviations from patrilineal patterns practiced by commoners in Dahomey may have functioned to maintain solidarity within the royal family and to allow it to grow relatively quickly. However, princesses' relative autonomy and ability to play central roles within their lineage, and by extension within the kingdom's political system, were contracting in the late nineteenth century.

Despite their political prominence and high social rank, the status of princesses was anomalous in Fon culture. A commoner wife who had been married with full payment of bridewealth ideally spent most of her adult life in the household of her husband. If she won the respect of his kin and was skilled in negotiating the shoals of lineage politics, she could assist her own children to reach lineage leadership positions and might be honored as an ancestor in her husband's family. In contrast, within

the families of their husbands, princess-wives, whose children were affiliated elsewhere, were assumed to have undivided loyalty to the royal lineage and were not integrated into their marital lineages. Typically, princesses established a separate household with the slaves and gifts that their
father presented to them at the time of their marriage. Their children
were royalty, yet they were curiously disadvantaged, being ineligible for
lineage office in the Alladahonu line. Finally, princesses could not be
punished for adultery, which meant that they, like men in Fon society,
controlled their own sexuality.

Our knowledge of the peculiar status of princesses is based mainly on
sources from the late nineteenth and the twentieth centuries. All of those
sources are at best ambiguous and at worst shrilly judgmental about
women born to the royal line. Some heap scorn on the princesses' "sexual
freedom," even though Fon culture was relatively permissive. Reactions
to a commoner wife's adultery, for example, ranged from pretending not
to notice to execution of the woman, depending upon the social rank of
both the husband and the wife. Nevertheless, the more common attitude
was, "If your wife is unfaithful, is that any reason to wish her dead? We
prefer to make accommodations." Other sources condemn princesses for
having liaisons with half-brothers, though the morals of their partners,
the princes and kings who took their sisters as wives, are not questioned.
The popular contempt reflected in these accounts was confirmed to
me again and again in the field. Men took it as a given that princesses
were faithless wives: "Royalty is capable of anything. They can never be
trusted. If, for example, you are married to a princess, and your enemies
put you in prison, she will go out and sleep with your enemies. She'll
sleep with your brother in your own house. A princess will always betray
you. Royalty has no morals, no ethics. They lie and cheat. All things
are permitted to them." [31] Contemporary princesses themselves reflected
popular stereotypes, complaining that they had difficulties in finding
men willing to marry them, yet boasting of their reputations as troublesome co-wives.

How are we to interpret this, and where if anywhere is there evidence
for something changing in the nineteenth century? There are three telling characteristics of nineteenth-century narratives about princesses that

point to change: the accounts are preoccupied with control over female sexuality; they are concerned with princesses only as wives; and they are consistently contradictory.

We have evidence that attempts were made in the nineteenth century to control princesses' sexuality, and control over sexuality generally correlates with attempts to control other aspects of women's lives. Burton says that "formerly, the royal ladies had only temporary husbands, visiting all men who pleased them. As this caused great scandals, the King has forbidden polyandry." Two sons of Glele offer corroborating testimony, saying that their oldest sister, the na daho, was responsible for enforcing proper behavior: "If her younger sisters did not respect their husbands, she would judge them. If they began to act like whores, she would correct them. She would judge disputes between her younger sisters and their husbands." Le Hérissé, too, confirms that princesses were no longer allowed to control their sexuality when he describes punishments for princesses' adultery, commenting that for a princess it was a minor infraction; at worst, the guilty woman spent some months confined at the home of the meu.[32]

Europeans in this period were also told that virginity was expected of princesses. Burton several times mentions the case of the twin first-born daughters of Glele and the yovoganon who lost their virginity to a nephew of the king. Le Hérissé similarly claims that princesses, like commoner girls, had to be virgins. Otherwise, an enraged king, their father, would supposedly take back the very numerous wedding gifts that he had provided.[33] Nevertheless, the twin daughters of Glele did marry the migan and the meu, and evidence from before and after this period, from the eighteenth and twentieth centuries, indicates very little concern on the part of Fon culture with virginity as a principle for anyone.

Second, the behavior and comportment of princesses was constantly discussed in their role as wives, as subordinates to husbands, rather than as sisters of the kings, as persons with a high degree of autonomy. The anthropologist Karen Sacks has argued that women as sisters in kin-corporate forms of social organization enjoyed relatively greater ability to influence events than they did in the subordinate position of wife, a finding that is consistent with Dahomean patterns. Discussing princesses only in the role of wife, then, is a subtle but telling distinction and commentary about their relative status. In early Dahomey, princesses had been married politically, and their marriages cemented alliances between Dahomey and neighboring kingdoms. In the mid–nineteenth century, princesses continued to marry in political alliances, though virtually all of the recorded examples are of princesses being married internally, to high-ranking officials of the kingdom. For example, the two oldest daughters of the king were always married to the migan and meu, the migan wedding the elder. Thus the na daho, the senior daughter of Glele who had authority over younger siblings, was also known as na migansi (literally, princess-wife of the migan). Lesser officials were given other women of the royal line in marriage.

Not only were princesses being seen more and more as wives of officials rather than independent members of the royal lineage, they were as such also more and more despised and distrusted. Le Hérissé notes that marriage to a princess could be problematic, because "flattered in his pride and desirous of taking full advantage of the benefits of the alliance, the husband of a princess would show himself to be full of attention for her; he would consult her in many circumstances, dress her beautifully, and finally give her precedence over his other wives. . . . But if, later, he had reason to complain about his wife, could he in good conscience go disparage her before the king? Could he denigrate before the giver the gift that had been given him?" Forbes raised the problem of marriage to a princess far more directly and bluntly, saying "no office under government is paid, and the offices . . . are subject to much espionage. In the house of each minister lives a king's daughter and two officers: these superintend the minister's trade, on which he pays tribute according to their report. . . . The whole system is one of espionage, cunning, and intrigue."[34] Forbes's description of a princess-wife as a spy in the household reflects images of royal female treachery that apparently became common in the nineteenth century. It evokes the memory of the legend of Na Geze, the daughter of Agaja who married the king of Whydah. By spying on her husband and his household, Na Geze was able to pave the way for the Dahomean victory over the kingdom of the Hweda. A myth that did not exist shortly after the 1727 conquest, the myth of Na Geze may well have been invented in the late nineteenth century, because it demonstrates vividly the dangers that popular thought of that period projected onto marital liaisons with princesses.

Visitors' accounts, when read closely, further raise questions about images of women and the way influences in gender attitudes were moving back and forth between Europe and Africa. Forbes, who spent a good deal of time visiting and being visited by ministers and prominent princes, clearly understood that those private visits of cordiality provided intelligence to him about the politics of the kingdom and gave members of the monarchy insights into European thinking. However, when the na daho, like her brothers, sent Forbes yams and fruit with an invitation to call, he interpreted her overture as sexually motivated and rebuffed it.[35] Was he right? Was she in fact seeking a sexual liaison, as befitted the reputation of princesses, or was she behaving as a member of the monarchy, a high-ranking princess who, like her brothers, needed to cultivate a foreigner for reasons of state? And how did the Dahomeans interpret the fact that Forbes refused to see her? How did such incidents, confirming the lack of access for women to European envoys, affect princesses' ability to participate at the center of power?

Princesses by the mid–nineteenth century were also becoming ahosi, members of the palace organization. Gezo had begun to appoint his brothers to high offices, a practice that Glele continued and expanded, and Behanzin assembled a monarchy that was nearly exclusively royal. We have evidence that by the time of Glele, princesses were being named to the ministerial posts paralleling the gbonugan daho. Yet such offices had to be held by women within the palace organization, by ahosi, persons who were by definition dependents or wives of the king. Children of Glele and Behanzin spoke to me with some embarrassment of the fact that many of Behanzin's most prominent wives were also his sisters.[36] Certainly, women in high-ranking positions within the palace exercised power, yet by exercising their power as wives rather than sisters, princesses lost the autonomy that had earlier characterized their political lives as royal equals to their brothers.

Finally, there is a great deal of ambiguity and contradiction about princesses that hints that attitudes toward them were in flux; by extension, that suggests their status was changing. Perhaps most striking is the account of the usually balanced Le Hérissé, whose own marriage to a daughter of Behanzin early in the colonial period must have compromised his official position from time to time. On the one hand, Le Hérissé argues that marriage to a princess was a great honor and mark of favor by the king; on the other, he claims that a man chosen to be king had to be born of a woman of commoner background, since princesses' morals were such that a king could never be sure of the paternity of his sons by women of royal blood. Princesses "go around spreading gossip, stirring up intrigues and . . . selling love."[37]

Princesses became the unwelcome gift-wives of high officials in the nineteenth century, but commoner men who were members of the gbonugan daho and commoner caboceers, the holders of other chiefly offices, were subject to other unwanted changes that signaled a consolidation of power within the hands of the royal lineage. They and their lineages must have watched with some consternation as Glele and later his son Behanzin systematically named their own brothers to offices formerly reserved for anyone *but* a member of the royal family. Along with women of the palace organization, they would have also shared concern at seeing Glele take another prince as his closest adviser and most intimate friend.

In the eighteenth century, the royal wives had been described both as close advisers to the king and as persons who were trustees of the king's wishes, particularly his wishes in the naming of an heir. By the reign of Glele, in addition to the several bokonon (diviners) who were central in advising the king, there was a male member of the royal family who was recognized as the king's confidant and best friend. That person was the Prince Adandejan, a son of Gnimavo, who was a son of King Agonglo. He was described by Burton as "a favourite at court," someone said to have been made very wealthy by his friend Glele, even though he was only a "lieutenant" of the migan. Nevertheless, Adandejan was acknowledged as the king's dearest friend and a close adviser. Adandejan, for example, was one of only three male courtiers present when Glele with "half-a-dozen 'ladies'" received Burton in private audience.[38] Some years later, Adandejan's son received his father's name and estate, and in turn made himself a friend of Behanzin. When the defeated Dahomeans were forced to sue for terms with the French invading forces in 1892 and 1893, it was Adandejan, usually in the company of one other trusted adviser of the king, who most often would be listed as envoy from Behanzin. In 1894, he would become the only adult male of the royal family to accompany the deposed king into exile.[39]

Religion and Royal Control ∿

The changing pattern of relations between the royal family and commoners in Dahomey was mirrored in the religious life of the kingdom. Kutome, the spirit world, was conceived as an exact image of Gbetome, the world of the living. In that sense, Fon culture inscribed its intellectual history on the realm of the spirits as the monarchy reordered and recreated the invisible world to suit an idealized conception of order and power as it existed, or should exist, in the visible world. We can read the record of the changing hierarchies of the gods and the altered patterns of officials responsible for their control to see the degree to which commoner families in the late nineteenth century had been distanced from access to power. Religious practices also hint of new conceptions of the center of power, of an image of an idealized monarch who would centralize and monopolize power in his own person as representative of all the kings who had gone before. Two major changes in religious organization underscore these new conceptions of power and who might legitimately wield it. The first was the development of worship that honored deified members of the royal family: the Nesuhwe, princes and princesses, and their more powerful and dangerous siblings, the tohosu. The second was the practice of Fa divination, which had begun to take center stage in the spiritual and decision-making life of the king and kingdom.

The word *Nesuhwe* (occasionally *lensouhwe*) does not appear in the literature until the nineteenth century, when people such as the Roman Catholic missionary Borghero remarked the "mysterious" divinity Nesu, who was worshipped in "obscure and hidden temples" around the city of Abomey. Nesuhwe celebrated the lives of the sons and daughters of the kings, though it did not memorialize all the children of all the kings. Clustered into congregations, each of which incorporated the children of a given king, Nesuhwe appears to have included only the most important direct children—for example, lineage officeholders such as the na daho (oldest daughter), the vigan (literally, chief of the children, the effective lineage head of that branch of the royal family), numerous zinkponon (titled holders of estates), and others said to have been of central importance during and after their father's reign. The numbers of royalty remembered and honored through Nesuhwe were 20 to 30 in each of the individual branches of the royal family, divided fairly evenly between men and women, though literally dozens of children were fathered by individual monarchs. For example, a census of the children of Glele and Behanzin taken after the fall of the kingdom found that 129 children of Glele and 77 of Behanzin's children had survived to maturity.[40] Venerated as vodun, these humans-turned-god were honored by adepts initiated into their worship, who would be possessed by their princely ancestors during ceremonies. Followers of Nesuhwe were theoretically all royalty, descendants within the various branches of the royal family of the vodun being honored. In fact, Nesuhwe and the related congregations dedicated to the tohosu were the only vodun to which members of the royal family might pledge themselves as vodunsi.

As spirits, the tohosu appear to have predated the Nesuhwe, though they were effectively subsumed under the category of "children of the king" (see chapter 3). Tohosu are said to have made themselves known to Fon culture initially at mid–eighteenth century, during the reign of Tegbesu. Originally born only in the royal family, tohosu were creatures with anomalous characteristics, whose arrival demanded ritual attention. "When a Tohosu comes to earth, it is in the body of an abnormal or monstrous infant. For a Tohosu, to be born is a sign of discontent, a call to order."[41] Tohosu might be declared at the appearance of any abnormality in a newborn, with signs that ranged from hair and teeth at birth to extreme physical deformities that were typically attributed to the most powerful of the royal tohosu. Even a spontaneous abortion or stillbirth might be considered a tohosu. If recognized, tohosu were said to be returned to the fluid world from which they had come; their name means, literally, king of the water, in the sense of a marsh or swamp. Eldest among the tohosu was Akaba's fearsome offspring Zumadunu, a creature born with six eyes and a growth on his buttocks so enormous that it dragged after him when he walked. Within a day he had transformed himself into a ball, and then a bird, which remained his central visual symbol. Significantly, the tohosu combined elements that were linked conceptually to both the deified members of the royal family and to the popular vodun. Children of kings, on the one hand, they were beings who belonged submerged within the blackness of swamps, areas that suggested the awesome supernatural, yet associated-with-nature powers of popular vodun. Tohosu were beings born of the royal lineage, yet originally their priests went north to Mahi country to learn how to worship them, just as priests had done for many other popular vodun that entered Dahomey. Perhaps this was the characteristic of the tohosu—that they were popular vodun imported yet transformed to descendants in the royal line—that prompted the monarchy to impose them as paramount over all the other gods. Whatever the reason, by the time of Glele, it was Zumadunu who reigned as first divinity in the kingdom of Dahomey.

During the eighteenth century, Zumadunu's priest and the titular head of all the tohosu was Mivede, who reported to Hwanjile, the kpojito of Tegbesu. Hwanjile, of course, had during that period assumed control over the regulation of all the vodun, reworking the hierarchy of the gods under the creator-deities, Mawu and Lisa, for whom she was a priest and benefactor. As heads of the realm of Kutome, Mawu and Lisa in turn suggested an eighteenth-century conception of power that balanced male and female, royal and commoner. We last saw Hwanjile in 1797, when she was implicated in the murder of Agonglo and was a member of the defeated side in the succession struggle that led to the reign of Adandozan. Whether it was because of that incident or because of a broader ideological change in definitions of leadership, by mid–nineteenth century Hwanjile and her protégé-vodun no longer controlled religious life, though she still remained titular high priest for Mawu and Lisa. Three other names are variously mentioned as key figures in the religious life of the late nineteenth century: the ajaho, the minister of religion appointed by the king; Mivede, the priest of Zumadunu; and the agasunon, the priest of Agasu, leopard-totem of the royal family. The ajaho's responsibilities exactly duplicated those formerly entrusted to Hwanjile: to be a liaison between the monarchy and the priests of the popular vodun, to regulate the appointment and investiture of priests, to authorize the installation of new shrines to vodun, to oversee the timing of ceremonies, and to be initial judge of offenses committed by followers of the vodun. Mivede and the agasunon were central to the long succession of rituals that honored the ancestors of the royal family, which by mid–nineteenth century were by law the primary ceremonies of the religious life of the kingdom.

The religious year in nineteenth-century Dahomey began with the honoring of the ancestors of the kings. These were the most important ceremonies of Customs. They involved a cycle of ceremonies in which the king, the agasunon, and the assembled court visited the spirits of each departed king and kpojito in order, offering prayers and sacrifices that reordered and reconfirmed the balance between Kutome and Gbetome. Immediately following the cycle of palace ceremonies in honor of kings and kpojito came the turn of the tohosu. Their rites were followed by the celebration of the Nesuhwe. It was weeks or months later, after the end of all the royal ceremonies, that commoner families were permitted to honor their ancestors and the priests of the popular vodun were allowed to perform their ceremonies. Even funeral ceremonies could not take place until the process of honoring the royal ancestors—kings and kpojito, tohosu and Nesuhwe—was complete. By delaying the honoring of the spiritual forces associated with commoner ancestors and the popular vodun, the monarchy kept the followers of those spirits under a severe constraint, because they risked suffering the displeasure of their own vodun while they waited for the royal ceremonies to be completed. In fact, what began to happen in the late nineteenth century was a social reordering that worked simultaneously to minimize the dangers of the religious system for the lower-ranking spiritual entities while it reinforced and reaffirmed the centrality of the royal lineage. The network that provided the framework for this reordering was the system of tohosu.

Each new reign in Dahomey produced a new branch of the royal lineage that included the descendants of all the sons and daughters of the king, plus literally hundreds of followers, wives, slaves, and other dependents. The members of each of these new sublineages established what was effectively a new quarter of Abomey. Their numbers incorporated the households of numerous high-ranking persons of commoner and slave origin who were part of or were attached to that king's monarchy to perform functions of some kind: they included, for example, ministers and officials, artisans established as ahosi, and priests of vodun imported during that reign. In these quarters of the capital city, the descendants of the monarchies of past reigns continued to reside in close proximity to each other. Sometimes individuals adopted the names of the princely line as their own; others maintained their lineage names but remained under the jural authority of the vigan, the head of their particular branch of the royal family. As the strict hierarchy for the honoring of the vodun was solidified in the time of Glele, commoner lines attached to particular branches of the royal family began to be permitted to recognize tohosu in their own families. These commoner tohosu could be honored at the same time as their royal-patron tohosu. Thus families attached to particular kings but not originally of royal birth could move up in the hierarchy of the vodun, effectively honoring their own tohosu-ancestor along with the tohosu of their particular branch of the Alladahonu line. They would simultaneously move up socially in the hierarchy of rank and privilege in a world where royal blood was increasingly the most significant marker. At the same time, major figures from a given reign such as the migan and the meu would become deified as vodun of the Nesuhwe of their branch of the royal family. In effect, tohosu and Nesuhwe began to draw virtually everyone in Abomey and—through the extended networks of kinship and service—everyone on the plateau and ultimately in the kingdom into relationships of subordination to one or another branch of the royal lineage.[42]

What was effectively happening in the late nineteenth century was a social and religious rearrangement that was based on a hierarchical vision of social structure. Members of the current ruling branch of the royal family were at the top of that hierarchy, followed in order by the previous branches of the royal line. Commoners, rather than standing as necessary partners with the Alladahonu, were relegated to a low social status, which they modified using the ameliorating vehicle of the tohosu to effect religious alliances with royalty. That same hierarchical vision of the primacy of the royal line was reified in the pattern of appointments to various high offices of the land, as sons and daughters of kings replaced commoners. Yet the sweep of royalty into control and the exclusion of commoners from power was never complete. Rather, there was a good deal of ideological tension and confusion, and there were curious inconsistencies in the patterns by which the late-nineteenth-century kings squeezed men and women of common birth out of high offices and replaced them with their close relatives. For example, both Glele and Behanzin named brothers and other princes to the ranks of the gbonugan daho and appointed ahosi-princesses as officials within the palace; yet in their exercise of power and their decision making, Glele and Behanzin did not depend fully on their own royal appointees, and sometimes do not even appear to have trusted them. The last kings of independent Dahomey as often as not worked with a tiny handful of male advisers, including a small number of bokonon or diviners of Fa. It is very likely that all of these individuals represented and reified the idea that power could and should be monopolized by a male absolute monarch.

During the reign of Tegbesu, the Fa (Ifa) system of divination was one of several competing systems for making decisions and foretelling the future. By the nineteenth century, it had become the predominant system. Freeman in the 1840s declared that Fa (Affar) was the most important "fetish" of the nation.[43] Fa flourished and was strengthened through the cultural links with Yorubaland that were the by-product of nineteenth-century warfare and the disintegration of Oyo. Yoruba-speaking diviners settled in Dahomey, and Dahomeans, including some sons of Gezo and Glele, went to Yorubaland to study Ifa in the families of their Yoruba-speaking mothers.

The first European to call attention to the central position of diviners of Fa at court was Burton, who was lodged in Abomey at the home of Glele's leading bokonon, rather than in the quarters of the meu, where visitors to Gezo's court had normally been housed. Burton describes the bokonon as the elderly son of Gezo's favorite diviner, a man who had predicted that Glele would be named king long before his appointment as vidaho. Glele thereafter trusted his word and was guided "in all his movements by his Buko-no."[44] The man was well-to-do, having received slaves and land from his patron, and he had some eighty wives, including a princess. At least two other bokonon, and possibly several more, were prominent advisors to Glele. Nugbodohwe, to whom Glele gave the revealing name "The house where truth is told," is generally cited as that king's principal diviner. Nugbodohwe, a central political figure, would take a stand against Glele's successor at the time of the king's death.[45] The other well-known diviner of Glele's era was Gedegbe, whose biography and personal philosophy anchor Maupoil's monumental study of divination.

The various bokonon of the king consulted Fa daily for virtually every decision to be taken; nothing was done without bokonon's advice. Knowledgeable as herbalists, the king's diviners also prescribed medicines to the palace inhabitants and on occasion to visiting Europeans who fell ill. Maurice Glélé argues that the bokonon in a sense shared power with the king—a perspective also shared by Maupoil.[46] The bokonon's very presence in the interior of the palace, and the nature of the belief system that they represented and manipulated, are telling signs of the changing ideological vision of the kingship and monarchy.

There were two characteristics of the Fa system of divination that distinguished it from other spiritual and ritual practices among the Fon: first, Fa focused on the male; and second, it was concerned wholly with the individual. As such, Fa contrasted starkly with Fon popular and royal deities. Women were typically the principal followers of vodun and held leadership positions in the chapter houses organized to worship them. Initiated into the sacred knowledge of the god, both female and male adepts communed directly with the spirits through the vehicle of possession, when the vodun would mount on their heads. The approach to the vodun was public and communal, set in open spaces of towns and villages and accompanied by music and dance that called all to witness. In contrast, Fa was private and hidden. Consultations were held within the closed interior spaces of compounds or in the secrecy of sacred forests. Unlike other vodun, Fa distanced the believer from the deity, requiring the intercession of a highly trained male specialist, the bokonon, for full consultation with the spirit world.[47] Anyone, male or female, could go to a diviner to seek knowledge of the unknown. However, following the patriarchal imperatives of Yoruba culture, Fa was centrally concerned with men's obligation to learn their destiny. At its deepest levels, Fa divination encouraged men to live their lives so as to build on the hidden knowledge of their fate, identifying and neutralizing dangers that otherwise were concealed from them, recognizing and taking advantage of opportunities, and generally promoting the fortunes of their patrilineage. Ideally, men at a relatively young age learned their kpoli, their sacred personal sign, through a retreat and ritual directed by a bokonon. Thereafter, they were expected to continue a lifelong quest for personal direction and certainty, their path guided by one or more bokonon. The system effectively demanded the building of an intimate intellectual and emotional relationship between a male client and his male adviser-diviner.

Not everyone was meant to pursue knowledge of personal destiny. A man's subordinates and followers, for example, might not need to know their kpoli—because they could be seen as sharing their leader's fate. More significantly, women's destinies were tied to and subsumed under those of their fathers and husbands. With the exception of some princesses and other relatively autonomous persons, women rarely learned their sacred signs, and even then were limited to the early stages of the lifelong process of discovery of personal destiny. The system of Fa divination thus assumed the subordination of women and reinforced it through its exclusively male priesthood and its view that only men as autonomous beings were worthy of personal destinies.

Like the Egungun and Oro societies, also imported from Yorubaland in the nineteenth century, the belief system of Fa was deeply concerned with issues of control over women. Perhaps most indicative of woman's lowly place in the gaze of Fa was the existence of the related vodun, Gbaadu, imported from Yorubaland by a bokonon of Glele. Known as Odu to Yoruba-speakers, Gbaadu represented the totality of knowledge of Fa, and was considered to be extremely powerful and dangerous, more dangerous and difficult to control than Fa himself. Indeed, Gbaadu's few male priests never met publicly, so dangerous were the approaches to their divinity. The vodun's danger was acute for wives of the heads of households who had installed Gbaadu in their homes, because the vodun instantly killed any woman who even thought about committing adultery. Women were absolutely forbidden to become adepts of Gbaadu. The hostility of the vodun to the female was emphasized by the list of ingredients needed to install Gbaadu in a new shrine: it included preserved female genitals, cut from a woman who died during pregnancy.[48]

What was the impact of all this on conceptions of power at the center of Dahomey? The practice of Fa has to have focused the attention of the men who were king on themselves and their personal destinies. The king was aho, the avatar of all his ancestors, the sum total of all those who had gone before. Conceptually, the practice of Fa must have contributed to a blurring of distinctions between individual and dynastic destinies, between king and kingdom. In private sessions with the bokonon of Fa, all that was important was the destiny of a single man. Gone were concerns for a kingdom made up of complementary parts, of alliances between an intrusive lineage and the owners of the land. Gone was a need to balance the interests of the royal lineage with the interests of commoners, of a necessity to integrate foreigners into a social order, of an obligation to balance male and female, of a need to ease tensions between inside and outside. All that mattered was the advice offered by Fa, as determined by the bokonon. Ironically, then, the late nineteenth-century kings pushed commoners out of high office to make room for their own siblings, but then turned for their most trusted counsel to men who had come from a foreign culture and enemy territory, priests who controlled a spiritual system that denied and negated many of the principles still proclaimed as the binding ideological cement of the nation.

Fa, the tohosu, and Nesuhwe had moved to a central position among the spiritual entities believed to participate in the vagaries of human existence. And what of the previous paramount spirits of the Dahomean hierarchy of the gods, Mawu and Lisa? Humans who set up new gods as central obviously risked the wrath of the older, displaced deities. Maupoil, reflecting the vision of the diviner Gedegbe, explains the transformation by noting that Mawu and Lisa together as creator deities continued to set the destinies of all human beings. Though they had divided the world of the gods among the various vodun, Mawu and Lisa reserved this ultimate creative act to themselves. Thus Fa, who revealed portions of their destiny to humans, was simply the voice of Mawu and Lisa. Yet in this role and in Maupoil's conception—and presumably in the conception of royal bokonon of the nineteenth century—Fa was superior to Mawu and Lisa, for without Fa, all other vodun were condemned to be silent, unable to be heard by humanity. Because Fa had to be consulted at virtually all decision-making moments, Fa was effectively supreme, because "whether it's a matter of a ceremony, of a sacrifice, of some problem identified in the practice of a cult, Fa is always consulted on the nature, time, place and length of measures to be taken. All the *vodun* are in this sense under his control. One can see the political importance invested in such a power; in any case, only the grand priests of Fa had continual access to the king of Abomey, who even gave them a site for consulting in the interior of his palace." [49] The royal conceptions of power relations were inscribed in the hierarchy of the vodun. There ruled the titular head of all, Zumadunu, a member of the royal dynasty, a being whose non-humanoid form made him a worthy and appropriate king, both over other deified humans and the popular vodun who had never existed in human form. But even Zumadunu did not rule alone. Fa challenged and effectively superseded Zumadunu's power and the power of all the other vodun through his control over communications between the seen and the unseen.

Succession in the Time of Glele and Behanzin ∿

The death of Gezo is described in detail and at relatively great length by Dunglas. Gezo was with his army returning from war waged in Egba territory near Meko in late 1858. In the vicinity of Ekpo, a village considered part of the kingdom of Ketu, King Gezo stepped down from his hammock and was shot and wounded by a young man who then managed to escape. Assuming that the gunman was from Ekpo, which the Dahomeans had attacked the previous February, the army turned and devastated the village. Meanwhile, the king was rushed back to Abomey. Gezo lingered for ten to fifteen days and then died of infection from the wound. Freeman was told what was essentially a confirming tradition—that Gezo had "caught a fever" on a war expedition to Po (Ekpo) and died. Later visitors heard the euphemism that smallpox had caused

Gezo's death, though a slow-moving report correctly noting the real cause reached the British Foreign Office in time to be misunderstood as information about Glele and forwarded to Burton in 1863.[50]

The accessions of Glele in 1858 and of his son Behanzin in 1889 were similar in many respects. Both men were recognized as heir long in advance of their fathers' deaths. As vidaho, each was permitted to develop the power base necessary to take and keep control. Both were visible and active at the courts of their fathers, and were well known to European visitors to Abomey. At the death of his predecessor, each vidaho was opposed by another prince. The rivals to Glele and Behanzin were allied with and promoted by powerful women of the palace organization. Each of the women champions of the would-be kings held the same office, that of the tononu, head of the household of the king. Although persons in the office of tononu were expected to die with the king, both women were exempted from the death requirement. The similarities of the accessions of Glele and Behanzin contrast with earlier succession struggles. Taken together, they suggest that the succession process had changed in significant ways, and they highlight the increasing efforts of the royal family to monopolize power in the kingdom.

There were at least three men named vidaho during the reigns of Gezo and Glele. Gezo selected Badahun, who took the name Glele on his enstoolment. Shortly after Glele consolidated his power as king, his son Ahanhanzo was named vidaho. When Ahanhanzo died in 1876, another son of Glele, Kondo, became the official heir, and it was Kondo who succeeded Glele under the name Behanzin. All three nineteenth-century vidaho enjoyed opportunities and privileges not known to their eighteenth-century predecessors.

Gezo had named Prince Badahun his vidaho at the latest by the 1840s. Badahun was introduced to Forbes in 1849 and was mentioned regularly by travelers in the 1850s. Some traditions claim that a son of Adandozan had been Gezo's vidaho for some twenty years after the coup of circa 1818, which suggests that Gezo may have waited to name his own vidaho until he had an adult son born to him after he had taken power. Whatever the case, Gezo appears to have decided to make sure that his vidaho would enjoy a strong enough power base to win the kingship without opposition. He set about instituting changes in the process by which a prince

8. A nineteenth-century king, probably Gezo, with attendants. Note the similarities with the dress of the women soldiers in the Paris photo (fig. 9). (Collection Musée de l'Homme, Paris)

became king in Dahomey. Those changes included strengthening the position of the vidaho and attempting to preempt a physical struggle within the palace.

Accounts based on nineteenth-century sources describe an education for heirs to the stool of Dahomey that put them at the center of the mon-

archy well before their father's death. As in the eighteenth century, potential heirs were reared in the households of ministers and other prominent
persons, being given land, wives, and slaves as they came of age. The
nineteenth-century mentors, however, tended to be the closest and dearest associates of the king. Badahun, the future Glele, grew up in the
household of Tometin, the royal meu and uterine brother of the king. He
remained Tometin's protégé throughout the lifetime of Gezo. In turn,
Glele's first vidaho, Ahanhanzo, was reared in the home of the king's
closest ally and friend, the prince Adandejan. Kondo, in contrast, was
an adult by the time he was named vidaho. Oral traditions are divided
about his upbringing and character. One source says that he was reared
by Hehegunon, a son of Gezo who became ajaho (minister of religion)
under Glele. Another claims that he was tutored by the deposed king
Adandozan, a tradition that is clearly meant to discredit him. Evidence
does suggest, nevertheless, that unlike Ahanhanzo, Kondo did not enjoy
a close personal relationship with his father.[51]

Each prince named to the position of vidaho would develop an estate
and build a palace on the outskirts of Abomey on land granted him by
his father. Jegbe, now a quarter of Abomey peopled by descendentss of
Glele, grew up around the palace established by Badahun. His palace
became a center where he received prominent visitors, including Europeans, and where he enjoyed rights that included the ability to pardon
fugitives from justice whom he chose to protect. Similarly, Ahanhanzo
had a residence near that of his mentor, Adandejan, where he received
and charmed visitors such as Skertchly. Kondo built Jime, which remains
the ancestral home of the descendants of Behanzin.

Unlike their predecessors, the vidaho of Gezo and Glele were not kept
away from politics, but took part in councils of state and were often present at private audiences of the king. Freeman, for example, spoke of night
meetings with Gezo that were attended by "two or three favorite wives,"
by the meu, and by the future Glele. Ahanhanzo and Kondo similarly
were present at court and active in public deliberations. Other sources
stress the role of the king in preparing the crown prince for power. Le
Hérissé claims that the king shared royal secrets with the heir, including

the secret history of the origins of the royal family, a history that was not revealed to outsiders until the twentieth century. Maurice Glélé similarly argues that the king instructed the vidaho privately in the history of the kingdom and how to govern it, having conversations with him each year at the closing of the ceremonies in honor of the royal ancestors.[52]

Despite the evidence that Gezo actively promoted Badahun and strengthened his position as vidaho, some twentieth-century historians have interpreted the succession from Gezo to Glele as a struggle between two factions, or parties, grouped respectively around one or the other. The faction allied with the king was said to have been progressive, modernizing, pro-European and committed to the ending of the slave trade and human sacrifice. The other faction, linked to Badahun, was conservative, militaristic, anti-European, and deeply committed to the continuation of human sacrifice. The enstoolment of Glele thus represented the triumph of reactionary forces and the negation of all the reforms that Gezo had instituted. In fact, as we have seen in the case of the king-as-prince and the enlargement of the ceremonial cycle, Gezo's monarchy had not really departed from the fundamental principles upon which the kingdom had been created. The monarchy had made a decision in early 1852 to sign a treaty with Britain promising to abolish the slave trade out of Whydah. Simultaneously, they moved to promote, aggressively, the production of palm oil and kernels. John Reid has shown that, when the economy continued to stumble by 1855–56, when a settlement with Abeokuta remained elusive, when a potential slave revolt was uncovered in 1855, and when cowry inflation threatened chaos, discussions began at court about the viability of the new policy. When the demand for slaves arose anew in 1857, the monarchy rapidly retreated from its apparent acquiescence to British demands.[53] In short, the issue of two opposing policy directions appears to have been settled more than a year before the death of Gezo.

Evidence also suggests that the so-called parties of the 1855–56 period were much less hard and firm than later interpretations have suggested. French observers in particular spoke of a party of resistance, a "national" party that had grown up around the crown prince in opposition to the

king. Supposedly allied with Badahun in this party was the meu. A closer
look at the European accounts, however, indicates a more complex situation. The meu in 1856, described as being about eighty years old, was
Voglosu, a commoner who had served King Adandozan and had been
part of the cabal that plotted the coup d'état against him with Gezo. English and French sources make clear that it was the meu, as opposed to
the migan, who was particularly influential at court. Freeman declared
that "he seemed to be, as it were, the King's second self." French visitors
concurred, grumbling that the meu was virtually always present in audiences and that no business could be transacted without him. In contrast,
the migan, supposedly the prime minister, rarely appeared in European
accounts. Forbes met him in 1850 and described him as a man in his
forties. This suggests that Atindebaku, the commoner migan first named
by Gezo, had died and been replaced (Ganse, the original migan of royal
blood, was still alive in 1849). It also suggests that the original members
of the monarchy of Gezo played a preponderant role in political discussions right up to the death of the king.[54]

Dr. Repin, a French visitor of 1856, believed that the meu was more
favorable to both the British and the Portuguese than to the French.
Anxious to get the king's agreement to a French request to establish a
trading settlement in Abomey, and believing that the meu was responsible for constraints on trading in Whydah, Repin struggled to see the
king outside the presence of his seemingly hostile meu. On the other
hand, Freeman believed that the meu was *not* favorable to the British
and complained that he was antimissionary and pro–slave trade. In fact,
one of the things that Meu Voglosu and Badahun appear to have had in
common was a less cordial manner with Europeans than that of Gezo.
But that does not necessarily mean that together they represented a distinct party or that they promoted a specific ideological position or policy
over any extended period of time. Indeed, Freeman enlisted the aid of
Badahun to bypass the meu. He appealed successfully to the male tononu, "by whose assistance we are enabled to counteract the old mewu's
intrigues." Freeman later worked out a scheme by which he received,
through the good offices of Badahun and the tononu, private access to
Gezo outside the presence of the meu.[55]

Obviously, given this evidence of the fluidity of individual relation-ships in court at a moment of changing policy, it seems mistaken to view the succession as a rivalry between Gezo and Badahun—a kind of oedipal encounter between father and son. Granted, Gezo was more than sixty years of age by 1858 and Badahun had had enough of a taste of power to be ready to rule in his own right. But there is no evidence that there were deep divisions between Gezo and Badahun just before the king's death. The king had named Badahun his heir and made no moves to remove him from that position. Freeman described father and son in 1856 as being "fondly attached"; Gezo seemingly withheld no secrets from his vidaho. And a French visitor of the period stressed the seriousness with which Badahun's views were heard at court.[56]

Why, then, does the reported policy split between Gezo and his son loom so large in European records of the time? The answer lies less in Dahomey and more in the British preoccupation or obsession with the slave trade and human sacrifice. Indeed, the diplomatic conversations be-tween British envoys and both Gezo and Glele are eerily similar, suggest-ing that the kings and their monarchies held essentially similar views. As we have seen, the Dahomean position on the slave trade had been clear virtually from the moment that Gezo insisted that he could stop the trade only in Whydah: the Dahomeans, including the king, would trade slaves as long as buyers came along the coast. Among the signatories to the 1852 treaty were several individuals later cited as opponents of the pact, which suggests that the decision to cooperate with the British, as well as the decision to return to openly trading slaves, was a collective one of the monarchy, not a policy made or upheld by the king alone. As for Gezo's perspective on human sacrifice, there was a persistent belief among Brit-ish observers at midcentury that the number of persons sacrificed was dropping, and that the king was moving toward the drastic reduction, if not the elimination, of human sacrifice in the kingdom. Yet the patterns of sacrifice apparent during midcentury are ambiguous at best.

The British visitors to Dahomey in the 1840s and 1850s sought evidence that the humanitarian efforts of their government were yielding positive results. Inevitably, travelers must have recorded their conversations with the king with an eye to their own reputations, to the mandates that they had been given, and to the impact that their words would have on their own constituencies: the British Foreign Office, missionary societies, and even the popular press in England. Gezo, and in his turn Glele, were adept at parrying British demands, or, more accurately, skilled at making arguments that visitors could find acceptable. For example, the Dahomeans knew that capital punishment was common in England. Following his first meetings with Freeman in 1843, Gezo consistently argued that the individuals sacrificed at Customs were all criminals, or at least war captives "who, if they could, would do the same." [57]

The belief of Europeans that only criminals were sacrificed persisted well beyond Gezo's death and was even used by detractors of Glele to emphasize his supposed brutality in comparison with the reforming Gezo. A French missionary who spent three years in Dahomey in the early 1860s wrote that "Guezo . . . tried in part to destroy the bloody institutions that he had inherited from his predecessors. Sacrifices to the gods took place only at long intervals; each time the human slaughter was less great and less pure: rather than innocent people, they killed only the guilty." [58]

Beginning with Duncan's 1846 visit, the British believed and constantly repeated their perception that Gezo had drastically reduced the numbers of individuals sacrificed. Duncan set the tone by declaring that the "intelligent and generous" Gezo had abolished human sacrifice "in a great measure," killing only "culprits condemned to death for offenses of the gravest character" and refusing to allow caboceers to perform human sacrifice. Subsequent embassies, while regretting that any sacrifice at all continued, still believed that Gezo himself was a reluctant instrument of ancient superstition. Forbes, for example, proudly proclaimed that the numbers had dropped from 240 sacrificed in 1848 to only 32 in 1849. Twentieth-century scholars have repeated the litany of fewer sacrificed, sometimes going so far as to argue that fewer were killed because of the positive influence of Chacha de Souza on the monarchy.[59] Yet this certainty that numbers of sacrifice victims had been reduced may have been related less to Gezo's conscience than to the European envoys' desires to convince their audiences of the effectiveness of their negotiations.

In fact, we have no idea how many persons were sacrificed at any given moment in Gezo's era, nor do we have reliable figures for the reigns of his predecessors or successors. One oral tradition claims that Gezo had mounted his coup d'état because Adandozan had reduced the number of sacrifices. Taken at face value, that tradition suggests that Gezo should have *increased* sacrifices. There was no set number of sacrifices in a given ceremonial cycle, and the European visitors knew that their "counts" of victims were guesses. Forbes himself, after asserting the dramatic drop in 1849, again counted 32 sacrifice victims during his visit of early 1850, but averred that "I have no doubt many more victims were sacrificed." The number of persons sent to Kutome most likely varied according to the circumstances at a given moment. Larger numbers might be despatched, paradoxically, in very good or very bad years, as thanksgiving for a well-fought war or especially abundant harvest, or alternatively as a plea for aid, particularly in a crisis.[60]

If in fact the numbers of sacrifice victims varied, why was Gezo said to have reduced them? Was it reasonable that Europeans had received the impression that there were fewer sacrifices late in the reign of Gezo? Or were British visitors in particular seeing what they wanted to believe rather than what was happening?

Dahomey had had a series of major wars and victories in the first two decades after Gezo's coup. The victory over Oyo and the ending of tributary status must have occasioned relatively large celebrations, with relatively large numbers of human sacrifices. The Oyo Customs permanently added at least a few sacrifice victims to the toll. A series of wars in the 1830s had ended by the early 1840s with the conquest of Mahi country to the north-northeast. These, too, would have been celebrated with unusually large numbers of sacrifices. In contrast, the late 1840s and the 1850s saw no triumphs of such stature. The only major military venture of the period was the 1851 attack on Abeokuta that ended in ignominious defeat. There followed several years when war and ritual both were relatively quiescent. Thus comments that European travelers of the 1840s and 1850s heard from long-time observers of the kingdom, that the numbers of victims were fewer than in the past, may have had some validity.

On the other hand, there is no hard evidence that the Gezo monarchy reduced the number of persons sacrificed in response to objections from

Europeans. Nor is there evidence that Gezo sincerely wished to abolish human sacrifice, which had long been a fundamental religious rite. Indeed, the principle of sacrifice in Dahomey was central, as it was in the Judeo-Christian tradition. The sacrifice of a human being was an extraordinary offering—the greatest gift that could be offered to the gods. When the French forcibly ended human sacrifice after the conquest, the Dahomean religious tradition continued to practice sacrifice as a sacrament, substituting cattle as the most valuable of creatures. And the belief in the efficacy of human sacrifice clearly continued into the twentieth century. An incident in the 1930s underlined its power. An ambitious son of Glele and chief of a district on the outskirts of Abomey was accused of having sacrificed a young girl in ancestral ceremonies, sparking an administrative investigation and search for the child that ended in some ambiguity. Nevertheless, the incident unambiguously underlined the primary importance of human sacrifice in the belief system of Dahomeans.[61]

Finally, factors following Gezo's death also contributed to the contrast between kings, because Glele through his filial piety gained a reputation for savagery in the first few years of his reign. Europeans had known for more than a century that the installation of a new king, the ceremonies called Grand Customs, required relatively large numbers of human sacrifices. Nevertheless, when the Glele monarchy performed Grand Customs in 1860, the king was roundly condemned by European critics for what they perceived to be a return to unacceptably high levels of human sacrifice. Ironically, Glele's Grand Customs were later believed in Dahomey to have been unacceptably small. On the morning of July 10, 1862, precisely two years after Grand Customs had been performed for Gezo, a severe earthquake struck Abomey. A Dutch visitor who met with the king later that day was told that the dead king was unhappy because the ceremonies for him had been inadequate. Three chiefs from the Egba Yoruba town of Ishagga, defeated earlier that year, were brought forward, were instructed to tell Gezo that Customs from then on would be better than ever, and were sent to the king in Kutome through decapitation.[62]

Two additional pieces of evidence have been used to suggest that Gezo was moving toward the abolition of human sacrifice. The king forbade killing within the palace at the time of his death. He also exempted certain officials from the requirement that they die when he died. However, that evidence could be related to Gezo's efforts to ensure the accession of his heir. Gezo had effectively integrated Badahun into his monarchy, making him one of the central figures surrounding the king, an innovation that positioned the prince well for a bid for power. But successions were also struggles for physical control within the palace. Gezo himself had faced serious opposition from armed women in the palace at the time of his coup. Thus a decree that forbade killing within the palace could well have been directed to the question of succession rather than to concerns about human sacrifice. In effect, Gezo appears to have tried to neutralize the palace as a factor in the succession of his designated heir.

There is no easy explanation for Gezo's motives in exempting certain high officials from the requirement to die with the king. However, it would have had at least one important effect. It would paradoxically have reduced the influence of the "saved" individuals in the politics of the palace and monarchy. The requirement that an official die with the king signaled trust and confidence; such a person would have had tremendous prestige, and power, by virtue of the certain knowledge that she or he would commit suicide when the king died. Those expected to accompany the king in death were certain high-ranking wives, eunuchs, singers and drummers—in short, palace officials who were very close to the person of the king. To exempt officials from the death requirement gave them life but also reduced their status within the political system. The struggles of previous eras had given commoners, and powerful ahosi in particular, a more direct role in the selection of the king, and in forming the monarchy that would rule in his name. Officials who died with the king were not members of the royal family. Like the prohibition on killing within the palace, the exemption of officials from the suicide requirement would have reduced the effectiveness of certain players in succession struggles, most notably eunuchs and certain high-ranking women within the palace.

What, then, was the nature of the contest at the time of the succession to Gezo and who was involved? The challengers were a prince named Huensu (or Ouinsou) and his ahosi supporter Yavedo. Huensu does not appear in accounts of the kingdom after the succession struggle, so it is possible that he was made to "disappear" after Glele consolidated his power.[63] Yavedo, however, occupied one of the most powerful offices within the palace, both before and after the accession of Glele. Her office and rank in the palace hierarchy, and the individuals with whom she was likely allied, suggest that the 1858 succession may have been a contest, not between forces allied with the dead Gezo and those linked to the crown prince, but between the palace organization and the royal family.

Yavedo was one of two persons within the palace who held the office of tononu, a title that Burton translates as "all must obey him [her]" from its component parts: *to* = country or people; *non* = mother, owner, or person responsible for a charge; *nu* = mouth. Yavedo's male counterpart was of necessity a eunuch, because the jurisdiction of the two tononu was limited to the palace. The tononu headed a group of officials called the utunon (owutunun); literally, those responsible for the body, in this case the body or person of the king. In essence, the utunon were officers of the king's household, charged with the private affairs of the king, as opposed to the gbonugan daho, the chiefs of the outside, who were responsible for the public affairs of the kingdom. The utunon included the royal treasurer or storekeeper, the head of the palace guard, the doctors and diviners who served the king, those who took care of his personal hygiene, and the people in charge of preparing his food and clothing. Collectively, the utunon were responsible for managing the palaces of the king, looking after the well-being of the king himself, supervising palace personnel, including messengers and palace guards, carrying on trade at Whydah on the king's behalf, and keeping the royal treasury and stores. The head bokonon, or diviners, of the king were considered part of the utunon, as was the kpakpa, who recruited girls to the palace organization in the late nineteenth century. Another prominent male member of the utunon was the royal treasurer or storekeeper, one Binazon during the time of Glele. His female counterpart was a woman named Videkalo. Oral traditions in Abomey assert that Binazon was the personal name of the kangbode or cambode, an officer seen by visitors to court in both Gezo's and Glele's reigns, though Burton implies that the offices were held by two different people. Among the responsibilities listed for the kangbode were control over the security of palace residents as well as foreigners visiting the kingdom.[64]

Individual women among the utunon were remembered by Abomeans as being the most powerful of the women of the palace. Indeed, if any position within the palace paralleled that of a common polygynous Dahomean's head wife, it was that of the tononu, the utunon's head. A son of Glele, for example, called his father's tononu, a woman named Visesegan, the "director" of the palace. A son of Behanzin called Visesegan a woman of "good character," a favorite of Glele, and a strong woman, though he acknowledged in classic understatement that she did not get along well with his father, Behanzin.[65]

This, then, was the position of the women who challenged the two vidaho, Badahun and Kondo. Though the tononu were normally expected to commit suicide on the death of the king, both Yavedo and Visesegan survived their husbands' deaths. Yavedo continued to be prominent at the court of Glele. Burton noted that she served as one of the "mothers" to his colleague, Mr. Dawson, though even by that early date Glele had already named Visesegan as his tononu.[66] Visesegan in turn survived the accession of Behanzin, though the new king almost certainly must have wished to see her dead, along with the prince that she supported in opposition to him.

The 1858 accession of Glele, then, was opposed by a woman who may have been the most powerful woman in the palace. But what woman or women *backed* Glele? As in the case of Gezo forty years earlier, Glele gave no woman credit for assisting him to become king. To the office of kpojito, the new king appointed a woman named Zoyindi, a Yoruba-speaker said to have been from Adakplame, six miles to the north of Ketu. However, Gedegbe, a diviner of Glele, claimed that Zoyindi was his elder sister and a daughter of the king of Save, a Yoruba kingdom that was located well to the north of Ketu.[67] Whatever her origins, the naming of Zoyindi to the position of kpojito met with opposition, judging from a song, retained by descendants of Glele, in which the voice of King Glele taunts unnamed persons opposed to Zoyindi:

Fortunately the king does not hold grudges
Otherwise I would chastise you severely
Because of all your intrigues attributable to your
Jealousy of my mother.

But what a good thing my father did
To serve justice in raising
Zoyindi to the rank of Kpojito.

Unlike all the other women named to the position of kpojito, Zoyindi is said by Abomeans to have been the biological mother of the king. Whether that fact would have been the cause of the negative reactions to her is not clear. What is clear is that the patterns of advancement in the palace were such that the highest-ranking and most politically active women were not those with sons who might compete for the stool. We can assume, then, that whatever her activities prior to the accession of Glele, Zoyindi was not in a position of great power or influence. Like Gezo before him, Glele was not rewarding a woman who had assisted him in reaching power. Indeed, the song suggests that Glele's father Gezo had selected Zoyindi, just as he had selected and ensured the accession of his son.[68]

Gezo had effectively changed the system of succession by naming a vidaho and helping him to consolidate power. As we have seen, in the eighteenth century, successions involved the struggles of coalitions of commoners allied with princes, of common women within the palace working with royal men outside it, but beginning with the reign of Gezo, the choice of the king would be decided well before the death of his predecessor. Moreover, it would be made by the king and members of the royal family. Nineteenth-century accounts routinely say that kings named their own heirs, though members of the royal family claim that it was the royal family that discussed the virtues of possible new vidaho. In either case, the succession system had been altered so that the decision was wholly within the royal family.

Obviously, the fact that the succession to Glele was contested indicates that there was opposition to the new system. Members of the palace organization—both women and eunuchs—had lost a good deal of power with the royal family's consolidation of control over the choice of king. Indeed, the accession of Glele confirmed a changed perception of the relationship between royal and commoner. If the eighteenth century was characterized by a recognition of the necessity of partnership between royal and commoner, the nineteenth was typified by royal pride and arrogance. More and more frequently, the interests of the royal family were defined as the interests of Dahomey. Rather than balance between royal and commoner, there began to be expressed an opposition between royal and commoner, and indeed between male and female.

One other lesson was to be drawn from Glele's accession. Once named vidaho, Badahun had been allowed, and even encouraged, to build a power base so strong that he could not be challenged effectively at the moment of his father's death. Assessing that experience, would-be kings in future might conclude that their best route to the royal stool would be through being named vidaho. But no longer would the problem be, as it had been in the eighteenth century, how to gain physical control over the palace and over one's rivals at the moment of the death of the king; rather, it would be how to be made vidaho long before the death of one's father, so that one might build an invincible base from which to seize power. Implicit in the changed position of vidaho was the danger, from the perspective of the monarchy, that a prince's power would become so great that he could threaten to usurp the power of the reigning king— that he might threaten to take effective control even before the death of his predecessor. As we have seen, that does not appear to have happened to the monarchy of Gezo. But the possibility of an overly ambitious vidaho became a problem for the Glele monarchy.

7

War, Disintegration, and the Failure of the Ancestors

The history of the royal family is by and large the history of Dahomey.

Maurice Ahanhanzo Glélé, *Le Danxome*

The Rise of Behanzin ∾

Burton does not mention meeting any vidaho during his 1863–64 visit, though Maurice Glélé claims that Prince Ahanhanzo had been named Glele's vidaho even before the 1858 death of his grandfather, Gezo. By 1871, however, Ahanhanzo was in place and actively playing the role of king-to-be: Skertchly met and much admired the young prince, noting that "A more generous, hospitable, intelligent young fellow I never met . . . and I felt more at home with Hahansu than I had done since leaving England." As vidaho, Ahanhanzo enjoyed a central place in court politics and ceremony. However, within fewer than five years of Skertchly's visit he had died under mysterious circumstances, and Kondo, the future Behanzin, had taken his place. Maurice Glélé, who is a direct descendant of Ahanhanzo, baldly states that Kondo caused the death of his brother. Other traditions claim that Ahanhanzo died of smallpox. But smallpox, as we have seen, was a euphemism for disorder and danger in relation to the kingship, a sign of irregular events that challenged legitimate authority.[1]

Traditions provided by members of the royal family differ widely over questions associated with Kondo, because Kondo/Behanzin, as the last king of an independent Dahomey, holds an ambiguous position in the historical record. A king who would be destooled by foreign invaders and cursed by members of the royal family, Behanzin is today also honored as a resister of colonial aggression. Behanzin's descendants, who have occupied influential positions of political and economic leadership in colonial and postcolonial Dahomey/Benin, have played no small part in the rehabilitation of their ancestor's historical reputation. The result is a series of traditions, most of which justify the stances of one side or another in the contested historical account of the fall of the kingdom and the naming of Agoliagbo as successor to Behanzin after the French conquest. Many traditions associated with the naming of Kondo as vidaho justify later events, as for example the comment of one prince, a man allied with the descendants of Agoliagbo, who said, "Kondo did things before the death of his father which he should not have done. For that, he had only a short reign." He went on to describe the choice of vidaho after the death of Ahanhanzo as a deadlock within the royal family. "The king was obligated to agree with the majority of his children. There were two candidates for vidaho, Sasse Koka and Kondo. Sasse Koka was the oldest of the children born after the coming of Glele. The family met for two days during which Wegbelu [later Agoliagbo] never spoke. On the third day, Glele asked Wegbelu for his opinion. He said, if you want peace, choose Kondo."[2] The rival to Kondo, Sasse Koka, was the protégé of Visesegan, Glele's powerful and ambitious tononu, and had been mentored in the home of Glele's diviner, Gedegbe.[3]

Naming Kondo to the position of vidaho did not in fact bring peace to the monarchy of Dahomey. The final thirteen years of the reign of Glele were characterized by a continued power struggle between Kondo and Visesegan. Though official heir, Kondo continued to be challenged by Visesegan up to and following the death of Glele at the end of 1889. A son of Glele commented that

> since Sasse Koka's mother, Visesegan, commanded all the palace, one could expect to see her son everywhere. He seated himself in councils of the family, like Behanzin. Yet he was not of the same rank as Behanzin. It was only because his mother commanded that he could act like Behanzin, that is, like the vidaho. People began to ignore Behanzin and to forget that he held first place. People began to assume that Sasse Koka was the first. Thus Behanzin chased him

away, told him to leave, that he had no right to be there. It was only because death had hurt Glele that he thought of Sasse Koka as a possible vidaho.[4]

The 1875–76 period was a key transition period for the Glele monarchy. It was a time of profound difficulty from which it may never have fully recovered. Three major events occurred in quick succession: the death of the Kpojito Zoyindi, the death of the vidaho Ahanhanzo, and a crippling blockade of Whydah by the British. Zoyindi died in early 1876, and Ahanhanzo's death probably occurred late that spring. Major ceremonies performed to honor Zoyindi were held in the fall of that year, about the same time that British warships appeared along the coast to impose a blockade. The blockade had resulted from a Whydah trade incident precipitated by Abomey, possibly at the instigation of Kondo, and apparently aimed at hurting the son of a recently deceased Afro-Brazilian trader and rival to the house of de Souza, one Jacintho da Costa Santos. The monarchy's handling of the blockade was a mix of verbal aggression and diplomatic passivity that left the matter to be settled by Dahomean officials at Whydah working with European factors and their home governments. The lack of direct and active participation by the monarchy in shaping the blockade settlement could have reflected a number of factors: Glele's personal despair at the ominous pattern of deaths, and particularly that of Ahanhanzo, who was said to have been beloved by him; the preoccupation of the monarchy with the grand ceremonies in honor of Zoyindi; or a certain level of ineptness at recognizing the new nature of incipient imperial challenge and negotiating effectively with it, an ineptness that in turn may have been related to the divisions at court following Kondo's appointment as vidaho.[5]

From the mid-1870s, Glele himself effectively and literally disappeared from view. He appears to have been in poor health and may have become blind, because evidence from as early as the 1864 visit of Burton indicates the onset of serious eye disease. In any event, no outsider recorded seeing Glele from 1875 until a French visitor described him in late 1889, just before his death. In the meantime, Kondo and Visesegan waged their bitter struggle for control. Its substance ultimately was over which prince would replace Glele—the vidaho or the man championed by the woman described as "Glele's favorite wife." Outside observers, as they had in the case of the accession of Glele nearly forty years before, interpreted the struggle as one over policy, in this case the policy question of appropriate responses to the growing threat of European imperialism. We need to look briefly at the nature of pressures on the monarchy at the end of Glele's reign to understand the circumstances of the death of Glele and struggle of Behanzin to consolidate power.

European Imperialism ∾

Three distinct political phases are discernible in the Dahomean experience of Europe from the 1840s to the 1890s. Those phases paralleled by and large the experience of dozens of other African states. During the first, from roughly 1840 to 1860, commercial relations were in transition. As the illegal slave trade became less and less viable, Europe pressed its demands for other products, sparking the transformation of the Dahomean export economy to one of commercial agriculture; specifically, the production of oil-palm products. French trading concerns and numerous coastal entrepreneurs, most notably individuals of the Afro-Brazilian community of Whydah, developed the bases for the export of palm oil and kernels. The British meanwhile were absorbed by their continued humanitarian efforts to negotiate the end of the slave trade and human sacrifice. During the second period, from about 1860 to 1880, rivalries grew among European powers for greater influence and ultimately greater control over Africa. Treaties began to be negotiated, and home governments tolerated increased shows of force, though they disavowed most efforts to commit metropolitan authorities to administrative control over African territories. Nevertheless, ambitious adventurers and politicians of many nationalities began to scheme and dream of expanding spheres of influence, connecting already existing interests along the coast and otherwise extending political control. The decade of the 1880s saw the explosion of imperial interest in Africa, systematized at mid-decade through the famous Berlin Conference, where European powers established principles for taking political control over African peoples and effectively agreed to avoid warfare with each other over issues of colonial territory.

Paralleling the political changes were changes in European perceptions of African peoples that ultimately provided rationale and justification for conquest and political subordination. Scholars have traced the growth of pseudoscientific thinking about race and nationality during this period and tracked the development of social Darwinism to its culmination at the turn of the twentieth century. In European and North American popular culture, Dahomey emerged from these debates as an archetype of depraved savagery, its name synonymous with barbarism. By the time French soldiers arrived on the coast, the French press had prepared them to fight against the "fameuses Amazones." Indeed, even before the conquest was complete, a troop of armed African women were exhibited in Paris's zoological gardens. Isabel Burton's preface to the memorial edition of her husband's book on Dahomey—written in mid-1893, when Behanzin had been defeated but not captured and the French were occupying but not ruling Dahomey—is indicative of the mood:

> Thirty years ago, no Europeans were at Dahome. None ventured into the interior to the Court of the Savage known as King Gelele. His time was spent in wars, his best troops being his many thousand Amazons, women crueller and fiercer than men. The prisoners were tortured, and their throats were cut. Whenever he required to send a telegram to his father, a man was slaughtered, and his soul was despatched with it. Women were cut open alive, in a state of pregnancy, that the King might see what it was like. Animals were tied in every agonizing position to die; impaling and cannibalism were common, and it was impossible to go out of one's hut without seeing something appalling.

At the same time that Isabel Burton was writing her preface, Dahomey was being featured at Chicago's Columbian Exposition of 1893, one of the most important of the series of world's fairs characteristic of the turn of the century in Europe and North America. The Dahomean exhibition in Chicago occupied the foot of the Midway, which ranked cultures from

9. Dahomean soldiers in Paris, 1893. (Collection Musée de l'Homme, Paris)

least to most civilized along its mile-long length and culminated in something called the White City. Should anyone miss the point, a correspondent for a popular monthly wrote of the Dahomeans that "sixty-nine of them are here in all their barbaric ugliness . . . as degraded as the animals which prowl the jungles of their dark land."[6]

Sadly, in the years leading up to the French conquest, Dahomey contributed to these racist stereotypes by consistently meeting Europe on Dahomean terms; that is, the kingdom responded to European powers as if they were other states of coastal West Africa. The monarchy stressed its bellicosity and belligerence, defiantly trading slaves, continuing human sacrifice, trumpeting gruesome executions, and literally parading examples of military ferocity before the eyes of Europe. The Dahomean ruling elite expected European nations to respond as their African neighbors did, with terror. By the late nineteenth century, however, European confidence in its moral, cultural, and technological superiority had reached a level that no non-Western nation could shake. Europeans believed that they practiced standards of human behavior far above those exemplified by the Dahomeans. By dramatizing what Europe increasingly saw as different, exotic, primitive, savage, and uncivilized, the Dahomean monarchy inadvertently provided justification for the colonial conquest launched against it.

Four European powers—Portugal, Germany, Britain, and France—were involved in the shifting patterns of negotiation, threat, intervention, and conciliation that proceeded intermittently for more than forty years before the conquest. Two—Portugal and France—tried to negotiate protectorates over portions of the kingdom. The others were players engaged by the monarchy as it parried the offers and demands of encroaching imperialism.[7]

Portuguese interests in Dahomey were fostered by prominent members of the Afro-Brazilian community of Whydah. Whydah itself remained the heart of lusophone culture along the Bight of Benin and continued to be the point from which most European visitors approached Dahomey. Nevertheless, Whydah was losing ground to other developing commercial centers along the coast. As palm-oil production increased in the interior, the problem of transport began to be resolved along waterways: from the interior, oil could be shipped in canoes down the Weme River valley to the east of Dahomey and along the Mono to the west. The lagoons and creeks behind the coast allowed traffic to move to exporting points as far east as Lagos and as far west as Agoue. Porto Novo in particular began to flourish, as oil poured out of the Weme valley through its trading houses and onward through the lagoons to Badagry and Lagos or across a strip of land to Porto Novo beach.

Meanwhile, tensions were growing between the monarchy and the Afro-Brazilian entrepreneurs. The Afro-Brazilians had fully accepted Dahomean authority over their lives. They were bilingual and bicultural. The households of their most prominent members resembled those of high-ranking Dahomeans. Afro-Brazilians took multiple wives, exchanged daughters with the king and other important princes, and maintained armed contingents of slaves who were sent to Abomey annually for war campaigns. Yet they still maintained links with Brazil and were loyal to Portugal as the European power of their cultural heritage. The death in 1849 of Gezo's great friend and ally Chacha Francisco de Souza had marked the ending of an era for the Afro-Brazilian community. Like all state titles in Dahomey, the title of chacha was inherited by a direct descendant of its previous holder, but the significance of the office, and its paramount position overshadowing even the office of the yovogan, had emerged from the close personal relationship between Gezo and de Souza. That relationship in turn had been founded on the slave trade. It had been cemented by Gezo's role as paramount producer of slaves from the interior and de Souza's role as mediator with European and Afro-Brazilian traders and shippers. Palm oil offered no such symbiosis. Having begun palm-oil production earlier than the monarchy and having the advantage of proximity to the coast, the Afro-Brazilians were in the position of being able potentially to derive greater wealth from the trade. In effect, the Afro-Brazilians as a group had become rivals of the monarchy in the commercial exploitation of oil palms, and in that competition they held the advantage. It is little wonder that they increasingly felt the pressure of closer surveillance and decreased trust by Abomey. By the 1870s and 1880s, imperialist fever rose; the Afro-Brazilian community began to split apart as individuals made choices of allegiance—to Dahomey, Portugal, or France.

French trading interests, meanwhile, had become the most prominent of all the European commercial interests. As the geographical configuration of the oil trade moved toward interior waterways, the French trading houses were drawn to outlets from the Weme River valley, specifically to Porto Novo and to a village called Cotonou, at the closest point of Lake Nokoue (sometimes called Lake Denham) to the sea. In fact, an outlet to the sea at Cotonou, though blocked by a sandbar, offered the closest transshipment point for loading seagoing vessels. Profiting from the ambitions of King Toffa of Porto Novo, who came to power in 1875, the French in the early 1880s reestablished a protectorate over Porto Novo that they had negotiated and then abandoned twenty years before. Meanwhile, they twice reconfirmed in writing—in 1868 and 1878—a verbal agreement with Dahomey made by French merchants in 1864 that recognized French rights to Cotonou. The protectorate treaties of 1868 and 1878 were used by the French government to legitimize their claims to Cotonou to their European rivals. Prior to the late 1880s, however, the French had

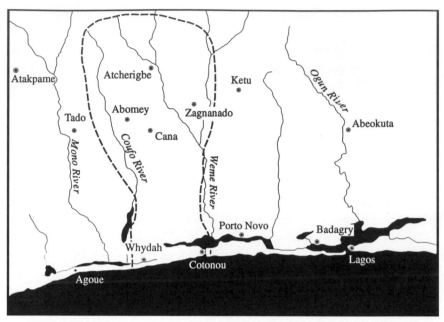

10. Dahomey and the Slave Coast at the end of the nineteenth century

not moved to invoke key sovereignty clauses, and Cotonou remained administratively under Dahomean control. Like the Afro-Brazilians in Whydah, the French were active cultural imperialists. Roman Catholic missionaries from Lyon arrived in Whydah by the 1860s, though the language of instruction, even in the French missionary schools, remained Portuguese until the end of the century. By the 1880s, a small Afro-French generation fathered by French traders had grown to adulthood and was ready to serve as cultural intermediary, and more specifically as translator, to those who would establish French rule in the area.

Many of the French actions along the coast of Dahomey were in fact prompted by British maneuvers. With long-standing commitments both to the east and west of Dahomey—in Lagos and the Gold Coast—the British took various actions hinting at an interest in linking their territorial holdings along the coast. Indeed, the French and British from the 1860s to the mid-1880s were like two boxers circling each other, constantly watching each others' moves, responding to threats, and delivering diplomatic jabs and feints as each sought advantage. But in a situation considerably more complicated than a boxing match, African political entities were also involved, seeking European alliances to gain leverage over their African rivals. Thus, for example, once Kondo had been made vidaho, Toffa requested the French protectorate over Porto Novo in order to have military backing in dealing with Dahomey; Toffa had been allied with Kondo's rival, the vidaho Ahanhanzo. His own competitor for the stool of Porto Novo, Sonjigbe, was allied with Kondo.[8] Similarly, the king of Ketonou, across the lagoon from Porto Novo, was enemy to Toffa; he welcomed a British protectorate over his territory, which controlled the shipping channel between the French possessions of Porto Novo and Cotonou. Following the Treaty of Berlin in 1885, the British and French were effectively committed to bilateral negotiations to resolve African territorial interests. Nevertheless, the British colony of Lagos would serve throughout Dahomey's struggle against the French as an outlet to contacts with Europe. British officials in Lagos regularly received Dahomean envoys and, judging from the content of communications, up to 1890 allowed the Dahomeans to believe that they might offer an alternative, in the form of a British protectorate, to French control.

West of Dahomey, the Germans by 1882 had established what would grow into the colony of Togoland. Their contacts with Dahomey were commercial and began to take effect only after 1889, as war between Dahomey and France drew closer. Trading arms for "free laborers" supplied by Dahomey, the Germans received manpower to help them consolidate their territory elsewhere in Africa. The Dahomeans at some point invited the Germans to establish a protectorate, but were rebuffed. Nevertheless, the Germans willingly provided the firepower that from their point of view kept at least one of their European rivals, the French, occupied.[9]

As other European interests on the coast grew and as relations with the Dahomeans continued to be uncertain, some members of the Afro-Brazilian community began to see a Portuguese protectorate as a means to reassert lusophone interests. After the French finalized protectorate treaties with Porto Novo in 1883 and with Grand Popo and Agoue in 1885, the fourth Chacha de Souza, Juliao, took the initiative to negotiate a treaty to establish a Portuguese protectorate over the Dahomean coast. In mid-1885 he received Portuguese officials from the island of São Tomé and accompanied them to Abomey. The signing of the treaty was celebrated in Whydah in the presence of the Portuguese governor of São Tomé; the monarchy even offered land for construction of a Portuguese residence and there was talk of a Dahomean embassy to Portugal. Not the least of the factors associated with Dahomean enthusiasm for the Portuguese connection was the provision for the supply by Dahomey of "free laborers" to be used on the plantations of São Tomé.

With the Germans and the Portuguese providing the demand and the legal subterfuge, the 1880s thus saw yet another revival of the slave trade. The French, meanwhile, were increasingly disturbed over the apparent rapprochement between Dahomey and Portugal and their negotiation of a protectorate. Threatened by the possibility that Portugal might usurp their own declared interests along the Bight of Benin, the French recognized that they needed to act to assert their rights over Cotonou. A confrontation was imminent, and by 1887 the pennies had begun to drop in Abomey.

The War with the French ～

Dahomean culture had changed profoundly in the years leading up to the late 1880s. Politically, a new vision of power and of who might appropriately wield it had affected the Dahomean power elite. That new vision was reflected in the religious hierarchy of the kingdom and confirmed in the changed process of succession, whereby members of the royal family exerted full control over the choice of king. Men of commoner birth had less and less access to offices of significance in the kingdom, while men of slave status who were highly skilled in divining, reaching for knowledge of matters unknown and unknowable, became closely linked to the person of the king and to the fate of the kingdom. Meanwhile, the population of the palace expanded. Its women ahosi were increasingly visible working for the benefit of the indivisible entities that were king and kingdom. But visibility and power were not synonymous. Dahomey in the late nineteenth century confirmed the theoretical arguments that Marxist feminist scholars would make a century later: that the overall status of women drops as internal slave classes grow.

An older system of partnership between male and female, royal and commoner, was disappearing. Yet much of the past remained in the actions and perspectives of the monarchy. Dahomean culture had changed a great deal. Still, there were striking continuities in the behavior patterns of the people associated with the monarchy as it faced European imperialism. As the health of Glele declined, the vidaho Kondo worked to position himself to be recognized as a legitimate power holder. Oral sources credit Kondo with a reputation variously described as a miracle worker, sorcerer, or magician, all suggesting the old idea that a king should be able to harness supernatural as well as earthly power. Policy decisions continued to be made collectively, albeit less often with the strong voices of commoner men or of women of the palace organization. Within the palace, the old system to some extent remained in place, because ambitious commoner women there had no option other than history as their model. Women worked to forge alliances with politically ambitious princes, to offer them help in gaining power, and to promote their own interests. Ironically, it was at this point, as the appropriateness of women's involvement in political life was being questioned, that a remarkably resourceful and enterprising commoner woman, Visesegan, became central in the political life of the kingdom.

In interpretations that echo those surrounding the accession of Glele in 1858, historians have argued that the struggle for power and the resistance to European imperialism involved two parties representing two different policy alternatives: Kondo and his allies represented a "traditionalist" viewpoint hostile to any and all protectorate arrangements with European powers, promoting warfare and human sacrifice. Visesegan was head of a "progressive" faction that, for its own commercial motives, promoted accommodation with European expansion and opposed war at all costs. This tidy dichotomy does not work. It is clear that there were at least two strong factions struggling over power well before the death of Glele, but their policy differences and directions may not have been as starkly different as history has claimed. Both groups were preoccupied with the succession struggle up to and throughout the period of the war with the French. Both were willing to accept European protectorates, but only to enhance their position vis-à-vis their Dahomean rivals. In essence, the imperialist challenge could not have come at a more difficult time for Dahomey, because it interrupted a struggle for power that was never fully resolved, leaving a disunited Dahomey to fight the French.[10]

There were two major clashes between Dahomey and the encroaching European powers prior to the death of Glele. The first led to the cancellation of the Portuguese protectorate over coastal Dahomey; the second involved the repudiation by Dahomey of the French protectorate treaties of 1868 and 1878. Historians typically argue that the crises occurred because of poor translations or misunderstandings of the original treaty terms; in the case of the Portuguese, it was said to be because of the existence of a second treaty stating different terms. But poor translation, misunderstanding, and substitute treaties were the least of the problem. The 1868 treaty with France, for example, declared that "the king of Dahomey . . . proclaims the ceding to H. M. the Emperor of the French for no compensation whatsoever the territory of Kotonou [Cotonou] with all the rights that he holds in this territory with no exception or reserve."[11] It would be absurd to assume that anyone discussed the full extent of meanings that France might place on such a clause with members of the court of Dahomey. The reality was that deception was a necessary basis for the negotiation of protectorate arrangements; otherwise, no one would have signed. On the other hand, the precise wording of the treaties themselves does not appear to have been the central concern of the Dahomeans; rather, the crises of 1887 with Portugal and 1889 with France were sparked by issues of economic consequence that touched on long-term Dahomean trade policies with European nations. Those issues had to do with the compensation of middlemen in overseas trade arrangements and the collection of customs duties at the coast.

Dahomey's quarrel in the case of the Portuguese appears to have been less with Portugal and more with the Chacha Juliao de Souza. In conjunction with the Portuguese treaty, de Souza had negotiated commercial arrangements for the export of laborers—in effect, a return to the slave trade. The chacha himself was agent for the "contracts" of the "laborers," and apparently either rewarded himself with overly generous commissions on each shipment of slaves or did not report fully to the monarchy on the financial arrangements. Someone denounced him, and de Souza was called to Abomey in the spring of 1887. His house was broken in the classic manner: he and several immediate relatives died in an Abomey prison and all his moveable goods and slaves were confiscated by the monarchy. Accounts of the incident do not make clear if the protectorate treaty was formally repudiated by Dahomey; in fact, it was renounced by Portugal at the end of 1887, but mainly in response to a long series of protests from France. There is no evidence from Abomey that the factions competing to control the kingship differed over responses to the Portuguese protectorate problem.[12]

The crisis with the French was another matter. The confrontation over Cotonou was precipitated by the European side. One of the requirements of the game of imperialism was that control over claimed territory be effective. Though the French at Cotonou had made moves that overstepped the normal bounds of commercial presence—for example, trying to cut an opening to the sea through the Cotonou bar—apart from the *X*'ed signatures of Dahomean officials on treaties, they had never received any real acknowledgment from Dahomey of their "legal" control over Cotonou. Tensions were intense between Dahomey and the French, in part because King Toffa of Porto Novo was using his status as a French protectee to taunt Dahomey, and the Dahomean army was making incursions into areas claimed by Porto Novo and hence "protected" by France.

In early 1889, the French began to push the issues of territoriality and protectorate status to a head by proposing a French customs post at Cotonou. The treaty of 1868 had expressly assured the Dahomeans that they would continue to administer Cotonou and collect customs. Now the French offered the Dahomeans 20,000 francs annually in exchange for the right to levy duties on merchandise passing through Cotonou but destined for their protectorate at Porto Novo. Dahomean officials on the coast refused to relay what they knew to be an unacceptable proposal to Abomey, and when letters were sent, the response was quick and unequivocal: the French at Cotonou should tell their superiors that Glele had run out of patience; he would never give up his rights to Cotonou, and the yovogan of Whydah and other caboceers who had signed the treaties of 1868 and 1878 had had their heads cut off. "Absolutely no one, not even the king of Danhomé, ever gives their possessions to any other nation." However, the French persisted, and by the fall of 1889, after letters and long-distance negotiations with the monarchy had led nowhere, they sent a relatively high-ranking official to Abomey to try to negotiate an effective treaty. Jean Bayol, the lieutenant-governor of Senegal, led a delegation to Abomey that spent six weeks, was granted only two royal audiences, and failed utterly to reach a new accommodation. Bayol left Abomey on December 28, 1889, and Glele died shortly thereafter, on December 30.[13]

However, the Bayol Mission produced a key document, dated early 1891, that casts both light and confusion on divisions in the court at the time of the death of Glele. Preserved in several copies and heavily used by historians, the document is a report by the mission's translator for the French, Xavier Béraud. Béraud was the eldest son of a French consular agent and a woman from Whydah. Educated in mission schools in Whydah, Porto Novo, and Lagos, he was fiercely loyal to France and correspondingly hostile to Dahomey. Indeed, the monarchy later broke the Béraud house in Whydah on grounds of the "treason of the Bérauds." Béraud's story of the actual negotiations of the Bayol Mission generally corresponds to accounts of Bayol himself—that the French offered an annual subsidy in exchange for the right to collect customs duties on goods entering Cotonou for Porto Novo. The Dahomeans responded that such an arrangement was impossible, and that if the French occupied Cotonou against the will of Dahomey, they would be struck by lightning; moreover, the treaties of 1868 and 1878 were invalid.[14]

Beyond the story of the formal negotiations, Béraud offers a behind-the-scenes account of discussions within the palace. I paraphrase it here:

> Visesegan, "the favorite of Glele who had great influence on him," argued to the king that times had changed. The whites wanted to occupy Kotonou, Godomey, and Whydah, and would pay rent to Dahomey, though they would stop warfare. That was the situation in Lagos and it worked fine. Glele replied that he wanted to continue to wage war and make human sacrifices. The Yoruba would make fun of him if he agreed to such terms and his father would be angry. Visesegan retorted that it would be better if he was angry with

his father, for if the whites made war against them, what would become of them? Would he expect to seek refuge in Yorubaland? Glele responded that he would rather die than give his country to the whites and poisoned himself on December 28.

Kondo succeeded under the name Behanzin and Visesegan plotted with several chiefs in the country to dethrone him and give the country to the whites. She was not the real mother of Kondo but the adoptive mother, for the custom in Dahomey is that the first wife or the favorite wife of the king is called Mother by the heir. Her fellow plotters were Binazon, Chodaton of Whydah, a creole named Nicolas who was chief of the Ganve quarter of Whydah, plus several others. Gouflé, who met with the plotters, told Behanzin about the plot. Behanzin imprisoned Visesegan and the other plotters and seized all their goods and slaves. He excused this crime to his people by claiming that it was Visesegan who had poisoned Glele.

People were sorry about the death of Visesegan, a woman who had much influence and in fact had exercised power in the latter part of Glele's reign. As a result Behanzin lost a good deal of prestige and authority. A rumor even reached Kotonou that a revolt against him was being prepared in Abomey. However, Behanzin regained face in May 1890 when Commandant Fournier [the naval captain who replaced Bayol] sent him gifts and later when a German Swiss named Barth came from Lagos to offer guns and cannons.[15]

Powerful and vivid, the Béraud account dramatically outlines the divisions between two competing factions. The general thrust of the split between supporters of Behanzin and Visesegan has since been confirmed by oral sources. Visesegan was a woman with important commercial interests; indeed, one historian claims she was spending her fortune earned in commerce trying to get control of the stool of Dahomey.[16] Béraud would have been familiar with the names of the Whydah people said to have been in league with her. Abomey oral sources have claimed that her allies additionally included at least three of the gbonugan daho—the migan, the ajaho, and the tokpo. On the other hand, Kondo is said to have had the support, among others, of Wegbelu (Agoliagbo), of the yovogan, of a woman named Hodafo, and of the diviner Gedegbe.

The Béraud account is also based on rumor and gossip and includes at least one stunning inaccuracy, all of which raise questions about its relative value as evidence. Its main error is the assumption that Visesegan had been killed. She did not die until 1912, and records of court cases in the first decade of the twentieth century show her still trying to reclaim individuals taken from her control by Behanzin. She could have temporarily disappeared from view, however, after her confrontation with Behanzin, leading Béraud to assume that she had been killed. The statement that Glele committed suicide is almost certainly untrue, although he could have died of poison. Kondo is rumored in oral traditions to have poisoned Glele, and Kondo probably had the most to gain from the death of his father. In fact, Glele is said to have died while Kondo was in Cana. Tokpa Mele, his brother, sent for him, decapitating an ahosi who had been a personal servant of Glele and had seen that the king was dead. Foul play is possible, but the king was clearly feeble and old; it is equally probable to assume that Glele's death at the end of 1889 was merely coincidence.

The struggle for the stool had been ongoing for years. Contemporary French sources and twentieth-century historical sources typically offer interpretations of the period of the late 1880s and the early 1890s that echo Béraud. Dahomey is shown divided over how to respond to the French crisis and the succession struggle becomes a background diversion from the central question, that of Dahomean-French relations. Yet it is plausible to argue that from the Dahomean point of view, the Europeans were mere players, albeit extremely powerful and dangerous ones, in a succession struggle. The task for a would-be king was to build alliances with one or another European nation in order to cement control and win recognition and legitimacy in Abomey. The actions of Kondo in the late 1880s can be seen in this light. If we assume that Visesegan and her coalition were promoting ties with the French, in order to secure his own power Kondo needed either to build an alliance with another equally strong European power or defeat the French—militarily or diplomatically. The historical record indicates that he tried both.

In late 1888, a small delegation representing Dahomey arrived in Lagos and was received by the British governor, Alfred Moloney. It was led by Fasinu, a son of Kondo who was twelve to thirteen years old and who asked in his father's name for a British protectorate over the kingdom. Questioning the woman coastal trader who was escort for Fasinu, Governor Moloney learned that Kondo was engaged in a struggle for the stool against a brother, Dahpeh, who was playing for French support and whose power base was Whydah. Kondo wanted to isolate his rival by closing the roads to Whydah and using Katanu (Ketonou?), a town that was part of the British protectorate, as an alternative port. Ironically, given Kondo's reputation as warmonger, this Dahpeh was described to the British as a bloodthirsty captain in the army, in contrast to the "more mild" Kondo. Dahpeh, apparently, would be the protégé of Visesegan, the prince otherwise known as Sasse Koka. Moloney took the protectorate request seriously, reporting it to London and keeping up negotiations with the Dahomeans for more than a year. Meanwhile, though, the French and British were negotiating a series of settlements over potential disputed territories in Africa and Asia. Over time, implicit recognition of French claims to the areas between Agoue and Porto Novo by the British meant that by February 1890, the acting governor of Lagos would write Behanzin that "there is no longer any question of the extension of British protection to the Kingdom of Dahomey."[17]

Meanwhile, with the death of his father, Behanzin began moving at top speed to consolidate his power and position. By the time of the initial burial of Glele at the beginning of January 1890, Behanzin was in control of the palace and the standing army. Now began his period of testing, when he needed to demonstrate the power that would legitimize his position as king. We do not know precisely when or how Visesegan and her associates in Abomey were confronted; we know only that Sasse Koka did not survive and that the French conquering forces later heard rumors that he had been poisoned. At some point Behanzin named his ministers, rewarding his brother Tokpa Mele, who had been with Glele at the moment of death, with the position of meu. Egbo, another brother, became migan. Guchili or Wegbelu (later Agoliagbo) became gau. Indeed, virtually all of Behanzin's top officials, both male and female, were siblings. In January 1890, he also visited Tado, in what is now Togo, for an investiture ceremony, and in February was similarly in Allada for ceremonial purposes. But Behanzin was not to have the luxury to establish his position firmly without outside threat.[18]

A rising imperial star before he reached Dahomey, Jean Bayol had fallen ill in Abomey, apparently from fright and frustration. After his failure to negotiate successfully and his return to the coast, Bayol seemed determined to force Dahomey either into acceptance of French terms or into war. At his insistence, the French moved new troops into Porto Novo and reinforced Cotonou. Both were done ostensibly because of fears of Dahomean attacks during the dry season, when Dahomey traditionally made war, and particularly in light of the death of Glele and the presumed need for captives for sacrifice. Assembling all the Dahomean officials of Cotonou in late February 1890, the French announced that they intended to occupy Cotonou and "protect" other key factories along the coast and lagoons. When the officials protested, they were held prisoner and allowed to assume that they might be turned over to Toffa and executed. The French expected the Dahomeans to respond by making hostages of eight French nationals resident in Whydah, which they did three days later. Then, on March 4, a large Dahomean army attacked the newly reinforced Cotonou garrison and was repulsed with heavy losses. A month later the Dahomeans attacked but failed to overcome a French force at a village called Atchoupa, about seven miles north of Porto Novo. Both sides then disengaged, the two groups of hostages were released, and Dahomey and the French fell into a long period of negotiation and formal agreement punctuated by occasional provocations and clashes. From May 1890 until the French invading forces came up the Weme River in the fall of 1892, the Dahomeans avoided sending large forces against the French. Meanwhile, the local French officials became thoroughly convinced that the only solution to the "problem" of Dahomey was its conquest, but until the spring of 1892 the French parliament was not willing to vote the necessary funds for war.

We have little direct evidence that can help us understand what was happening in the court of Dahomey up to and during the war against the French in the fall of 1892. The contemporary written records are limited to the course of negotiations and correspondence between the French and Dahomey. Save for the Béraud report, they say little of the succession struggle. Oral accounts provided by members of the royal family begin a scant decade after the events, the first being the account provided to

Le Hérissé by Agbidinukun, a brother of Behanzin. Working separately in the early 1970s, Luc Garcia and I collected valuable oral commentaries on internal debates from surviving children of Glele, Behanzin, and Ago-liagbo. Still, it is hard for historical memory, whether oral or written, to imagine and convey the thinking and motivation that were involved on the Dahomean side, and that could not have been common knowledge at the time. Moreover, our knowledge of the end of the story—the ultimate defeat of the kingdom and the establishment of the colony of Dahomey—and the sense of inevitability associated with it distort our retrospective thinking. Using oral evidence and our understanding of Dahomean culture we can speculate, though, that Behanzin and his monarchy found themselves in an anomalous position. They controlled the palace and army, and Behanzin was in the process of performing the requisite ceremonies for recognition of his position as king. Yet the king's authority in Dahomey had traditionally been earned through a prince's demonstration of his ability to concentrate and channel supernatural and physical power. It was not enough simply to have been named vidaho. Indeed, Behanzin as heir had struggled to have his position accepted and acknowledged, yet his claims to the stool had been challenged both before and after the death of Glele by a formidable rival.

The opposition to Behanzin had argued that some form of accommodation needed to be made with the French. According to Agbidinukun, Behanzin was aware that it would be dangerous, indeed foolhardy, to provoke war with the French. He resisted the incursions toward Cotonou demanded by his brothers, but nevertheless saw the monarchy goaded into war on the coast.[19] Had the Dahomean army succeeded in defeating the French at Cotonou, driving them into the sea with the sharpness of a shark's attack, the visual emblem chosen by the new king, the Behanzin monarchy would have been vindicated. Overrunning the French garrison would have been seen as a demonstration of his abilities and evidence of the blessing of the royal ancestors on the new king. The failure at Cotonou made a decisive victory over the French imperative for Behanzin. A new plan was devised. The French would be lured out of Porto Novo into an area to the north that would be unfamiliar to them. A sudden murderous attack would keep them pinned down while the Dahomean army made a flanking move to attack Porto Novo itself. If the plan worked, not only would Toffa be punished, but the French might decide to leave the coast of Dahomey altogether.

As it turned out, the decisive confrontation was at Atchoupa, and the French realized when attacked that they needed to retreat to the unprotected Porto Novo. Managing to form and hold a disciplined square, they held off waves of attackers, the most vicious of whom were said to have been women soldiers. Porto Novo was saved and Behanzin's position further weakened. According to royal informants, "plots began to percolate again with even greater vigor. This time doubt even crept into the ranks of the close supporters of Behanzin, and everyone began to wonder if his removal from office might in the end save the kingdom from certain destruction." [20]

Nevertheless, Behanzin managed to remain in power. How did he do it? Béraud's suggestion—that gifts sent by the French in May 1890 and a later visit by a German merchant gave Behanzin the respect he needed—may point to the answer. Certainly, the French unwillingness to press militarily could have been interpreted in Abomey as weakness, and from the Dahomean perspective a series of incidents seemed to confirm French hesitation, even fear, to confront Dahomey. Behanzin had demanded in mid-March 1890, for example, that the French hostages write a letter "to the king of France" telling him that Bayol had launched an unjust war against Dahomey. Behanzin opined that he would long since have had Bayol's head for such misbehavior. Three weeks later, the French envoy was called home, presumably to be punished. The French pushed for a peace treaty that was signed in October 1890. Their motive was to gain time, but the monarchy may not have understood that.

Another telling incident occurred in February–March 1891, when a mission of French military officers bringing numerous gifts to Abomey, but whose main purpose was espionage, were persuaded by Dahomean authorities to enter the city carrying palm branches, a public sign of submission. Later, the French wrote conciliatory letters to Behanzin protesting in the mildest possible terms that the Dahomean army had attacked villages under French protection. This strategic retreat of the French must have helped Behanzin consolidate power. It appeared to demonstrate that belligerence was successful in dealing with European threats. But there was another factor, too, that would have favored Behanzin— the revival of the slave trade and the prosperity, and influx of arms, that it brought.

More than five thousand men, women, and children were embarked from Whydah during the three years from May 1889 to May 1892. They were sent to Belgian, German, and Portuguese territories in Africa, and specifically to the Belgian Congo, Cameroon, and São Tomé. Both Dahomeans and Europeans acknowledged that they were slaves. The major trading partners were German firms, and the largest customer by far was Germany. In exchange, the Dahomeans imported war matériel. By November 1891, the French administrator at the coast was estimating that at least five thousand rapid-firing rifles had reached Abomey. Mobile artillery was an important addition to the Dahomean arsenal at this time, as were early machine guns that had been captured from the French in the Franco-Prussian war of 1870. By 1892, the Dahomeans possessed what were probably the best and most up-to-date imported weapons of any point in the history of the kingdom. The German merchants obligingly provided technical assistants to train Dahomeans in the use of the new guns. About a half-dozen Afro-Brazilians also worked with the Dahomean forces, and some ultimately fought with them, along with four Europeans who would be captured and executed by the French.[21]

Meanwhile, the final funeral ceremonies for Glele, the Grand Customs, were postponed, though preparations were being made for them. Slave raiding and wars were carried out to the east as well as southwest of Dahomey to gain captives for trade and sacrifice. At the same time, consultations with the ancestors and gods had advised strongly against war with the French. However, by the spring of 1892 the French Chamber of Deputies had voted the modest funds needed for war. The French provoked an incident with a gunboat on the Weme River and the Dahomeans attacked, obligingly providing a casus belli. Insisting that his warriors had fired without orders, Behanzin wrote a number of letters apologizing and offering to negotiate. But it was too late. The French had the funds and men to invade, and Behanzin's letters went unanswered.[22]

By twentieth-century standards, the French war against Dahomey was small and brief. An expeditionary force of some twenty-two hundred fighters, whose goal was to occupy Abomey, departed from Porto Novo on August 17, 1892 and entered Abomey precisely three months later. Nevertheless, it was neither a simple nor an easy conquest. The French force was resisted virtually all along its journey up the Weme River valley and overland to Cana and Abomey. Despite planning the campaign for more than a year, the French were seriously hampered by logistics problems. Their intelligence was weak, their guides were next to useless, and their resupply system was inadequate, leaving them without water for more than a week at one point. Luc Garcia estimates the effective forces on the Dahomean side to have totaled eight thousand; of those, the standing army was roughly two thousand, one-third of whom were women soldiers. The Dahomean army tried an array of classic tactics against their enemy—predawn surprise attacks, ambushes, attempted ruses—along with newer ideas such as an artillery bombardment at 3:00 A.M. and fighting from fixed positions in trenches and behind thick mud fortifications. Its most successful attacks were guerrilla—small, deadly strikes against patrols, firing on gunboats from the underbrush lining the Weme, shooting at European officers through the thick morning mists. The French wrote glowing reports of the bravery of the Dahomeans, and particularly the women, who, with guns in one hand and short swords in the other, would assault bayonet lines manned by soldiers literally beyond their reach.[23]

Midway through the war, another attempt was made to remove Behanzin from power. The king was away from Abomey when his brother and migan, Egbo, and "his mother," apparently Visesegan, made their move. Rushing back to the capital, Behanzin and his allies managed to put down the coup and imprison the plotters. Egbo later died in prison "of smallpox." His house was broken and his children imprisoned. Abomey oral tradition implicates Porto Novo in the plot, on grounds of the enmity between Toffa and Behanzin that dated back to the time of the vidaho Ahanhanzo. Egbo, tradition suggests, had allied with Behanzin's old enemy Toffa as a prelude to settling with the French.[24]

By late October, the French were nearing Cana and it was clear to the Dahomeans that they could not stop the invaders. Envoys began to arrive at the French bivouacs offering gifts and asking to negotiate, which was the usual form of surrender in the Gbe-speaking area. Agbidinukun told Le Hérissé that 10,000 francs, yams, two cannons, and a finger fashioned of silver were sent to the commanding officer, Alfred-Amédée Dodds. Meant as a gift to the president of France, the silver finger was designed to symbolize the linking of Dahomey to France, like the attachment of the finger to the hand. For the monarchy, "we thought thus to obtain the retreat of the soldiers of the colonel for, when we had unfortunate wars with the Yoruba, we would give them money, and they would leave the country." Waiting for specific instructions from Paris, Dodds indicated that settlement terms would include at the least the acceptance of a protectorate over Dahomey, the payment of a war indemnity, and the abolition of the slave trade and human sacrifice. The monarchy agreed in principle, save for the occupation of Abomey by the French. Then, when much harsher terms were made specific, the monarchy accepted all. Unable or unwilling to meet Dodds's demand for a good-faith payment of seven million francs, eight cannons, and two thousand rapid-firing guns within a twenty-four-hour period, Behanzin and his court fled Abomey, leaving the city aflame. For the next year the monarchy remained intact but invisible to the French, who stayed encamped at Goho on the eastern outskirts of Abomey. France had defeated Dahomey, all agreed, yet the kingdom had not been conquered. And for the moment, the royal family seemed to be united behind Behanzin, for they followed him north from Abomey.[25]

The monarchy-in-exile set up its center at Atcherigbe on the southern bank of the Zou River, thirty-one miles north of Abomey along the frontier of the territory under effective Dahomean control. Dahomean outposts and sentinels controlled the roads south to Abomey, as well as the roads southwest to Aja country and southeast to the region of Agonli. The exiles, whose numbers were estimated at between two thousand and six thousand persons, were supplied with foodstuffs from both Aja and Agonli, and farms were also cleared and worked in the area of Atcherigbe. The Dahomeans were able, at least during the early months of 1893, to reach Lagos, and despatched a delegation to Europe by way of the British colony to negotiate directly with the president of France or, barring that, to mount a press campaign that would turn other European nations against the French. As early as April, however, the numbers of followers of the court began to thin as people returned to their homes. There was illness in the camp, and provisions dwindled. Nevertheless, the Dahomeans were said to be reconstituting their army, and reports consistently estimated larger numbers of female than male troops.[26]

In December 1892, word had reached the French that Customs were being performed at Atcherigbe in honor of Glele; they were not, however, Grand Customs, the final funeral of the deceased king, which needed to be celebrated in Abomey. That month, there was a literally unbelievable report that six thousand Nagots (Yoruba-speakers) had been taken to Atcherigbe to be sacrificed. In February 1893, the French heard that prisoners who had been incarcerated at Abomey were being sacrificed in ceremonies, and in April that chickens were being substituted for human beings. Certainly, Behanzin's relationship to his ancestors has to have become a central question for the monarchy in the months after the court fled Abomey. How had the ancestors allowed the Dahomeans to be defeated in war? Had Behanzin offended them, and what must be done to placate the ancestors? How could it be that defeat was not followed by negotiation and payment of tribute? What did the French want? Should Behanzin take the unprecedented step of going personally to negotiate with them?[27]

Meanwhile, communications between the monarchy and the French at Goho were regular and conciliatory. In December 1892, Dodds had formally declared Behanzin destooled, and the French searched for a replacement who had the authority to rule. In correspondence, the king consistently avoided acknowledging his deposition, though he conceded that he had lost the war and offered suggestions for settlements. The French were obliging in the early months of 1893, and even considered dividing the kingdom in such a way that Behanzin would be left as ruler over the Abomey plateau. However, the king resisted requests that he surrender, even though the French encouraged him to come to Allada rather than Whydah or Cotonou, under the assumption that proximity to the sea was spiritually dangerous to his person. By July, the French were refusing to negotiate further with envoys and demanded that the king arrive in person. Behanzin sent messages that he was north of the Zou and unable to cross the rain-swollen river.

Dodds, meanwhile, made a three-month trip to Paris to win support and funds for a final campaign against Dahomey. He returned with authorization to assemble a military force that was slightly larger than the original army of invasion. Operations began in mid-October 1893 with four columns that were coordinated to form a pincer to capture the king. By early November, the French were advancing and it was clear that the end was near. What was left of the court and royal followers divided into two groups. Behanzin, fleeing with a handful of wives and children, effectively became a fugitive. The others surrendered or were captured. Siblings of the king and other members of the royal family were kept at Goho by the French.

What happened next is a matter of dispute. Only the end of the story is clear. Guchili, the former gau, or minister of war, became king in January 1894 and took the reign name Agoliagbo, from a praise-phrase: "Watch out! The dynasty from Allada has stumbled but, thanks to the French, it has not fallen." The enstoolment took place at Goho in the presence of the French authorities and virtually all the prominent brothers and sisters of Behanzin. Behanzin gave himself up ten days later, during the night of January 25–26, 1894.

There are deep divisions between the descendants of Behanzin and Agoliagbo that date from this period and are openly acknowledged on all sides. Those divisions persist and have even been played out in national politics in the postcolonial period of Dahomean-Beninese history. What is odd is that the oral traditions about the accession of Agoliagbo as they have been recounted since the 1930s claim that there was a good deal of solidarity and unanimity within the royal family over the selection of Agoliagbo as king. In short, the oral traditions as recounted over the past seventy years offer no explanation for the reality of fissures within the royal family. The events of the moment as recorded by French sources, on the other hand, which are complemented by the turn-of-the-century account of Behanzin's brother, Agbidinukun, provide telling glimpses into some of the tensions that appear to have emerged after the military defeat of a monarchy not yet fully acknowledged.

According to French military records, virtually all of the principals of the royal family and their entourage were assembled at Goho by mid-November 1893, including two of Behanzin's closest advisors, Adandejan and Yehome, who had served frequently as envoys between the king and the French. Behanzin himself continued to elude the French columns, and the court waited. Agbidinukun tells of meeting with General Dodds on November 7 as part of a delegation of twenty-five persons. Offering to accept a protectorate and asking for a treaty to end the war, the delegation was spurned by Dodds, who said flatly, "You are only chiefs. I can't deal with you. Behanzin must come here." Days, then weeks, passed. Villagers remained loyal to Behanzin, who apparently moved easily around the countryside, sometimes literally in view of French troops, who could not distinguish him from other Dahomeans. Yet the situation was impossible. Dodds had made clear that Behanzin could not continue as king; someone else had to be chosen. As Dunglas imagines the scene, the court talked politics, and "those who were absent were always in the wrong." Two persons, a brother and sister of Behanzin, began to negotiate on behalf of the royal family. One was Tokpa Mele, who was alodokponugan for the royal family, the senior brother of the reigning king who served as titular head of all members of the royal family. The second was Yaya Migansi, the na daho, firstborn twin daughter of Glele and his yovoganon. She was described by the French as a "woman of mature age, of a remarkable intelligence [who] appeared to exercise a real influence on her brothers." After royal family discussions, Dodds was told that Guchili was the choice of the royal line to replace Behanzin.[28]

Agbidinukun offers one of several pictures of the family meeting about the choice of a new king, which apparently took place at the compound of the war chief, Soglo, at Wawe, about two miles southeast of the French camp at Goho. Guchili, who had fallen into the hands of the French about two weeks later than other members of court, maintained that he had been designated by Behanzin to become king. The family members were wary, and insisted that Guchili take a sacred oath swearing to the truth of what he claimed. The substance of the family conference was the process of administering the oath. Later, when Behanzin was captured, the royal family members discovered that Guchili had lied, and Behanzin cursed him.[29]

In contrast, oral traditions that date to later periods claim that Behanzin and Guchili worked together to arrange for the gau to be accepted by the French as ruler. The plan was that Guchili would become regent for Behanzin, who would go to France to negotiate the peace personally; on Behanzin's return, Guchili would relinquish the stool. This version was first articulated by Paul Hazoumé in the 1930s. He argues that when Behanzin heard that the French might select a prince of whom he disapproved, the king secretly made his way to the compound of Soglo, where he met with Guchili and several of his other brothers. The plan was made and sworn with an oath. In order to convince the French to accept Guchili, the gau was to pretend that he disagreed with Behanzin and had abandoned the king. Other sisters and brothers would similarly surrender to the French and pretend to be against Behanzin. Hazoumé thus turns evidence of strife within the royal family into theater. "The anger and the curses of Gbèhanzin against Goutchili, when the deposed king learned of the submission of his brother to the French and his enthronisation, . . . were reported to the general and his staff simply to fool the French." The effect of Hazoumé's version, obviously, is to cast into question all interpretations that suggest that the royal family was not in full agreement with the actual events as they unfolded. It argues that the royal family did not agree with Behanzin's destoolment and was unified in its support for both men. Several later accounts drawn from members of the royal family similarly suggest that not only were Behanzin and Agoliagbo in agreement, but that Soglo, the only principal involved who was not a member of the royal family, is to be blamed for trickery and treason. Others stress royal family fears that an enemy of the dynasty, someone like Toffa, would have been named king if the family had not presented its own candidate.[30]

Abomey oral traditions of the mid- and later twentieth century, then, have argued that a sense of solidarity within the royal family existed in face of the French conquest; in short, that a united royal family resisted the imposition of colonial rule. An anticolonial tradition had become important by the fourth decade of the twentieth century, but, as Luc Garcia points out, it "passes in silence over the treason of the direct entourage of the king, as revealed in the reports, in order to retain only that of Soglo." In fact, Behanzin "had been abandoned by his most faithful companions." The French records suggest less a situation of treason and betrayal than the final scene in a long and hard-fought succession struggle. French interference had added a new and unforeseen element to the contest, and, as Agoliagbo was to learn, a king enstooled under French colonial authority was a king in name only. Nevertheless, the despatching of a delegation of "three of the most aged among the great caboceers" to Behanzin on January 27 smacks of succession politics. Archival records simply say that the message to the king announced that he was destooled and that his reign would be seen as not having happened. One of the French officers present at Goho recounts the bitter message in stronger terms: "I am charged to tell you that you are no longer part of the house of Allada. You poisoned your brother Sasse, you poisoned your father. The gods have abandoned you. Your reign has been worse than that of Adandozan. You have lost Dahomey. You no longer exist for us." The French accounts, then, suggest that at least some members of the royal family were not only complicit in the enstoolment of Agoliagbo, but made clear to Behanzin that he had been discredited and replaced.[31]

One other mystery remains about the end of Behanzin's reign. Virtually all of the king's most trusted supporters were gone from him during the two months from mid-November to the enstoolment of Agoliagbo on January 15. The king then waited another ten days before surrendering to the French. Where was Behanzin during that period and what was he doing? What was happening to his tiny group of fugitives, consisting mainly of women and children, while decisions were being made at Goho? A report from General Dodds to his superiors, dated January 20, gives us some hints. First, Dodds notes that he received a letter from Lagos indicating that the messengers that the monarchy had sent to France in early 1893 had returned and were asking to communicate with the king. Was Behanzin perhaps waiting and clinging to the hope that his emissaries might be effective? Their news in fact was not good. No one except newspaper reporters had been willing to speak with them, and they had failed utterly either to meet with French officials or to foment a press campaign against the French actions in Dahomey. Though the messengers promised that they would convince Behanzin to give up, Dodds refused to let them communicate with Behanzin. Interestingly, Dodds's

11. King Behanzin in exile. The king's son, Ouanilo, stands on the right in front of Adandejan. Five wives went with the king. Identified in this photo by descendants of Behanzin were Etchiome and Vidotote, seated on either side of the king, and Agbajaten, Agbopanu, and Menuswe standing behind. (Collection Musée de l'Homme, Paris)

comment about the letter from Lagos indicates that the French, even though they were never able to locate Behanzin, were able to communicate with him on a regular basis. We know, too, that communications continued, at least at intervals, between Behanzin and individuals who had submitted to the French.[32]

Dodds also reported that December 30 was the anniversary of the death of Glele and the season for annual offerings to the royal ancestors. It was Behanzin's sacred duty to perform ceremonies honoring his ancestors. The king was known to have left Atcherigbe and traveled south past Abomey to the banks of the Coufo River, southwest of the capital. There, claimed French intelligence in January, "Behanzin has just sacrificed near the Couffo his principal wives, numerous inhabitants of Whydah and some of the children of his brother Egbo."[33]

The only other indication of what was happening near Behanzin, particularly in those ten final days after Agoliagbo had become king, comes from the period after the former king had given himself up. Behanzin and a relatively large entourage of wives, servants, and children were taken from Goho on January 28 and transported by boat down the Weme to Cotonou. There they stayed until February 11, when the French steamer *Segond* departed for Martinique, in the West Indies, where Behanzin and his companions would remain for nearly a decade. During the days that the royal party waited, Behanzin had a series of conversations with the French officer Tahon, who was charged with his confinement and care. Tahon, sympathetic to the former king and respectful of him, left a memoir of their talks that provides a dramatic and moving account of the war and its aftermath. Here is the account as told through a translator. "At the beginning of the war I was protected by my father, the great Glélé, and I had successes. At one point, at the engagement at Dogba [a surprise attack on a French bivouac along the Weme, 18 September 1892], I even believed I would be able to push the French back to the sea, but from that moment on I was abandoned and despite the envoys that I sent to him [Glele] each evening—my bravest warriors— nothing worked." Behanzin then recounted how the French advance continued, and how he and his entourage were forced to abandon Abomey and the other important cities of the kingdom to flee to Atcherigbe. There,

> heartbroken, dispirited, I no longer knew who to rely on, being convinced that my envoys sent to Glélé did not complete their missions; I thus appealed to my aged mother and asked her to sacrifice herself for her son and country by consenting to go herself to intervene with her husband. She agreed, but with the single provision that her head be cut off by me, her son, and that the execution take place on the banks of the sacred river, the Couffo. After the execution I waited eight days, then seeing nothing happen of advantage to me, and recognizing to the contrary that the French columns

were closing up, and fearing to be betrayed and delivered to my brother who would have immediately put me to death, I preferred to appeal to the feelings of generosity of the French government. I now await my fate.[34]

And thus the short reign of Behanzin ended in an act of devotion and desperation.

Agoliagbo and the Aftermath of the French Conquest ∼

The deposition of Behanzin by the French marked both the end of the succession struggle to follow Glele and the end of the independent kingdom of Dahomey. Having orchestrated the enstoolment of Agoliagbo, the French administrators of what was then known as "Dahomey and Dependencies" expected the new king to become a loyal subordinate willing to promote the French colonial project. Agoliagbo was to take orders from the *résident* (administrator) of Abomey, who in turn was answerable to the governor of the colony. The kingdom he was to rule was reduced in territory to the Abomey plateau and the Agonli region, an area of rich farmland between the Weme and Zou rivers. Agoliagbo, like his brother Behanzin, began his reign with a monarchy that effectively consisted of members of the royal family. He eventually settled his entourage in an older portion of the central palace in Abomey and set artisans to work refurbishing and replacing royal regalia lost in the war with the French.

Conflict between Agoliagbo and the French was inevitable, since both expected to control the fundamental resources of people and land. The French began releasing slaves and sending them to their homes as early as January 1894, the month that Agoliagbo was installed. They reported that many of the wives of Behanzin refused to become part of the palace of the new king. Agoliagbo had no coercive power to force their obedience. The king was permitted to keep a portion of taxes collected, but it was not nearly sufficient to match the royal income of autonomous Dahomey—or to keep members of the royal family content. The monarchy of royal siblings could not hold. Within a year of his enstoolment, six of Agoliagbo's brothers and one sister had gone into exile at Allada because the king could not provide for them. By November 1894, Tokpa

Mele, who with the na daho had led the royal lineage to their choice of Agoliagbo as king, visited the French administrator to ask that the king be replaced. Agoliagbo in turn complained that three of his brothers had threatened that if he did not behave as they wished, "we will replace you." [35]

Problems came to a head in the region of Agonli, east of Abomey. Presumably in order to ease tensions on the Abomey plateau, the monarchy turned to Agonli for the resources demanded both by the French administration and Dahomean cultural imperatives: porters for the French and soldiers for French ambitions in Madagascar; food for the funeral celebration in honor of Glele; and women to repopulate the palace. When the people of Agonli rebelled in 1894 and 1895, the French detached the region from the kingdom, simultaneously complaining of Agoliagbo's "weak political sense and the disaffection that the Dahomean people have for a king so ignorant of his best interests." Later that year, the governor of the colony visited Abomey and threatened to replace Agoliagbo with a brother who might "better understand the conditions under which he had to exercise his prerogatives and powers." In response, the king appears to have worked harder to be accommodating to the real rulers of his kingdom, which was now reduced in size to the Abomey plateau alone. The French soon began to congratulate themselves that Agoliagbo "seems to have given up all inclinations toward independence." Proclaiming the population of the downsized kingdom to be malleable and easily governed, the administrator of Abomey exulted that "we are perfectly obeyed in this region formerly so warlike; they like our authority and appreciate the benefits of order, peace and individual liberty." Nevertheless, Agoliagbo asserted his autonomy a final time in 1898, objecting to an annual tax that was to be collected by the king and levied on everyone more than ten years of age. Confident of their authority and comfortable that the Dahomeans would not protest, the French responded by abolishing the kingdom itself. Agoliagbo was exiled to the Congo in 1900 and the area of the plateau was divided into eight cantons, each headed by a chief who was either a prince of the Alladahonu line or a close ally of the royal family. [36]

The two central institutions of state power and authority, the monarchy and the palace, had effectively dissolved well before Agoliagbo's unwilling departure from Dahomey. When Agoliagbo was enstooled, members of his family had formed a kind of monarchy, an entourage around the king, and offices had been awarded. But Agoliagbo can hardly be said to have had a monarchy in the old sense, that of a coalition of individuals who had sought power together and then ruled with and in the name of the king. Later, when the French divided the plateau into cantons, it was deliberately to diffuse power, to keep any single prince from claiming the authority of the royal stool. The canton chiefs and their urban counterparts, the chiefs of the quarters of the city of Abomey, set up what became a series of hereditary would-be fiefs ruled by descendants of Glele and their close associates. Each of these princely chiefs created his own mini-court that duplicated on a much-reduced scale the old grandeur of Dahomey, and a number of them over the years competed for recognition as king. As they sat in formal authority over the plateau, the collective body of chiefs—all male, and virtually all members of the royal family—perpetuated the form of late-nineteenth-century monarchies, but without the central and centralizing figure of a king and without the experience of common purpose that provided unity to monarchies of the past.

As for the palace, relatively large numbers of its population in the late nineteenth century had consisted of slaves or free Dahomean women forcibly recruited to become ahosi. The war with the French decimated the women warriors, and many other palace women slipped away in the chaos that followed the 1892 defeat and flight from Abomey. Agoliagbo tried with little success to force women back into the palace organization, and after 1900, the canton chiefs similarly attempted to build up their polygynous households. French administrators grumbled from time to time about chiefs trying to extort women from the villagers under their authority; in fact, women themselves appear to have refused to perpetuate versions of the palace in the twentieth century. As late as the 1970s, various women described life within the households of canton chiefs as lacking in opportunity and interest. Many women coerced into marriage with a chief, I was told, would use their talents and energies to flee and then negotiate marriages with other men.

But despite the disappearance of the two central organs of the king-dom's authority and power, vestiges of the old system remained, as did signs of a continuation of trends and processes that were operating in the days of the kingdom. For example, the men of the royal family continued the nineteenth-century trend toward the exclusion of women from the exercise of power. Colonial authorities were predisposed to consider women's participation in politics inappropriate, and princes clearly did little or nothing to clarify women's earlier roles to the French. Both com-moner women of the palace and princesses had been central to public affairs in the eighteenth century and had been losing their prerogatives, rights, and good repute toward the end of the nineteenth. Yet documents surviving in the Benin National Archives suggest that women were in fact still attempting to engage the colonial authorities and participate in po-litical negotiation. For example, in 1904 Le Hérissé, then administrator of Abomey, forwarded correspondence to the French governor related to a group of princes who were pressing the administration to reinstate the kingship. Among the letters was one in which Prince Gbohayida dis-cussed strategies with Prince Aho, warning "another piece of advice I have to give you, is not to bring any women with you any more, as you did the other day in meeting the administrator of Abomey, because women these days have confused and complicated nearly all of our busi-ness."[37] Similarly, occasional references appear in the archives to the four wives of Behanzin who returned to Abomey following the deposed king's death in Algeria, where he had been transferred in 1906. The women fre-quently met with the administrator of Abomey, usually to urge the return of Behanzin's remains to Dahomey. Reports make clear that the French saw them as a nuisance. What is telling of the Dahomean perspective, though, is that the women do not appear to have been accompanied by any other members of the royal family in their visits to the colonial au-thorities. In short, they were not visibly backed by the princes, who were in positions of civil authority in the French administration and who would have been the expected supporters for missions of this nature. Is this evidence of continuing hostility toward those closest to Behanzin? Or is it an indication of princely unwillingness to cooperate with women who formerly held important positions in the palace?

Royal authority and prestige remained dominant on the Abomey plateau in the twentieth century in part because the colonial state preserved
and supported it. French power had superceded the power of the Alladahonu, and over time Dahomey and its populations would be profoundly changed by the colonial enterprise. But one striking element of
the colonial period is the degree to which the French accepted and became part of Dahomean patterns of power relations. Decisions made in
colonial courts of law in Abomey in the first decade of the twentieth
century, for example, consistently sought a middle ground in which the
authority of members of the old regime was preserved while a degree of
personal choice was permitted to former slaves and other dependents.
Two cases involving high-ranking women are indicative.

In 1906, Visesegan, the favorite wife of Glele and nemesis of Behanzin,
went to court to claim as hers the children of a woman named Djoleme.
Djoleme had been a slave purchased by Visesegan during the reign of
Glele and kept within the palace organization; she had secretly taken a
lover and become pregnant. When found out, Djoleme and the lover
were both imprisoned. Freed when the French conquered Abomey, the
young woman was then kidnapped into Aja country. The lover found her
there and brought her back to Abomey. She and the lover then lived
together "with the consent of Visesegan" and she bore her mate three
more children. Visesegan argued that because Djoleme was a dependent/
slave who had not been married with proper payment of bridewealth,
the children were members of her household. Le Hérissé, the administrator of Abomey at the time, ruled that since technically slavery no
longer existed, Djoleme was free. However, since the young woman had
no other family, he asked that she recognize Visesegan as her mother.
Djoleme agreed, which legitimized Visesegan's claim to control over the
children by confirming the younger woman as a member of Visesegan's
household. A daughter of Djoleme's was sent to reside with Visesegan and
serve her.

In another case, the Kpojito Agontime appeared in court to ask permission to give a girl named Bodjo over to the control of a vodunon or
priestess of the cult of Nesuhwe. Bodjo was the daughter of a woman
named Nasi, who was "under the power of the Kpojito," a euphemism

for slave status. The spirit of the Kpojito Adonon had possessed Nasi, the mother, and Agontime argued that Adonon would later mount the daughter as well. The court effectively supported Agontime's rights by ruling that giving Bodjo to the priest would be slavery and could not be allowed; however, Agontime had the right to give the girl in marriage and receive the bridewealth payments. The court records can be read for many signs of continuity and change on the Abomey plateau, and for indications of women's attempts to have the colonial authorities confirm their previous autonomy. At the same time, though, they speak eloquently to the complexity of interpersonal negotiations of status in the colonial period, and of French efforts to preserve older status relations.[38]

There is a final telling example of the ways in which the French colonial authorities were co-opted into Dahomean forms of political relationship. Princesses and women dependents of the royal family in the colonial period became wives of French administrators, creating ties of cooperation and kinship that echoed the old patterns of interaction with neigboring states, with European slave traders resident in Whydah, and with the Afro-Brazilian elites. Branches of the royal family that descended from the nineteenth-century monarchs in particular maintained and enhanced their positions in the colonial state through cultivating ties with colonial administrators in this way. Often, those ties were strengthened through marriage.[39]

The most compelling example of the way that the colonial system became Dahomean, a story that is yet to be told in full, concerns the children of Behanzin. As was usual when an individual was discredited in Dahomey, the wives, children, and other dependents of Behanzin appear to have shared in the shame of their father at the moment of his destoolment. Scattered in the wake of the conquest, their mothers refusing to enter the palace of Agoliagbo, they nevertheless maintained some sense of cohesion. By an astute strategy of marrying some daughters to French administrators, sending some sons to serve in the French military, and educating family members to understand and participate in the emerging order, the Behanzin branch of the royal lineage gradually reconstituted itself, emerging as a leading family in late colonial and postcolonial Dahomey. Alliance and accommodation through marriage was of course an old stategy in Dahomey. Its operation in the early twentieth century was an echo of the earliest days of the kingdom, when a beleaguered group of strangers needed and used the talents of all—women, men, strangers, and friends—to create a nation. That observation brings us both to the beginning and the end of our story. But it may also point to an important object lesson in how unity needs to be built and maintained within an imagined community that we call a nation-state. ∾

8

Reprise

Dahomey was born as a by-product of the Atlantic slave trade. Its founders forged a kingdom on a small plateau north of the state of Allada, in an area subject to the dangers and insecurities brought by slave raiding. The peoples of that Abomey plateau shared an identity that they continue to share, even though, paradoxically, the composition of the population was constantly changing over the course of the roughly two hundred years of the known history of Dahomey. It was an identity built of a shared language family and common historical experience, of cultural ties extending probably as far as the area we today call Ghana. But a collective identity does not preclude tensions. Dahomey was built by conquest—village by village, household by household, individual by individual. Its founders were intruders on the plateau, outsiders with ambitions that they carried out through military means. Whether or not they were kinsmen, the founders of Dahomey at some point accepted and acknowledged one lineage among themselves—the Alladahonu—as hereditary rulers, and a male leader of that lineage as king.

The Alladahonu kings ruled with and through two key overlapping institutions. The first was the monarchy—a coalition of powerful individuals closest to the king who acted as ministers of state and close advisers. The second was the palace—the thousands of persons who made up the household of the king and managed the affairs of state. Certain women were simultaneously members of both institutions. Individuals in the monarchy and palace exercised power in the name of the king. But the king himself was neither a cipher nor a despot. Individuals who became king were not simply thrust into power, nor did they seize power and rule absolutely. Rather, a small number of sons of a king were potential kings. The men who became king proved their merit through demonstrating their leadership abilities—to attract followers, to form alliances with individuals of talent and ambition, to garner the support of supernatural powers, and to win and hold power with the people who would become their governing coalition. Some Dahomean kings, their monarchies, and their palaces governed with particular skill and acumen; others made poor decisions or let matters drift. In either case, agency, the question of who acted and made decisions, never lay wholly in the hands of any one element: king, monarchy, or palace. Rather, the balance among the individuals who made up those institutions was constantly being renegotiated.

Over time, there were dramatic changes in the origins and gender of the individuals who made up the monarchy and palace. Though the changes were gradual, they contrast starkly when compared at mid–eighteenth and mid–nineteenth century. At the earlier moment, Dahomey was effectively at its height. Having more than doubled its size in the 1720s, the kingdom had faced constant security crises as it tried to maintain control over the coast and survive attacks from the powerful empire of Oyo to the northeast. The task of the monarchy and palace of the early eighteenth century was consolidation and integration—consolidation of territory and administration, and integration of outsiders into the institutions of state. By mid–eighteenth century, stability and prosperity had been achieved. Dahomean military power had been sufficient to protect the earlier conquests, and a political settlement with Oyo had allowed Dahomey to trade tribute for an end to invasions of the Abomey plateau. The slave trade was bringing luxury imports along with integration into a broader, international, capitalist commercial system. Religious institutions were quiescent and ritual accommodations were in place that bound the ruling invaders to the previous politicoreligious authorities.

How had this been achieved? The state grew through co-opting the services of many: members of the royal family, people who lived on the plateau before the arrival of the Alladahonu and their companions, and individuals captured in war or purchased in the slave trade who for various reasons were kept within the kingdom. Those who participated at the centers of power and came to be part of the monarchy and palace included women as well as men, royalty, commoners, and slaves. There were generous rewards for the powerful in the kingdom. titles, imported goods, land, tribute-paying villages, wives and slaves, and rights to trade, which promised even more wealth. Twentieth-century Dahomeans described the kingdom as a meritocracy, and that interpretation by and large fits the evidence of the eighteenth-century kingdom. Individuals outside the special circle of royalty earned their rewards through loyal service to the palace and monarchy. Nevertheless, members of the royal family had rights by birth to portions of this largesse; a monarchy that failed to provide generously for the king's siblings did so at its peril.

Women had arguably reached a pinnacle of power and influence by mid–eighteenth century. At its high point, the former captive from Aja country, Kpojito Hwanjile, ruled in tandem with her protégé, King Tegbesu. Openly acknowledged as one of the keys to Tegbesu's successful climb to the royal stool, Hwanjile was instrumental in reordering the deities and their earthly servants, the priesthood, under state control. The ideological vision of the monarchy of Tegbesu's time was reflected in the other world, Kutome, where Hwanjile placed a pair of creator gods, Mawu and Lisa, to reign supreme. Like Hwanjile and Tegbesu, Mawu and Lisa were neither siblings nor spouses, but rather a female-male pair who worked together to create and recreate the world. The model of royal succession demonstrated by Hwanjile and Tegbesu typified the age. At the center of king making was the palace. Ambitious princes of necessity had to be linked to women of the palace: it was the women who held the balance of power in succession struggles, who had the ability to assist one coalition or another to win physical control, and to have the name of one particular prince uttered and accepted as his father's choice. Later, when a new king's position was secure, it was palace women who advised and counseled kings. It was likely also women in the palace who were instrumental in recruiting brothers, fathers, and other talented men to become ahosi for eighteenth-century kings.

Dahomey at mid–nineteenth century at first glance appeared even stronger than a hundred years before. Its king was the vigorous Gezo, who had allied with Afro-Brazilians on the coast to seize power from a man said to have been both incompetent and cruel. Seemingly open to influence from Europe, Gezo was courted by European envoys seeking the cessation of the slave trade and pursuing advantages in the emerging commerce in palm oil. The transition in major exports from slaves to palm products was being made with little apparent social or political disruption. Dahomey was well known as a military power and boasted a unique army of women that was widely feared in the region. Freed from Oyo suzerainty, Dahomey was still absorbing outsiders and their culture and was being visibly enriched by Yoruba-speaking peoples who had fallen victim to the warfare beyond the kingdom's eastern frontier.

But the story of the nineteenth century is one of appearances and deceptions. In retrospect, one senses a certain desperation at the center, a fear that control was being lost. Royal revenues from the overseas trade had declined and the imported goods that were needed to demonstrate prestige and attract clients were harder to come by. The transition from slaves to palm oil was placing the ruling coalition of Dahomey at a serious disadvantage. Coastal plantations owned by Afro-Brazilians were far more convenient to shipping points than was the Abomey plateau, and small producers might process and sell palm-oil products outside of royal control. By mid–nineteenth century, the monarchy was responding to the decline in resources by moving toward greater coercion: taxes were increased and collected with greater rigor; there was stricter surveillance of individuals with state responsibility; and larger numbers of women and slaves were being put to work on production for the royal treasury. Militarism was increasing, even though by mid–nineteenth century the only state strong enough to overrun Dahomey, Oyo, had long since disappeared.

Most importantly, the centers of power were being reconfigured. Gezo had instituted changes in both the monarchy and the palace. He had come to power from outside the system, with the support of a coalition of his siblings and a group of Afro-Brazilian traders. Gezo opened the way to greater royal influence by naming brothers and sisters to his monarchy alongside the commoners who were the usual officials of the kingdom. With the demands of the royal family for support a given, and with resources continuing to decline, it had become efficient to name brothers and sisters to high office. Once the precedent was set, his successors would name members of the Alladahonu royal lineage to their monarchies and depend far less on commoners or slaves, and particularly on those commoners from within the territorial limits of Dahomey. During the nineteenth century, fewer and fewer men and women of talent outside the royal lineage were welcomed to power.

At mid–nineteenth century, Dahomey was still absorbing neighboring peoples and their cultures. But they were arriving in larger numbers than in earlier periods and they tended to be exclusively Yoruba-speaking. Though many were integrated into households and communities, many others remained permanently and visibly in slave status, working on palm-oil plantations that were being created on the Abomey plateau. The Dahomean army, female as well as male, was increasingly staffed with Yoruba-speakers. As in the past, some of the newcomers reached the highest levels of influence in the state; increasingly, however, these powerful individuals were males, who rose through their knowledge of the occult, applying their skills as bokonon or diviners of the Yoruba-derived system of Fa. By midcentury, women advisers to the king were beginning to find their roles challenged both by brothers of the king and by his bokonon.

Paradoxically, within the palace women were more desired yet increasingly distanced from power. The population of the palace had increased dramatically in the first half of the nineteenth century. But it was the *labor* of women that was sought, as women increasingly were being brought into the palace organization to process palm oil, to work at numerous other royal industries, and to fill the ranks of the army. Meanwhile, women's participation on the highest political levels was being systematically eroded. The palace appears to have resisted Gezo's coup, or at best, the palace did not produce large numbers of women who actively advanced his cause. Gezo had taken a crucial step that diminished women's powers by altering the succession process. Beginning with Gezo's choice of heir, nineteenth-century vidaho were selected by the royal family and groomed for power. Princes no longer needed to build coalitions in alliance with powerful women of the palace. Mentored by male elders in the royal family, they consolidated their monarchies well before the death of their fathers.

There were, however, still influential and powerful women within the palace. For example, Visesegan already held an important office at midcentury. Later, she would lead the opposition to Behanzin, operating in the old way by allying with a prince to seek control with him. Apparently intimately linked to Glele through ties of deep trust, she spoke with the authority of the king. Yet she and her faction lost their bid to win ascendancy, and Behanzin in 1890 became the third successive nineteenth-century king to gain control of palace and monarchy without the acknowledged help of palace women.

To argue that this process of social change in a political elite was occurring, I have taken oral accounts and the words of nineteenth-century travelers and read through them, looking for other meanings behind their words. Europeans' conversations with King Gezo, for example, were rich in deceptive meanings. In the 1850s, Gezo reassured visitors that he had stopped selling slaves overseas. He spoke a technical truth, even though his alter ego, Gakpe, still traded, and even though the principle that the slave trade was an acceptable form of commerce remained unchanged. Gezo also told visitors that only criminals were sacrificed at Customs. He was correct, because captives of warfare were by definition enemies, and hence criminals. Europeans and some historians heard, however, that only people who had committed grievous crimes were condemned to be sacrificed. Gezo insisted that his women warriors could not be asked to cultivate the soil. He was right, because their status as soldier freed them of the drudgery of farm labor. But Gezo knew full well that his was an agricultural nation, and that most of his subjects spent their time farming.

There were other signs in nineteenth-century Dahomey that what was being said or seen masked other realities. Customs showed the court as a state at work, but it was also political performance. The emphasis on military power and might, with high officials at court performing military dance and women warriors storming make-believe defenses, made Dahomeans appear a violent and war-loving people. Yet the army that fought was made up mainly of slaves, and its pattern of success in the nineteenth century differed little from the past. The equilibrium between royal and commoner typified by the royal dyad, king and kpojito, was visible in the ceremonial life of the kingdom in the nineteenth century. Indeed, balanced complementary opposites at the court of Dahomey were seemingly without end: king and kpojito, male ministers and female ministers, officials of the left and officials of the right, the inside (the palace) and the outside (the kingdom as a whole). Following the lead of the royal oral tradition, twentieth-century historians have enshrined in their analyses that vision of complementary doubles and the necessity for inclusiveness: man and woman, royal and commoner, Dahomean and foreigner. Yet the ideology of complementarity performed publicly masked a changing religious hierarchy that reflected more accurately the political realities of the late nineteenth century.

Religious life in Dahomey was manipulated by the monarchy in the belief that the world of the spirits, Kutome, was a mirror image of the visible world of humanity, Gbetome. The reordering of the hierachies of the gods by successive monarchies can be read as intellectual history that reveals the changing conceptions of power relations by those at the kingdom's center. If Mawu and Lisa, the creator gods of the mid–eighteenth century, represented a vision of complementarity and partnership, Zumadunu, who supplanted them in the nineteenth century, represented the arrival of royalty as solely supreme. Zumadunu was a monstrous tohosu, a king of the waters. Yet Zumadunu was not just a spirit-king but the son of an earthly king, a creature said to have been fathered by King Akaba and hence eligible to rule as king on earth. Every king after Akaba was linked to a tohosu double, a fearsome being who embodied the supernatural powers said to be within the control of the king. All the tohosu and all the other deities, royal and popular, by the late nineteenth century were aligned under Zumadunu, who reigned as supreme deity. By that point, commoner tohosu were being recognized and honored, yet all under the aegis of branches of the royal family. In effect, the vodun also were participating in the strict social hierarchy and tighter control over Dahomean life that was characteristic of the period. Part of the hierarchy, yet in a sense outside it, lurked Fa, the deity of divination. Present in the eighteenth century but only as one of a number of competing vodun of divination, Fa moved to center stage in the nineteenth. It was only through divination—and ideally Fa divination—that humanity was able to know the unknown, to have a communications link with the invisible, to come into direct contact with the vodun. Decisions large and small were dependent upon the good offices of Fa. But more importantly, Fa offered men knowledge of their personal destiny. Fa and Zumadunu together proclaimed the centrality of the male within the royal lineage.

How and why did the people of Dahomey, women and commoners, accept this changing religious ideology? Behaviors can be forced and co-operation to some extent coerced, but spiritual beliefs persist, sometimes the more strongly the greater their suppression. The monarchy allowed the so-called popular vodun to persist, and thrive, in Dahomey. They and their priests were accommodated with grants of land and financial subsidies. In exchange, the monarchy exercised a degree of control over their leadership and their ceremonial life. With the possible exception of Gu (the Yoruba Ogun), who was directly linked to the war-making power of the state in the nineteenth century, none of the popular vodun was closely tied to the central government in the way that Shango, for example, was linked to the strength of Oyo. In fact, Sakpata, the deity commonly associated with smallpox, was a focus of opposition to the monarchy. That opposition, as Sakpata, took the form of a questioning of the legitimacy of the dynasty.

Legitimacy was a question that ran like a stream through the kingdom's history, sometimes as quiet and still as a river at the end of the dry season and sometimes flooding with the violence of torrential rains. Questions of legitimacy were raised at several levels: the right of the dynasty to rule; the right of the state to establish its authority over kin groups; and the suitability of an individual to become king. Successions were periods of flood, when the monarchy was recreated through violent struggle at the center, involving the palace, powerful outsiders, and the royal family in the choice of a man to rule as king. Successions and their immediate aftermaths also were periods when broader questions of legitimacy were raised, particularly in the eighteenth century, about the dynasty's right to rule. Signs of unrest and rebellion, which typically emerged early in the reigns of new kings, were expressed at least in part through religious movements and metaphors. The creation of the office of kpojito, for example, provided a ritualized accommodation between the intruding founders of Dahomey and the older owners of the earth. The reordering of the hierarchy of the gods during the reign of Tegbesu and the concessions made to the vodun and their priests spoke of responses to challenges to the legitimacy of the dynasty. And at the end of the eighteenth and beginning of the nineteenth centuries, the followers of Sakpata appear to have contested the right of the Alladahonu to rule Dahomey. Sakpata's strength was effectively acknowledged through the distance that the monarchy kept from the vodun and the regular use of Sakpata as metaphor for disorder and political danger.

Tensions between the state and kin groups were constant, too, because loyal service to the monarchy undercut allegiance to kin groups. For example, state titles with their accompanying wealth overshadowed lineage elders and their authority. The population of the palace was a social microcosm of the kingdom, one that tied kin groups to the state, willingly or not, and held out the promise of wealth to be gained by the collectivity should their kinswomen reach high levels of power. Moreover, the palace acted as a conduit of information between the center and the population at large, enabling the monarchy to tap popular reactions and to convey its own perspectives to the populace. In the late nineteenth century, the monarchy effectively tried to supplant the sacred basis of lineage ties by realigning family rituals and integrating them into the various branches of the royal family.

The Alladahonu lineage had arrived on the Abomey plateau as part of a small band of strangers. With skill and determination they had built a state, expanding their own ranks by integrating peoples of relatively diverse backgrounds into their lineage and dependency relations. Their wealth was human—their children and dependents, their slaves sold overseas or kept at home, their human offerings to the ancestors and gods, and their tributary peoples who brought annual gifts. At their most successful, they had fostered opportunities for strangers and slaves, commoners and captives, men and women; all these could share in wealth and power through the monarchy and the palace. They had eagerly entered and embraced a system of commercial capitalism that offered rich rewards but was beyond their control. When the system changed, and opportunities narrowed, they reacted by consolidating, contracting their sights to the narrow interests of their lineage, and limiting power to their men. State power in the end in Dahomey became wholly dynastic and patriarchal, its exercise limited to male members of the royal lineage. Yet at that very moment, Dahomey itself was being absorbed into the larger imperialism of Europe. It would become the task of the descendants of the Alladahonu and their neighbors nearly a century later to create anew a polity in which individuals of talent and skill, whatever their background or sex, might play a role.∼

Notes

Chapter 1 ⟲ Along the Slave Coast

1. Gayibor, "Mémoire," 53. Other prominent apologists for the slave trade include Snelgrave, Smith, and Dalzel. Strongest among the abolitionist voices is Atkins. For a discussion of abolitionist and antiabolitionist perspectives, see Law, "Dahomey."

2. Quénum, *Pays*, 19.

3. An exception to the pattern is the palace and shrine to Akaba, traditionally known as the second king of Dahomey, located to the north of the central palace complex. Law has argued that this physical evidence, along with a king list collected by Norris in the early eighteenth century, show that the remembered order of kings is mistaken, and that Akaba in fact was the first Dahomean king ("History and Legitimacy").

4. Mercier and Lombard, *Guide*, 9.

5. Hazoumé, *Cinquante ans*, 33.

6. ASA, Commandant.

7. Hazoumé, *Pacte*, 28–31.

8. Le Hérissé, *Royaume*, 158–59, 209.

9. Forbes, *Dahomey*, 2:77.

10. Dalzel, *History*, 127–28; Mercier and Lombard, *Guide*, 14–15.

11. Hazoumé, "Tata Ajachè;" Morton-Williams, "Yoruba Woman."

12. Jones discusses the complex possible meanings of observations repeated by several travelers in "Semper Aliquid Veteris."

13. Bulfinch Lamb's letter to Jeremiah Tinker, "From the great King Trudo Audati's Palace of Abomey, in the Kingdom of Dahomey in 1724," is printed in two sources: Smith, *New Voyage,* 171–89, and Forbes, *Dahomey,* 1: appendix A. Lamb in 1731 delivered a letter purportedly dictated to him by Agaja to the court of George I of England. The British Commissioners for Trade and Plantations, to whom it was submitted, declared it a forgery. Even as such, it reflects Lamb's observations from his sojourn in Dahomey. It is reprinted in Law, "Further Light."

14. I am grateful to Robin Law for providing a copy of "Réflexions" for my use.

15. The two-volume *Dahomey* is the central work produced by Herskovits on Dahomey. Maupoil notes errors in information provided by Herskovits's principal

informant in "Géomancie," 65, fn. 1, and 75, fn. 1. Blier criticizes his field methods in "Field Days."

16. E.g., Polanyi, *Dahomey*; Sacks, *Sisters*.

17. Law has pointed out that even in the precolonial period, Dahomeans drew on written records of the past to discuss contemporary issues, citing precedent from the written works of various Europeans ("History and Legitimacy," 432–34).

18. Law, "History and Legitimacy," 434–35. See also Lombard, "Moyen," 152.

19. For a discussion of perpetual kinship and positional succession, see Vansina, *Kingdoms*, 27.

Chapter 2 ∾ From Dahomey's Origins to 1740

1. Le Hérissé, *Royaume*, 2.

2. Skertchly, *Dahomey*, 36.

3. Le Hérissé, *Royaume*, 47–48.

4. Manning estimates that 90 percent of all slaves exported from the Bight of Benin were Gbe- (Aja-) or Yoruba-speaking peoples and hence from areas within 120 miles of the coast (*Slavery, Colonialism, and Economic Growth*, 32).

5. Norris estimated that the speed of his hammock was at least five miles an hour (*Memoirs*, 140).

6. Smith, *New Voyage*, 192–93.

7. "Captain Phillip's Journal," 218.

8. Robertson and Klein suggest an overall ratio of two or three men to each woman (*Women and Slavery*, 4). Geggus argues that the overall proportion was somewhat lower, in the range of 179 males to 100 females ("Sex Ratio"). Law similarly describes relatively high proportions of males to females for the area around Whydah for just before the turn of the century (*Slave Coast*, 167–68). In negotiating trade terms with the king of Dahomey in 1727, Snelgrave expressed his preference for a ratio of three men to every woman (*New Account*, 73).

9. Bosman, *Description*, 337.

10. Manning (*Slavery, Colonialism, and Economic Growth*, 27–31) says that his estimates of slave exports may be considered accurate to within ± 20 percent.

11. Akinjogbin, *Dahomey*, 63–64; Law, "Slave-Raiders," 48–49; "Captain Phillip's Journal," 219; Bosman, *Description*, 345. For sale of the king's women in Dahomey, see Pommegorge, *Description*, 166, and Dalzel, *History*, 146.

12. Law, "History and Legitimacy," 431–56; Bertho, "Parenté," 121–32; Chapman, "Human Geography," 79–101; Le Hérissé, *Royaume*, 273.

13. Norris, *Memoirs*, xiv; letter of Delisle, quoted in Law, "Dahomey," 242. It is possible that Agaja was referring to independent lineage compounds when he

used the term translated into French and then English as "country." Twentieth-century descendants of Hangbe, for example, wrote of her "principality," meaning her large compound near Abomey's center. Lamb reported a similar boast by Agaja from the 1724–26 period, but with different numbers of conquests. Lamb presumably altered Agaja's claims to fit what he believed to be reality by saying that Agaja's grandfather had conquered one kingdom and his father nine. His brother fought seventy-nine battles in the process of subduing "several petty kingdoms," and Agaja himself "fought two hundred and nine battles, in which I have subdewed many great kings and kingdoms." The full Lamb text is reproduced in Law, "Further Light," 211–26.

14. Lamb's estimates (see Law, "Further Light") cannot always be trusted. He also estimates the distance from Whydah to Abomey at two hundred miles, when in fact it is closer to sixty. See Smith, *New Voyage*, 182–83. Coastal kings also had massive households; the wives of the king of Whydah grew in numbers from Barbot's estimate of two hundred in 1682 to Phillip's three thousand in 1694 and to Bosman's four thousand to five thousand in 1697–99 (Hair, Jones, and Law, *Barbot*, 2:648, fn. 12).

15. Labat, *Voyage*, 2:96–97. Bosman's observation is quoted in Smith, *New Voyage*, 206.

16. Mercier, *Civilisations*, 289–90; Forbes, *Dahomey*, 2:14; interview, Sagbadju Glele, 26 March 1972.

17. Snelgrave, *New Account*, 135.

18. The European who recorded the news of warfare in Dahomey was William Baillie, who wrote from Whydah, 18 Jan. 1718 (Law, *Slave Coast*, 267). Law argues convincingly that Agaja's succession was circa 1716 rather than 1708, as Norris believed (Law, "Ideologies," 339, fn. 4).

19. Accounts of Hangbe include Coissy, "Règne," 5–8; Le Hérissé, *Royaume*, 7; interviews, Sagbadju Glele, 25 July 1972; Kinhwe, 7 March 1973; elders, house of Hangbe, 9 June 1972, 20 July 1984; Glélé, "Royaume," 46–47.

20. Burton, *Mission*, 4:268; Akinjogbin, *Dahomey*, 60–62; Law, "History and Legitimacy," 442; Law, *Slave Coast*, 266–67 and 275, fn. 59. Burton's first two editions of *Mission* were in two volumes. The 1893 edition, which is used in these citations, was part of a larger, multivolume collection of his works. In it, the materials of vol. 1 of the first edition appear as vol. 3, and vol. 2 becomes vol. 4.

21. Interview, elders, house of Hangbe, 9 June 1972.

22. Interview, Kinhwe, 7 March 1973; Foà, *Dahomey*, 13. Dunglas collected two oral accounts saying that Akaba died of smallpox during the course of a war campaign and that Hangbe, who resembled him, took charge of the Dahomean army in his place ("Contribution," part 1, 97).

23. Law, "Ideologies," 339, fn. 4.

24. There is ritual evidence of an ambiguous relationship between children of princesses and the royal lineage. In 1973, during the two-week-long cycle of annual ceremonies performed by the children of Behanzin, descendants of princesses stole one of the goats waiting to be sacrificed. Later, the goat was returned and money was given to the thieves. The na daho had no explanation except that the children of princesses were "precious" to the family. A similar incident of ritual mischief was witnessed by Forbes during ceremonies in 1849 (*Dahomey*, 2: 130–31).

25. Atkins, *Voyage*, 119; Akinjogbin, *Dahomey*, 77. Those who disagree with Akinjogbin include Henige and Johnson, "Agaja," 57–67; Johnson, "Bulfinch Lambe," 345–50; Ross, "Anti-Slave Trade," 263–71; Law, "Dahomey," 237–67; Law, *Slave Coast*, 300–308. Nevertheless, Akinjogbin's thesis has proved irresistible to several writers whose goal has been to synthesize West African history. Interestingly, Beninese historians have by and large followed the lead of the oral sources and have not shown themselves to be overly concerned with the question of motivation in the conquest of Allada and Whydah. Much to the consternation of foreign visitors, descendants of one of Dahomey's most famous slave traders, Francisco Félix de Souza, in 1992 used an eighteenth-century slave-traders' argument to justify the de Souza ancestor's work, suggesting that had slaves not been traded to Europeans, they would have been offered as human sacrifices in Abomey (C., "Ouidah," 40).

26. Law provides an excellent description of the taking of Allada and Whydah that is based on contemporary European sources (*Slave Coast*, 278–87). See also Akinjogbin, *Dahomey*, 39–71.

27. Akinjogbin, *Dahomey*, 69–72; Law, *Slave Coast*, 284–85; and Law, "Neglected Account," 323–24.

28. Gavoy, "Notes," 53–56. See also Dunglas, "Contribution," Part 1, 149–53; and Hazoumé, "Conquête," 41–45.

29. Snelgrave, *New Account*, 10–12, 13–14.

30. Norris, *Memoirs*, 68.

31. Ibid., 92–93.

32. Snelgrave describes the "Camp" of the king as being about forty miles inland from Jakin and "near a very great ruin'd Town, late the principal place of the Kingdom of Ardra" (*New Account*, 28). Modern Allada grew up around a Dahomean palace located slightly more than a mile from Togudo, the old center of the kings of Allada.

33. Law, "Further Light," 218; Snelgrave, *New Account*, 24–66.

34. Snelgrave, *New Account*, 36–48.

35. Ibid., 77–78.

36. Ibid., 39; Smith, *New Voyage*, 195.

37. Lamb, in a letter purportedly written in 1726 and delivered in 1731, numbers Agaja's palaces at seven, but in a letter written from Abomey in 1724 he claims eleven. Law, "Further Light," 217–18; Smith, *New Voyage*, 183.

38. Snelgrave, *New Account*, 34–35, 38–39; Law, "Further Light," 219.

39. Van Dantzig, *Dutch*, 94; Edwards, *Life*, 9, 22; Lander, *Records*, 2:191; Bosman, *Description*, 396; Snelgrave, *New Account*, 126.

40. AN, P. K. Glélé, "Royaume," 78.

41. Snelgrave, *New Account*, 27; Van Dantzig, *Dutch*, 295; Le Hérissé, *Royaume*, 38–41; SOM, "Réflexions," 52. See Law (*Slave Coast*, 84–85) for a description of the office in neighboring kingdoms.

42. Norris, *Memoirs*, 4. Though no title is given, a Dutch trader visiting Dahomey in 1733 was received by two important officers, the migan (Taminga) and "the King's First and Supreme Councillor," who may well have been the meu (Van Dantzig, *Dutch*, 295).

43. Le Hérissé, *Royaume*, 42; Law, *Slave Coast*, 325, 335 37. Obichere has collected a list of the individuals said to have served as gau. It begins with the reign of Wegbaja ("Change," 243).

44. Labat, *Voyage*, 2:59–60, 98, 250–51; Law, *Slave Coast*, 324–28.

45. Snelgrave, *New Account*, 98–106.

46. Dalzel, *History*, 68.

47. Le Hérissé, *Royaume*, 133; interview, Aho, 3 May 1972; Forbes, *Dahomey*, 2: 135; Burton, *Mission*, 4:270–71. Names are given in the twentieth-century oral tradition for kpojito to the kings prior to Agaja. However, names are frequently cited for persons who purportedly held offices prior to the known historical creation of such offices, a practice that helps enshrine the sense of immutability in Dahomean institutional structures.

48. Author's field notes, Hountondji family, Abomey, 1984. Much of this discussion draws on oral accounts collected by Blier ("Path") in 1985–86 and by a team of researchers directed by Albert Tingbe-Azalou ("Mythe et Inceste") in 1992–93.

49. Law, "History and Legitimacy," 450.

50. Burton, *Mission*, 4:111; Blier, "Path." Law argues that it was Wegbaja who effectively declared Dahomey's independence from Allada suzerainty in 1715 and that for that reason he is remembered as the first king. He cites a king list published by Norris to claim that Wegbaja was in fact the second king of the Dahomean dynasty, not the first ("History and Legitimacy," 437–39).

51. Dunglas's history of Dahomey, which is based in the main on oral tradi-

tions, describes a series of disputes between the Alladahonu and the chiefs who were ainon, "owners of the land." All the disputes were resolved by the killing of the chief and the seizure of the land by the Alladahonu ("Contribution," part 1, 85–87). Fuglestad argues that the Alladahonu never accommodated themselves with an earlier religious authority, and thus, by conquering lands without recognizing the appropriate earth gods, the Dahomean dynasty was never seen as legitimate in the eyes of its subjects. Paradoxically, it was at the same time liberated to use force alone in the conquest of territory, and hence could enjoy greater military success ("Quelques réflexions," 493–517).

52. Maupoil, "Géomancie," 530–31, fn. 2; Burton, *Mission*, 4:97; Maurice Glélé indirectly confirms Dakodonu's distance from the royal lineage by saying that no member of the royal family could ever be named agasunon. He also reinforces the likelihood that these politico-ritual accommodations were made during the reign of Agaja by saying that the agasunon began to live at Wawe (where he still resides) during the reign of Agaja (*Danxome*, 65–67).

53. Tingbe-Azalou, "Mythe et Inceste," 18–19; Blier, "Path," 403. A different account of Adonon's origins that I collected from Da Adonon, the head of the descendants of Adonon in Abomey, conflated her identity with that of Aligbonon and claimed that she was a sister to Dakodonu (interview, 22 Dec. 1972). Though it contradicts the notion that Adonon was wife to Dakodonu, such a tradition hints that Dakodonu and his family were not of the Alladahonu lineage.

54. Adonon in interviews, 13 and 16 Oct. 1972. Weme Jigbe was the home of Yahaze, a king that oral tradition claims was defeated by Akaba. Burton heard that a war against Weme Jigbe was waged during the reign of Akaba. These accounts suggest that the war against Yahaze could have been the one in which Adonon lost her son (*Mission*, 4:268). Interestingly, Adonon refused to allow her wealth to be incorporated into the patrilineage of her birth. A story told through the idiom of marital relations describes a break between the kpojito and her own patri-kin. Supposedly the family of Adonon sent a daughter to the household of the king to serve Adonon. Adonon's husband, Wegbaja, made the young woman pregnant, a serious moral violation that normally was considered grounds for divorce. However, Adonon's father negotiated an accommodation with Wegbaja, and the sister received two villages, many retainers, and a new name, Ajakije, meaning "what the brother-in-law did was pleasing to the father." Supposedly because of this incident, Adonon ruled that no member of her patrilineage should inherit her position, and all subsequent Adonon have been drawn from among the descendants of Akaba or Agaja. Interview, Adonon, Gbonugan Gohonu, and Hangbesi, 16 Oct. 1972.

55. Dalzel, *History*, 176; Burton, *Mission*, 3:158; SOM, Rapport Journalier; ANB, Rapport adressé; Dunglas, "Contribution," part 2, 16; Herskovits, *Dahomey*,

2:47. So far as I can discern, Le Hérissé was the first to use the term *kpojito* in print (*Royaume*, 28).

56. Labat, *Voyage*, 2:79, 92; Snelgrave, *New Account*, 151; Rattray, *Ashanti*, 81–82.

57. Mercier, *Civilisations*, 284; Law, *Oyo*, 70–71.

58. Burton, *Mission*, 3:235; Duncan, *Travels*, 1:253–54. Skertchly describes a ceremony honoring three of the early kings in which the agasunon and King Glele appear to have stood near each other. He says nothing about if and how they greeted each other (*Dahomey*, 396).

Chapter 3 ∽ The Age of Tegbesu and Hwanjile

1. This discussion is based in part on concepts of African power outlined by Arens and Karp in their introduction to *Creativity of Power*, x–xxix.

2. Dunglas, "Contribution," part 1, 144–45.

3. Ibid., 146–47; interview, Agessi Voyon, 28 April 1972; Yomana, 10 June 1972; Fengbe, 14 Oct. 1972. Heviosso is known in Yoruba-speaking areas as Shango; Sakpata is Shoponna.

4. Yomana, 6 June 1972.

5. Le Hérissé, *Royaume*, 31, 299–300.

6. Law, *Slave Coast*, 280–81, 287–88, 290–93.

7. Dalzel, *History*, 60; Law, *Slave Coast*, 325–26; Le Hérissé, *Royaume*, 300–1; Norris, *Memoirs*, 6–10. Norris dates Tegbesu's accession to 1732 and the meu's rebellion to 1735. Letters from factors at Whydah, however, place the date of Agaja's death in 1740 (see Akinjogbin, *Dahomey*, 107; Verger, *Flux*, 172). If Norris was correct about the object of the meu's revolt but wrong about the date, we can assume that the meu's rebellion took place in the early 1740s.

8. Law, *Slave Coast*, 319–20; AN, P. K. Glélé, "Dan-hô-min," 49.

9. Dalzel, *History*, 7; M'Leod, *Voyage*, 39; Le Hérissé, *Royaume*, 7. Describing Whydah, both Bosman and Marchais report that the elder son was selected unless there were good reasons to put him aside (Bosman, *Description*, 366–366a; Labat, *Voyage*, 2:50). Later authors who claim that the firstborn was the usual heir include Forbes, *Dahomey*, 1:27; Le Hérissé, *Royaume*, 7; Quénum, *Pays*, 17; AN, P. K. Glélé, "Dan-hô-min," 46.

10. Another term, less commonly used, was *degenon* or *degenon daho*. Its etymology is unclear. *Degenon* means old man in contemporary Fongbe usage. The term reportedly was used among ministers at court and may have been a more familiar appellation. See Segurola, *Dictionnaire*, 1:116; interview, Aho, 21 Jan. 1972.

11. SOM, "Réflexions sur Juda par les Sieurs de Chenevert et Abbé Bulet," 72. Norris states that the heir apparent of Tegbesu was given a patrimony called Povey (*Memoirs*, 2). Accounts from Whydah in the eighteenth century and Porto Novo

in the nineteenth also claim that the king's sons were kept far from the court (Labat, *Voyage*, 2:52; "Dahomey," 18).

12. The five kings who ruled for more than twenty years were Agaja, Tegbesu, Adandozan, Gezo, and Glele (see table 1, p. 49). Le Hérissé (*Royaume*, 8) says the heir was the first son born after the king was named heir. Norris (*Memoirs*, 4) says the heir was the first son born after the king was enthroned, as does Quénum (*Pays*, 17). Marchais reports that in Whydah it was the first son born after coronation (Labat, *Voyage*, 2:51).

13. SOM, "Réflexions," 6; Le Hérissé, *Royaume*, 8.

14. Norris, *Memoirs*, 4, 85. Dunglas ("Contribution," part 1, 165–66) names the "Council of Ministers." However, he may be projecting backwards from his knowledge of the late nineteenth century, when a "Council of Ministers" was central to many decisions at court, including the choice of Behanzin as heir.

15. SOM, "Réflexions," 72–73; see also Pommegorge, *Description*, 188.

16. Bosman, *Description*, 366a; Dalzel, *History*, 222; Norris, *Memoirs*, 130; Dunglas, "Contribution," part 3, 20.

17. Pommegorge, *Description*, 188. For Dahomey, see SOM, "Réflexions," 72; for Whydah, see Labat, *Voyage*, 2:52; for Porto Novo, see "Dahomey," 18.

18. Pires, *Viagem*, 78. Pommegorge, *Description*, 188. A similar scene appears in Norris, *Memoirs*, 105, involving the heir apparent.

19. Bay, "Royal Women," 208–9.

20. Law has traced changes in accounts about Tegbesu from a contemporary view that he was a usurper to a twentieth-century version that claims he was the designated heir. See "History and Legitimacy," 441–42.

21. Interview, Sagbadju Glele, 25 July 1972; Verger, *Notes*, 450; Herskovits, *Dahomey*, 2:104; Maupoil, "Géomancie," 47, fn. 1.

22. Maupoil, "Géomancie," 70.

23. Maupoil, "Géomancie," 64; Herskovits and Herskovits, *Outline*, 35; Herskovits, *Dahomey*, 2:104.

24. Herskovits records an oral tradition that claims the following as vodun imported by Hwanjile: Mawu, Lisa, Sakpata, Heviosso, Gu, Dan Aidowhedo, Nesuhwe, Tovodun, Fa, Menona, Boko-Legba (*Dahomey*, 2:104). Le Hérissé credits to Hwanjile or Tegbesu the following: Mawu, Lisa, Heviosso, H'lan, and the tohosu (*Royaume*, 102, 112–13, 121–22). Most other sources list only Mawu, Lisa, and the hunter deity Age. These three latter vodun remain under the direction of Hwanjile in a sanctuary located adjacent to the palace of Akaba and facing the central palace of the kings. It is clear that both Mawu and Lisa were known in Dahomey before their elevation by Hwanjile. The distinction being claimed may be the specific shrines brought from Aja or the joining of the two as chief deities.

25. SOM, "Réflexions," 75. The priests of the snake deity of Whydah by the late eighteenth century reportedly received 20,000 cowries (about £2.5 sterling) every six months and had been given four female slaves to work their fields. At annual ceremonies for the vodun, the monarchy would provide a sacrificial cow, brandy, and 20,000 cowries (Labarthe, *Voyage*, 131–32).

26. Herskovits, *Dahomey*, 1:229–33.

27. Maupoil, "Géomancie," 46–47.

28. Herskovits and Herskovits, *Outline*, 35, 36; Maupoil, "Géomancie," 48; Le Hérissé, *Royaume*, 303.

29. Yai, "Vodun to Mawu," 10–29; Verger, *Notes*, 438, 504–6; Herskovits and Herskovits, *Outline*, 11, 14. Glélé, *Danxome*, 100. See also Palau Marti, *roi-dieu*, 215, and Mercier, *Civilisations*, 284.

30. Law, *Slave Coast*, 327–28; Akinjogbin, *Dahomey*, 120; Norris, *Memoirs*, 50.

31. Le Hérissé, *Royaume*, 33.

32. Norris, *Memoirs*, 9–10, 85–86.

33. Le Hérissé, *Royaume*, 37; interview, Nondichao, 7 September 1994.

34. Norris, *Memoirs*, 85–86, 98; SOM, "Réflexions," 7, 52; Pires, *Viagem*, 51. Norris confuses the duties of the ajaho with those of the sogan.

35. Interview, Agbado, 17 June 1972.

36. Chenevert and Bulet appear to be referring to this legal status when they claim that "all the boys and girls born of ministers and officers are placed in the hands of the King who disposes of them as he pleases" (SOM, "Réflexions," 7).

37. Interview, Fengbe, 14 Oct. 1972.

38. Le Hérissé, *Royaume*, 39–41.

39. Ibid., 51; Law, "Slave-Raiders," 50–51; Snelgrave, *New Account*, 37; SOM, "Réflexions," 11; Law, "Royal Monopoly," 565.

40. Pommegorge, *Description*, 208–9; Dalzel, *History*, 208–10; SOM, "Réflexions," 20.

41. Manning, *Slavery, Colonialism, and Economic Growth*, 43; Law, "Royal Monopoly," 567. See also Law, *Slave Coast*, 212–13 for a comparison with Allada and Whydah.

42. Dalzel, *History*, "Introduction," x. See discussion of the question of purchases of captives in Law, "Royal Monopoly." Law in the end comes to believe that all war captives were monopolized by the king ("Slave-Raiders," 49). Le Hérissé states unequivocally that only the king "had the right to possess war slaves." However, his description, which is drawn on evidence from the late nineteenth century, implies that the captives that he discusses are those taken by soldiers dependent upon the king (*Royaume*, 52).

43. Law, "Royal Monopoly," 562; Duncan, *Travels*, 2:264.

332   Notes to Pages 107–114

44. Snelgrave, *New Account*, 37–38; Law, *Slave Coast*, 174–75. Burton similarly witnessed the giving of relatively small sums to soldiers of the king (Burton, *Mission*, 4:149–50). Le Hérissé reports that soldiers were given the equivalent of five francs and a wrapper (approximately two yards of cloth); this was when slaves fetched 160 to 320 francs, probably in the late nineteenth century (*Royaume*, 90).

45. Dalzel, introduction to *History*, xii. Since the king paid his accounts with these shortened strings, both he and the women who strung the cowries benefited.

46. Le Hérissé appears to be speaking solely of warriors of the king when he describes the system. He calls the amount given by the king "in no sense a payment but a simple gift capable of inspiring courage" (*Royaume*, 52).

47. Agbo, *Histoire*, 44–45. Agbo consistently refers to the period of time between the conquest of Whydah by Dahomey and the conquest of Dahomey by France as the period of Dahomean "domination" or "occupation."

48. Snelgrave, *New Account*, 66 (a misprint; the page in fact is 82)–88.

49. Norris, *Memoirs*, 40–48. See also Law's discussion of the relative veracity of the Norris account in "Slave Trader," 229–30. Law, "Royal Monopoly," 563–64.

50. SOM, "Réflexions," 53; Verger, *Notes*, 240, 525–31.

51. Law, "Further Light," 218–19; Pommegorge, *Description*, 159–60. The question of whether or not the Dahomean kings were considered to be divine in the same sense as their Yoruba-speaking counterparts became a point of scholarly controversy in the twentieth century. See Palau Marti, *roi-dieu*.

52. Norris, *Memoirs*, 108. A twentieth-century oral historian in Abomey, Vincent Kinhwe, similarly claimed that certain of the class of palace women called the kposi wore veils of beads (interview, 24 March 1972).

53. Beginning with Tegbesu, traditions assert, the kings of Dahomey refused to continue to receive the sacred scarification marks that were visible signs of the leopard Agasu because, once marked by Agasu, no one could thereafter look them in the face. The person designated to receive the scars instead was the ajahutonon, the priest of the vodun-founder of the royal line of Allada (Le Hérissé, *Royaume*, 10–11). In fact, except for moments when they consumed food or drink, the kings of Dahomey were never recorded as having concealed their faces.

54. Johnson, *History*, 57–63; Law, *Oyo*, 68; Norris, *Memoirs*, 94; Pires, *Viagem*, 51, 59, 60. The functions of the legede were similar to those of another Oyo institution, that of the *ajele*, palace slaves of the alafin who resided in provincial towns to watch over the loyalty of subordinate rulers. See Law, *Oyo*, 110–13.

55. Pommegorge, *Description*, 172.

56. Johnson, *History*, 60–61; Law, *Oyo*, 68–69.

57. Pommegorge, *Description*, 168; Akinjogbin, *Dahomey*, 118, fn. 2; Burton, *Mission*, 4:25.

58. Johnson, *History*, 62; Agbado, 17 June 1972.

59. Ibid., 57; Law, *Oyo*, 69, 186.

60. SOM, "Réflexions," 53; Norris, *Memoirs*, 100.

61. Norris, *Memoirs*, 86. Norris appears to confuse the ajaho's duties with those of the sogan. He says that the jahou "is master of the horse." Dalzel, *History*, 163; Pires, *Viagem*, 100; Le Hérissé, *Royaume*, 43, 52; Mercier and Lombard, *Guide*, 13–14.

62. Dalzel, *History*, 158–64.

63. Dalzel, *History*, xx, 224; Norris, *Memoirs*, 16, 83, 92; Dunglas, "Contribution," part 1, 168.

64. Nardin, "reprise," 93; Blanchely, "Dahomey," 534–37; Brue, "Voyage," 59.

Chapter 4 ∿ The Struggle to Maintain the State

1. SOM, "Réflexions," 3; Gayibor, "Mémoire," 52.

2. Akinjogbin provides a useful political and economic overview of this period in *Dahomey*, 141–201.

3. Pommegorge, *Description*, 204; Law, *Slave Coast*, 92–93; Norris, *Memoirs*, 87, 99. See also Dalzel, introduction to *History*, xi.

4. Pommegorge, *Description*, 164–65; SOM, "Réflexions," 7; Dalzel, introduction to *History*, xii; 170–71.

5. Akinjogbin, *Dahomey*, 134. Seventeenth and early eighteenth-century descriptions of the organization of trade in Allada and Whydah are comparable to nineteenth-century descriptions of the trade in Dahomey. It seems reasonable to assume, then, that the organization of the trade in late eighteenth-century Dahomey was similar. See Law, *Slave Coast*, 209–12, for Allada and Whydah, and see Law, "Royal," 560–61, for Dahomey.

6. Cruickshank, "Report." Manning takes issue with Cruickshank's estimate, which in fact had been given him by the slave dealer Francisco Felix de Souza. He argues that the king's gross revenue was only $40,000 (*Slavery, Colonialism, and Economic Growth*, 48 and fn. 78). Manning, however, compares Cruickshank's estimate of *total* revenues derived from the trade (including customs duties and fees, plus proceeds from the sale of the king's slaves) to his own calculation of only the revenues from the sale of the king's slaves. Moreover, Manning uses a lower per-slave price and a lower number of slaves exported than does Cruickshank. Cruickshank errs in assuming that the king paid a customs duty of $5 on each of the three thousand slaves that he sold. Thus his $300,000 estimate should be reduced by $15,000.

7. Norris, *Memoirs*, 87; Dalzel, introduction to *History*, xx–xxi.

8. Adande, *Récades*, 13; Skertchly, *Dahomey*, 454–55.

9. Pommegorge, *Description*, 189; Norris, *Memoirs*, 112.

10. Skertchly, *Dahomey*, 216–17. See also Duncan, *Travels*, 1:264, and Burton, *Mission*, 3:252. Ironically, when the French conquered Abomey and entered the palace in late 1892, they reported that they had found "a good deal of cloth" but little else (d'Albeca, "Dahomey," [August 18, 1894], 112).

11. Norris, *Memoirs*, 93–94; Forbes, *Dahomey*, 2:213–42.

12. Norris, *Memoirs*, 71, 146; SOM, "Réflexions," 46, 48.

13. Verger, *Flux*, 165; Smith, *New Voyage*, 173.

14. Law, *Slave Coast*, 269, and "African Response," 283; Argyle, *Fon*, 81–89; and Reid, "Aristocrats."

15. Hazoumé, *Pacte*, 19–26; Le Hérissé, *Royaume*, 64; Herskovits, *Dahomey*, 2:91–92. See also Pires (*Viagem*, 87–88) for an account of a turncoat priest who offered the supernatural secrets of Oyo military strength to the Dahomean king.

16. Norris, *Memoirs*, 54; Dalzel, *History*, 182–88. In the interim, the Dahomean army was nearly routed in a surprise attack.

17. Snelgrave, *New Account*, 56–58. The story of Na Geze (chapter 2) is another example of the genre. Dalzel, *History*, 167–68.

18. Dalzel, *History*, 201–2. See also Dunglas, "Contribution," part 1, 150 and 168–69.

19. Pommegorge, *Description*, 164–65; Norris, *Memoirs*, 37, 56; Dalzel, *History*, 163–64, 185–88; Akinjogbin, *Dahomey*, 116.

20. Pommegorge, *Description*, 162, 181; Snelgrave, *New Account*, 77–78; Dalzel, introduction to *History*, xi.

21. Evidence for gender roles in this period can be frustrating at best. Barbot writes that "the men and women of Juda [Whydah] are generally large, industrious and strong. . . . They make their principal occupation going to war whenever they have an opportunity. In time of peace they cultivate their lands in such a way that you see none empty or unoccupied." (Hair, Jones, and Law, *Barbot*, 2:641). Does Barbot mean what he seems to say—that both sexes both made war and farmed? No other contemporary writer says that women were included in the army of Whydah. Moreover, other contemporary visitors name only women as farmers. Could Barbot have meant that men warred and women farmed? Or should we take him literally, at his word? The Dutch visitor Olfert Dapper in the seventeenth century similarly implies that women and men fought when he says "in time of war nobody is exempt, except old people and small children" (quoted in Law, *Slave Coast*, 99).

22. Law, "Further Light," 217. See Law, *Slave Coast*, 58–63, for a discussion of the demography of the area in the sixteenth to nineteenth centuries. Unfortunately, apart from numerous seventeenth- and early eighteenth-century accounts claiming that the area was densely populated, we have no knowledge of the total

population of Whydah and no even reasonably accurate means to estimate it. Manning has argued that the Slave Coast was severely depopulated as a result of the slave trade. He charts his data on a graph that appears to indicate some half a million fewer persons in the Bight of Benin (roughly the same area as the Slave Coast) in 1850 as compared with 1730. Nevertheless, when we compare mid-nineteenth-century estimates that give the *total* population of Dahomey at two hundred thousand to Lamb's claim of an army of five hundred thousand in the 1720s, we get a sense of Lamb's exaggeration of numbers of soldiers (Manning, *Slavery and African Life*, 67).

23. Norris, *Memoirs*, 12–13, 21, 38–39, 75; Dalzel, *History*, 10; Labat, *Voyage*, 2:237.

24. Snelgrave, *New Account*, 126.

25. D'Almeida-Topor, *Amazones*, 33–36; Law, "Amazons," 245–60. Apparently written for a popular audience, d'Almeida-Topor's book is of limited value as a historical work because of its inaccurate citations and uncritical use of written and oral traditions on a subject that is particularly susceptible to mythmaking.

26. Dalzel, *History*, 176. Dunglas identifies Agoonah as the area near the confluence of the east and west Coufo Rivers, about thirty-one miles northwest of Abomey ("Contribution," part 2, 15). However, Dalzel later says that Kpengla died at Agoonah following the defeat of Ketu (*History*, 204). Since Ketu is east-northeast of Abomey, Agoonah may in fact be the area called Agonli or Agoni, which lies east of Abomey between the Zou and Weme Rivers. Historical patterns repeated themselves in 1977, when a band of mercenaries landed at Cotonou's airport to attempt a coup d'état. In the aftermath, President Mathieu Kerekou called out the entire civilian population—male and female—to bring whatever arms they had and defend the nation.

27. Dalzel, introduction to *History*, xi; Pommegorge, *Description*, 162; Forbes, *Dahomey*, 2:88; Degbelo, "Amazones"; interview, Yomana, 10 June 1972.

28. Le Hérissé, *Royaume*, 52; SOM, "Réflexions," 52.

29. Norris, *Memoirs*, 13; Dalzel, *History*, 163.

30. Pommegorge, *Description*, 223–35. Norris records an English version of the same incident (*Memoirs*, 56–59).

31. Berbain, *Comptoir*, 65; SOM, "Réflexions," 53. Antonio Vaz Coelho, a free black born in Brazil, offered European technologies and skills and fought with the Allada troops against the Dahomeans. Marchais comments that African smiths were skilled at repairing guns and that the Africans shot well (Labat, *Voyage*, 2:242–43).

32. Labat, *Voyage*, 2:237–39; SOM, "Réflexions," 76. Smith similarly describes warfare on the Gold Coast (*Voyage*, 217–18).

33. Smith, *Voyage*, 182; Norris, *Memoirs*, 12–15. Norris says the Oyo war in question began in 1738; Law and Akinjogbin prove that the date was in fact later. See Law, "Slave Trader," 226–27.

34. Snelgrave, *New Account*, 56–58.

35. Smith, *New Voyage*, 183; Norris, *Memoirs*, 99.

36. Though ideally marriages were made only to serve the interests of lineages and not individuals, the choices and opinions of both the female and male partners were normally taken into account and played an important role. See, for example, for this period Labarthe, *Voyage*, 128.

37. Labat, *Voyage*, 2:80.

38. Europeans made much of a handful of ahosi who had been born of marriages between European traders and African women at the coast and whom they pitied at being incorporated into the palace. Sally Abson, the daughter of the English factor Lionel Abson, is the most famous of these. See M'Leod, *Voyage*, 79–86, 124; Pires, *Viagem*, 93.

39. Manning, *Slavery and African Life*, 67–68; Le Hérissé, *Royaume*, 291.

40. Reade, *Savage Africa*, 53.

41. Norris, *Memoirs*, 86; Snelgrave, *New Account*, 78.

42. Herskovits, *Dahomey*, 2:72–79. Herskovits's account of the census is controversial and was specifically denied by Dahomeans in the 1930s when Maupoil tried to corroborate it. The method of reckoning that Herskovits describes, however, was witnessed by Norris in the 1770s (*Memoirs*, 91).

43. Interview, Kinhwe, 1 February 1973. See also Maupoil, "Géomancie," 460, fn. 2.

44. Norris, *Memoirs*, 99. Law has argued that marriage was more polygynous along the Slave Coast than elsewhere in West Africa; i.e., that powerful individuals took more women as wives than in neighboring areas (*Slave Coast*, 65).

45. Bosman, *New and Accurate*, 214–15; Norris, *Memoirs*, 98–99; Law, *Slave Coast*, 54–55. Finding relative stability in the price of chickens from 1750 to 1850, Law remarks that the price of prostitutes rose "precipitously" over those years.

46. Norris, *Memoirs*, 88. Kpengla tried to fix the price of women slaves at an artifically low twenty-six heads of cowries (Dalzel, *History*, 213). At midnineteenth century, another visitor reported that the cost for a palace woman was 30,000 cowries (Guillevin, "Voyage," 292–93).

47. Pires, *Viagem*, 67.

48. Labat, *Voyage*, 2:79.

49. Pires, *Viagem*, 84.

50. Norris, *Memoirs*, 108, 130; SOM, "Réflexions," 6. Six does not appear to have been a sacred or symbolic number in Fon culture, which tends to support

the possibility that there were in fact six wives of Tegbesu recognized as mothers of potential heirs. That particular number is not used in conjunction with any other king.

51. Pires, *Viagem*, 59.

52. Dalzel, *History*, 161–62, 224; Pires, *Viagem*, 84.

53. Norris, *Memoirs*, 18–19; Dalzel, *History*, 165–66, 211; Le Hérissé, *Royaume*, 303–4. In the case of the Mahi and Kpengla, Dalzel's own account of the final defeat of Mahi by Dahomey makes it likely that the Mahi sought peace and assisted Dahomey because they had become a subordinate state.

54. Pires, *Viagem*, 52, 84, 98; SOM, "Réflexions," 73.

55. Norris, *Memoirs,* 127–28. Of Tegbesu's successors, two (Agonglo and Kpengla) appear to have died prematurely, and Adandozan was removed from power, living for another forty or fifty years.

56. Ibid., 4; SOM, "Réflexions," 72–73; Glélé, *Danxome*, 106; Dalzel, *History*, 203; Pires, *Viagem*, 68–70.

57. Pires, *Viagem*, 70; Moulero, "Guezo," 51–59; Hazoumé, *Pacte*, 110–12. The Herskovitses claim that four kings died of smallpox; however, they do not list the names and I have been unable to find associations with smallpox for any kings other than Kpengla, Agonglo, and Gezo (Herskovits and Herskovits, *Outline*, 18). Agaja, Gezo, and Glele were reportedly pockmarked. Both Moulero and Hazoumé claim that the death of Gezo was kept secret for a period of time, with Hazoumé insisting that the king's death was not announced until the third dry season afterwards, or three years later, during an epidemic of smallpox. Hazoumé is contradicted by European sources, who note that the Grand Customs in honor of Gezo were held in July and August 1860.

58. Herskovits and Herskovits, *Outline*, 16–18; Herskovits, *Dahomey*, 2:131–34.

59. Herskovits, *Dahomey*, 2:137.

60. Ibid., 2:144; Verger, *Notes*, 253.

61. Le Hérissé, *Royaume*, 128–29; Verger, *Notes*, 240–41. In contrast, Le Hérissé says that Sakpata was proscribed during the nineteenth-century reigns of Gezo and Glele (*Royaume*, 128).

62. Buckley, "God," 187–200; Bosman, *New and Accurate*, 366a; Labat, *Voyage*, 2:90–91. See also Smith, *Voyage*, 206, and Norris, *Memoirs*, 5. The only suggestion of comparable mayhem in Dahomey is made by Dalzel in his description of the death of Kpengla in 1789 (*History*, 203–4).

63. Pires, *Viagem*, 73–75; Le Hérissé, *Royaume*, 179. Dalzel's description of mourning for Kpengla in 1789, which was probably influenced by descriptions of Whydah, says rather illogically, "No provisions were exposed to sale during the space of several days after [Agonglo's] accession, which afforded a pretext for the

commission of many disorders; but the interference of the tamegan [migan] soon put an end to all confusion" (Dalzel, *History*, 223). The idea of disorder in the sense of robberies, pillages, and the settling of scores is also strongly disputed by Glélé in *Danxome*, 108.

64. Letter of Guestard cited in Akinjogbin, *Dahomey*, 153–54; Norris, *Memoirs*, 23–24, 105; interview, Agbado, 23 June 1972; Dunglas, "Contribution," part 2, 3–4.

65. See, for example, Akinjogbin, *Dahomey*, 153–54.

66. Norris, *Memoirs*, 128–29. Dunglas records an oral tradition describing a fight within the palace "shortly after" his enthronement ("Contribution," part 2, 6–7).

67. Dalzel, *History*, 204–5, 222–23.

68. Pires, *Viagem*, 70–71; Verger, *Flux*, 249, fn. 72. Edouard d'Almeida adds that others involved in the plot were the agasunon, the ajaho, the meu, and the migan ("Dahomey," 2:355). If d'Almeida's account is accurate, the involvement of the migan and meu would seem to contradict Pires's testimony.

69. Pires, *Viagem*, 77–80, 85. See also Verger, *Flux*, 230–31 and 249, fn. 72.

70. Labarthe, *Voyage*, 124; Labat, *Voyage*, 2:92–93; Hair, Jones, and Law, *Barbot*, 2:641; SOM, "Réflexions," 73. Pires similarly notes that among those who were sent to accompany Agonglo were women singers and dancers (*Viagem*, 74).

71. Ellis, *Ewe-Speaking Peoples*, 127; Skertchly, *Dahomey*, 446; MAE, Lartique; Le Hérissé, *Royaume*, 180.

72. Pires, *Viagem*, 76; Le Hérissé, *Royaume*, 16–17. Though Europeans were sometimes present at Grand Customs, no one appears to have left a detailed eyewitness account prior to the Grand Customs in honor of Gezo that were performed in 1860.

Chapter 5 ～ The Implications of Cultural and Commercial Change

1. Pires, *Viagem*, 70; Verger, *Flux*, 251–58. Additional missions were sent to Lisbon in 1804 and 1811 under the reign of Adandozan.

2. SOM, "Réflexions," 10.

3. Adoukonou, *Jalons*, 95; interview, d'Oliveira, 22 March 1972; Pires, *Viagem*, 93–94. During the reign of Gezo, Francisca Olivier de Montaguère, granddaughter of Sophie, was sent to the palace of Abomey to maintain the shrine to the god of Christianity.

4. Several accounts give 1788 as the date of de Souza's arrival in Whydah (e.g., Turner, "Bresiliens," 88–89; de Souza, "Contribution," 17; Hazoumé, *Pacte*, 28, fn. 1). Verger claims a date of 1803 (*Flux*, 240), which seems more likely. Hazoumé, for example, appears to confuse Franciso Félix with his brother Jacinto José de Souza, who was named governor of the Portuguese fort in 1804.

5. Turner, "Bresiliens," 88–100; de Souza, "Contribution."

6. Interview, d'Oliveira, 22 March 1972; d'Oliveira, *Visite*; Hazoumé, *Pacte*, 29–30.

7. Hazoumé, *Pacte*, 28; Aguessy, "Mode," 244; Glélé, *Danxome*, 117, 122; Dunglas, "Contribution," part 2, 44–48; interview, Dosso-Yovo, 9 Nov. 1972.

8. Glélé, *Danxome*, 116–18. See also Djivo, *Guezo*, 21. Akinjogbin uses the image of the perforated pot to argue that it was used metaphorically by the Alladahonu founders of Dahomey to describe a wholly new conception of the relationship of individuals to the state. Rather than a conception of the state as a family, with the king as father, the pot represented a state in which each subject was required to fill the holes in order to keep the water, which symbolized the king, in place. Akinjogbin acknowledges that the metaphor of the pot dates only to the reign of Gezo, though he without hesitation applies it to a setting nearly two hundred years before (*Dahomey*, 25, esp. fn. 1). A perforated pot clearly was a popular metaphor in the late nineteenth century. Skertchly saw one being paraded in 1871. It was said to be a magical pot representing the army of Dahomey ready to attack Abeokuta, because water poured into it would not flow out the holes (Skertchly, *Dahomey*, 254). A perforated pot was also pictured in a bas-relief in Glele's portion of the central palace in Abomey. It was photographed in 1911 and published in Waterlot, *Bas-Reliefs*, plate XVI-A.

9. Dunglas, "Contribution," part 2, 43–44.

10. Ibid., 46–47.

11. Glélé, *Danxome*, 115–26; Hazoumé, *Doguicimi*, 78–79; MMS, Freeman typescript, 172; Maupoil, "Géomancie," 134; Dunglas, "Contribution," part 2, 48. A later French visitor, Répin, claimed that Gezo was "brought to power by women soldiers who revolted against his own brother" (*Tour*, 99). Since this is the only account to suggest support of Gezo by armed women, and a number of other independent accounts suggest otherwise, I suspect that Répin misunderstood information he was given about Gezo.

12. Glélé, *Danxome*, 126.

13. Le Hérissé, *Royaume*, 33; Glélé, *Danxome*, 156; Forbes, *Dahomey*, 2:243, 247.

14. Verger, "Culte," 21.

15. Dalzel, *History*, 223; Hazoumé, *Pacte*, 31–32; Glélé, *Danxome*, 109. See also Herskovits, *Dahomey*, 2:64. Those arguing that Agontime did return include Sagbadju Glele, interview, 29 July 1972; Kinhwe, interview, 25 March 1972; Aho, interview, 23 May 1972; Dunglas, "Contribution," part 2, 63–64; and Verger, "Culte," 21. Herskovits (*Dahomey*, 2:64) records the tradition, claiming that Agontime spent twenty-four years in the Western Hemisphere and then adds a contradictory comment that she returned about eighteen years before Gezo's death, or in about 1840.

16. Verger, "Culte," 19–24. Verger's work was inspiration for a novel about

Agontime by Gleason (*Agotime*). Both Aho (interview, 23 May 1972) and Elder Dosso-Yovo (interview, 9 Nov. 1972) also claimed that Agontime was taken to the Brazilian province of Maranhaõ, but they may have received their information from Verger's work. Dosso-Yovo testified with certainty that Agontime had arrived in Whydah in 1815, because, he said, the ship bringing her back to Dahomey had passed that carrying Napoleon to St. Helena.

17. Interview, elders, house of Na Agontime, 8 Sept. 1994; interview, Solde and Agonhun, 8 Sept. 1994.

18. Like the oral traditions, this tradition dates the voyages associated with Agontime to early in Gezo's reign. Don João VI became king in 1816 and returned his court to Portugal in early 1821.

19. Verger, "Culte," 20–21; interview, Dosso-Yovo, 9 Nov. 1972.

20. Verger, "Échanges," 747–48. Contemporary Abomeans affirm that the Yemadje family's founder also was brought as an ahosi from Tendji, but they were uncertain if he was of the same lineage.

21. Forbes, *Dahomey*, 2:24–27.

22. Herskovits, *Dahomey*, 1:21; Le Hérissé, *Royaume*, 318. These sentiments are echoed in the songs of the official court historians, the kpanligan, who call Gezo the second founder of the kingdom because Gezo freed Dahomey from Oyo (interview, Nondichao, 8 Sept. 1994).

23. Robertson, *Notes*, 268. Law provides an excellent account of the freeing of Dahomey from Oyo in *Oyo*, 267–73.

24. Forbes, *Dahomey*, 1:31 and 68.

25. Le Hérissé, *Royaume*, 52; d'Albeca, "Dahomey," (18 Aug. 1894).

26. Interviews, Akati, 30 July 1984, and Badiji, 3 Oct. 1984; Dunglas, "Première attaque," 18.

27. Interview, Dosso-Yovo, 9 Nov. 1972.

28. Ibid. See also Skertchly, *Dahomey*, 455. P. K. Glélé classifies glesi among the ranks of the slaves, calling them kannunmonvi (literally slave child or child of a slave) (AN, "Dan-hô-min," 85).

29. McCoskry to Campbell, as cited in Reid, "Aristocrats," 420.

30. Manning, *Slavery, Colonialism, and Economic Growth*, 51–53. Reid ("Aristocrats") has produced a detailed study, archivally based, of the politics of the transition from the slave trade to the palm-oil trade in Dahomey. Many of the points made in this brief discussion are elaborated in his work.

31. Reid, "Aristocrats," 422–24. See reviews of the literature in Law, "Royal Monopoly."

32. Manning, *Slavery, Colonialism, and Economic Growth*, 99; Reid, "Aristocrats," 348–50.

33. Law, "Royal Monopoly," 555–77; Reid, "Aristocrats"; Coquery-Vidrovitch has argued that the oil trade was effectively complementary to the slave trade ("Traite," 107–23), a position persuasively argued by Soumonni in "Compatibility," 78–92. Domingos Jose Martins, biggest trader along the coast in the late 1840s, claimed the two trades were complementary: he had made $80,000 in the previous year from oil alone, but he wasn't sure whether oil or slaves were more profitable (Forbes, *Dahomey*, 2:85).

34. Law provides evidence from Abeokuta of the contempt men had for the work of preparing and marketing palm oil. He also describes a visitor to Whydah in the 1840s who saw a team of men tramping oil out of palm fruit and directed by "a kind of overseer," which suggests supervised slave labor ("Trade and Gender," 199, 205).

35. Manning, *Slavery, Colonialism, and Economic Growth*, 99. See also Skertchly, *Dahomey*, 33–34.

36. Herskovits, *Dahomey*, 1:30. Abomey is sometimes cited as an exception to the gender division of labor in agriculture, on the basis of a mid-nineteenth-century comment by Forbes that "in the neigbourhood of Abomey, unlike the rest of Africa, men labour in the fields and the women are only employed in carrying water" (*Dahomey*, 1:31). As Law observes, the visibility of women as water carriers around Abomey could have been related to the need for large quantities of water for processing palm oil ("Trade and Gender," 202). On the other hand, the lack of corroborating evidence that women were *exempted* from other labor in order to carry water, as Forbes implies and Law accepts, is difficult to accept, particularly in light of Burton's strong assertion in the early 1860s that women hoed, sowed, and reaped (*Mission*, 4:166, 168). See also Skertchly (*Dahomey*, 82) for evidence that women worked with hoes in rural areas of the kingdom.

37. Manning, *Slavery, Colonialism, and Economic Growth*, 49; Law, "Trade and Gender," 205–6.

38. Smith, *New Voyage*, 183; Dalzel, *History*, 129; M'Leod, *Voyage*, 38; Forbes, *Dahomey*, 1:14 and 2:190; SOM, Rapport de route; Le Hérissé, *Royaume*, 27.

39. Pommegorge, *Description*, 165; Skertchly, *Dahomey*, 454–55; interview, elders, Soude family, 4 June 1972; Burton, *Mission*, 4:45; Le Hérissé, *Royaume*, 78; interview, Adjanahudegbo, 18 Oct. 1972. See also Hazoumé's fictionalized account of recruitment in *Doguicimi*, 131.

40. Forbes, *Dahomey*, 2:152; Skertchly, *Dahomey*, 417, 444.

41. MMS, Freeman typescript, 322; Duncan, *Travels*, 1:240. European visitors of the mid–nineteenth century consistently called the women soldiers "amazons." Some appeared to be likening the Dahomean soldiers to the female warriors of Greek mythology; others used the term in a pejorative sense, implicitly

contrasting Dahomean women with a Victorian ideal of ladylike behavior. The appellation has continued to be used by twentieth-century scholars; it is rejected in this work, save for its occasional use in quotations, because it unnecessarily emphasizes the exotic and reinforces misleading and negative images.

42. Duncan, *Travels*, 1:226.

43. Forbes, *Dahomey*, 1:78; Burton, *Mission*, 4:145.

44. Commodore Wilmot to Rear Admiral Sir B. Walker, 29 Jan. 1863, in Burton, *Mission*, 4:237; Burton, 3:182; Duncan, *Travels*, 1:226; Répin, *Études*, 91–92, 94; Burton, "Present State," 407; Skertchly, *Dahomey*, 384.

45. Burton, *Mission*, 3:178; Répin, *Tour*, 92; Burton, "Present State," 407; Skertchly, *Dahomey*, 457.

46. Le Hérissé, *Royaume*, 67; Law, *Slave Coast*, 192, 222–23; Forbes, *Dahomey*, 1:157–59; Skertchly, *Dahomey*, 502.

47. D'Almeida-Topor, *Amazones*, 40, 174; Foà, *Dahomey*, 257; SOM, Rapport journalier; ANB, Hocquart; Duncan, *Travels*, 1:227. Not all sources agree that women went into combat. A missionary stationed in Whydah for three years in the early 1860s claimed that a reserve army of women "guarded" the city while only the men went to war (Laffitte, *Dahomé*, 103–5), and a source from the end of the century claimed that men went to war as warriors and women only as carriers of supplies (Foà, *Dahomey*, 254).

48. Skertchly, *Dahomey*, 257.

49. Amegboh, *Behanzin*, 69.

50. Quénum, *Pays*, 57.

51. Law, "African Response," 292.

52. Ross, "Autonomous," 149; Forbes, *Dahomey*, 1:134.

53. Degbelo, "Amazones." There is no evidence from the period that clitoridectomy was practiced anywhere in Dahomey. However, a number of sources from the eighteenth century up to the present describe the massaging of the labia of young girls, supposedly in order to enlarge them to enhance sexual pleasure (Dalzel, *History*, xviii; Adams, *Remarks*, 74–75; Herskovits, *Dahomey*, 1:277–85; and interview, Loko, 4 Feb. 1973).

54. Le Hérissé, *Royaume*, 68; Burton, "Present State," 406.

55. Degbelo, *Amazones*, 170.

56. Forbes, *Dahomey*, 2:108.

57. Dunglas, "Première," 17.

58. MMS, Freeman typescript, 324; Burton, *Mission*, 3:126; Bowen, *Adventures*, 149. A similar story was reported after the fall of the kingdom, when a delegation from the town of Cove, from which women had regularly been taken for service

in the palace, came to Abomey to reclaim them. Of the women contacted, only one was willing to return home (ANB, Rapport mensuel).

59. Duncan, *Travels*, 1:234; interview, Agbalu Glele, 26 Oct. 1972; Hazoumé, "Tata Ajachê."

60. Forbes, *Dahomey*, 2:143.

61. MMS, Freeman typescript, 279; MMS, Freeman, "Journal"; Forbes, *Dahomey*, 2:66, 90; Duncan, *Travels*, 2:61–62; Burton, *Mission*, 3:213–14. Law mistakenly believes that Yewe was the meunon because she was responsible for working with the British and the meu was generally responsible for relations with foreigners ("'Amazons,'" 255).

62. Burton, *Mission*, 3:243; interview, Agbalu Glele, 9 Sept. 1972.

63. Forbes, *Dahomey*, 2:71.

64. Skertchly, *Dahomey*, 52, 89, 154; Chaudoin, *Trois mois*, 50.

65. Forbes, *Dahomey*, 1:70; 2:178–79; Skertchly, *Dahomey*, 25, 396; interviews, Fengbe, 30 July 1972, and Agbalu Glele, 26 Oct. 1972.

66. Dalzel, *History*, xii; Skertchly, *Dahomey*, 60; Forbes, *Dahomey*, 2:183–84.

67. Interview, Avloko, 27 Feb. 1973; Chappet, *Côte*, 23; Foà, *Dahomey*, 192; interviews, Aho, 3 May 1972, and Kinhwe, 24 March 1972; Le Hérissé, *Royaume*, 72; Maire, *Dahomey*, 51.

68. Delange, *Arts*, 70.

69. Burton, *Mission*, 4:11.

70. Interview, Sagbadju Glele, 26 March 1972.

71. Maupoil, "Géomancie," 123; MMS, Freeman typescript, 316; d'Almeida, "Dahomey," 335, fn. 1.

72. Le Hérissé, *Royaume*, 26.

73. Burton, *Mission*, 4:257; Béraud, "Note," 376.

74. MMS, Freeman typescript, 306; Burton, *Mission*, 4:58; Skertchly, *Dahomey*, 271.

75. Skertchly, *Dahomey*, 271–72; Burton, *Mission*, 4:59; Coquery, "Blocus," 383–84.

76. Mercier, "Fon," 232.

77. Law, "Human Sacrifice," 85, fn. 175; Reid, "Aristocrats," 337–44. All three arguments are discussed in Bay, "Trail," 1–15.

78. MMS, Freeman typescript, 306; Skertchly, *Dahomey*, 271; Burton, *Mission*, 4:59.

79. Following the conquest, the crown found its way into the collection of the Musée de l'Homme in Paris.

80. Duncan, *Travels*, 2:220.

81. Forbes, *Dahomey*, 2:19–20. The incident is also described by Fanshawe in his journal entry of 13 May 1850 (PRO, Journal). Two decades later, Skertchly would grumble at seeing a nonfunctioning clock in a home in Whydah that it was "truly a prophetic emblem of the utter insignifance of the value of time with the Dahoman" (*Dahomey*, 13).

82. Portions of this argument are made by Reid ("Aristocrats," 316–80), Law ("African Response"), Yoder ("Fly and Elephant"), and Ross ("Autonomous," 116–55). It is Ross who believes that Gezo was killed by courtiers of Dahomey once his policies had been discredited and Glele had obtained the upper hand (152–55).

83. Skertchly, *Dahomey*, 433–34.

84. Reid, "Aristocrats," 344 and 294–95. Reid argues that Gezo generally was behind the revived slave trade after 1857, and particularly the trade through Prya Nova.

Chapter 6 ∼ The Decline of Dahomey

1. Interview, Agodeka Behanzin, 3 June 1972.

2. Forbes, *Dahomey*, 2:15–19.

3. Ibid., 1:15; Burton, *Mission*, 3:230.

4. Skertchly, *Dahomey*, 367.

5. This eyewitness account is by a missionary, Father Borghéro. The version quoted is a translation by Ellis (*Ewe-Speaking Peoples*, 193–95). The French original is printed in Laffitte, *Dahomé*, 106–9.

6. Aguessy, "Mode," 97; Forbes, *Dahomey*, 2:56–57; PRO, Fanshawe.

7. Skertchly, *Dahomey*, 140, 347–49, 444; Burton, *Mission*, 3:146. In their lists of the most prominent ministers of state, Skertchly, Burton, and Forbes all omit the gau.

8. Interview, Agodeka Behanzin, 3 June 1972. Confirmed in interview, Savakonto, 30 Jan. 1973; interview, descendants of Agbalu Glele, 13 Sept. 1972.

9. Parrinder, *Story*, 65–72; Aublet, *Guerre*, 304–5.

10. Forbes, *Dahomey*, 1:16–17; Dunglas, "Première attaque," 16; Dunglas, "Deuxième attaque," 47–57.

11. Burton, *Mission*, 4:165.

12. Le Hérissé, *Royaume*, 86.

13. Skertchly, *Dahomey*, 84.

14. Le Hérissé, *Royaume*, 82–88. Though sources generally claim that the king returned virtually all the property of deceased individuals, the de Souza family claims that Gezo kept some two-thirds of Francisco Félix de Souza's estate on his death in 1849 (de Souza, *Famille*, 43).

15. Burton, *Mission*, 3:33.

16. Skertchly, *Dahomey*, 16; interview, Codjia, 27 Feb. 1973; Forbes, *Dahomey*, 1:111–12. Another prominent family broken by the monarchy in the 1870s was that of one of the handful of ahisigan, principal traders of the monarchy, Quénum. A logbook of cases settled by the *commandant de cercle* of Abomey in the early years of the twentieth century has a large number of cases involving *wemesi*, persons who were made slaves because of a crime against the state committed by their head of family (ASA, Peines). See also Burton, *Mission*, 3:58.

17. For example, Le Hérissé (*Royaume*, 37–44) lists seven: the migan, meu, yovogan, adjaho, sogan (king's horseman), topo (minister of agriculture), and akplogan (governor of Allada). Glélé (*Danxome*, 128–39) also names seven, though he places in a separate category the yovogan and akplogan, on grounds that they were physically distant from Abomey. For him, the others are the migan, meu, gau, ajaho, and binazon (treasurer). Dunglas ("Contribution," part 1, 91–93) lists eight: the migan, meu, ajaho, gau, kposu (second to the gau), sogan, akplogan, and binazon.

18. Duncan, *Travels*, 1:275; Foà, *Dahomey*, 270–71.

19. Répin, *Tour*, 83; Burton, *Mission*, 4:240; Mercier and Lombard, *Guide*, 17; Skertchly, *Dahomey*, 432; interview, Aho, 21 Jan. 1972. Glele knew at least conversational Portuguese, the lingua franca of trade in the nineteenth century (Dunglas, "Deuxième attaque," 43).

20. Chaudoin, *Trois mois*, 269–70.

21. MMS, Freeman typescript, 311. See also Valdez, *Six Years*, 1:339. Forbes (*Dahomey*, 2:82) testifies to the ease with which female relatives could enter and exit the palace.

22. Maupoil, "Géomancie," 162; Chaudoin, as quoted in Dunglas, "Contribution," part 3, 46–47.

23. Mercier and Lombard, *Guide*, 20. Confirmed in Savonkonton interview, 30 Jan. 1973; interview, Sagbadju Glele, 25 July 1972.

24. Falcon, "Religion," 22; Aguessy, "Mode," 383; interviews, Kinhwe, 24 March 1972, and Aho, 24 Oct. 1972.

25. Forbes, *Dahomey*, 2:90; MAE, Lartique; Chaudoin, *Trois mois*, 270. See also Mercier and Lombard, *Guide*, 20.

26. Herskovits, *Dahomey*, 1:110–11; UCB, Bascom, 274. Herskovits describes this system in operation at Jime, which was the personal palace of Behanzin; hence, his informant appears to have been referring to the reign of that king.

27. Le Hérissé, *Royaume*, 27. Agbalu Glele, a son of King Glele, reaffirmed the image of the kposi having no particular duties save to accompany the king and

hold objects for his personal use (interview, 11 Sept. 1972). Le Hérissé claims that there were about forty kposi; however, he may be accepting as literal a symbolic use of the term forty: forty and forty-one are used in Fon culture to suggest a perfect or ideal number. Maupoil provides a telling anecdote about one of Gezo's herbalists who was once summoned to the palace to minister to a sick person. When the man discovered that his patient was a kposi, he was so intimidated that he refused to approach her. Reassured by the king that he could speak to Kpede, the woman, he ended up being renamed Masikpede, "Don't be afraid of Kpede" (Maupoil, "Géomancie," 143, fn. 2.).

28. Forbes, *Dahomey*, 2:238; Burton, *Mission*, 4:241. Burton's comment suggests a constantly changing group of women; new wives were regularly acquired by the palace during the course of a king's reign. That view is supported by three descendants of Abomey royalty (interviews, Camille Behanzin, 13 July 1972, Aho, 3 May 1972, and Agbalu Glele, 9 Sept. 1972).

29. Skertchly, *Dahomey*, 262. See discussion of the problem of the roles of the kposi in Bay, "Royal Women," 181–88.

30. Quénum, *Pays*, 19; interviews, Aho, 3 May 1972; Agbalu Glele, 11 Sept. 1972; Kinhwe, 24 March 1972; Ellis (*Ewe-Speaking Peoples*, 127) claims that they died with the king.

31. Maupoil, "Géomancie," 87; interview, Feliho, 18 September 1972.

32. Burton, *Mission*, 3:243. Royal informants included Aho, 21 January 1972, Agbalu Glele, 9 Sept. 1972, and Sagbadju Glele, 26 March 1972. The quote is from Sagbadju. Le Hérissé, *Royaume*, 77.

33. Burton, *Mission*, 3:149, 243; Le Hérissé, *Royaume*, 222.

34. Le Hérissé, *Royaume*, 31–32; Forbes, *Dahomey*, 1:34–35. See also 1:111.

35. Forbes, *Dahomey*, 2:184.

36. For example, Glele's meunon (Wahuton) and Behanzin's miganon (Yovoda), meunon (Edolo), and gaunon (Jikada) were all sisters of their respective kings. Glele had two kposi who were his nieces. Interview, Savakonton, Jime, 30 Jan. 1973.

37. Le Hérissé, *Royaume*, 34–35.

38. Burton, *Mission*, 3:147; 2:180–81; Hazoumé, *Pacte*, 4. The Englishman Burton sensed a certain rivalry between Adandejan and the bokonon, with whom he was lodged.

39. Thirty-five years later, doing fieldwork in Dahomey, Herskovits found a curiously contradictory system of institutionalized friendship. Everyone was said to have a Best Friend, an intimate companion who knew the innermost feelings and desires of his or her friend. It was the Best Friend who spoke at a person's funeral and who indicated the choice of the deceased for his successor. There are

intriguing echoes of kingly succession disputes in Herskovits's portrayal of a Best Friend as the repository of the true wishes of a man, and particularly his description of the hypothetical example of a man who had earlier announced his successor but changed his mind. Since renouncing the heir publicly would bring shame on the heir's family, a man in such a situation would secretly tell only two persons: the newly-chosen heir and the Best Friend. The Best Friend in turn would announce the real choice only at the man's death. The Friend was described as a beloved, lifelong companion. Oddly, though, as Herskovits pointed out, the Best Friend was institutionalized; it was effectively an office, with two lesser-ranking Friends in the wings, ready to replace the Best Friend, should he die before his companion. Herskovits was clearly puzzled by the logical constraints of such a system. He suspected that the institution was not as widespread as people claimed, and noted that a son of the deceased often played the role of Best Friend (Herskovits, *Dahomey*, 1:88–92; 239–42).

40. AMR, Borghéro. See also Skertchly, *Dahomey*, 472. ANB, Contrôle des Chefs.

41. Verger, *Dieux*, 189.

42. Houseman, et al., "Note"; interview, Legonon and Houseman, 29 July 1984.

43. MMS, Freeman typescript, 188.

44. Burton, *Mission*, 4:99.

45. Ibid., 4:99; Glélé, *Danxome*, 74. A Ketu woman who had been a slave in the palace claimed that the king had "about four babalawo [diviners]." Shown a photo of Gedegbe published in Maupoil's book, she identified him as one of the king's diviners (UCB, Bascom).

46. Glélé, *Danxome*, 74–75.

47. Maupoil found that women were occasionally known to have been diviners in Yorubaland; in Dahomey, however, he could find evidence of only two women who ever consulted Fa as bokonon. One was a daughter of King Kpengla and the other a daughter of the king of Dassa, who ruled during the period of Glele. She was also a wife of Behanzin ("Géomancie," 153–54).

48. Maupoil, "Géomancie," 84–111.

49. Ibid., 69.

50. Dunglas, "Contribution," part 2, 90–101; MMS, Freeman typescript, 175; Burton, *Mission*, 3:xviii. Abbé Moulero has recorded a slightly different version in "Guezo," 51–59. The attack on Ekpo in early 1858 fulfilled the conditions of the prophecy recorded by Forbes, that "if war was made on Katoo, the king would be killed" (*Dahomey*, 1:20).

51. Interview, Sagbadju Glele, 28 March 1972. Kakaï Glele, as quoted by Coquery ("Blocus," 381), claims that Kondo was mentored by the diviner Gedeghe

However, Gedegbe is also credited with training a man who ultimately challenged Kondo, Sasse Koka.

52. MMS, Freeman typescript, 284; Glélé, *Danxome*, 104–5; Le Hérissé, *Royaume*, 8–9. These intimate conversations between king and prince are fictionalized in Hazoumé's *Doguicimi*.

53. Ross, "Autonomous," 143–65; Law, "Human Sacrifice," and "African Response"; Reid, "Aristocrats," 385–91. Yoder's account of party politics in Dahomey recognizes the reality of factions, but makes major errors in discerning individuals belonging to the factions ("Fly and Elephant"). My interpretation of the king-as-prince differs from Reid's. He argues that the king-as-prince was invented to allow the monarchy to produce and sell palm oil, an activity otherwise demeaning to a warrior aristocracy.

54. Vallon, "Royaume," 342; MMS, Freeman typescript, 284–85; Répin, *Tour*, 86; Forbes, *Dahomey*, 2:62. Gezo, of course, had retained two meu when he was enstooled—Voglosu and Tometin, his uterine brother and later the mentor to his son Badahun. Both had been plotters in the coup that brought Gezo to power and both were among the oldest and closest associates of the king. Forbes listed both the "Mayo" and "Toh-mah-tee" as recipients of royal gifts in 1849, which suggests that both men were still alive in the 1850s. Burton reported in 1864 that To-metti "has lately succeeded his father, who was one of Gezo's brothers" (*Mission*, 4:83, fn. 2).

55. Répin, *Tour*; MMS, Freeman to Beecham and Freeman to General Secretaries. In fact, when Répin finally did reach the king outside of the presence of the meu, the king still denied the French the right to establish a factory in Abomey, just as he had denied that right to the English and just as he regularly denied European religious missions the right to set up operations in the capital.

56. MMS, Freeman typescript, 176–82; Vallon, "Royaume," part 1, 341.

57. Burton, *Mission*, 4:185; Cruickshank, "Report"; Duncan, *Travels*, 2:305.

58. Laffitte, *Dahomé*, 88.

59. Duncan, *Travels*, 2:305; Forbes, *Dahomey*, 1:33; Ross, "Autonomous," 70–71; Law, "African Response," 283–84. Law relates human sacrifice specifically and solely to Dahomean militarism. "Human sacrifice in Dahomey . . . involved principally war captives, whose sacrifice served to celebrate Dahomian military prowess. . . . Ending Dahomey's involvement in slave-trading would necessarily imply undermining Dahomian militarism, which in turn would necessarily involve an attack on human sacrifice" (283–84).

60. Forbes, *Dahomey*, 2:171. Law argues that Gezo initially increased the number of sacrifices but in the 1840s reduced them in response to British demands and the encouragement of Francisco Félix de Souza ("Human Sacrifice," 53–87).

61. In 1853, Gezo made an offer to the British to abolish human sacrifice. Received with skepticism, it would appear to have been a bargaining chip for negotiations; in any event, no one ever called the king's bluff. See discussion in Law, "Human Sacrifice," 83–84. The chief involved in the incident in the 1930s was Justin Aho, who was accused in 1937 of killing Telli (Atelli), a young apprentice of a trading woman (interview, Aho, 23 May 1972).

62. Dunglas, "Première attaque," 46.

63. Dunglas, "Contribution," part 2, 102; d'Almeida, "Dahomey," 1:153. Burton was told that an older brother, a "notable drunkard" named Godo, had been set aside (*Mission*, 4:137, fn. 2).

64. Burton, *Mission*, 3:151, 153; AN, P. K. Glélé, "Dan-hô-min," 67; Skertchly, *Dahomey*, 128. Bouët credits the cambode with helping Gezo gain power. He remained a central powerful figure enjoying the trust of Gezo through the 1850s (Répin, *Tour*, 84, 87). Sources typically assume that binazon (Binazon) was the name of an office, rather than a personal name.

65. Interviews, Sagbadju Glele, 25 July 1972, and Agodeka Behanzin, 3 June 1972.

66. Burton, *Mission*, 3:152. Yavedo was also seen by Skertchly in 1871 (*Dahomey*, 265).

67. Dunglas, "Contribution," part 2, 102; interview, Aho, 3 Feb. 1972; Maupoil, "Géomancie," 136. A witness in a court case in the early 1900s testified that Zoyindi was a "soeur de fetich" (fetish sister) with Gedegbe (ASA, Peines). Olabiyi Yai indicates that such a term may mean a woman who has been initiated to some degree into Fa (personal communication, 18 Nov. 1996).

68. D'Almeida, "Dahomey," 2:417. Burton recorded rumors speculating about who Glele's biological mother might have been, one arguing that she was Mahi and another that she was a Euro-African associated with the French factory at Whydah (*Mission*, 3:158). Such rumors suggest that Zoyindi, whatever her origins, was not the biological mother of the king.

Chapter 7 ∽ War, Disintegration, and the Failure of the Ancestors

1. Glélé, *Danxome*, 103, 124–25; Skertchly, *Dahomey*, 159. Maupoil argues that Kondo had his sorcerers cause Ahanhanzo's death from smallpox ("Géomancie," 138, fn. 1). A Yoruba slave woman, who had been resident in the palace in the late nineteenth century, testified in 1951 that "people said that Kondo poisoned a man" (UCB, Bascom, 274).

2. Interview, Aho, 23 May 1972. This appears to be a standard version maintained by descendants of Agoliagbo and their allies. I also collected it from Agoliagbo (interview, 24 July 1972) and from his son Andre Agoliagbo (3 March 1973).

3. Interview, Agodeka Behanzin, 3 June 1972.

4. Interview, Agbalu Glele, 29 September 1972. See also Aguessy, "Mode," 189.

5. Accounts of the blockade may be found in Coquery, "Blocus," Dunglas, "Contribution," part 3, 12–13, and Foà, *Dahomey*, 33–36. Ross speculates on the basis of a sudden change in Dahomean trade policy that Ahanhanzo was overthrown in May (214–15).

6. Burton, *Mission*, 3:xi–xii; *Frank Leslie's Popular Monthly*, as quoted in Rydell, *All*, 66. The best discussion that I know of the growth of British racism is Curtin, *Image*.

7. Valuable sources for details of the coming of imperialism to Dahomey and the French war against the kingdom include Turner, *Bresiliens*; Cornevin, *République*; and Garcia, *Royaume*.

8. Glélé, *Danxome*, 206–7.

9. ANB, de Souza à Rodriguez.

10. See, for example, Garcia, "Archives," 196–99; d'Almeida, "Dahomey," 2:335–36.

11. The full text is printed in Cornevin, *République*, 289–90.

12. Turner, *Bresiliens*, 256–60. See also de Souza, *Famille*, 55–57. Garcia suggests that de Souza's dealings with the French had additionally compromised his position (*Royaume*, 44).

13. Garcia, "Archives," 194–95; Cornevin, *République*, 317–18. Sources disagree on the precise date both of Glele's death and of Bayol's departure from Abomey. Bayol left either December 27 or 28, and Glele is said to have died sometime between December 28 and December 30. I have accepted the dates mentioned by Behanzin himself in a letter to the president of France dated April 17, 1890, and quoted in Dunglas, "Contribution," part 3, 45. Ironically, in light of the Dahomean exhibition at the Chicago Exposition three years later, one of the gifts presented to Glele by the Bayol mission was a stereoscope set with photos of the Paris Exhibition of 1889.

14. Garcia, *Royaume*, 51–53. Dunglas claims that Mme. Béraud was from Whydah ("Contribution," part 3, 16).

15. ANB, Rapport, 12 mars 1891. Garcia (*Royaume*, 69) gives a citation for the document as ANB, Rapport, janvier 1890. A copy also exists in France (SOM, Rapport, 12 mars 1891).

Goufle (Gounfle) was the sogan of Glele. If Béraud's account is correct, he was playing an appropriately loyal role to the monarch (see chapter 3, 116–17).

16. D'Almeida, "Dahomey," 2:335.

17. PRO, Africa No. 365, Africa No. 386.

18. D'Albeca, "Dahomey," 111; Chaudoin, *Trois mois*, 182. Garcia argues that

Behanzin moved against Visesegan only after a peace treaty with the French was signed in October 1890 (*Royaume*, 27). However, a son of Behanzin claimed that Sasse Koka was already dead by the time Behanzin named his ministers, which suggests that the threat of Visesegan and her protégé was dealt with at an earlier point (interview, Agodeka Behanzin, 3 June 1972). Garcia also suggests that links to Tado might have been related to a desire to build alliances against the French (*Royaume*, 82).

19. Le Hérissé, *Royaume*, 338–40.

20. Sagbadju Glele and Agodeka Behanzin as quoted by Garcia (*Royaume*, 79–81).

21. Garcia, *Royaume*, 94, 98.

22. Le Hérissé, *Royaume*, 344–45.

23. There are numerous accounts of the war, including a number of published diaries by French participants. One of the most thorough contemporary accounts is Aublet, *Guerre*. Garcia's *Royaume* is the most thorough and balanced treatment by a professional historian.

24. Glélé, *Danxome*, 206–8; interview, Ougoton, 29 June 1972. Although he gives no dates in the text, Aublet places his mention of the coup attempt between 29 Sept. and 2 Oct. in his narrative of the war (*Guerre*, 246). Garcia links Visesegan to Egbo as her "adopted son" (*Royaume*, 26).

25. Le Hérissé, *Royaume*, 347. See also Garcia, *Royaume*, 234. The war indemnity was set at the strikingly high sum of 15 million francs, and fully one-half was demanded in cash within twenty-four hours as a sign of good faith. The highest price per head paid for the slaves sent out of Dahomey between 1889 and 1892 had been 500 francs. If we assume that price for each of the five thousand sold, the total income from the renewed slave trade was 2.5 million francs, of which a good deal had been spent on arms.

26. ANB, de Souza à Rodriguez. The delegation was not received by any officials in France, though they did meet with a French counsul in Liverpool on their arrival from Lagos in early November 1893 (Garcia, *Royaume*, 242–44).

27. ANB, Renseignements.

28. Le Hérissé, *Royaume*, 349–50; Dunglas, "Contribution," part 3, 103; SHA, Rapport.

29. Le Hérissé, *Royaume*, 351–52.

30. Interview, Andre Agoliagbo, 3 March 1973; Hazoumé, *Pacte*, 34–38; Glélé, *Danxome*, 214–15; Garcia, "Archives," 191; Dunglas, "Contribution," part 3, 105. See also Emmanuel, *Traités*.

31. D'Albeca, *France*, 194; Garcia, "Archives," 191, 192, 203. How, then, do oral traditions explain the acknowledged divisions between the descendants of

Behanzin and Agoliago? Essentially, they argue that the feud derives from factors in play after the essential decision had been arranged—that Behanzin became angry because Gedegbe told Guchili of the decision to make him ruler before the king did, or that Behanzin's children became angry when Agoliagbo claimed all the wives and goods of the king (Glélé, *Danxome*, 217; Dunglas, "Contribution," part 3, 107–8).

32. SOM, Correspondence. Agbidinukun suggests that Behanzin placed a great deal of hope in the possibility of success by the envoys sent to Europe (Le Hérissé, *Royaume*, 339–40, 348–49).

33. SOM, Correspondence. Two sources claim that among those sacrificed were Behanzin's Afro-Brazilian artillerymen, Georges de Souza and Jose Quenum (interview, Dosso-Yovo, 9 Nov. 1972; d'Albeca, "Dahomey," 126).

34. Tahon, *Carnets*, 65–66. Three other sources acknowledge this incident: Moulero, "Conquête," 67; AN, P. K. Glélé, "Royaume"; and Leprince, *Deux*.

35. Newbury, "Note," 151; ANB, Correspondences.

36. ANS, Rapport, 1895; ANS, Rapport, 1896; Mikponhoue, "Administration."

37. ANB, Gbohayida.

38. ASA, Peines.

39. A list of children born of these unions who were in residence on the Abomey plateau in 1928 includes names of twenty-six children, their mothers, and their European fathers. Fully seventeen of the mothers are identifiable as women of the royal family or families of ruling chiefs. ASA, List.

Glossary

Adandozan—seventh king of Dahomey (1797–1818)

Adonon—first kpojito of Dahomey (c. 1716–1740)

Agaja—third king of Dahomey (c. 1716–1740)

Agasu—mythical being said to be the son of a princess of Tado and a leopard; founder of the royal family of Dahomey

Agasuvi—literally child(ren) of Agasu; the royal family of Dahomey

agbajigbeto—literally hunter in the reception area; spy

Agoliagbo—eleventh king of Dahomey (1894–1900)

Agonglo—sixth king of Dahomey (1789–1797)

Agontime—sixth kpojito of Dahomey (1818–1858)

ahosi—dependent, follower, subordinate, or wife of the king

ahovi—child(ren) of the king; princes, or princesses

ajaho—minister of religion, head of the secret police

Akaba—second king of Dahomey

Alladahonu—people from Allada, specifically the royal family of Dahomey

anato—free person, commoner

Behanzin—tenth king of Dahomey (1889–1894)

bokonon—diviner of the Fa system of divination

Chai—third kpojito of Dahomey (1774–1789)

daklo—woman within the palace who conveyed messages between the king and visitors

Fa—god of divination; system of divination derived from the Ifa system of Yoruba culture

gandoba—women slaves given to retainers outside the palace whose female children returned to service in the palace

gau—war chief

Gbetome—visible world, land of the living

Gezo—eighth king of Dahomey (1818–1858)

Glele—ninth king of Dahomey (1858–1889)

Hwanjile—second kpojito of Dahomey (1740–1774)

Hweda—people of kingdom along the coast conquered by Dahomey in 1727; name of kingdom usually transcribed Whydah or Ouidah

joto—spiritual presence of an ancestor in one of his/her descendants

Kamlin—eighth kpojito of Dahomey (1889–1894)

Kanai—ninth kpojito of Dahomey (1894–1900)

kannumon—slave, captive

Kentobasin—fifth kpojito of Dahomey (1797–1818)

Kpengla—fifth king of Dahomey (1774–1789)

kpo—leopard, totem of the royal family of Dahomey

kpojito—literally, she who whelped the leopard; the reign-mate to the king

kposi—adept of the spirit of the founder of the royal family; class of high-ranking wives of the king

Kutome—land of the dead; kingdom of the shadows

legede—messengers of the kings, popularly called half-heads because of their characteristic way of alternately shaving one side of the head

Lisa—creator god made head of all the spirits by kpojito Hwanjile

Mawu—creator god made head of all the spirits by kpojito Hwanjile

meu—second minister, responsible for territory south of Allada, responsible for members of royal family

migan—prime minister, chief executioner

na daho—literally eldest princess, title of senior daughter of the reigning king

Nesuhwe—cult dedicated to the deified members of the royal family

Sakpata—group of deities linked to the earth and popularly associated with smallpox

Senume—fourth kpojito of Dahomey (1789–1797)

sogan—chief of the horse, master of the horse

Tegbesu—fourth king of Dahomey (1740–1774)

tohosu—king of the waters; abnormal child believed to be spirit creature

tohwiyo—mythical being, often a wild animal, acknowledged as founder of a clan

vigan—literally chief of the children; head of the branch of the royal family descended from a given king

vodun—god, deity

vodunon—person responsible for a god; priest; "mother" of a god

vodunsi—dependent, follower, initiate of a god; adept of a god; "wife" of a god

Wegbaja—first king of Dahomey

yovogan—chief for foreigners; "chief of the whites," responsible for trade relations in Whydah

zinkponon—literally mother or owner of the stool; titleholder

Zoyindi—seventh kpojito of Dahomey (1858–1889)

Zumadunu—tohosu-child fathered by King Akaba, head of all the deities in the nineteenth century

Bibliography of Sources Cited

Published Materials

Adams, Captain John. *Remarks on the Country Extending from Cape Palmas to the River Congo*. London, 1823.

Adande, Alexandre. *Les Récades des rois du Dahomey*. Dakar: IFAN, 1962.

Adoukonou, B. *Jalons pour une théologie africaine: essai d'une herméneutique chrétienne du vodun dahoméen*. Paris: Lethielleux, 1979.

Agbo, Casimir. *Histoire de Ouidah*. Avignon: Pressses Universelles, 1959.

Aguessy, Honorat. "Du Mode d'existence de l'état sous Ghezo." Thèse de troisième cycle, Univ. de Paris, 1970.

Akinjogbin, I. A. *Dahomey and its Neighbors: 1708–1818*. Cambridge: Cambridge University Press, 1967.

Amegboh, Joseph. *Behanzin, Roi d'Abomey*. Paris: ABC, 1975.

Arens, W., and Ivan Karp. *Creativity of Power*. Washington DC: Smithsonian Institution, 1989.

Argyle, W. J. *The Fon of Dahomey*. Oxford: Clarendon Press, 1966.

Atkins, John. *A Voyage to Guinea, Brasil and the West Indies*. 1735. Reprint. London: Frank Cass, 1970.

Aublet, E. *La Guerre au Dahomey, 1888–1893*. Paris, 1894.

Barbou, Alfred. *Histoire de la guerre au Dahomey*. Paris, 1893.

Bay, Edna G. "Belief, Legitimacy and the *Kpojito*: an Institutional History of the 'Queen Mother' in Precolonial Dahomey." *The Journal of African History* 36, no. 1 (1995): 1–27.

———. "The Royal Women of Abomey." Ph.D. diss., Boston University, 1977.

———. "On the Trail of the Bush King: A Dahomean Lesson in the Use of Evidence." *History in Africa* 6 (1979): 1–15.

———. "Servitude and Worldly Success in the Palace of Dahomey." In *Women and Slavery in Africa*, edited by Claire C. Robertson and Martin A. Klein. Madison: Univ. of Wisconsin Press, 1983.

Béraud, Xavier. "Note sur le Dahomé." *Bulletin de la société de géographie* 12, 5th series (1866): 371–86.

Berbain, Simone. *Le Comptoir Français de Juda au XVIIIe siècle*. Mémoires de l'IFAN, no. 3. Paris: Larose, 1942.

Bertho, Jacques. "La Parenté des Yoruba aux peuplades de Dahomey et Togo." *Africa* 19, no. 2 (1949): 121–32.

Blanchely, M. "Au Dahomey." *Les Missions Catholiques* 23 (1891): 534–37.

Blier, Suzanne Preston. "Field Days: Melville J. Herskovits in Dahomey." *History in Africa* 16 (1989): 1–22.

———. "The Path of the Leopard: Motherhood and Majesty in Early Danhomè." *Journal of African History* 36, no. 3 (1995): 391–417.

Bosman, William. *A New and Accurate Description of the Coast of Guinea*. 1705. Reprint, with introduction by J. R. Willis and notes by J. D. Fage and R. E. Bradbury. New York: Barnes & Noble, 1967.

Bouët, Auguste. "Le Royaume de Dahomey." *Illustration* 20 (24 July 1852): 59–62.

Bowen, T. J. *Adventures and Missionary Labours in Several Countries in the Interior of Africa from 1849 to 1856*. 1857. Reprint, with introduction by E. A. Ayandele. London: Frank Cass, 1968.

Brue, A. de. "Voyage fait en 1843 dans le royaume de Dahomey." *Revue coloniale* 7 (1845): 55–68.

Buckley, Anthony D. "The God of Smallpox: Aspects of Yoruba Religious Knowledge." *Africa* 55, no. 2 (1985): 187–200.

Burton, Richard F. *A Mission to Gelele, King of Dahome*. 1864. 2 vols. The Memorial Edition of the Works of Captain Sir Richard F. Burton, vols. 3 and 4. Edited by Isabel Burton, London, 1893.

———. "The Present State of Dahome." *Transactions of the Ethnological Society of London* 3 (1865): 400–8.

C., Fara. "Ouidah, cité de tolérance." *Jeune Afrique*, no. 1682 (1–7 April 1993): 40.

"Captain Phillip's Journal of his Voyage from England to Cape Mounseradoe in Africa; and thence along the Coast of Guiney to Whidaw, the Island of St. Thomas, and so forward to Barbadoes." Vol. 6 of *A Collection of Voyages and Travels*. Edited by A. Churchill. London, 1732.

Chapman, D. A. "The Human Geography of Eweland." In *Première conférence internationale des Africanists de l'Ouest* 1 (1950): 79–101.

Chappet, E. *La Côte des Esclaves: rapport sur le mémoire de M. le Docteur Féris*. Lyon, 1881.

Chaudoin, E. *Trois mois de captivité au Dahomey*. Paris, 1891.

Coissy, Anatole. "L'arrivée des 'Alladahonou' à Houawé." *Etudes dahoméennes* 13 (1955): 31–32.

———. "Un Règne de femme dans l'ancien royaume d'Abomey." *Etudes dahoméennes* 2 (1949): 5–8.

Coquery, Catherine "Le blocus de Whydah (1876–1877) et la rivalité franco-anglaise au Dahomey." *Cahiers d'études africaines* 2, no. 3 (1962): 373–419.

Coquery-Vidrovitch, Catherine. "De la traite des esclaves à l'exportation de l'huile de palme et des palmistes au Dahomey: XIXe siècle." In *The Development of Indigenous Trade and Markets in West Africa.* Edited by Claude Meillassoux. London: Oxford Univ. Press, 1971.

Cornevin, Robert. *La République Populaire du Bénin.* Paris: Maisonneuve & Larose, 1981.

Cruickshank, B. "Report by B. Cruickshank of his Mission to the King of Dahomey." *Parliamentary Papers* 9 (1850): Appendix K.

Curtin, Philip. *The Image of Africa: British Ideas and Actions, 1780–1850.* Madison: Univ. of Wisconsin Press, 1964.

"Dahomey à la fin du XIXe siècle, Le" *Études dahoméennes* 9 (1953): 18–23.

d'Albeca, Alexandre L. "Au Dahomey." *Le Tour du monde* 68 (4 Aug. 1894): 65–80; (11 Aug. 1894): 81–96; (18 Aug. 1894): 97–112; (25 Aug. 1894): 113–28.

———. *La France au Dahomey.* Paris, 1895.

d'Almeida, Leslie Edouard Ayikwe. "Le Dahomey sous le règne de Dada Glèglè." Thèse de troisième cycle, Université de Paris, 1973.

d'Almeida-Topor, Hélène. *Les Amazones.* Paris: Rochevigne, 1984.

d'Oliveira, Th. Constant-Ernest. *La Visite du musée d'histoire d'Abomey.* n.p., 1970.

Dalzel, Archibald. *The History of Dahomy, an inland Kingdom of Africa.* 1793. Reprint, with an introduction by J. D. Fage. London: Frank Cass, 1967.

de Souza, Norberto Francisco. "Contribution à l'histoire de la famille de Souza." *Études dahoméennes* 13 (1955): 17–21.

de Souza, Simone. *La Famille de Souza du Bénin-Togo.* Cotonou: Éditions du Bénin, 1992.

Degbelo, Amélie. "Les Amazones du Danxomè, 1645–1900." Mémoire de maîtrise d'histoire, Université Nationale du Bénin, 1989.

Delange, Jacqueline. *Arts et peuples de l'Afrique Noire.* Paris: Gallimard, 1967.

Diamond, Stanley. "Dahomey: A Proto-State in West Africa." Ph.D. diss., Columbia University, 1951.

Djivo, Adrien. *Guezo: la rénovation du Dahomey.* Paris: ABC, 1977.

Duncan, John. *Travels in Western Africa, in 1845 & 1846.* 2 vols. 1847. Reprint (2 vols. in 1). London: Johnson Reprint, 1967.

Dunglas, Edouard. "Contribution à l'histoire du Moyen-Dahomey," parts 1, 2, and 3. *Études dahoméennes* 19, part 1 (1957): 7–185; 20, part 2 (1957): 3–152; 21, part 3 (1958): 7–116.

———. "Deuxième attaque des Dahoméens contre Abeokuta (15 mars 1864)." *Études dahoméennes* 2 (1949): 37–58.

————. "La première attaque des Dahoméennes contre Abéokuta (3 mars 1851)." *Études dahoméennes* 1 (1948): 7–19.

Edwards, Paul, ed. *The Life of Olaudah Equiano, or Gustavus Vassa the African.* Harlow, Essex UK: Longman, 1989.

Ellis, Alfred Burden. *The Ewe-Speaking Peoples of the Slave Coast of West Africa.* London, 1890.

Emmanuel, Karl. "Les Traités de Protectorat Français dans le Dahomey." Thèse de troisième cycle, Université de Toulouse, 1970.

Falcon, Paul. "Religion du vodun." *Études dahoméennes*, n.s. 18–19 (1970): 1–211.

Foà, Édouard. *Le Dahomey*. Paris, 1895.

Forbes, Frederick E. *Dahomey and the Dahomans.* 2 vols. 1851. Reprint. London: Frank Cass, 1966.

Fuglestad, Finn. "Quelques réflexions sur l'histoire et les institutions de l'ancien royaume du Dahomey et de ses voisins." *Bulletin de l'IFAN* 39, ser. B, no. 3 (1977): 493–517.

Garcia, Luc Messanvi. "Archives et tradition orale." *Cahiers d'études africaines* 16, no. 61–62 (1976): 189–206.

————. *Le royaume du Dahomé face à la pénétration coloniale.* Paris: Karthala, 1988.

Gavoy, Administrateur. "Notes historiques sur Ouidah." *Études dahoméennes* 13 (1955): 53–56.

Gayibor, Nicoué Lodjou, ed. "Mémoire contenant des observations sur quelques points de la côte de Guinée visitées en mil sept cent quatre vingt six par la corvette le Pandour, et sur la possibilité d'y faire des établissements." In *Textes et documents d'histoire de l'ancienne Côte des Esclaves (Anlo-Genyi), 1660–1835.* Cotonou: Université Nationale du Bénin, 1976.

Geggus, David. "Sex Ratio, Age and Ethnicity in the Atlantic Slave Trade: Data from French Shipping and Plantation Records." *Journal of African History* 30 (1989): 23–44.

Gleason, Judith. *Agotime: Her Legend.* New York: Grossman, 1970.

Glélé, Maurice Ahanhanzo. *Le Danxome.* Paris: Nubia, 1974.

Grandin, Commandant. *A l'assaut du pays des noirs. Le Dahomey.* Paris, 1895.

Guillevin, M. "Voyage dans l'interieur du royaume du Dahomey," *Nouvelles annales des voyages* 2 (June 1862): 292–93.

Hair, P. E. H., Adam Jones, and Robin Law, eds. *Barbot on Guinea: The Writings of Jean Barbot on West Africa, 1678–1712.* 2 vols. London: Hakluyt Society, 1992.

Hazoumé, Paul. *Cinquante ans d'apostolat.* Lyon, n.d.

———. "La Conquête du royaume houédah par les Dahoméens au XVIIe siècle." *Bulletin de l'enseignement de l'Afrique Occidentale Française* (1921): 41–45.

———. *Doguicimi*. Paris: Larose, 1938.

———. *Le pacte de sang au Dahomey*. 1937. Travaux et mémoires de l'Institut d'Ethnologie 25. Reprint. Paris: Institut d'Ethnologie, 1956.

———. "Tata Ajachê soupo ma ha awouinyan," parts 1–3. *La Reconnaissance Africaine* 1 (1925): 7–9; 2 (1925): 7–8; 3 (1925): 7–8.

Henige, David, and Marion Johnson. "Agaja and the Slave Trade: Another Look at the Evidence." *History in Africa* 2 (1976): 57–67.

Herskovits, Melville J. *Dahomey: An Ancient West African Kingdom*. 2 vols. New York: J. J. Augustin, 1938.

Herskovits, Melville J., and Frances S. Herskovits. *Dahomean Narrative*. Evanston: Northwestern Univ. Press, 1958.

———. *An Outline of Dahomean Religious Belief*. Memoirs of the American Anthropological Association, no. 41. Menasha WI: American Anthropological Assn., 1933.

Houseman, Michael, et al. "Note sur la structure évolutive d'une ville historique." *Cahiers d'études africaines* 26, no. 104 (1986): 527–46.

Johnson, Marion. "Bulfinch Lambe and the Emperor of Pawpaw: a Footnote to Agaja and the Slave Trade." *History in Africa* 5 (1978): 345–50.

Johnson, Samuel. *The History of the Yorubas*. 1921. Reprint. London: Lowe & Brydone, 1969.

Jones, Adam. "Semper Aliquid Veteris: Printed Sources for the History of the Ivory and Gold Coasts, 1500–1750." *Journal of African History* 27, no. 2 (1986): 215–35.

Labarthe, P. *Voyage à la côte de Guinée*. Paris, 1803.

Labat, R. Père. *Voyage du Chevalier des Marchais en Guinée, isles voisines, et à Cayenne*. 2 vols. Paris, 1730.

Laffitte, M. l'Abbé. *Le Dahomé: souvenirs de voyage et de mission*. 6th ed. Tours, 1883.

Lander, Richard. *Records of Captain Clapperton's Last Expedition to Africa*. 2 vols. London, 1830.

Law, Robin. "An African Response to Abolition: Anglo-Dahomian Negotiations on Ending the Slave Trade, 1838–77." *Slavery and Abolition* 16, no. 3 (Dec. 1995): 281–310.

———. "The 'Amazons' of Dahomey." *Paideuma* 39 (1993): 245–60.

———. "Dahomey and the Slave Trade: Reflections on the Historiography of the Rise of Dahomey." *Journal of African History* 27, no. 2 (1986): 237–67.

————. "Further Light on Bulfinch Lambe and the 'Emperor of Pawpaw': King Agaja of Dahomey's Letter to King George I of England, 1726." *History in Africa* 17 (1990): 211–26.

————. "History and Legitimacy: Aspects of the Use of the Past in Precolonial Dahomey." *History in Africa* 15 (1988): 431–56.

————. "Human Sacrifice in Pre-colonial West Africa." *African Affairs* 84 (1985): 53–87.

————. "Ideologies of Royal Power: The Dissolution and Reconstruction of Political Authority on the 'Slave Coast,' 1680–1750." *Africa* 57, no. 3 (1987): 321–44.

————. "'Legitimate' trade and gender relations in Yorubaland and Dahomey." In *From Slave Trade to 'Legitimate' Commerce: The Commercial transition in nineteenth-century West Africa*, edited by Robin Law. Cambridge: Cambridge Univ. Press, 1995.

————. "A Neglected Account of the Dahomian Conquest of Whydah (1727): The 'Relation de la Guerre de Juda' of the Sieur Ringard of Nantes." *History in Africa* 15 (1988): 323.

————. *The Oyo Empire c. 1600–c. 1836*. Oxford: Clarendon Press, 1977.

————. "The Politics of Commercial Transition: Factional Conflict in Dahomey in the Context of the Ending of the Atlantic Slave Trade." *Journal of American History* 38, no. 2 (1997): 213–33.

————. "Royal Monopoly and Private Enterprise in the Atlantic Trade: The Case of Dahomey." *Journal of African History* 18, no. 4 (1977): 555–77.

————. *The Slave Coast of West Africa, 1550–1750*. Oxford: Clarendon Press, 1991.

————. "The Slave Trader as Historian: Robert Norris and the History of Dahomey." *History in Africa* 16 (1989): 219–35.

————. "Slave-Raiders and Middlemen, Monopolists and Free-Traders: the supply of slaves for the Atlantic trade in Dahomey, c. 1715–1850." *Journal of African History* 30, no. 1 (1989): 45–68.

————. "Warfare on the West African Slave Coast, 1650–1850." In *War in the Tribal Zone: Expanding States and Indigenous Warfare*, edited by R. Brian Ferguson and Neil L. Whitehead. Santa Fe NM: School of American Research Press, 1992.

Le Hérissé, A. *L'Ancien royaume du Dahomey*. Paris: Larose, 1911.

Leprince, Jules. *Mes Deux premiers voyages*. Coulommiers, 1897.

Lombard, J. "Le Moyen de contrôle social dans l'ancien Dahomey." *Le Monde non Chrétien*, n.s. 38 (April-June 1956): 145–57.

M'Leod, John. *A Voyage to Africa*. 1820. Reprint. London: Frank Cass, 1971.

Maire, Capitaine. *Dahomey*. Besançon: Cariage, 1905.

Manning, Patrick. *Slavery and African Life*. Cambridge: Cambridge Univ. Press, 1990.

———. *Slavery, Colonialism, and Economic Growth in Dahomey, 1640–1960*. Cambridge: Cambridge Univ. Press, 1982.

Mattei, Commandant. *Bas-Niger, Bénoué, Dahomey*. Grenoble, 1890.

Maupoil, Bernard. "La Géomancie à l'ancienne Côte des Esclaves." Thèse pour le doctorat ès lettres, Université de Paris, 1943.

Mercier, Paul. *Civilisations du Bénin*. Paris: Société continentale d'éditions modernes illustrées, 1962.

———. "The Fon of Dahomey." In *African Worlds*, edited by Daryll Forde. London: Oxford Univ. Press, 1954.

Mercier, Paul, and J. Lombard. *Guide du musée d'Abomey*. Porto Novo: IFAN, 1959.

Mikponhoue, Hugues Theodore. "L'Administration coloniale française dans l'ancien royaume du Danhome de 1894 à 1920." Thèse du U. E. R. d'Histoire, 1975.

Morton-Williams, Peter. "The Yoruba Kingdom of Oyo." In *West African Kingdoms in the Nineteenth Century*, edited by Daryll Forde and P. M. Kaberry. London: Oxford Univ. Press, 1967.

———. "A Yoruba Woman Remembers Servitude in a Palace of Dahomey, in the Reigns of Kings Glele and Behanzin." *Africa* 63, no. 1 (1993): 102–17.

Moulero, Abbé Th. "Conquête de Kétou par Glele et conquête d'Abomey par la France." *Études dahoméennes*, n.s. 4 (May 1965): 61–68.

———. "Guezo ou Guedizo Massigbe." *Études dahoméennes*, n.s. 4 (May 1965): 51–59.

Nardin, Jean-Claude. "La reprise des relations franco-dahoméennes au XIXe siècle. La Mission d'Auguste Bouët à la cour d'Abomey (1851)." *Cahiers d'études africaines* 7, no. 25 (1967): 59–126.

Newbury, Colin. "A Note on the Abomey Protectorate." *Africa* 29 (1959): 146–55.

Norris, Robert. *Memoirs of the Reign of Bossa Ahadee, King of Dahomy*. 1789. Reprint. London: Frank Cass, 1968.

Obichere, Boniface I. "Change and Innovation in the Administration of the Kingdom of Dahomey." *Journal of African Studies* 1, no. 3 (1974): 235–51.

Palau Marti, Monserrat. *Le roi-dieu au Bénin*. Paris: Berger-Levrault, 1964.

Parrinder, E. G. *The Story of Ketu*. Ibadan: Ibadan Univ. Press, 1967.

Pires, Vicente Ferreira. *Viagem de Africa em o reino de Dahomé*. Edited by Clado Ribeiro de Lessa. São Paulo: Companhia Editora Nacional, 1957.

Polanyi, Karl. *Dahomey and the Slave Trade*. Seattle: Univ. of Washington Press, 1966.

Pommegorge, Pruneau de. *Description de la nigritie*. Amsterdam, 1789.

Quénum, Maximilien. *Les ancêtres de la famille Quénum*. Langres: Dominique Guéniot, 1981.

————. *Au pays des Fons*. 3rd ed. Paris: Maisonneuve et Larose, 1983.

Rattray, R. S. *Ashanti*. 1923. Reprint. New York: Negro Univ. Press, 1969.

Reade, W. Winwood. *Savage Africa*. London, 1864.

Reid, John. "Warrior Aristocrats in Crisis: The Political Effects of the Transition from the Slave Trade to Palm Oil Commerce in the Nineteenth Century Kingdom of Dahomey." Ph.D. diss., University of Stirling, Scotland, 1986.

Répin, Dr. "Voyage au Dahomey." *Le Tour du monde* 7 (1863): 76–109.

"Report by B. Cruickshank Esq. of his Mission to the King of Dahomey." *Parliamentary Papers* 9 (1849), appendix K.

Robertson, Claire C., and Martin A. Klein. "Women's Importance in African Slave Systems." In *Women and Slavery in Africa*, edited by Claire C. Robertson and Martin A. Klein. Madison: Univ. of Wisconsin Press, 1983.

Robertson, G. A. *Notes on Africa*. London, 1819.

Ross, David. "The Anti-Slave Trade Theme in Dahoman History: An Examination of the Evidence." *History in Africa* 9 (1982): 263–71.

————. "The Autonomous Kingdom of Dahomey, 1818–1894." Ph.D. diss., University of London, 1967.

Rydell, Robert W. *All the World's a Fair*. Chicago: Univ. of Chicago Press, 1984.

Sacks, Karen. *Sisters and Wives*. Urbana: Univ. of Illinois Press, 1982.

Segurola, B. *Dictionnaire Fon-Français*. 2 vols. 1963. Reprint. Cotonou: Centre Catéchétique de Porto Novo, 1968.

Skertchly, J. A. *Dahomey As It Is*. London, 1874.

Smith, William. *A New Voyage to Guinea*. 1744. Reprint. London: Frank Cass, 1967.

Snelgrave, William. *A New Account of Some Parts of Guinea and the Slave Trade*. 1734. Reprint. London: Frank Cass, 1971.

Soumonni, Elisée. "The Compatibility of the slave and palm oil trades in Dahomey, 1818–1858." In *From Slave Trade to 'Legitimate' Commerce: The Commercial transition in nineteenth-century West Africa*, edited by Robin Law. Cambridge: Cambridge Univ. Press, 1995.

Tahon, Général. *Carnets du Général Tahon: Avec les bâtisseurs de l'Empire*. Paris: Bernard Grasset, 1947.

Tidjani, A. Serpos. "Notes sur le mariage au Dahomey." *Études dahoméennes* 6 (1951): 27–107.

Tingbe-Azalou, Albert. "A propos de mythe et inceste dans l'ancien royaume du Danxome." Cotonou, 1993.

Turner, J. Michael. "Les Bresiliens—The Impact of Former Brazilian Slaves upon Dahomey." Ph.D. diss., Boston University, 1975.

Valdez, Francisco Travassos. *Six Years of a Traveller's Life in Western Africa.* London, 1861.

Vallon, A. "Le Royaume de Dahomey." *Revue maritime et coloniale* 1, part 1 (1860): 341–45.

———. "Le Royaume de Dahomey." *Revue maritime et coloniale* 3, part 2 (1861): 329–58.

Van Dantzig, A., ed. *The Dutch and the Guinea Coast, 1674–1742: A Collection of Documents from the General State Archive at the Hague.* Accra: Academy of Arts and Sciences, 1978.

Vansina, Jan. *Kingdoms of the Savannah.* Madison: Univ. of Wisconsin Press, 1966.

Verger, Pierre. "Le Culte des vodoun d'Abomey aurait-il été apporté à Saint-Louis de Maranhon par la mère du roi Ghézo?" *Études dahoméennes* 8 (1952): 19–24.

———. *Dieux d'Afrique.* Paris: Paul Hartmann, 1954.

———. "Echanges de cadeaux entre rois d'Abomey et souverains européens aux XVIIIe et XIXe siècles." *Bulletin d'IFAN* 32, série B, no. 3 (July 1970): 741–54.

———. *Flux et reflux de la traite des nègres entre le Golfe de Bénin et Bahia de Todos os Santos.* Paris: Mouton, 1968.

———. *Notes sur le culte des orisa et vodun.* Mémoires d l'IFAN, no. 51. Dakar: IFAN, 1957.

Waterlot, Em. G. *Les Bas-Reliefs des Bâtiments royaux d'Abomey.* Paris: Institut d'Ethnologie, 1926.

Yai, Olabiyi. "From Vodun to Mawu: Monotheism and History in the Fon Cultural Area." *Sapina Newsletter* 4, nos. 2–3 (1992): 10–29.

Yoder, John C. "Fly and Elephant Parties: Political Polarization in Dahomey, 1840–1870." *Journal of African History* 15, no. 3 (1974): 417–32.

Archives

Benin

Archives Nationales du Benin (ANB)

Controle des Chefs, Abomey et Allada, c. 1925.

Correspondences du 16 avril au 16 decembre 1894. Série E. Dossier I, II, and III, Expéditions de 1890–94.

F. de Souza à Candido Rodriguez, avec Behanzin à Acherigbe, 25 mars 1893.

Gbohayida à Aho, 13 juin 1904.

Hocquart, M. "Rapport Politique." 9 février 1891.

Rapport adressé par l'interprète X. Béraud à Monsieur le Résident de France aux Établissements du Golfe de Bénin, 12 mars 1891. Dossier 1E3, Register X.

Rapport de l'interprète Xavier Béraud, janvier 1890. Dossier K.

Rapport mensuel, juillet 1895.

Rapport sur les négotiations entamées avec Béhanzin, n.d.

Renseignements du 27 novembre 1892 au 26 septembre 1893.

Archives de la Sous-Préfecture d'Abomey (ASA)

Commandant de Cercle d'Abomey au Gouverneur du Dahomey, 19 avril 1935.

List nominatif des métis du cercle d'Abomey, 24 février 1928.

Peines Disciplinaires et Conciliations, nov. 1905–nov. 1908.

England
Public Record Office (PRO)

Africa No. 365. CO 879/29.

Africa No. 386. CO 879/31.

Journal of Arthur Fanshawe. FO 84/827.

Methodist Missionary Society, London (MMS)

Freeman, Thomas Birch. "Journal of a Journey to Badagry, Aku and Dahomey—1842–43." Biog. W. Afr. 2, Stack QI.

Freeman, Thomas Birch. Typescript of untitled book, n.d. Biog. W. Afr. 5, Stack QI.

Freeman to Beecham, 12 March 1855. Copy Book 18, Biog. W. Africa 4, Stack QI.

Freeman to General Secretaries, London, 20 July 1855. Copy Book 22, Biog. W. Africa 4, Stack QI.

France
Archives Nationales, Section Outre-Mer (SOM)

Rapport de route: Mission à Abomey de M. le Lt. Gouverneur Jean Bayol, nov.– déc. 1889. Dah. 3, Dossier 1.

Rapport journalier: Mission à Abomey de M. le Lt. Gouverneur Jean Bayol, 21 nov.–28 déc. 1889. Dahomey 3, Dossier 1.

Correspondence, Dah. 1, Dossier 13.

Rapport adressé par l'interprète X. Béraud à Monsieur le Résident de France aux Etablissements du Golfe de Bénin. Dahomey 3, Dossier 2.

"Réflexions sur Juda par les Sieurs de Chenevert et Abbé Bulet." 1776. Aix-en-Provence, Dépôt des Fortifications des Colonies: Côtes d'Afrique, ms. 111.

Archives Nationales, Paris (AN)

Glélé, Pogla K. "Le Royaume du Dan-hô-min: tradition orale et histoire écrite." 1971.

Service Historique de l'État-major de l'Armée, Vincennes (SHA)

Rapport sur les Operations du Corps Expeditionnaire du Dahomey en 1893–94. Dahomey Carton 1.

Ministère des Affaires Étrangères (MAE)

Lartique, J. "Relation du voyage à Abomey." Mémoires et Documents, tome 51 (1838–62).

Italy

Society of African Missions, Rome (AMR)

Borghéro, R. P. "Journal de la Mission du Dahomey, 1860–1864."

Senegal

Archives Nationales du Sénégal (ANS)

Rapport politique mensuel, juillet 1895. 2G1—31.
Rapport politique mensuel, juin 1896. 2G1—32.

USA

University Archives, Bancroft Library, University of California at Berkeley (UCB)
William R. Bascom, 1950–51. Yoruba Field Notes. 1—Meko—1–360.

Interviews and Personal Communications

Adjanahudegbo, Da. Zagnanado, 18 Oct. 1972.
Adonon, Da. Abomey, 22 Dec. 1972.
Adonon, Na, Gbonugan Gohonu, and Da Hangbesi. Abomey, 16 Oct. 1972.
Adonon, Na. Abomey, 13 Oct. 1972.
Agbado, Da. Abomey, 17 and 23 June 1972.
Agessi Voyon, Da. Abomey, 28 April 1972.
Agoliagbo, Andre. Gbindo, 3 March 1973.

Agoliagbo, Da. Gbindo, 24 July 1972.

Aho, René. Abomey, 21 Jan., 3 Feb., 3 and 23 May, and 24 Oct. 1972.

Akati, Gounon Simon. Abomey, 30 July 1984.

Author's field notes, Abomey, 1972–73.

Avloko, Na. Whydah, 27 Feb. 1973.

Badiji, Christophe. Hoja, 3 Oct. 1984.

Behanzin, Da Agodeka. Jime, 3 June 1972.

Behanzin, Da Camille. Abomey, 13 July 1972.

Codjia, Da. Brazilian Quarter, Whydah, 27 Feb. 1973.

d'Oliveira, Ernest. Abomey, 22 March 1972.

Descendants of Agbalu Glele, Gbindo, 13 Sept. 1972.

Dosso-Yovo, Da. Whydah, 9 Nov. 1972

Elders of the house of Hangbe. Abomey, 9 June 1972, 20 July 1984.

Elders of the house of Hountondji. Abomey, 3 July 1984.

Elders of the house of Na Agontime, Tindji. 8 Sept. 1994.

Elders of the Soude family. Abomey, 4 June 1972.

Feliho, Alexis. Abomey, 18 Sept. 1972.

Fengbe, Philippe. Agbagnizon, 30 July and 14 Oct. 1972.

Glele, Da Agbalu. Abomey, 9, 11, and 29 Sept. 1972, 26 Oct. 1972.

Glele, Da Sagbadju. Abomey, 26 and 28 March, 25 and 29 July 1972.

Kinhwe, Vincent. Abomey, 24 and 25 March 1972, 1 Feb. 1973, 7 March 1973.

Legonon, Blandine, and Michael Houseman. Abomey, 29 July 1984.

Loko, Léonard. Cotonou, 4 Feb. 1973.

Nondichao, Bachirou. Abomey, 7 and 8 Sept. 1994.

Ougoton, Da. Jime, 29 June 1972.

Savakonton, Na. Jime, 30 Jan. 1973.

Solde, Na, and Da Agonhun. Abomey, 8 Sept. 1994.

Yai, Olabiyi. personal communication, 18 Nov. 1996.

Yomana, Da. Abomey, 6 and 10 June 1972.

Index